Journalism, Satire, and Censorship in Mexico

JOURNALISM, SATIRE, AND CENSORSHIP IN MEXICO

EDITED BY
Paul Gillingham,
Michael Lettieri, and
Benjamin T. Smith

University of New Mexico Press | Albuquerque

Library of Congress Cataloging-in-Publication Data
Names: Gillingham, Paul, 1973– editor. | Lettieri, Michael, 1983– editor. |
    Smith, Benjamin T., editor.
Title: Journalism, satire, and censorship in Mexico / edited by Paul Gillingham,
    Michael Lettieri, and Benjamin T. Smith.
Description: Albuquerque: University of New Mexico Press, 2018. |
    Includes bibliographical references and index. |
Identifiers: LCCN 2018016227 (print) | LCCN 2018020477 (e-book) |
    ISBN 9780826360083 (e-book) | ISBN 9780826360076 (pbk.: alk. paper)
Subjects: LCSH: Press and politics—Mexico—History—20th century. |
    Press and politics—Mexico—History—21st century. | Freedom of the press—
    Mexico—History—20th century. | Freedom of the press—Mexico—History—
    21st century. | Censorship—Mexico—History—20th century. | Censorship—
    Mexico—History—21st century.
Classification: LCC PN4974.P6 (e-book) | LCC PN4974.P6 .J68 2018 (print) |
    DDC 079/.720904—dc23
LC record available at https://lccn.loc.gov/2018016227

Cover photograph by Nacho Lopez courtesy of the Fototeca National del INAH
Designed by Felicia Cedillos
Composed in Minion 10.25/14.25

For David Bailey, Mirsada Šakić-Hatibović and Javier Valdez Cárdenas

Contents

Illustrations

Tables

Foreword

Killing the Messenger
The Perils of Committing Journalism

JUDITH MATLOFF

It started out like so many safety training sessions I have conducted for reporters. The journalists from northern Mexico gathered in a safe place to learn how to avoid being murdered. Nearly everyone in the room had lost a co-worker or had received death threats from drug gangs that target the media. Their offices had been shot at. Sinister text messages demanded they drop investigations.

The writers and photographers craved tips on survival. Mexico is one of the most dangerous places to be a journalist, due to the impunity of narcos and the complicity of the very officials entrusted with protecting citizens. Since the 1990s, more than ninety media workers have been killed and over twenty have gone missing. Seven were murdered in the first half of 2017 alone.[1] Many reporters have gone into hiding, and still more have been silenced by fear or intimidation.

In 2006 Mexico set up a special prosecutor's office to investigate crimes against freedom of expression. But it is ineffectual, having obtained only three convictions in the hundreds of cases lodged.

A reporter from the state of Chihuahua described her daily ordeal. A white car tailed her every morning as she drove her small daughter to kindergarten. It was always the same maneuver. As soon as she pulled out of her driveway the sedan followed in pursuit, a couple of car lengths behind, but never so close that she could see the driver's face in the rear-view mirror. The journalist was pretty sure he represented the Zetas, one of the most vicious syndicates. The group had killed several colleagues and phoned threats to at least a dozen more.[2] The driver would follow as she dropped the child at school and then continue behind her most of the way to the office. A single mother, she dreaded leaving her daughter orphaned or having her harmed. How could she live with that? The journalist felt guilty, torn, desperate. Every day when she put her bag down at the office she saw the empty cubicle of a photographer who had been assassinated by the *malos* (bad men).

What could she do? I raised a couple of possibilities for the group. The reporter could try divergent routes, I ventured. She could vary the time she left the house. She could travel in convoy with a friend or relative. Someone else could take the girl in the mornings. The mother could drive with an emergency number on speed dial, ready to press if the man got too close to her car. Or take a defensive driving class.

Her expression dulled as we brainstormed more options. Circle the block several times. Get a bulletproof car ("Too expensive"). Hire armed guards ("Can't afford that either"). Change jobs ("And work where?"). Move to another town (same problem). More proposals, none viable. As we ran out of ideas, she said in a flat voice: "They'll get me if they want to."

Tragically, she was right. Safety is a fatalistic matter in Mexico, and the customary preventive measures won't withstand the dangerous juggernaut. Impunity is so rife, and the collusion between organized crime and law enforcers so profound, that only self-censorship saves lives.[3] That's why so many Mexican media professionals have stopped reporting on the violence.

I've been conducting these security workshops on and off for several years now, going from north to south, east to west. Veracruz, Jalisco, Veracruz again, Nuevo Laredo, Chihuahua City, Ciudad Juárez, Nuevo León, Chiapas, Mexico City. I've worked with journalists from nearly all of the thirty-one states. They all share the same lament: contingency planning goes only so far.

Risk assessment is the linchpin of security plans. You identify the worst-case scenarios and then figure out how to mitigate them. Who are the hostile parties? What is their modus operandi? Are you likely to be kidnapped or murdered at home? Seized outside the office? Are they snooping on your Facebook communications? Do they target relatives as well? Will they email a warning before cutting off your head? Do they string tortured bodies from bridges?

Then you work backward. Set up a communication plan with a trusted person who knows where you are hour by hour. Be vigilant about your surroundings. Safeguard digital and mobile communications to prevent eavesdropping or the hacking of accounts. Be wary of narco spies planted in the newsroom. Don't leave the computer switched on when you go to the restroom; don't leave cell phones on the desk. Don't broadcast your plans or post family snapshots on social media. Cover stories in a group.

But that only works so far. What's the point of reporting threats to police who may be working with the bad guys? What if your boss refuses to take you off the police beat? The sheer variety of what can go wrong is staggering in Mexico. You can't stay away from the front line, because you live on it. And that front line is ever mutating. The violence has so many actors and variables that following one line of caution isn't enough. Different syndicates control different plazas, or markets, in different parts of the country. Stratfor, a geopolitical intelligence firm, illustrates this balkanization in its periodic maps of cartel control.[4] They show how the landscape changes from year to year as groups chase away rivals or new ones splinter off. These shifting sands make it doubly hard to keep track of infiltration into the judiciary and law enforcement. There are a lot of underpaid cops willing to take bribes among the two federal, thirty-one state, and hundreds of municipal police forces.

I have spoken to dozens of Mexican journalists across the country, and nearly all say that appeals for transfers to safer beats or for hiring armed sentries are laughed off. Salaries are low—the average monthly wage is US$650—and employment so scarce that reporters are often scared to push for their rights. Forget about strong unions. "My editor expected me to return to work right after being beaten," one reporter from a border town told me.

Without money, lawyers, or sympathetic bosses, journalists improvise. One police reporter in the state of Guerrero goes to Alcoholics Anonymous meetings, not for a booze problem but because he needs to vent somewhere. He figures that the narcos drink heavily so this is a safe environment to talk about his fears. Other journalists drive across the border to the United States once a week to get a break from the relentless pressure. They don't talk to family about their work and have removed their children's pictures from

Facebook to make it harder for abductors to kidnap them. Others have given up successful careers, or fled town.[5]

That didn't work, though, for Rubén Espinosa, a photographer from Veracruz, one of the worst states for the assassination of journalists. He told the media advocacy group Article 19 that he was followed in several locations and given sinister looks. He relocated to Mexico City, previously a safe haven for journalists. Not anymore. Espinosa was shot dead there soon after.

Ironically, Veracruz has a mechanism set up to protect journalists. The Commission for the Care and Protection of Journalists was formalized in late 2012 to provide measures such as alerting authorities in cases of emergency. It followed the creation of the National Mechanism to Protect Human Rights Defenders and Journalists. If it worked properly, a small circle of people would weigh a request for, say, bodyguards, panic buttons, or assistance in relocation. Then a committee would analyze the severity of the situation and, hopefully, take action before the applicant was killed.

However, many Mexican journalists harbor a distrust of the government, so they don't reach out. A sampling of journalists from five states whom I surveyed in late 2015 scoffed at the notion of asking for state-sponsored help, since half of the aggressions reported against journalists come from authorities. The body that oversees the mechanism is the Secretaría de Gobernación, not a robust champion of free speech. Several of the 200-odd journalists who have actually sought protective measures report painfully slow responses. And the panic buttons don't always work.

The federal system was based loosely on one in Colombia, another Latin American nation where cartels have tried to intimidate the media. The Colombian mechanism, among other measures, finances armed bodyguards or plane tickets so that threatened journalists can fly to other locales. The Mexican initiative, however, lacks the same teeth.

In addition, Colombia enjoys conditions that are more favorable to building solidarity. Competitors collaborate on investigations and coordinate publications, and they even staged a news blackout to protest a killing. That level of collaboration is unthinkable among Mexico's fragmented media.

Also, the world of journalism in Mexico is alienated from the rest of civil society; the general populace often views reporters as irresponsible vultures, which is not the case in Colombia. And often media workers in the hinterland lack links with colleagues in other towns, including Mexico City, where power lies. In some cases, the publishers of Mexican newspapers live across the border in the United States, and have little, if any, contact with reporters. Colombian journalists tend to be better connected.

Furthermore, unlike their Colombian equivalents, Mexico's media giants seem disinterested in lobbying for protection as a group, according to the Center for International Media Assistance.[6] This leaves provincial reporters out on a limb with no strong advocates in the seat of government. In contrast, the influential national media in Bogotá have joined forces with the political elite, which had been similarly targeted by the Medellín drug cartel.

"Almost all of the attacks in Mexico have been far from the capital city, carried out against local targets, and thus drawing little sustained national attention," noted a report by the center. "There is almost no contact among the local and national media in Mexico, no coordinated efforts by publishers and editors to develop a common strategy to protect their journalists."[7]

Mexico also lacks a robust judicial system to bring killers to justice. In 2013, Mexican lawmakers approved an amendment to the constitution that made attacks on journalists a federal crime, and gave federal authorities the power to prosecute in situations that would normally fall under local or state jurisdiction. However, the legislation has failed to yield prosecutions.

Abandoned in these ways, Mexican journalists are making their own security arrangements. A loose network called Periodistas de a Pie has reached out to Colombian reporters for tips. Over the past couple of years, seasoned experts have flown to meet with their counterparts from Mexico. The common language facilitates communication, as does an understanding of what it's like to deal with the shadowy world of drug gangs. "We believe that we can serve as a useful example for Mexicans," said Ignacio Gómez, the former head of Colombia's leading press freedom group, Fundación para la Libertad de Prensa (FLIP).[8] He has lost track of how many seminars FLIP has conducted in Mexico for colleagues facing danger.

The workshops have spawned an informal association of reporters, from Ciudad Juárez to Oaxaca, who share things—the names of affordable psychologists, a couch if someone needs to escape town, photocopies of counter surveillance guides. And they have begun to form local chapters in order to lobby as a group to win officially sanctioned protection.

One regional leader is Rocío Gallegos, an editor of *El Diario de Juárez*, from the border town that long held the dubious distinction of being the world's homicide capital. Things got so bad in Juárez in 2011 that *El Diario* begged the drug lords to define the rules so that its journalists knew what was off-limits. "What Do You Want from Us?" asked the editorial, which ran on the front page.

The editors never got an answer, so Gallegos took matters into her own hands. In 2012, she created an informal association of independent-minded reporters fed up with self-censorship.[9] They team up on stories and invite experts to explain such things as password protection and altering routines. They regularly check on each other's emotional state. It's sort of a combination support group and professional development union. "We established alliances between individual journalists so that we can watch each other's backs," explained Gallegos. "Scoops take second place."

The word is spreading. A reporter from Chihuahua city who attended one session left so fired up that she formed her own chapter back home. Members are vetted to ensure they are not serving as informants for drug dealers; distrust in the newsroom is a common complaint. "We had to take the initiative," said Patricia Mayorga a prominent local journalist. "No one else was looking after us." That's for sure. Last year she fled Mexico after receiving death threats and following the murder of a close colleague, Miroslava Breach Velducea.

Safety remains especially elusive for reporters in places like the border city of Nuevo Laredo, where the Zetas command such terror that many people won't utter the name out loud. In 2013, *El Mañana* newspaper announced that it would stop covering violent disputes among rival groups after a second grenade attack against its offices in two months. Residents of the town rely on Facebook and other social media to learn about shootouts, which are often referred to by the euphemism "parties." This leaves journalists wondering again how they can do their job properly.

"Collaboration wouldn't work, because we don't cover news anymore," dryly noted Daniel Rosas, the online editor of *El Mañana*. "I like the idea though."

The mother of the kindergarten student similarly self-censored. She changed beats and stays away from sensitive stories. When I last checked, the white car had stopped following her. She was still alive. Unable to work freely, but still alive.

Notes

1. By the time you read this, it will be out of date. For (varying) current statistics and reports, see the Committee to Protect Journalists, https://cpj.org/americas/mexico/2017 and https://cpj.org/killed/americas/mexico; Reporters Without Borders, "Mexico," https://rsf.org/en/mexico; Article 19, "Latinoamérica," https://www.article19.org/pages/es/latin-america-translation.html (all accessed Nov. 9, 2017).
2. For one reporter's experiences with the Zetas, see Corchado, *Midnight in Mexico.*
3. Cacho et al., *La ira de México.*
4. See https://worldview.stratfor.com/image/geography-mexican-drug-cartels (accessed Sept. 8, 2017).
5. For groundbreaking investigative journalism, see Javier Valdez Cárdenas's award-winning work from Sinaloa, *Narcoperiodismo* and *The Taken.* Valdez Cárdenas was murdered outside his newspaper office in May 2017.
6. See http://www.cima.ned.org (accessed Sept. 8, 2017).
7. Farah, *Dangerous Work,* 23.
8. See https://www.flip.org.co/index.php/es (accessed Sept. 8, 2017).
9. Self-censorship characterizes both reporters and reported; many victims of violence do not engage with the authorities, since they fear being suspected of being narcos themselves. For stories, see Turati, *Fuego cruzado.*

Acknowledgments

This book relied on the support and funding of multiple institutions. Most important, we would like to thank the Center for US-Mexican Studies at the University of California, San Diego (UCSD). The center hosted a two-day conference in May 2014 on the history and contemporary state of journalism in Mexico, organized by Michael Lettieri. That conference provided the basis for this edited collection. We thank all the conference attendees, the wonderful and efficient administrators at UCSD, and the fantastic, smart, and engaged postdoctoral students at the center. Special thanks to Gema Santamaría, Sam Quinones, David Shirk, Peter H. Smith, Alfredo Corchado, and Froylán Enciso.

We must also thank the Arts and Humanities Research Council (AHRC) in the United Kingdom. As part of a larger research grant, the AHRC funded a workshop in August 2015 on contemporary journalism and the war on drugs. This allowed Benjamin Smith not only to resume conversations with two of the standout contributors to this volume, Javier Garza Ramos and Paul K. Eiss, but also to meet many other media studies experts, journalists, and NGO workers. Special thanks to Freedom House (Mexico), Colectivo de Análisis de la Seguridad con Democracía, El Colegio de la Frontera Norte, Mariclaire Acosta, Raúl Benitez, Ioan Grillo, Duncan Tucker, Nina Lakhani, José Brambila Ramírez, and Alex Aviña.

We also thank the British Academy, which provided a BA Small Research Grant for Benjamin Smith to put together a history of the twentieth-century

Mexican press. That history provided the inspiration for much of this work. Finally, we thank the Global History and Culture Centre at the University of Warwick, and in particular Giorgio Riello, who provided additional funding and support for the 2014 UCSD conference.

Beyond these institutional debts, we also owe a lot to the three anonymous readers of the text, who provided so much provocative and useful commentary; to the ever sharp and engaged Clark Whitehorn at the University of New Mexico Press, with whom we have worked before and will hopefully work again; and to Andrew Paxman, who has provided continued knowledgeable input into this project.

Acknowledgment pages are not the space for eulogies; there is more than enough death in this book. But during the making of this volume three people passed away, all of whom have a link to our interest in the subject of the press and politics. The first is David Bailey, Benjamin Smith's mentor at Michigan State University and one of the kindest and most generous people Smith ever had the pleasure to spend time with (though not enough). The second is Mirsada Šakić-Hatibović, winner of the International Women's Media Foundation award for courage in journalism; she was brave not just on the front lines. The third is Javier Valdez Cárdenas, who attended the 2014 workshop, wrote some of the best investigative journalism on Mexico's contemporary drug war, and provided the basis for much of Everard Meade's work on Mexican journalism in this time of crisis. He was executed outside his newspaper, *Ríodoce*, on May 15, 2017.

Introduction | # Journalism, Satire, and Censorship in Mexico

PAUL GILLINGHAM, MICHAEL LETTIERI,
AND BENJAMIN T. SMITH

R isky criticism, satire, and censorship have a long history in Mexico. As soon as Hernán Cortés captured Tenochtitlan the first libels appeared, daubed daily on the whitewashed walls of his Coyoacán headquarters. They ranged from artfully composed verse to the unprintable "palabras que no son para decir en esta relación" (words with no place in this chronicle), and Cortés's reaction was first to match wits with his scurrilous critics, then to disdain them ("pared blanca, papel de necios," white wall, fools' paper), and finally to ban them.[1] Bernal Díaz del Castillo is silent as to what happened next, but the assumption—given the timely deaths of various of those inconvenient to Cortés—must be that the threats worked to silence the dissidents.[2] Thus began some five centuries of censorship. Churchmen burned books (and occasionally their authors); kings banned printing presses and treatises on indigenous people; dictators deployed violence both improvised (Santa Anna) and systematic (the penitentiaries of the Porfiriato, with their presidential suites for journalists).[3] The revolutionary governments took an evolutionary step forward, coercing less and co-opting more. To that end, politicians used multiple subsidies ranging from the formal (lavishly paid adverts, cheap newsprint, generous loans) to the informal—but inspirational— payoffs to individual hacks. The Mexican rulers of the *dictablanda*—a state

that combined authoritarian and democratic elements and that exerted tenuous control over markedly autonomous local societies—smoothly and comprehensively censored the twentieth-century media: happily handing out carrots
to an oft-complicit press, prepared when needed to pick up the stick.[4] In short,
the arch-Machiavellian Cortés might well be painted as a worthy predecessor
of the arch-Machiavellian Institutional Revolutionary Party (Partido Revolucionario Institucional, PRI).

So, at least, runs an old and powerful story, which until recently ended
on an uplifting note with the democratization of the print press in the
1980s and '90s.[5] Yet as the contributors to this book argue, such an eman-
cipatory narrative no longer holds. These authors come from varied professional backgrounds. Many are historians, drawn to examine the complex
roots of the contemporary situation. Some, like Judith Matloff and Rafael
Barajas, are journalists forced by necessity to ponder the old assurances of
press liberalization. Others, like Javier Garza Ramos and Jacinto Rodríguez
Munguía, combine investigation of the past with concern for present-day
problems to bridge both professions. Finally, scholars such as Everard
Meade and Paul Eiss have turned from history to contemporary cultural
commentary to discern patterns and dislocations in our new and shocking
reality. The diversity of approaches, methodologies, and assumptions is
inevitable and self-evident. Yet amid that diversity, the chapters are linked
by three common observations, which also structure this book.

First, as even a cursory glance at the headlines suggest, journalism is more
dangerous, and consequently more constrained, now than at any other point
in modern Mexican history. Since 2006 reporters have been murdered at a
far greater rate than at the PRI's peak.[6] There is no longer a liberal story of
press democratization with a happy ending.[7] Second, the new scrutiny and a
shift from memoir and polemic to history have knocked the linchpin out of
any simple dichotomies of domination and resistance from an earlier print
world. A world in which an authoritarian conservative president (Gustavo
Díaz Ordaz) helps bring the most influential opposition journalist (Julio
Scherer) to power; or where a conservative Mexico City mayor (Ernesto Uruchurtu) props up a genuine opposition outlet (*Política*); or where another
unpopular president (José López Portillo) funds an opposition daily (*Unomásuno*) is a world considerably more complex than any just-so story can tell.[8]
(Perhaps, as Everard Meade suggests in this volume, it is one in which both

liberal teleologies and Gramscian imaginaries break down.) Third, this empirical shift toward a new narrative complexity parallels comparative and conceptual shifts in studies of the media in other times and places. It is now clear that globalized media competition does not inevitably translate into more democratic flows of information or newly empowered consumers. The press in the United States is no historical yardstick, bent as it is by its own pressures of commercial imperatives, state co-optation, "fake news," and violence.[9] Above all, censorship is not a solely political phenomenon, existing in Manichaean opposition to freedom of expression. As several authors demonstrate, censorship can also be market-driven, or criminal; it involves complex relations of "complicity, collaboration, and negotiation" between censors and the censored.[10] In Ana María Serna Rodríguez's description, it is "a cultural-political practice emerging from a multiplicity of sites, voices, and subjectivities."

Old Stories, New Histories: Mexico's Print Culture until 1910

Mexican historians have begun embracing what Robert Darnton terms the "new history" of communication.[11] Delving into Mexicans' relationships with printed texts, they have started to chip away at old liberal certainties.[12] The Inquisition, for example, was depicted by liberals such as Vicente Riva Palacio (in both papers and novels) as an efficient machine of totalitarian censorship; in reality inquisitors lacked enough copies of their lists of banned books to cover New Spain (and only updated them every twenty years anyway).[13] At the other end of the colony, the late eighteenth and early nineteenth centuries were times of widespread enthusiasm for France's revolutionaries and evil-minded attacks on Spaniards, bureaucrats, and churchmen. Across the hierarchies of this increasingly literate culture, readers got their hands on the newspapers, gazettes, and satirical pamphlets that transmitted new and dangerous ideas. Some publications, newspapers, and tracts were explicitly political; others were spaces of backdoor commentary, such as the medical journals in which doctors and folk healers discussed innovative ways to view society, or the thin religious booklets with commentaries on and prayers to unsettlingly heterodox saints.[14] People read them together in the new spaces of Enlightenment sociability: the Masonic lodge, the economic society, the café, the reading group.[15] The printed word traveled well beyond the page and the literate, as authors both drew on and developed a critical vernacular culture through the cries of the pamphleteer sellers, the carefully rehearsed rhetoric of public readings, and the plays, songs, gossip, rumors, letters, and libels.

This public sphere swelled dramatically during and after the wars of independence. Tumultuous discussions of autonomy, democracy, and the church echoed through the newly established town halls, and a newborn electorate—which initially included poor people, indigenous people, and Afro-Mexicans—responded with votes, insurrections, and their attendant manifestos.[16] A new, vocal, and often contrarian generation of newspapermen and pamphleteers emerged in both the capital and the provinces.[17] They met from the start with tides of censorship, which ebbed and rose according to regime.[18] Article 17 of Agustín de Iturbide's constitution ordered writers to make "a rational sacrifice of the right to think and manifest ideas freely, neither attacking nor alluding to, without prior censorship, the Catholic religion, ecclesiastical discipline, the moderate monarchy, the emperor's person, independence, and the union."[19]

Journalists deserved stiff jail sentences, Antonio López de Santa Anna decreed twenty years later, because Mexico's ruinous condition was down to "the continuous and scandalous abuse of freedom of the press."[20] Such legislation was backed up by force. Between 1831 and 1832 numerous printing shops were closed and editors arrested; in the late 1830s journalists were incarcerated in Mexico's nastier jails, such as San Juan de Ulúa.[21] Censors, though, could still be evaded: under Santa Anna *Le Trait d'Union* used an improbable combination of French and fashion commentary to criticize the president.[22] Such satire ran too deep in Mexican culture to eradicate with legislation; it was the dominant tone of pamphlets from the beginning, its targets running across society, its power to harm recognized in laws that specifically targeted nicknames, sarcasm, and ridicule.[23] Even priests, it seemed, were satirists; in Tabasco one padre was murdered for his verses mocking the governor.[24] During the Reform era, satire only intensified, including both the Horatian mode of irony and mockery (often general) and the Juvenalian tradition of bitter vituperation (often personal). Satire was seen in written polemics and in the first political cartoons, which took up one of the four pages of *Mi Sombrero*, launched in 1860 and later rebaptized *La Orquesta*, and which quickly spread to other papers.[25] With the liberal party triumphant, political debate between relatively large, established newspapers such as *El Siglo XIX* and *El Monitor Republicano* peaked.[26]

The story of the Porfiriato was long one of the death of these press freedoms through persecution and subsidy: the suppression of juries devoted to assessing cases of press freedom, the serial jailings of journalists, the closure of mainstays such as *El Monitor Republicano*, and the unfair competition of the larger, cheaper, commercial papers that received extensive official subsidies.[27] As Pablo Piccato notes in this volume, however, "the influence of the press did not diminish." There was, as even Daniel Cosío Villegas noted, a continual rumble of criticism across the period, from both liberal and conservative editors—why else, after all, the prison suites?—and as Claude Dumas and Zamudio Vega observe in their study of the main conservative newspapers, there was "the slightly chaotic but constant existence of an opposition press."[28] Set piece battles still broke out, as when *El Demócrata* reported the Tomóchic massacre in the guise of a novel.[29] Cartoons survived and grew more refined; coverage of and commentary on social issues and crime provided half-hidden critiques of the dictatorship. (Not always hidden either: one José Guadalupe Posada cartoon in *El Diablito Rojo* explicitly rebuked Díaz for the Creelman interview.)[30]

Beyond the broadsheets of the capital, censorship was even less complete. In the poorer suburbs, workers-turned-journalists resisted patronizing official discourses and sought to create alternative and critical stories of working-class culture and masculinity.[31] Their satirical papers traveled far beyond the capital: by 1906 the popular *La Guacamaya* (which styled itself a "newspaper of gossip and good humor, agile and a teller of truths, not puffed up or snobby, scourge of the bourgeoisie and defender of the Working Class," according to its masthead) had a print run of 29,000 and was sold in Orizaba, San Luis Potosí, Aguascalientes, Toluca, Parral, and Guanajuato.[32] Alongside these imports, radical newspapers emerged in the provinces and borderlands, tapping Reform era traditions of criticism, exposure, and debate.[33] Revisionism concerning the incomplete nature of Porfirian censorship is not, perhaps, all that surprising; the same roundabout but effective communication systems—gossip, songs, libels, pamphlets, the gutter press, Kremlinological signs in the big papers—and the same weakened grasp of provincial information flows are evident in other states where authoritarian dreams outpace reality, such as ancien régime France.[34]

Visions of the More Recent Past

While authoritarian dreams were likewise hard to realize under the post-revolutionary governments, a similar reassessment is only just beginning in studies of twentieth-century Mexico's newspaper industry, traditionally subject to profoundly normative and negative assessments. That post-revolutionary press, commentators have held, was "submissive and unconditional"; newspapers were "factual deserts," "timid, over-sensational, often influenced by official optimism and possibly more concerned over profits than honest and objective presentation of the news."[35] Technology was primitive, and many publications lacked "the installations, the humans, or the equipment that modern newspapers need."[36] Print runs were so short that many owners "neither competed for readers nor formed public opinion independently."[37] Owners were businessmen first and editors second, principally concerned with using their papers to further their commercial ends. *Novedades*'s owners were "car salesmen"; Rodrigo de Llano, the editor of *Excélsior*, was more publicity agent than newsman; Regino Hernández Llergo, the owner of *Hoy*, was "very intelligent but extraordinarily corrupt"; the media mogul José García Valseca was immortalized in Carlos Fuentes's revolutionary-turned-plutocrat, Artemio Cruz.[38] The journalists were apparently even worse: lazy, unprofessional, ill-educated, profiteering drunkards, whom Mexicans colloquially dismissed as coyotes, blackmailers, *pícaros* (blaggers), *lambiscones* (brownnosers), journalism merchants, and gangsters.[39]

Although commentators held that institutional and coercive forms of censorship were rare, they argued that official control of newspapers was effectively absolute. The press was "one of the sectors of the country where subordination to power was most obvious."[40] Shared ideological positions on anticommunism, national progress, and economic stability united officials, editors, and journalists.[41] Financial incentives, including discounted newsprint, government advertising, cheap loans, and regular payoffs—the *sobornos* (bribes) known in slang as *igualas* (fees), *embutes* (bribes), *sobres* (envelopes), or *chayotes* (squashes)—tightened these bonds.[42] Formulaic press releases laid down clear party lines; stories wrote themselves.[43] In

Mexico's newsrooms, "censorship extended and implanted itself as something natural"; all journalists knew "the limits of what they could write"; and self-censorship was the rule, something like the "scissors in the head" of East German writers.[44] Empty eulogy, fawning, and flattery of officials were all commonplace, while the "core features of the political system—presidential authority, official corruption, state violence and electoral fraud etc.—were decidedly off limits."[45] If journalists occasionally transgressed the boundaries, owners and editors silenced or sacked them.[46] At best, the print media were "a free press which does not make use of its freedom"; at worst, freedom of expression was a "great lie" that "was subject to so many limits, it does not exist."[47]

As a result, the political influence of newspapers was perceived as extremely limited. They were echo chambers *avant la lettre*. "The mass media were in essence ineffective, they persuaded those already persuaded and could inhibit those still on the fence, but they did nothing more."[48] State control, high prices, elitist subject matter, and an obscurantist, overly elaborate prose alienated the majority of potential, if semiliterate, readers.[49] The press acted as little more than an elite talking shop, "read by politicians for its hidden messages, used by the government to float controversial ideas and exploited as a forum for infighting between different political mafias."[50] Public opinion was "the patrimony of the initiated," a narrow and exclusive section of the privileged class; in short, the public sphere was not all that public.[51] If Mexicans outside the inner circle did read the newspapers, they either imbibed a one-way stream of "unified messages and symbols reinforcing regime legitimacy" or they did so with cynicism.[52] Writing in the 1970s, Cosío Villegas argued that the "incredulity of the immense majority of readers" was such that Mexicans "didn't simply judge journalists as liars, but took it as a rule to believe exactly the opposite of what they wrote."[53] One popular dictum held that "the person who reads nothing is better educated than the one who only reads the newspapers."[54] If everyday Mexicans did exchange political opinions, they did so through rumor and gossip, around the water fountain, in the market, over a coffee, or inside their families.[55] If they sought to challenge state authority, they did so not through print media but rather through rituals, ranging from choreographed riots to savvy disruptions of official celebrations, "spaces in which people could express ideas that were not allowed in the public sphere."[56]

Such negative assessments of the press have considerable weight—and some empirical backing. Large parts of the story, however, rest on political polemic, normative approaches, and questionable comparisons. Right-wing critics have drawn on a romanticized teleology of Western press freedoms to denigrate the Mexican press for its technological backwardness, moribund commercial policies, lack of professionalism, and political subordination.[57] In the twenty-first century such an approach has been bolstered by theorists of media democratization, who argue that it took increased commercialization and competition to bring innovation, professionalization, and a new level of public debate on power.[58] For observers on the left the story is more political and individual than commercial, centering on the role of Julio Scherer and his generation in combating state control. For influential writers like Vicente Leñero, Carlos Monsiváis, and Elena Poniatowska, the pivot was *Excélsior*'s challenge to the state from the 1968 student massacre until the 1976 expulsion of Scherer and his allies from their newsroom.[59] The unintended consequence of this governmental coup against Mexico's only serious independent newspaper, what cartoonist Rius called the "Pinochetazo of *Excélsior*," was the launch of several new opposition publications. Scherer founded the pathbreaking weekly *Proceso*; other "civic pioneers" founded the dailies *Unomásuno* and *La Jornada*; and these, finally, guided Mexico to the sunlit liberal uplands of a free press.[60]

If right- and left-wing narratives of oppression and emancipation differ on process and details, they share three flawed assumptions. First, they exaggerate the coherence and power of the state. Even in its pomp, the PRI's grasp on Mexico was weak, the regime a dictablanda by necessity. Regional autonomies, central factionalism, and a fundamental shortage of money and manpower all made totalitarian press control impossible.[61] The laws governing information flows were aggressive, but went largely unenforced. There was only one dedicated censorship agency, the Comisión Calificadora de Publicaciones y Revistas Ilustradas (Assessment Commission of Publications and Illustrated Magazines), which was set up to deal with the moral threat of comic books. It subsequently expanded to include sports, *nota roja* (crime), and soft porn magazines, yet it was rarely very effective, and what censorship did take place came on an ad hoc basis from the Ministry of the Interior.[62] Second, they are heavily based on Mexico City's broadsheets, the self-declared *gran prensa*, and the writings of their

stalwarts. The hegemonic narrative of oppression and (post-1968) resistance has lent Julio Scherer (among others) what Arno Burkholder terms a
"mystifying halo"; this undermines critical study and condemns the rest of
the press to accusations of state control, corruption, and essential civic
irrelevance. Whether coming from before '68 or from outside the city, other
print media are generally ignored or dismissed.[63] Provincial newsmen,
Monsiváis wrote, were devoted to "banality, adulation, local credulity, and
parochial anticommunism."[64] Critical newspapers like *Por Qué?* were "tabloid" and "exaggerated," their denouncements the "fruits of desperation
and not careful reflection."[65] The nota roja enthusiasts of tabloids and crime
magazines were "sensationalist" and "bloody."[66] Yet these media did provide forums for criticism and debate; they constituted a fourth (not Cosío
Villegas's "fifteenth") estate.[67] As Piccato notes in this volume, "The trade
still involved many of the values of nineteenth-century periodistas de combate: integrity, concern about reputations, and a close relationship with
readers." Finally, critics of all stripes underestimate notably the strength of
Mexican civil society under the PRI. Censorship was widely deplored (even
by the censorious), and its ultimate manifestation, the murder of journalists, was politically perilous, toppling regional politicians from mayors to
governors.[68] The net effect was the survival of a broad range of media, consumed by readers who did not always know much about political journalism but knew what they liked.[69]

Toward a New History of the Press, 1910–1970

This book is a collective history of that broad range of print media. The
authors apply the revisionist scrutiny of earlier periods to the twentieth century, above all to the time of the PRI, 1929–2000. In doing so, they do not
throw the baby out with the bathwater; on the contrary some contributors
convincingly reinforce parts of the traditional narrative. Press manipulation
and journalistic self-censorship were rife. The single intelligence document
that Jacinto Rodríguez Munguía unpacks, a carefully considered proposal
for subtle and total press manipulation, lends a new weight to belief in the
Orwellian fantasies (though not capacities) of sectors of the ruling class.
Andrew Paxman's case study of the Puebla press is a detailed substantiation
of how some of those fantasies were realized by hard-line governors. In other

chapters, however, old suppositions go down the plughole. Some of the contributors make it clear that provincial newspapers, metropolitan cartoons and crime pages, newsmagazines, and even trade publications collectively provided considerable political news and critical commentary.[70] Renata Keller's chapter on *Política* depicts a powerful leftist magazine that until 1967 took on any and all comers, including, in defiance of "the so-called unwritten rules of Mexican journalism," the president. On the other side of 1968, Vanessa Freije shows how censorship frequently intensified rather than silenced controversy. The sum is a book that recognizes ambiguities and considerable temporal and geographical variation in the interactions of press, politicians, cultural managers, and readers. Starting and finishing with the tragic stories of the press of our time, however, the volume raises unsettling questions: at the structural level of how much politically controversial debate goes on in the public sphere, has all that much changed? In extremis, has change run in the opposite direction, from debate to diversion and silence? Are there more limits to what can be written in a formally democratic Ciudad Juárez, or Michoacán, or Acapulco, or Veracruz than there ever were under single-party rule?

Ambiguities, of course, are nothing new in this history. The revolutionaries wrote press freedom into the 1917 Mexican Constitution, making it illegal to shutter or destroy printing establishments or to close down papers for defamatory articles. They also wrote the 1917 press law, which made it illegal to even "covertly" criticize individuals, and a penal code that promised up to two years' imprisonment for any journalist threatening the public peace through "discrediting, ridiculing, or destroying the fundamental institutions of the country" or "insulting the Mexican nation or its political entities."[71] Yet for all the repressive aspects of the press laws after the death of President Francisco Madero, who had been savaged mercilessly by the papers he initially protected, and even when set against revisionist versions of Porfirian press history, the revolution was, as Serna Rodríguez and Piccato demonstrate in this volume, a clear rupture. By the 1920s popular demands were "channeled through both formal and informal routes, . . . [and] journalism acquired its primordial function as the intermediary between public opinion and the state."[72]

During the revolution and the decades immediately following, radical workers' newspapers flourished; voicing their demands was the key to success.[73] But so did their opponents: Catholic organs, like the earnest Cristero newspaper *La Epoca*; their vituperative hard-line conservative successors, the tabloids *Hombre Libre* and *Omega*; and the mouthpieces of the regional bourgeoisie, like *El Siglo de Torreón, El Dictamen, El Diario de Yucatán*, and *El Porvenir.*[74] The expanded industry of mass-produced nationals, like *Excélsior, Novedades, La Prensa*, and *El Universal*—which walked a delicate line between official support and overt criticism—also flourished. As flagships of the revolutionary state's liberal credentials, they were often given a long rope. But this could be yanked fairly aggressively, particularly at times of political tension, to keep them in line.[75] If journalists changed, so too did the structure of media ownership. By the early 1940s it had undergone its own revolution: the old owners, like the aristocratic Rafael Reyes Spíndola, had gone, and ambitious businessmen from the lower middle classes, like José García Valseca, had taken their place. Moreover, two of Mexico's biggest dailies, *La Prensa* and *Excélsior*, were owned by worker cooperatives.[76]

If the early post-revolutionary decades witnessed an overhaul of press discourses and structures, it was the midcentury that saw a genuine change in print readership. This had multiple causes: education, better communication, a soaring birth rate, relative prosperity, and comparatively little competition from other media forms. Revolutionary schooling and literacy programs paid off: in 1940, 42 percent of adults were literate; by 1970, the number was 76 percent. These new readers lived in towns and cities of a new size—the 1960 census found more Mexicans in town than country—where newspapers, often local, were readily available.[77] Both local and national papers traveled farther and quicker on the new road networks, often by using the free second-class mail granted to the press by President Lázaro Cárdenas.[78] Print media now reached far beyond the immediate environs of the printshop. Economic growth also mattered. Increased advertising gave owners greater financial support: between 1963 and 1970 annual spending on advertising increased from 1.6 billion pesos to nearly 4 billion.[79] For some, the big sixty-centavo broadsheets remained out of reach, but for many the twenty-centavo or thirty-centavo tabloids and local eight-page weeklies did not cut too far into rent and food. Finally, while other media made inroads they had yet to dominate the market. Radio listening, intense since the 1930s, complemented rather than supplemented newspaper reading. Television, the future, was limited to Mexico City and provincial capitals until the 1970s, and until then

Televisa's newsreaders tended to repeat the front pages of the newspapers anyway.[80] The sum of these changes was a veritable explosion of newspaper production, far outpacing population growth. In 1930 there were 44 dailies in Mexico; by 1974 there were 256.[81]

Their readers were not evenly spread across class or place. The capital's three main broadsheets—*Excélsior, El Universal, Novedades*—lost ground in relative terms, their readership growing slower than the population and much slower than that of the tabloids.[82] While they faced competition from new broadsheets, more significantly they failed to reach much beyond middle- and upper-class residents of the capital. Dull subject matter, limited sports and crime, clunky language, oft-impenetrable columns, and a distinct air of snobbery put off workers, students, teachers, taxi drivers, and clerks. In 1970 an Informex survey concluded that even Scherer's *Excélsior* rarely penetrated beyond professionals, merchants, and industrialists.[83] But Mexico City tabloids like *La Prensa, La Prensa Gráfica, Últimas Noticias, Ovaciones,* and *Tabloide* saw circulation soar. "We are the main newspaper in Mexico," claimed *La Prensa's* editor as early as 1942, "because in reality we are [a] truly popular newspaper and can sustain ourselves without great problems."[84] By 1960, the twenty-centavo *Tabloide* allegedly sold over 150,000 copies per day.[85] Ten years later, *La Prensa* had a certified circulation of 185,361, and *Ovaciones* was outselling *Excélsior* by more than two to one.[86] Content was key: scandal, sports, crime, and celebrity news sold. But so was language. Roberto G. Serna, the editor of *Zócalo*, insisted that his journalists employ a style that "was colloquial, anecdotal, seasoned with jokes and wordplay," using "the greatest amount of popular terms but without losing grammatical form."[87] These papers were designed for Mexico City's working class, and they worked.

Provincial newspapers were also often success stories. Scholars have regularly denigrated the regional penetration of the press, using statistics which show that per capita readership at the national level was relatively low, around one issue per ten inhabitants.[88] Changes in villages and hamlets are difficult to see, and some anthropologies suggest minimal (if politically important) readership.[89] But taking into account the urban-rural divide, more focused approaches reveal a burgeoning regional industry—a genuine readers' revolution. In cities across the country owners claimed to produce more papers than there were households. Even allowing for deliberate overestimates and sales in the hinterlands, the figures are startling. In 1967 Monterrey's five dailies produced around 241,000 copies for 114,000 house-holds. In Mérida notarized counts of *El Diario del Sureste*, *El Diario de Yucatán*, and *Novedades de Yucatán*'s circulations totaled 101,900 copies for 28,000 households.[90] In the same year, an extensive US government survey estimated that 79 percent of urban Mexicans read their local newspapers regularly.[91] If you were literate and you lived in a town or city, you read the press.

The precise extent, rhythms, and mechanisms of state censorship are still to be established. That the state attempted to control the press is beyond doubt. Initially attempts were ad hoc and comprised a distinctly dictablanda mix of personal approaches, bribery, threats, and violence.[92] By the mid-1960s, as Rodríguez Munguía demonstrates in this volume, there were those in government who sought to construct "an invisible tyranny" through conscious, subtle, and total manipulation of the mass media. Many owners, editors, and journalists embraced this, both for ideological reasons and for financial gain.[93] In the national broadsheets some targets, like the president, and some themes, like military violence, were forbidden.[94] And particularly after 1948 print satirists were sparse, incomprehensible, or nonexistent.[95]

But this fails to tell the whole story of pressure on print media. Private enterprises also tried their hands at censorship. Up until the 1960s the powerful Monterrey group had a censor in the newsroom of *El Norte*, who would redact or change sensitive stories on strikes and workers' rights.[96] (In the twenty-first century, as Javier Garza Ramos and Rafael Barajas argue in this volume, such pressure has increased, far outweighing the censorship attempts of the state.) Furthermore, even during the mid-twentieth century official censorship was far from complete. In the provinces local governments lacked the cash to accomplish anything near "an invisible tyranny." Instead they relied on irregular bouts of dirty tricks, violence, and intimidation to shut up or punish the critical press.[97] As Paxman's chapter demonstrates, even when they succeeded the process was lengthy and open to some haggling: faced with the Ávila Camacho *cacicazgo*,[98] *La Opinión de Puebla* took years to bend entirely to Maximino's will.

Because censorship was irregular, spaces for criticism, debate, and popular input were relatively commonplace. In the nationals, the crime news, cartoons, and to a lesser extent photographs served these roles. By the 1940s most broadsheets and all the tabloids ran the nota roja, though *Excélsior*, "wanting to cooperate with authorities and educational centers of the country oriented toward the popular classes" had piously forsworn bloody crime news in 1930.[99] The crime pages were implicitly political. They probed suspicious murders, exposed government corruption, and suggested links between the upscale restaurants of the "lawyerocracy" and the spit-and-sawdust cantinas of professional hitmen.[100] As Piccato has argued, "crime news was the terrain on which civil society addressed the separation between truth and justice, the disjuncture between people's knowledge about the reality of criminal acts and the state response to these acts."[101] The crime pages also encouraged popular interaction. They experimented with readers' polls; letters pages were stacked with amateur detectives' theories; and crime magazines ran collaborative columns like "You Are the Judge."[102] As the Sonoran crime journalist Cesar Vallejo made clear, "I believe the crime page has the most contact with the people, with reality. I believe that it is the most human, the nearest to the problems of the people."[103]

During the immediate postwar era, anticommunist cartoonists dominated the national newspapers. Most cartoonists condemned perceived left-wing movements, including the 1958 teachers strike, the 1959 railway workers strike, and the 1968 student movement. In 1954 the US National Editorial Association even employed the caricaturist Rafael Freyre to support US intervention in Guatemala.[104] But right-wing cartoonists also mercilessly mocked the regime's claims to revolutionary policy. In *Presente*, Antonio Arias Bernal's cartoons not only lampooned the president's cronies but also critiqued Miguel Alemán directly. He was less Mr. Colgate, the beaming president, and more a buck-toothed buffoon locking up the constitution.[105] Meanwhile more radical, left-leaning cartoonists were emerging. By the 1950s, illustrated satire had taken over from written press or stage versions of the genre. Abel Quezada led the way with complex and scathing cartoons, images that drew on Posada's tradition of the visually grotesque while pioneering the multiple boxes and long texts that characterized his successors. Quezada's fifty-year career in many ways epitomized the censorship of his times. His contribution to *Ovaciones* of June 10, 1950, savaged the self-censorship of the reporters accompanying a presidential tour:

Of course [the journalists'] patriotism, combined with the excellence of the banquet, led them not to see, for example, that on Sunday, May 21, in Ixtepec, Oaxaca, while they were eating opulently in Alemán's company, soldiers were marshaling a queue outside of people piling up to eat the leftovers; and neither did they see, perhaps through studying too closely the president's smile, a banner that was displayed on the 5th of June in Motul, Yucatán, which read "Mr. President, we the *ejidatarios* of Motul are dying of hunger."[106]

After the ensuing ten days of attacks from his colleagues, Quezada resigned with an elegant final cartoon on absent press freedoms; within months he was back at work, unabashed; in 1976 he was expelled along with Scherer and company from *Excélsior*; in short order he was at work once more.[107]

Eduardo del Río, also known as Rius, followed, earning a living wage in the tabloids *Ovaciones* and *La Prensa* before running scathing cartoon supplements in left-wing magazines like *Política*, *Sucesos*, and *Por Qué?* and publishing his own comic book, *Los Supermachos*. In his autobiography the cartoonist admitted that in *Política* he "published some of the most violent cartoons that post-revolutionary Mexico had ever seen." By 1968 he and three other cartoonists set up a cooperative, which put out *La Garrapata: El Azote de los Bueyes*, a supremely critical selection of pro-student cartoons.[108] Even more officialist cartoonists started to undermine state policy. Jorge Carreño's frontispieces for *Siempre!* "contribut[ed] to the gradual erosion of presidentialism."[109] And by the 1960s caricature had become "the foundation for the creation of popular political culture."[110]

Photographs could also offer counterhegemonic versions of contemporary news. By their very nature they were more open to interpretation than were written texts. Although editors tried hard to control the visual presentation of controversial events through apposite selection and calculated caption writing, they were not always successful. Alberto del Castillo Troncoso's careful studies of photographic representations of the student movement in 1968 reveal that even the most bourgeois broadsheets occasionally acknowledged students' demands through oversight or deliberate error. After soldiers used a bazooka to open the doors of the Instituto Politécnico Nacional (National Polytechnic Institute), university rector Javier Barros Sierra led a student march through Mexico City. Even the notoriously conservative *Heraldo de México* acknowledged the march's popular support, showing the applauding people hanging out of the Miguel Alemán housing complex in the center of town. Similarly, on August 31, 1968, the newspaper included a picture of two older women walking down the street with crossed arms in support of the student strike. There was no caption. Readers were free to interpret the photograph as demonstrating that civil society was beginning to back the revolt.[111]

If space within the gran prensa existed but was somewhat limited, other print media were much less controlled. Provincial newspapers ran the gamut from exceptionally officialist (and dull) through the strictly commercial (and apolitical) to a degree of focused political radicalism unthinkable in the Mexico City dailies. This was due to the federal government's drive and ability to control the capital's public sphere, but also to the lesser importance of electoral politics there. There were no elected positions to fight over in Mexico City, whereas the oft-bitter competition for state and municipal offices in the provinces made local politics and local reporting far more significant. The provincial press was consequently far less docile or predictable than traditionally thought and distinctly more willing to enter into personalized opposition—in the main against regional politicians, but also concerning the president.[112] The growing number of papers in the García Valseca, Bercun, and Healy publishing chains did make coordinated central influence easier, but even they periodically entered into local politics with a critical vigor; meanwhile some independent newspapers were genuinely independent. A 1960 Ministry of the Interior survey of regional papers could not find overt government influence in 41 percent of the titles, and the agents classified the editorial stance of 50 percent as either independent or oppositional.[113] Some critical papers were sober centralist broadsheets, such as Guadalajara's El Informador; others were radical tabloids, such as La Verdad de Acapulco, the port's left-wing stalwart for some twenty years. All used their editorials for virulent political attacks; some extended this criticism overtly into their reporting, while others used "structural slyness"—the meaningful juxtaposition, the mock-innocent aside—to undermine their oficialista coverage.[114] They exercised an everyday, qualified but meaningful press freedom that was absent in Mexico City.

Right-wing and left-wing magazines also provided ample space for relatively free, informed journalism. The Partido Acción Nacional's paper, La Nación, was much more than a party political organ. Coverage of electoral fraud was particularly acute, revealing how dirty tricks and violence curtailed the PAN's popular candidate for the Baja California governorship in 1959 and Salvador Nava's independent run for the San Luis Potosí position two years later.[115] On October 15, 1968, the paper ran an extremely bloody front-page photograph, which showed three dead students at Tlatelolco, above the headline "Huichilobos Returns to Tlatelolco."[116] Left-wing magazines were also overtly critical. As Renata Keller argues in this volume, *Política* broke all the "unwritten rules of the press," attacking Adolfo López Mateos's treatment of workers, supporting political prisoners, revealing the increasing repression of opposition, and openly ridiculing presidential candidate Gustavo Díaz Ordaz.[117] In the mid-1960s, *Sucesos* under Mario Menéndez took up the role of countercultural critic, publishing investigative reports into official corruption and providing a road map for radical change in the form of extensive, favorable interviews with Fidel Castro and guerrillas in Venezuela, Guatemala, and Colombia.[118] Finally, in early 1968 Menéndez started *Por Qué?*, a sensationalist tabloid weekly replete with bloody nota roja visuals of state violence.[119] These magazines transformed politics, becoming required reading for a generation of students and opposition activists.[120]

Union magazines also provided forums for debate and critique. During the late 1950s the electricians' publication, *Solidaridad*, became what José Luis Gutiérrez Espíndola terms "a tribune of the labor insurgency." Tips on tactics were exchanged, and sympathetic strikes were offered coverage and support. Such open discussions were well liked. Backed by union dues, the magazine hit an estimated print run of 10,000–12,000 per month, more than Vicente Lombardo Toledano's increasingly official *El Popular*.[121] As Michael Lettieri demonstrates in this volume, *El Informador Camionero* likewise provided a relatively open, critical forum for the nation's bus workers.

Reform and Good-Bye, 1970–2000

During the 1970s, relations between the state and the national print media changed. President Luis Echeverría announced a new period of "political opening," and front stage he encouraged "independent, honest and timely journalism." "If he means it, this would be [a] clear departure from what currently exists in Mexico," observed the US ambassador.[122] His press secretary,

Fausto Zapata, reiterated the shift. "We don't want to supplant our reality with rigged information. . . . The government doesn't want to disguise problems but resolve them."[123] This was partly theater. During the *sexenio* (six-year term), Echeverría's government used state pressure or allies in the private sector to close down *Por Qué?*, usurp control of *El Universal* and García Valseca's *Sol* chain, and most famously harass and then take over *Excélsior*.[124] But the statement was not wholly spurious either: back stage Echeverría confessed to *Excélsior*'s head, Julio Scherer, that he thought too much censorship "thins the blood, weakens the juices, and makes a real man a eunuch."[125] Echeverría's successor, José López Portillo, took a similar line, reforming Article 6 of the constitution to include the "public right to know" and starting a debate on the state's relationship to the mass media.[126]

Such opinions shaped the new tone of national newspapers. Political columns in particular started to offer greater space for public discussion. These had started as elitist, money-making enterprises. Salvador Novo had punned on their name and termed them *calumnias políticas*, "political calumnies."[127] Carlos Denegri's "Miscelánea" in *Excélsior* provided the model. Described by Scherer and Monsiváis as "a flatterer without scruples, precious beyond measure, and a specialist in the abuse of power," Denegri sold his column to the highest bidder.[128] During the early 1970s, however, more critical writers came to the fore. As Vanessa Freije has shown, columnists like Manuel Buendía, Miguel Granados Chapa, and Julio Manuel Ramírez (the pen name for the combined skills of Julio Scherer, Manuel Becerra Acosta, and Fernando Ramírez de Aguilar) revealed government corruption, denounced poor policy, and increasingly included popular voices in their columns. Even the "front pages of the mainstream press could be quite confrontational."[129]

The work of these writers also opened space for the expansion of a more independent, left-wing press. At first this included relatively marginal magazines like *Punto Crítico*, *La Fragua*, and *El Causa del Pueblo*, which were established by former members of the student movement and members of the Communist Party. There were also publications linked to specific movements, like the Colonia Rubén Jaramillo's *Frente Popular* and the Chihuahua Comité de Defensa Popular's *El Martillo*.[130] But by the 1980s this newly critical press also included large-scale, industrially produced newspapers and magazines with national reach like *Proceso*, *Unomásuno*, and *La Jornada*.[131] Even if they failed to acknowledge it, most were inspired by Menéndez's *Por*

Qué? They were written in a simple, accessible language, engaged with the actual problems of Mexico's working classes, and paid attention to the competing voices of civil society. They embraced civic journalism; *El Martillo* even contained a special section devoted to the "denunciations" of the people, which, its editors argued, "laid bare the classist character of the actual system."[132] Like *Por Qué?*, the new publications often aped the format and concerns of the nota roja, continuing the tradition of using crime news to expose politicians' corruption, repression, and criminal collusion.[133] This led to accusations of *amarillismo*, or yellow journalism. It also meant they were read.

In the provinces, the critical spaces afforded by local newspapers endured and broadened. As Javier Garza Ramos shows in this volume, even the big, industrial regionals were increasingly linked to the country's growing democratization movements. In the late 1970s, Coahuila's *El Siglo* and *La Opinión* gave ample coverage to opposition politicians and investigated claims of electoral fraud. Freed from the control of the Garza Sada family, Monterrey's *El Norte* did the same. In 1985 the newspaper pioneered the system of placing unaffiliated observers in polling stations. These observers countered the official party's claims to a clean sweep and offered in-depth coverage of the losing PAN candidate's protests that there was vote rigging. In fact, the ongoing abrasive quality of regional newspapers both foreshadowed and helped create change at the national level. They provided editors, journalists, and stringers unencumbered by traditions of self-censorship or close relations to metropolitan elites; they printed stories from the frontiers of state repression; they provided spaces for national journalists' more subversive critiques; and at times they even provided cash backing. *El Norte's* Junco family started up the national *Reforma*; Jorge Alvarez del Castillo, the owner of Guadalajara's *El Informador*, gave Scherer the start-up money for *Proceso.*[134]

By the late 1980s such changes had shifted the press coverage even of national elections. In 1970 only the PRI's candidate had appeared on the news pages of the major nationals. *Excélsior* averaged around three mentions per issue; the more obsequious (and indebted) *El Universal* averaged around eighteen. Opposition candidates went virtually unmentioned.[135] By 1988 reporting had changed. The press now reflected the more plural, democratic elections. The proportion of coverage given to each party was almost the same as their proportion of the popular vote. The PRI, which had received around 90 percent of mentions in 1970, now garnered 55 percent, only 4 points higher than its share of the vote. By the end of the decade the print segment was by far the most independent of the mass media. In comparison, television stations focused over 90 percent of their coverage on the PRI candidate.[136]

Yet while political constraints on the print media fell during democratization, cultural and commercial constraints rose. Television replaced newspapers as citizens' primary source of information. Ownership increased: by 1990 over 90 percent of households had access to TVs.[137] So did TV watching: by the last decade of the twentieth century Mexicans watched more television than people in any other nation.[138] And so did television's role as a means of delivering the news. In 1958, only 50 percent of urban Mexicans had ever watched a TV, and only 11 percent got their news from the device. In comparison, 72 percent read the news. Thirty years later, the roles had reversed: 89.6 percent of Mexicans got news from the TV; less than 50 percent read papers or magazines.[139] Not coincidentally, television's triumph overlapped with the creation of a rival to Televisa's monopoly, TV Azteca. The new broadcaster brought a degree of pluralism to the small screen even as it put pressure on the newspaper business. In the twenty-first century, the popularity of another technological innovation—the internet—would generate another, even more significant revolution in how Mexicans received the mass media, and it too threatened the printed press.

Mexico's Contemporary Press, 2000–2017

A good story might end here, perhaps on election night 2000, after more than two decades of increasingly independent national journalism marked by the liberties taken by the writers of *Proceso* or *Reforma* or *La Jornada* in attacking *priistas*, or the cartoon savagings in El Fisgón's popular collection *El sexenio me da risa*, or the gleeful coverage of the *pistoleros*, psychics, and Swiss bank accounts of the president's brother, Raúl Salinas. Yet the spaces for reporting and debate that opened up during democratization have proved a lot less open or secure than seemed possible on that ecstatic night; there is no happy ending.

Instead, contemporary print journalists face four major pressures. The first is commercial, founded on problems that newspapers face everywhere in the twenty-first century: as Javier Garza Ramos points out in his chapter, "digital technologies have changed reading habits; advertising budgets are being allocated in other media; and newspapers have not found a way to monetize their websites and digital products." The second is cultural: the internet provides a multiplicity of new routes from event to report at the same time as it sucks money and consumers out of professionalized "old" media. The third is political: the rise of powerful, autonomous governors (or what political scientists term "subnational authoritarianism") and the return of authoritarian practices in many places outside Mexico City.[140] The fourth is criminal: journalists trying to do their job face unprecedented violence from cartels and compromised politicians. As Judith Matloff reports in the foreword to this volume, "many Mexican media professionals have stopped reporting on the violence" because "impunity is so rife, and the collusion between organized crime and law enforcers so profound, that only self-censorship saves lives."

On the surface, Mexico's newspaper industry appears economically robust. A glance at a Mexico City newsstand shows five established nationals, a handful of more specialized or regional titles, and a range of editorial lines. Yet circulation is in decline, and Mexico's largest newspaper, *Reforma*, sold fewer copies in 2015 than *Excélsior* did in 1970.[141] Moreover, these dailies, as in the past, do not enjoy truly national distribution: Mexico City represents 49 percent of *Milenio*'s circulation, 60 percent of *Reforma*'s, 76 percent of *Excélsior*'s, and 85 percent of *El Universal*'s.[142] And perhaps most important, the fragmentation of the newspaper industry is endemic. The more successful nationals share readers and advertising with a host of smaller, less-independent organs. Since revenue is spread so thinly, most are forced to rely, at least partially, on government funding.[143]

While the relationship of the national print media to politics is less overt than that of the broadcast media, regional papers still rely on government subsidies and advertising, in many cases more than before because businesses have substantially cut the commercial advertising that supported some independence.[144] Moreover, with journalists' pay abysmally low—averaging around US$650 per month—economic pressure is not just institutional, but also individual.[145] As Rubén Espinosa observed, penury is as responsible for stifling free expression as are narco traffickers.[146] The result is a new censorship, exercised by politicians of all stripes. In a Kafkaesque case in 2015, the governor of Baja California reacted to critical coverage by taking out full-page newspaper ads announcing that his administration would no longer take out newspaper ads.[147]

At the cultural level of technological consumerism, internet journalism actually helps make this censorship possible; while *Reforma* was quick to adopt a paywall for its portal, the net effect of the explosion of online-only news sites has been to defund the print press. Yet their competitive success is not based on advertising alone. Unlike in the United States, where the portals of the *Huffington Post* or *Slate* are less important than those of print publications like the *New York Times* or the *Atlantic*, in Mexico online-only news sites host some of the best reporters and columnists. Nationally, *SinEmbargo* and *Animal Político* are widely read and influential. On a regional level, internet news sites such as Puebla's *Lado B*, Veracruz's *Plumas Libres*, or *Valor por Tamaulipas* provide critical material in places where criticism is particularly difficult. Access to these sources, however, is limited to the relatively well-off: though smartphones are starting to penetrate, less than half of Mexican households have internet connections, and these are far more prevalent in cities than in the countryside.[148] Web-only outlets also face the same problems of charging for their work as do newspapers and consequently struggle to sustain their journalists and business. Some come up with creative solutions: *Animal Político* allows readers to contribute via "subscriptions" of eighty pesos per month, which fund prizes for their reporters.[149] Yet much of the best work is unpaid and hence of uncertain longevity.

Parallel to the growth of formal online journalism, the internet has driven the expansion of informal citizen journalism. In some cases this feeds stories to traditional media, as when a cell-phone video captured a federal official's daughter threatening to have her father close a restaurant (a threat which was made good).[150] More important, such images combine with reporting to fuel blogs and social media crucial in exposing corruption and human rights abuses. At its peak the most notable, *El Blog del Narco*, had 25 million visitors a month and a greater readership than *La Jornada* or *Milenio*. The blog, founded by a journalist known only as "Lucy" and an unnamed computer scientist, posts anonymous reportage and gory images of violence; it neither censors nor (understandably but disturbingly) verifies. In places it has lived up to its origin story of fearless citizen journalists filling the vacuum created by violent censorship in the provinces; nationally it is to some extent an aggregator, at times reproducing without attribution articles from mainstream media, which in turn use the blog as a source. As Paul Eiss argues in this volume, websites such as *El Blog del Narco* provide a space where old and new media converge, where "violence and pressure . . . generate the context and impetus for a new form of news media production, arguably of a reach equal to or even greater than conventional mass media journalism." The crowd-sourced nature of such production, though, means that it flows not just from the keyboards and cell phones of the citizenry, but also from those of state and criminal actors. Narcos do not automatically despise citizen journalists; they also use them, whether to strike poses, to threaten, or to issue press statements.

Among the chaff the rise of internet journalism has also provided a lot of wheat, particularly significant given the political pressure on traditional media. In the twenty-first century, journalists have enjoyed far greater latitude to launch targeted, specific attacks on abuses of power at the highest levels. Yet censorship has endured and increased. In 2011 President Felipe Calderón came to an arrangement with media outlets, including *El Universal* and *Excélsior*, to set highly restrictive "editorial criteria" for narco reporting, justified as silencing the cartels' efforts at public relations. In Tijuana, President Enrique Peña Nieto's administration stopped releasing information on drug war homicides or policing, and subsequently launched a national "Nueva narrativa en material de seguridad" (New narrative on security issues) encouraging the press to attribute all violence to narcos and to avoid criticism of state violence.[151] Such measures are indirect effects of crime; politicians have also engaged in censorship with the more direct function of self-interest. The most prominent example was the Carmen Aristegui case, in which an investigation into a construction company's exchanges of favors with Peña Nieto led to the reporter's firing. This backfired, generating yet more negative publicity and giving Aristegui new platforms, including a more popular website, international speaking tours, and new newspaper columns. Aristegui, however, was already one of the most visible journalists in Mexico before the scandal; her success was unsurprising. Provincial journalists have been less fortunate. In extremis, the drug wars provide cover for old-fashioned political killings. In Veracruz, for example, it is highly improbable that the seven journalists who have disappeared and the eighteen who have been murdered between 2010 and 2016, many of whom were covering corruption and social movements, were all victims of narco violence.[152] While Veracruz is notorious, it is not all that distinctive; according to one sample, half of the recent violence reported against journalists came from state and not criminal actors.[153]

It is also provincial journalists who have borne the brunt of criminal censorship. Precise quantification of the violence is difficult since the motivations for some killings are murky while lesser acts of violence go unreported, but the Committee to Protect Journalists' count of twenty-nine murders during the period 2006–2017 is deeply conservative. A mere two of these victims came from the national media.[154] In Nuevo Laredo, for example, *El Mañana* has had its editors and publishers kidnapped and four of its staffers killed or disappeared. Sustained violence has led to new sets of unwritten rules about what can and cannot be written. (These vary from place to place: in Culiacán and Tijuana, there was—at least until the 2017 execution of Javier Valdez Cárdenas—more open coverage of narco trafficking in the weekly newspaper *Ríodoce* and the magazine *Semanario Zeta*.) After a second of *El Diario de Juárez*'s journalists was killed in 2010, the editor famously ran an editorial acknowledging the cartels as the "de facto authorities" and asking them to "explain to us what you want from us, so we know what to abide by. . . . It is impossible for us to do our job under these conditions. Tell us, then, what you expect from us, as a newspaper."[155] Following the editorial, *El Diario de Juárez* stopped covering drug-related topics, a decision mirrored by *El Mañana* and other papers. National media and civil society organizations have been relatively disinterested in the crisis, in part due to Mexico's marked metropolitan-provincial divide, in part due to historical disdain for journalists in general. Yet as Paul Gillingham and Javier Garza Ramos demonstrate in this volume, freedom of information was once stronger in the states than in the capital. With the inversion of that past a substantial part of Mexico's public sphere has gone dark.

In 2017 Mexico was ranked 147th in Reporters Without Borders's World Press Freedom Index, the lowest in mainland Latin America. By this algorithm journalists in Nicolás Maduro's Venezuela or Rafael Correa's Ecuador enjoyed greater liberties to publish and be damned. The combined effect of political, commercial, and criminal censorship has left Mexico allegedly outcompeted in press freedoms by Afghanistan, Burma, Russia, and Zimbabwe.[156] When mixed with revisionist work that recovers earlier press freedoms, this is an end point that is really no end point at all. The history of the Mexican press does not, in fact, conform to any of the standard plots. It is not a story of overcoming a monster, or a heroic quest, or a rebirth, or an inevitable rise, or a decline and fall. It is certainly no comedy; neither, despite the contemporary crisis, is it an unalloyed tragedy. However, its similarity to the broader, ambiguous, and messy narrative of modern Mexico has not escaped us.

Notes

1. Díaz del Castillo, *Historia verdadera*, 418.
2. They included Moctezuma; Cortés's first wife, Catalina; and the disputatious king's treasurer, Julián de Aldarete.
3. Lafaye, *Quetzalcóatl y Guadalupe*, 273, Piccato, *Tyranny of Opinion*, 36–39, 185.
4. Or in Mexican terms, *pan o palo*. For the concept of post-revolutionary Mexico as a dictablanda, see Gillingham and Smith, *Dictablanda*, 1–43.
5. Lawson, *Building the Fourth Estate*; Hughes, *Newsrooms in Conflict*.
6. Between 1940 and 1960, nineteen journalists were murdered, nearly half of them between 1959 and 1960; since the late 1990s as many as ninety have been killed, although it is not always possible to link their murder to their work. Smith, *The Mexican Press and Civil Society*, ch. 5; "Libertad de prensa o demagogia," *El Chapulín*, Jan. 10, 1960; Matloff, this volume.
7. As Garza Ramos and Paxman demonstrate in this volume, there has also been a marked growth of commercial and political censorship.
8. Burkholder de la Rosa, "El olimpo fracturado," 1343–44; Keller, this volume; Vanessa Freije, pers. comm., Aug. 6, 2014.
9. Meade, this volume. The United States currently ranks 43 in the World Press Freedom Index, one place below Burkina Faso. Reporters Without Borders, "2017 World Press Freedom Index," https://rsf.org/en/ranking# (accessed Aug. 1, 2017). John Nerone and Roger Streitmatter emphasize that violence has curtailed US press freedoms, in particular those of radical papers, while Timothy Cook has explored the state's role in financially supporting the mainstream. In such a context, Mexico's history of the press looks closer to those of the United States or Western Europe than previously allowed. Curran and Park, *De-Westernizing Media Studies*; De Burgh, *Making Journalists*; Nerone, *Violence against the Press*; Streitmatter, *Voices of Revolution*; Cook, *Governing the News*. For critiques of the myth of US press freedom, also see Gitlin, *The Whole World Is Watching*; Herman and Chomsky, *Manufacturing Consent*.

10. See Garza Ramos and Barajas, both this volume; Darnton, *Censors at Work*, 234.

11. Darnton, "What Is the History of Books?," "An Early Information Society," and *Forbidden Best-Sellers*. Two key nodes of this shift have been the Instituto Mora's Seminario de Historia de la Prensa, now run by Ana María Serna Rodríguez, and the edited collections of Celia Del Palacio Montiel, including *Siete regiones*, *Rompecabezas de papel*, and *Violencia y periodismo*.

12. Piccato, *Tyranny of Opinion*, 23–26.

13. Ortiz Monasterio, *Historia y ficción*, 244, 309; Nesvig, *Ideology and Inquisition*.

14. For an overview of this historiography, see Piccato, "Public Sphere in Latin America"; Uribe-Uran, "Birth of a Public Sphere"; Annino, Castro Leiva, and Guerra, *De los imperios a las naciones*; Guerra et al., *Los espacios públicos*; Torres Puga, *Opinión pública*; P. Ramírez, "Enlightened Publics for Public Health"; Taylor, *Shrines and Miraculous Images*, 49–52.

15. Uribe-Uran, "Birth of a Public Sphere"; Guerra et al., *Los espacios públicos*.

16. Guardino, *Time of Liberty*, 156–222; Fowler, *Forceful Negotiations*.

17. By 1831 there were three major opposition newspapers in Mexico City and six in the provinces. Ríos Zúñiga, "Una retórica para la mobilización popular," 756–57. Also see Coudart, "Función de la prensa," 93–104; Clark de Lara and Speckman Guerra, *La república de las letras*.

18. There was a certain correlation between conservatism and increased press curbs.

19. Rojas, "Una maldición silenciada," 36–37.

20. Piccato, *Tyranny of Opinion*, 37.

21. See Ríos Zúñiga, "Una retórica para la movilización popular," 756.

22. Covo, "La prensa," 698–99.

23. Rojas, "Una maldición silenciada," 38; Piccato, *Tyranny of Opinion*, 39. For the colonial roots of satire, see Johnson, *Satire in Colonial Spanish America*.

24. Rugeley, *River People in Flood Time*, 107.

25. Leal, "El contenido literario," 330–31. The historiography of political cartoons is dense; see Gantús, *Caricatura y poder político*; Barajas, *El país de "El Ahuizote"* and *El país de "El Llorón de Icamole."*

26. Pérez-Rayón, "La prensa liberal," 145–70; Cosío Villegas, *La República Restaurada*.

27. This was especially true of *El Imparcial*, with its peak circulation of over 100,000 copies daily. Buffington, *Sentimental Education*, 11, 240.

28. These were *La Voz de México*, *El Tiempo*, and *El País*. Cosío Villegas, *El Porfiriato*, 2:525–27; Dumas and Vega, "El discurso de oposición."

29. Piccato, *Tyranny of Opinion*, 53.

30. The Creelman interview of 1908 was a lengthy conversation between the American journalist James Creelman and President Porfirio Díaz. Replete with

sycophancy and promises of free elections, it led to intense political mobilization for the 1910 presidential election. Those mobilized, subsequently disappointed by the rigging of the election, launched the revolution. *El Diablito Rojo*, Mar. 16, 1908, reproduced in Buffington, *Sentimental Education*, 120.

31. Buffington, *Sentimental Education*; Díaz, "The Satiric Penny Press."

32. Díaz, "The Satiric Penny Press," 502–4; Buffington, *Sentimental Education*, 9.

33. Lomnitz, *The Return*, 82–89. For skepticism as to how deeply the opposition messages in cartoons actually penetrated, see Gantús, *Caricatura y poder político*, ch.1.

34. In the mid-eighteenth century France's chief censor did not know how many cities outside Paris had inspectors of the book trade to enforce censorship. (The answer was two.) Darnton, *Censors at Work*, 59–60; Darnton, *Forbidden Best-Sellers*, 131.

35. Rodríguez Castañeda, *Prensa vendida*, 13; Stevens, *Protest and Response*, 34; Cline, *Mexico*, 185–86.

36. Cosío Villegas, *El sistema político*, 75.

37. Riva Palacio, "Culture of Collusion," 22.

38. Scherer García and Monsiváis, *Tiempo de saber*, 19–20; Gómez Arias, *Memoria personal*, 123; Fuentes, *Artemio Cruz*.

39. Castellaños, *México engañado*, 37–41; Luquín, *Análisis espectral*; Nichols, "Coyotes of the Press"; Rodríguez Castañeda, *Prensa vendida*, 13; G. Ramírez, *Los gangsters*.

40. Volpi, *La imaginación*, 34.

41. Servín, "Propaganda y guerra fría."

42. Bohmann, *Medios de comunicación*, 285–95.

43. Monsiváis, *A ustedes*, 54.

44. Granados Chapa, "Aproximación," 49–50, Darnton, *Censors at Work*, 84.

45. Lawson, *Building the Fourth Estate*, 25.

46. Riva Palacio, "The Nightmare," 109.

47. Cosío Villegas, "The Press," 279; Miguel de Mora, *Por la gracia*, 34.

48. Carlos Monsiváis quoted in Secanella, *El periodismo político*, 121.

49. Ibargüengoitia, *Instrucciones*, 91–92, 101–2; *Por Qué?*, Sept. 10, 1970.

50. Alan Riding quoted in Adler, "Media Uses and Effects," 84.

51. Monsiváis, *A ustedes*, 48.

52. Hughes, *Newsrooms in Conflict*, 50.

53. Cosío Villegas, *El sistema político*, 76.

54. Granados Chapa, *Nava Si! Zapata No!*, 33.

55. Cosío Villegas, *El sistema político*, 79.

56. Lomnitz, "Ritual, rumor y corrupción," 35.

57. Many of the early studies of the Mexican press adopted this tone, for example, Erlandson, "Press of Mexico." One of the first US works to buck this trend was the pathbreaking Cole, "Mass Media of Mexico."

58. Hallin, "Media, Political Power," 91; Calmon Alves, "From Lapdog to Watchdog," 183–84.

59. Leñero, *Los periodistas*; Scherer García and Monsiváis, *Tiempo de saber*; Monsiváis and Poniatowska in Brewster, "The Student Movement," 171–90.

60. Rodríguez Castañeda, *Prensa vendida*, 135–77; Hughes, *Newsrooms in Conflict*, 120–21; Lawson, *Building the Fourth Estate*, 66–69.

61. Gillingham and Smith, "Paradoxes of Revolution."

62. The commission brought only seven publishers to court between 1944 and 1953, and only four paid any fines; one editor of a pornography magazine simply refused to meet with the agency and went unsanctioned. The commission's weakness may have been in part because under President Alemán it lost its office in the Ministry of Public Education, furniture, files, and office equipment. It was, however, later used to shut down critical magazines in 1969, 1974, and 1986. Rubenstein, *Bad Language*, 117–18; Loret de Mola, *Denuncia*, 140–50; "Mexico's President Admonishes Media Sector for Exalting Violence," WikiLeaks, Kissinger Cables, Sept. 6, 1974, https://www.wikileaks.org/plusd/cables/1974MEXICO07626_b.html; "Revistas picardías mexicanas," June 3, 1969, AGN/DGIPS-2959A.

63. Burkholder de la Rosa, *La red de los espejos*, 16; Piccato, this volume.

64. Monsiváis, *A ustedes*, 60.

65. Trejo Delarbre, *La prensa marginal*, 115–16.

66. Erlandson, "Press of Mexico," 2, 103.

67. Gillingham, this volume; Piccato, "Murders"; Cosío Villegas, *El Porfiriato*, 525.

68. For example, the murder of *El Mundo*'s editor, Vicente Villasana, caused the fall of the Tamaulipas governor and the collapse of the Portes Gil cacicazgo. Informe, Apr. 9, 1947, AGN/DGIPS/794/exp. 9; *El Mundo*, Apr. 10 and 14, 1947.

69. What editors thought those preferences to be is clear in the promises of mastheads, which were designed to pull in readers and which from the Porfiriato to the PRI hawked the independence, truthfulness, courage, humor, and zeal of their papers.

70. See chapters by Pablo Piccato, Ben Smith, Michael Lettieri, Paul Gillingham, Roderic Ai Camp, Javier Garza Ramos, and Everard Meade. All translations in this book are by the contributors unless otherwise indicated.

71. Castaño, *El régimen legal*, 80–130.

72. Serna Rodríguez, "Periodismo, estado y opinión pública," 57.

73. Garcíadiego, "La prensa"; Piccato, this volume; Lear, *Picturing the Proletariat*. For a full bibliography, see Serna Rodríguez, "Prensa y sociedad."

74. Curley, "Anticlericalism"; Del Palacio Montiel, "La prensa católica"; Lewis, *Life in a Mexican Village*, 201; Fallaw, *Religion and State Formation*, 8, 29; Borrás, *Historia de periodismo mexicano*, 148–56; Fallaw, "Politics of Press Freedom"; Nolan, "Relative Independence"; Esquivel Hernández, *El Norte*.

75. Tactics ranged from financial pressures to the murder of editors. Burkholder de la Rosa, "Construyendo una nueva relación" and *La red de los espejos*; Armistrad, "History of *Novedades*"; Fernández Christlieb, *Los medios*, 22–23.

76. Serna Rodríguez, "Prensa y sociedad," 126.

77. INEGI, *Estadísticas históricas de México* (2000), CD-ROM.

78. Erlandson, "Press of Mexico," 137–38.

79. *Crónica de la publicidad en Mexico*, 24; Annual Marketing Report 1970, Thomas Sutton Papers, Duke University, Durham, NC; Ferrer, *Cartas de un publicista*, 143.

80. *Directorio de Medios* (Aug. 1967); González de Bustamante, *Muy buenas noches*, 33. In 1967 the US government surveyed 9,411 inhabitants of over thirty Mexican towns and cities: 87 percent of the upper and upper middle class, 79 percent of the middle class, and 57 percent of the lower middle and lower class got their national news from newspapers. In the same year, only 50 percent of households in Mexico City owned televisions. "Effectiveness of Newspaper Supplement," 1967, NARA/RG306/MX-6702.

81. The total number of current affairs and news publications increased from 244 in 1940 to 1,249 in 1970. *Anuario estadístico compendiado.*

82. For detailed readership figures, see Smith, *The Mexican Press and Civil Society*, ch. 1.

83. Jiménez de Ottalengo, "Un periódico mexicano."

84. Quoted in Piccato, *History of Infamy*, 71.

85. *Medios Publicitarios Mexicanos* (May–Aug. 1960).

86. The two editions of *Ovaciones* sold a total of 337,900. Cole and Hester, *Mass Communication*, 17.

87. Sánchez García, *El Plumaje del Mosco*, 165–66.

88. González Casanova, *Democracy in Mexico*, 89; Bohmann, *Medios de comunicación*, 127–32; Rodríguez Castañeda, *Prensa vendida*, 154.

89. Of 800 residents of one small Morelos village, no more than 10 regularly read newspapers. Fromm and Maccoby, *Social Character*, 46.

90. The figures for circulations and households are drawn from *Directorio de medios* (Aug. 1967).

91. "Effectiveness of Newspaper Supplement."

92. Smith, this volume.

93. The best introduction to the means of control is Rodríguez Munguía, *La otra guerra secreta.*

94. In the most extensive quantitative analysis, Louise F. Montgomery in "Stress on Government" found that both *Excélsior* and *Novedades* almost never criticized the president between 1950 and 1970. An example of the control of coverage of the military is the suppression of reporting on the La Trinitaria massacre in 1955; see informe, Aug. 24, 1955, AGN/DGIPS-2014B.

95. Smith, this volume.

96. Esquivel Hernández, *El Norte*, 59–61, 67–68.

97. Smith, *The Mexican Press and Civil Society*, ch. 5.

98. A "cacicazgo" is the territory and informal organization ruled by a cacique (political boss) and their clan.

99. Sloan, *Death in the City*, 114.

100. "Lawyerocracy" comes from Bernal, *The Mongolian Conspiracy*.

101. Piccato, "Murders," 195.

102. *Guerra al crimen*, Sept. 1952; Piccato, "Murders," 197–99.

103. Quoted in Robles, *Retrato hablado*, 210.

104. Pensado, *Rebel Mexico*, 95–96.

105. Smith, this volume.

106. *Ovaciones*, June 10, 1950. "Ejidatarios" are farmers on state-granted, collectively held lands.

107. *Ovaciones*, June 20, 1950. Quezada was also a target of private censorship, as when a bullfighter outraged by his mockery tried to beat him up (but got the wrong man). *Ovaciones*, Mar. 1, 1950.

108. Del Río, *Rius*, 166–70.

109. Zolov, "Jorge Carreño's Graphic Satire," 13.

110. Barajas, *Sólo me río cuando*, 19.

111. Del Castillo Troncoso, "El movimiento estudiantil," 76, and "Fotoperiodismo y representaciones," 153. See also Mraz, *Looking for Mexico*; Del Castillo Troncoso, *Rodrigo Moya* and *Ensayo*.

112. Gillingham, this volume.

113. "Relación de periódicos de las diferentes entidades federativas de la república," June 11, 1960, AGN/DGIPS/1279.

114. Gillingham, this volume.

115. "Rosas Magallón: Gobernador electo," *La Nación*, Aug. 6, 1959; "San Luis Potosí: Un pueblo escarnecido," *La Nación*, Sept. 24, 1961.

116. *La Nación*, Oct. 15, 1968. "Huichilobos" is the term the Spanish conquerors applied to the Aztec war god, Huitzilopochtli.

117. See also Sánchez Sierra, "Crisis mística."

118. For example, Mario Menéndez, "Basta ya," *Sucesos*, July 8, 1967.

119. Del Castillo Troncoso, "La visión de los vencidos."

120. Keller, this volume.

121. Gutiérrez Espíndola, *Prensa obrera*, 55; "Report on prensa latina," Aug. 20, 1960, NARA/RG59/1961-1963, box 22.

122. US embassy report, June 7, 1971, Subject Numeric Files, Culture and Information, NARA/RG59/1970-3/PPB, M1-1-70, box 431.

123. Rodríguez Baños, *Libertad de expresión*, 32.

124. "Figueroa Kidnapping Case," *Por Que?*, in WikiLeaks, Kissinger Cables, Sept. 13, 1974, https://wikileaks.org/plusd/cables/1974MEXICO07855_b.html; "Conversation with Fausto Zapata," WikiLeaks, Kissinger Cables, July 31, 1976,

https://wikileaks.org/plusd/cables/1976MEXICO09834_b.html; Fernández Meléndez, *Nadie supo nada*; Burkholder de la Rosa, *La red de los espejos*.

125. Scherer García, *Los presidentes*, 129.
126. Borrás, *Historia de periodismo mexicano*, 76–77.
127. Novo, *La vida en México*, 27.
128. Scherer García and Monsiváis, *Tiempo de saber*, 148.
129. Freije, "Exposing Scandals, Guarding Secrets," 380.
130. Trejo Delarbre, *La prensa marginal*.
131. Sánchez Ruíz, "Los medios de comunicación," 416.
132. Quoted in Trejo Delarbre, *La prensa marginal*, 121.
133. Trejo Delarbre, *Mediocracía*, 167.
134. Hughes, *Newsrooms in Conflict*, 120; Freije, this volume; Miguel Ángel Granados Chapa, "Males y (re)medios," *Proceso*, Nov. 2001.
135. Secanella, *El periodismo político*, 157–58.
136. Sánchez Ruíz, "Los medios de comunicación," 428.
137. Correspondence with Andrew Paxman, Sept. 2016.
138. Paxman, "Cooling to Cinema."
139. International Research Associates, "A Study of Audience Opinions of 'El Mundo en Marcha,'" 1958, NARA/RG306/IRI Mex, 20; Durand Ponte, "La cultura política."
140. Gibson, *Boundary Control*.
141. In order of daily circulation according to the National Registry of Print Media (PNMI): *Reforma* (133,446 copies), *La Jornada* (107,659), *Milenio* (86,825), *El Universal* (57,594), and *Excélsior* (26,983). Also important are *El Norte* (131,138, principally in Monterrey), *El Financiero* (91,923), *El Sol* (67,190), and *El Economista* (35,291). Data from the Secretaría de Gobernación's Padrón Nacional de Medios Impresos; and García Rubio, "Radiografía de la prensa diaria."
142. As in the past, tabloids and sports papers all sell better: *La Prensa* has the highest paid circulation in the country (over 276,000 copies) and is growing.
143. See Andrew Paxman, "El Heraldo: Parte del problema," *Arena Pública*, June 15, 2017, http://arenapublica.com/blogs/andrew-paxman/2017/06/15/6042/el-heraldo-de-mexico-la-prensa-en-mexico-periodicos-mexicanos.
144. Garza Ramos, this volume.
145. Matloff, this volume.
146. "Interview with Rubén Espinosa," http://rompeviento.tv/RompevientoTv/?p=2003 (accessed Sept. 6, 2016).
147. "Mexican Politicians Accuse Media of Extortion," *San Diego Union-Tribune*, Mar. 13, 2015.
148. "Mexico: Country Report," Freedom House, https://freedomhouse.org/report/freedom-net/2014/mexico (accessed Sept. 6, 2016).
149. In January 2015 the site announced a competition for three grants of

20,000 pesos (approximately US$1,300) for investigative reports, with the final selection occurring via an online poll of the contributing subscribers. "Conoce los tres reportajes que financiarán los Amigos de Animal," *Animal Político*, Mar. 9, 2015, http://www.animalpolitico.com/2015/03/conoce-los-tres-reportajes-que-financiaran-los-amigos-de-animal.

150. In the wake of the video, the father was forced to resign. Damien Cave, "Bad Reviews for Patron at Restaurant in Mexico," *New York Times*, Apr. 29, 2013, http://www.nytimes.com/2013/04/30/world/americas/restaurant-patrons-behavior-is-panned.html?_r=0.

151. Eiss, this volume; Adela Navarro Bello, "Mexico between Politics and Organized Crime," public lecture at University of California, San Diego, Apr. 23, 2013, https://vimeo.com/66334672.

152. "Attacks on Journalists in Veracruz, Mexico," Trans-Border Institute, http://sites.sandiego.edu/tbi-foe/attacks-on-journalists-in-veracruz (accessed Sept. 6, 2016).

153. Matloff, this volume.

154. Committee to Protect Journalists, https://cpj.org/killed/americas/mexico (accessed Aug. 1, 2017). The CPJ's rigorous protocols make its estimates lower than those of Reporters Without Borders or the International Federation of Journalists.

155. "'Explain to Us What You Want from Us': Juárez Newspaper Publishes Editorial Addressing Cartels after Another Reporter Gunned Down," *Democracy Now*, Sept. 23, 2010, http://www.democracynow.org/2010/9/23/explain_to_us_what_you_want.

156. "2017 World Press Freedom Index," Reporters Without Borders, https://rsf.org/en/ranking (accessed Aug. 1, 2017).

Notes for a History of the Press in Mexico

PABLO PICCATO

In this chapter I propose a general outline of the history of print journalism in Mexico. The premise is that there is such a history, instead of a series of isolated chapters in which the press is merely the mouthpiece of political actors or social groups—as the subject has been treated by most scholars until recently. Newspapers and magazines evolved according to a multiplicity of factors, including institutional changes, economic development, technological advances, and literary fashions. Above all, it was the business of gathering and distributing news and opinions for an increasingly broader public that defined their trajectory between the mid-nineteenth century and the latter half of the twentieth. The politicized "writing market" that Ángel Rama proposed as the driving source of demand for journalism in modern Latin America was certainly there but, despite common opinion, the state itself was not the exclusive factor in this demand.[1] There were different readers and different ways to read newspapers, and censorship is only one among many variables that explain the transformation of journalism in Mexico. Specifically, rethinking the connections between business and politics offers a more promising path for new research in the field.

As with most syntheses, this one might be defined by its omissions and its reliance on the work of others—although the two are in no way related. There is a considerable literature on the history of newspapers and journalists, but most of it keeps to a very narrow focus on specific periods, names, or titles. There are many regional variations to the patterns that have been studied mostly in Mexico City. Other chapters in this volume show the autonomy and impact of the press in smaller localities or specific periods and, in some cases, the more direct forms of coercion exercised against journalists outside the capital. In an attempt to propose a general framework, I proceed chronologically, starting with a brief mention of the early press after independence, then focusing on the moment of the greatest influence of the nineteenth-century *periodismo de combate* (literally, journalism of combat, perhaps best translated by the English term "attack journalism" although recently that phrase has picked up its own distinct US cultural baggage), a romantic vision of the role of journalists as people of honor, representatives of public opinion willing to engage in rhetorical and physical fights over their ideas. I then rush through the Porfiriato, when that vision was domesticated, and the revolution, when it became much less relevant, and finally I discuss in greater length the emergence of what I call "industrial newspapers" after the armed phase of the revolution. I stop at the 1940s because at that time a structure was established in which large newspapers that were close to the government and commercially viable established their domination over the public sphere for the next four or five decades. The contemporary landscape of Mexican journalism includes the legacies of periodismo de combate and industrial newspapers: honor and business are not antinomic, since journalists are still apt to exploit their reputation as part of their capital, and opinion is as valuable a commodity as news.[2] The relationship between the state and owners or editors remains an important variable, but if history is any guide it is not the only one to shape the transformations and successes of the main organs of the Mexican press into the twenty-first century.

The density, contents, and size of newspapers and magazines were determined, above all, by the demand from readers and, to a lesser extent, by the availability of certain key factors in the production of those periodicals (capital, technology, and the labor of writers, photographers, and printers).[3] The oldest sociological truism about the history of journalism is that since Mexico had low levels of literacy, the press was only a reflection of upper-class concerns and had a limited impact on the lives of the majority of people. Furthermore, the argument goes, the press was merely a source to understand some aspects of high politics, a by-product of political elites' lives. Demand was indeed expressed in the number of copies sold but, I argue, it did not reflect a hierarchical structure but a diversity of expectations about the contents of the newspapers and the possible connections between readers and producers. As I show, in the case of Mexico it is harder to measure demand than to trace the changes in those expectations. State actors intervened in this market (through subsidies, protection, censorship, or persecution), but they could not determine the demand for different kinds of opinions or news. In other words, for Mexican publications to satisfy the market demand and survive financially, large printings and economies of scale were less important than the labor-intensive need to maintain a variety of journalistic offerings. The increasing diversification of readers was probably the most important factor that continually strengthened demand, in some cases countering official attempts to limit the topics of public discussion in the press. I propose that without considering the public sphere as a broad dimension of political and economic life (in other words, the demographic and economic bases of public debates) we misrepresent not only high-level politics but also the participation of popular sectors in revolutionary, dictatorial, and democratic politics.[4]

Republican Experiment

Going back to the last days of the colonial period and the era of the 1810 insurgency, scholars of the press in Mexico have argued that newspapers were born politicized, a product of the needs of the different parties in dispute, almost indistinguishable from pamphlets. The titles published then had a small circulation but an outsized influence as vehicles of enlightened ideas on the intellectual history of independence and early liberalism. Yet many of these early publications contained diverse information, starting with the *Gazeta de México*. They followed a model in which the periodical press was intended to be an encyclopedic channel of useful knowledge on a variety of topics, while politics was only beginning to be defined as an autonomous realm of public life. The news was conceived in the broadest terms: papers covered viceregal court activities, treasury accounts, runaway slaves, a needle retrieved from a servant's hand with a magnet.[5] Reading the press made it possible for any enlightened person to critically engage other subjects of the empire and the government. Impelled by events in the Iberian peninsula, prominently the 1808 abdication of King Charles IV, autonomists and other factions began to use the press as a weapon, producing political manifestos and news sheets. After independence the politicization of many aspects of public life was evident in new periodicals, although the scarcity of printing presses still limited the number of titles.[6] Multiple press regulations were passed by republicans and monarchists, liberals and conservatives—so many that if we take legislation as an indicator of conceptions of political representation, free speech was a higher priority than elections during much of this formative period. Public opinion, in the perspective of the liberal groups that eventually prevailed in the second half of the nineteenth century, was a more effective and precise representation of the popular will than was the vote. As a consequence, the public sphere was the central stage of political antagonism—although the historiography is only gradually beginning to identify it as a discrete realm, despite the importance attributed to the early press.[7]

Journalism as a profession only appeared in recognizable form during the middle decades of the nineteenth century, when professionals began to turn out a regular product and survive, albeit with difficulties, from it. This early journalism was centered on opinion rather than reporting and drew much of its authority from the literary competence and broad cultural perspective of editors and staff writers. It is best remembered through enterprises such as *El Monitor Republicano*, edited by Vicente García Torres between 1844 and 1896. The consolidation of journalism as a business centered on opinion and backed by writers' honor took place during the Restored Republic (1867–1876). Protected by the 1861 press law, which established that written offenses would be tried in front of a jury and was only fully enforced after the defeat of the French intervention, journalists were able to criticize public men with a ferocity that would not be found again for many years. Although taming opposition newspapers was not out of the question for the Benito Juárez (1858–1872) and Sebastián Lerdo de Tejada (1872–1876) presidencies, and even that of Manuel González (1880–1884), censorship did not work well against liberal, often fiercely personalist writers and editors. The journalists' attacks or apologies were only as effective as their reputations as men who would defend their words with actions. As a result, newspapers of the period were self-referential, commenting on each other's columns and engaging in debates that, in a few cases, ended up in duels. If a government official brought a libel accusation to a jury, skillful journalists saw only an opportunity for more advertisement of their reputation as men of honor and seldom risked fines or imprisonment.

These practices were not an idiosyncratic feature of Mexican journalists but an expression (common in other countries too) of the central importance of honor for the profession. It was necessary to be a man of honor in order to represent public opinion and, when necessary, challenge other public men. Conversely, those whose honor was vulnerable or in doubt (because they had been traitors, criminals, cuckolds, etc.) could not speak publicly. Women and those without education were excluded for the same reason. Journalists like Ireneo Paz and Santiago Sierra saw themselves as warriors of the pen willing to die for their beliefs, including those concerning the virtues of candidates for the presidency. They were also ready to challenge each other's reputation, leading in their case to the duel in 1880 in which Sierra was killed by Paz. Both sides in this encounter exemplified the complexity that journalism had gained by then. Paz was a versatile editor in the mold of García Torres: he produced different kinds of books and periodicals out of *La Patria*'s presses, wrote in a variety of genres, and opposed the authoritarianism of the Porfirian regime. Sierra and his brother Justo, writing from *La Libertad*, were ideologues of the "conservative liberalism" that eventually would constitute the foundation of late Porfirian authoritarianism and the hegemony of positivism.[8] For all of them, the romantic gestures of personal polemics and dueling were not incompatible with the idea of making a living from journalism and helping the advance of scientific politics. Honor was, in fact, a requirement of progress.

Based on a romantic view of their own trade and a Rousseauean definition of public opinion that included the criticism of individuals, journalists appointed themselves as judges of the reputations of all citizens, particularly those who were involved in public life. Attacks were not based on ideology. As Justo Sierra argued, support for a candidate did not mean a departure from the dictates of conscience.[9] The public writer's subjectivity, the inner sanctum of his conscience, could not be examined without challenging his integrity, yet it could be relied upon for a rigorous assessment of others' characters. Honor protected the autonomy of this realm, since it postulated the essential integration of external reputation and self-esteem. Such status was not built on political alliances but, in the case of journalists, on the competence to write in any literary format. Guillermo Prieto (poet, journalist, orator, politician) was the most glorious example of this reservoir of honor and skill that the Restored Republic's press was able to tap. A close collaborator of Juárez during the conflicts against conservatives and French invaders, Prieto proved that bartering reputations was not the only contribution of journalism to public life. Praising another *letrado* (educated person) of his time, Francisco Zarco, Prieto implicitly praised himself and described that

> transcendental literary genre, so typical of our century, that is journalism.
> . . . The newspaper is like the action of the idea, the militant idea. It
> encompasses and focuses all literary genres, criticism, philosophy,
> sciences, customs. . . . It is the reflection of the entire society, lives for
> a moment, [and] its fragments fall into pieces . . . to form a sort of
> geological layer that registers in their entirety, still breathing, the ideas,
> concerns, habits in their most intimate details (from the philosophical
> editorial to the fashion and food advertisement), and helps in the
> reconstruction . . . of an era, a society, a civilization. Since the newspaper
> was invented the past ceased to exist for history.[10]

Although the Restored Republic was a free-spirited and democratic era in the history of the Mexican public sphere, it was also characterized by some shameless pandering to politicians' purses. Periodismo de combate thrived, it is argued, thanks to the political needs of caudillos and camarillas, particularly at the times of elections. Even though these newspapers did not have great circulation, they could be influential by undermining politicians' reputations. Subsidies from public officials or candidates came in the form of subscriptions, jobs, or direct payments. Writers, however, rarely became permanent speakers on behalf of a single sponsor or program: they switched sides according to the needs of the political market while claiming to maintain their adherence to broad liberal principles. This was possible, indeed necessary, because diversity of opinions was a requirement of the writing market. Polemics increased sales and enhanced the social capital of journalists. While *periodistas de combate* never reasonably expected to make large sums of money, some of them did convert their social capital into status and government positions later in life. As a result, we need to view with some skepticism the argument of Justo Sierra and even historian Daniel Cosío Villegas that newspapers like *La Patria, El Monitor Republicano,* and *El Siglo XIX* created the acrimony that eventually caused the fall of the Restored Republic and the authoritarianism of

Porfirio Díaz. This kind of journalism preceded 1861 and survived through the first years of the Porfiriato.[11]

Cosío Villegas's *Historia moderna de México* provides a strictly political reading of the press during this period. Later research shows that, following Prieto's description, there was a robust reading market for different kinds of products. As a literary genre, journalism had the ability to borrow from a diversity of languages and formats. Newspapers were written in a style that was closer to oratory than to the terser journalistic prose of the twentieth century. Their authors were in many cases gifted public speakers, and they often transcribed parliamentary speeches from Mexico and elsewhere. Poems could be intermixed with the news. Reading newspapers aloud in cafés, on street corners, and in other public spaces was a common practice that expanded their audience beyond educated groups.[12] Newspapers were at the center of a larger cultural industry. The presses that printed *El Monitor Republicano* and other dailies, like Ireneo Paz's *La Patria*, had enough capacity to produce other publications after the newspaper finished with its daily run, usually in the hundreds of copies. García Torres's machines, which he acquired over time, also published novels, calendars, histories, official reports, travelogues, and devotional books. Thus, *El Monitor* managed to survive political instability and cater to the curiosity and literary tastes of diverse readers. The press could also be good business for writers and publications concerned with religious themes.[13] Readers were interested in fashion, opera, literature, and the serial publication of canonical novels like Manuel Payno's *Los bandidos de río Frío*.[14] Even in the Porfirista *La Libertad* personal politics only appeared in combination with other content that editors and readers may have seen as more transcendent.[15] The number of periodicals continued to grow throughout the second half of the nineteenth century—even though literacy rates barely changed.

Authoritarian Expansion

The beginning of the end for this period in the history of Mexican journalism was the 1882 constitutional reform that abolished the press juries and placed press offenses in the hands of politically appointed penal judges. These judges used their ample discretion to punish offenders against individual or national honor, and they justified their sentences with the *doctrina psicológica*—which held that, much like a writer's judgment of character, the reasoning needed to adjudicate a crime against someone's reputation was essentially subjective and could not be reproduced outside the mind of each judge.[16] Díaz and state governors were now able to more effectively censor opposition writers by accusing them of libel against public officials. Yet this was not just a ruse to deploy censorship. As Rafael Barajas has shown, this restrictive turn was ostensibly intended to curtail frivolous gossip, extortion, and duels, and it was not opposed by most journalists.[17] We can see simultaneously—under the influence of positivism—the emergence of the idea of honor as a private good that had to be protected by the state. During these years, in which Mexico was becoming more closely integrated with the economies of other countries, trustworthiness was becoming too valuable an asset to be left in the hands of the narcissistic journalists of the romantic era.

This transformation did not mean the end of journalism as a business, but the beginning of a deep transformation in the way journalists wrote about personal reputations. For *periodistas de combate*, after all, honor was a commodity: they could increase theirs by attacking that of others. Under the pyramidal structure of patronage consolidated under Díaz, and given their meager salaries, some journalists now took a more tactful approach with the goal of eventually reaching a respectable job. Federico Gamboa admitted that he was an example of this: facing the choice to continue working in embattled Filomeno Mata's *Diario del Hogar* and struggle with penury and government hostility or to seek a career in diplomacy and writing through his family connections, he chose the latter.[18] While the regime took away with one hand, it gave with the other: subsidies became more systematically administered as Díaz's regime consolidated, in part because the personalist disputes for the presidency became tamer. As libel became the object of penal punishment, trading in honor now offered higher risks and lower profits than other forms of intervention in public life. The idea that the private lives of public men had to be off-limits for journalists was firmly established then and has survived into the twenty-first century, when we again see charges of defamation used against journalists.

The influence of the press did not diminish during Díaz's presidency, however. Florence Toussaint Alcaraz puts the number of newspapers founded during the Porfiriato at 2,579. Smaller opposition newspapers survived outside Mexico City, and a few were found even in exile. The number of publications may have decreased during the second part of the period, in part because elections did not create the same demand for opinions as in the time of the Restored Republic. Print runs, however, seem to have increased. The earlier newspapers had sold hundreds of copies, but sales were now in the tens of thousands. According to a US reporter, in 1905 *El Imparcial* sold 75,000 daily copies, *El Popular* 50,000, *El Mundo* 30,000, *El Diario de Jalisco* 20,000, and the English-language *Mexican Herald* 10,000. These numbers might be debatable, but they fit with the higher literacy rates in urban areas and readers' interest in themes other than just politics. When electoral competition heated up again by the end of the regime, some opposition newspapers like *El País* circulated, according to some sources, up to 200,000 copies. There was no centralized authority to collect and verify these numbers, though. Most information comes from newspapers' own daily reports on street sales—although they only shared that information when it served their purposes.[19] Some newspapers survived with lower print runs but a loyal readership. *El Diario del Hogar*, despite its political involvement, continued to present itself as a newspaper "for families" and to publish recipes, fashion notes, poetry, and fiction.[20]

But it is the success of *El Imparcial*, established in 1896, that best attests to the continuing importance of the media during the Porfiriato. The newspaper founded by Rafael Reyes Spíndola introduced important changes: faster and cheaper printing methods, a lower price per copy (one cent, against six for its competitors), broader distribution, use of images, and reporting in a way that deemphasized opinion and matters of honor. *El Imparcial*'s favorite way to deal with adversaries was now complete silence about them, rather than personal accusations. Its publishers no longer needed to print books or pamphlets in order to secure their cash flow. *El Imparcial* has been praised as the first modern newspaper in an era that elsewhere in Latin America saw the emergence of other large, commercially successful newspapers. New printing machines made possible lower costs and greater outputs;[21] they could print up to 65,000 copies a day. *El Imparcial* was criticized for lowering the cultural level of its intended readers, but it represented, in fact, the first systematic effort to create a mass audience. Its reports were written in a very different tone from the periodismo de combate: not for educated men who knew members of the political elites on a personal basis, but for a broader range of urban readers, including women and those who might not be so interested in politics. Writing to Secretario de Hacienda José I. Limantour in 1902, Reyes Spíndola calculated that four people read each copy of his newspaper, and he predicted that the number of readers would continue to grow in the following years.[22]

El Imparcial's innovation has merit from a contemporary point of view, but it should be taken with a grain of salt if we consider that the large subsidy it received from the treasury basically ran the competition out of business. Reyes Spíndola's project combined business and politics in such an integrated way that his example cast a shadow over the industry in subsequent decades. After all, he embodied the mix of private and public interests that defined the domination of the technocratic clique of the *científicos* (scientists) over national politics during the glory days of the Porfiriato. Reyes Spíndola's management of the newspaper staff dispensed with the comradeship that had characterized earlier newsrooms. He did not expect his employees to last more than a few years. While in the past some journalists had become well-known writers or recognized figures in politics and diplomacy, at *El Imparcial* most of the staff remained low-paid workers who did not sign their articles, and they lacked the elevated goals that animated their predecessors. Efficiency extended to the calculations of the newspaper's political effects. In the same memo to Limantour, Reyes Spíndola argued that supporting his newspaper was more convenient for the government than repressing others "that could start annoying with their foolishness." He manipulated prices, continued to receive the subsidy from the government, and engaged in other business undertakings, building an insurmountable advantage over his competitors.[23]

Despite Reyes Spíndola's understanding with Limantour, there was never any centralized political control of the press during the Porfiriato. The most important internal division within the political elite was between Limantour and his científico allies and Bernardo Reyes. Although both Limantour and Reyes were part of Díaz's cabinet, the battle over their qualifications to succeed the aging dictator took place by proxy, through newspapers subsidized by each side. In fact, evidence of Reyes's intervention in an article against Limantour led to the former's resignation from the cabinet in 1902.[24] By the eve of the revolution, newspapers on different sides of the succession battle were playing important roles. Electoral agitation was triggered by the publication in 1908 of an interview of Díaz by US journalist James Creelman. In

1909 Luis Cabrera gained public prominence with his polemic against Limantour about the subsidy to *El Imparcial* and the personal benefits obtained by members of the científico circle. *Antireeleccionismo* (antireeleccionism) played out in local publications too, and violence against opposition journalists seems to have increased.[25] Attacks against free speech were among the recurrent themes in *Regeneración*, the most influential opposition publication from a liberal and anarchist stance, established in 1900 and eventually published from exile.[26]

Revolution and Consolidation

During the early phase of the Mexican Revolution, in the transition out of Porfirio's long rule, most political actors attributed a central role to the press. For moderate Porfiristas, Reyistas, Maderistas, and other antireeleccionistas increasing the weight of public opinion through Congress and the press was the best way to prevent a massive and uncontrollable popular rebellion.[27] Although the premise of these projects was that public opinion consisted of the voices of the educated middle sectors of modern Mexico, not the masses from the cities and countryside, the impulse to expand the public sphere continued after the departure of Díaz. Printings of revolutionary newspapers, particularly *Nueva Era* and *El Demócrata*, grew from 1911. Reactionary publications became particularly virulent and personal in their opposition to President Francisco Madero, printing caricatures that suggested his diminished masculinity or the rebels' lack of civilization. *El Imparcial*, under the editorship of Salvador Díaz Mirón, embraced a violent rhetorical tone that echoed the tradition of periodismo de combate but had more ominous implications in a completely different political context: civil war meant that violence outside the code of honor was a legitimate way to deal with adversaries. Madero was overthrown and killed in 1913 along with his brother, Gustavo, editor of *Nueva Era*. When General Victoriano Huerta had to leave power, the threat turned against those who had supported him in the press. Díaz Mirón had to shave his moustache in order to escape through Veracruz to exile in Cuba and Spain.[28] In the context of the civil war, disputes about honor were no longer formalized, and any revolutionary plebeian who felt insulted could use his gun and skip the niceties of dueling. The factions in conflict after the defeat of Huerta paid for their own newspapers and invested considerable effort and resources to obtain favorable press coverage in the United States, but the role of the press seems to have dissipated during the years it took for the constitutionalists to prevail over the other revolutionary armies since the massive popular mobilization subordinated the demand for freedom of speech to other social and political goals, such as agrarian reform, food distribution, and unionization.[29]

It is not surprising therefore to see that the revolution did not lead to a radical expansion of free speech. New legislation introduced important changes in terms of the protection of newspapers as businesses, but it also maintained the use of honor as a rationale for control. Madero's government proposed a press law in October 1912 that empowered the government to fine, arrest editors and reporters, and force them to correct news items that were not accurate. The new regulation was necessary, the government argued, because the 1871 penal code, which since 1882 had been the sole regulation for press offenses, had not adapted to the "systems of publicity that prevail nowadays, because back then newspapers had a purely partisan character, different from the current focus on the news, which through the publication of articles lacking any truth are causing alarm in the society and encouraging the weak-minded to rise up in arms against the established government." The law was not approved by Congress but included a novelty that would be incorporated into later codes: the printing presses, which in the past had been seized by judges as part of their prosecutions of libel, could no longer be expropriated because "newspapers constitute a property and as such cannot be infringed upon."[30]

The constitution of 1917 did not reestablish the press jury but did include protections for newspaper vendors and other employees against incarceration, and it prohibited the seizure of printing presses and other properties of newspapers. The material penuries that Filomeno Mata, now a heroic figure, and others had endured during the Porfiriato inspired this reform. Paradoxically, the basic mechanisms to control the press through the protection of honor, which had been used against Mata and others, remained in place. Venustiano Carranza decreed a press law in April of that year with the ostensible justification of preventing the kind of personal attacks that Madero had suffered during his government. The new law went further than any previous legislation in the breadth of the definition of offenses against private individuals: a statement that "expose[d] any person to hate, scorn or ridicule, or could cause them a loss in their reputation or their interests," regardless of its form of transmission ("by mail, telegraphy, telephone, radio telegraph, messages or any other means") could be punished with up to two years of prison. The law also specified penalties for insults aimed at the president.[31]

The Carranza press law would not be applied in the following decades as often as the doctrina psicológica had been under Díaz because the relationship between newspapers and political power evolved toward a new system. The constitution's protection for the property of companies laid the foundation for the development of journalism as a productive and competitive business with great material benefits for the top echelons of the profession. The new legal framework combined with technological changes, continuing growth in demand, and a pro-business attitude in the government to open a new era in the history of Mexican newspapers. *El Universal*, established in 1916, and *Excélsior*, in 1917, initiated a long-lasting model—what I call "industrial newspapers" because of their scale, use of labor, and business structure. These dailies were characterized by large circulations and modern rotary presses, the ample use of visual resources, famous columnists, many pages of advertisements, including several of classified ads, and in general a diversity of offerings for readers. They continued the tradition of *El Imparcial* in terms of staff management although now they had to deal with unions—thus enhancing the importance of political support from the government. Unlike Reyes Spíndola's daily, however, they sought other forms of revenue to limit their reliance on state subsidies. After some rocky moments in the 1920s and 1930s, their directors, managers, and editors developed close connections with political elites, including Mexico's presidents. In order to preserve a reputation of independence, they also maintained editorial lines that could contradict certain aspects of official policies, often in the areas of foreign relations and social policies. They targeted a broader audience of readers through different sections, with urban middle-class readers as their central but not exclusive target.

Félix Fulgencio Palavicini is emblematic of the entrepreneurial and political spirit behind these newspapers. He edited *El Antireeleccionista* in the early years of the struggle against Díaz, and Carranza put him in charge of the constitutionalists' propaganda efforts. He participated in the 1916–1917 Constitutional Congress and became editor of *El Universal* after acquiring the government's stock in the company. He sought diverse opportunities for growth but did not reject subsidies related to content. Besides support from Carranza, he received money from clients such as the British-owned oil company El Águila and probably the German government. His newspaper attacked the United States during World War I, but was also receptive to its influence later on. This promiscuity might explain Palavicini's break with Carranza and in 1923 his departure from the newspaper after falling out with Álvaro Obregón and Plutarco Elías Calles.[32] *El Universal* nevertheless continued to grow in the following decades, relying on advertisement sales and improved relations with the country's presidents.

Excélsior was founded by Rafael Alducín, a businessman who used his experience in previous magazines *Revista de Revistas* and *El Automóvil de México* to set up the new daily. He also incorporated new machinery. He died in 1924, and his widow, Consuelo Thomalen, became the owner. She was forced to sell the newspaper to a group of politicians close to the government in 1928, after its coverage of the trial of José de León Toral and Concepción Acevedo de la Llata for the murder of Álvaro Obregón prompted attacks from Gonzalo N. Santos and other members of the Chamber of Deputies, a boycott of official advertisements, and obstruction of its circulation.[33] In 1932, facing bankruptcy, members of the *Excélsior* staff asked for the support of Calles to form a cooperative. Calles obliged, despite his past hostility toward the newspaper. As a cooperative, *Excélsior* maintained a conservative line without breaking with the government and was able to grow commercially through the tenure of editor Rodrigo de Llano, who remained at the helm until his death in 1963.[34] Diversification was also key for expansion. In 1936, the unused capacity of the machinery acquired by Alducín allowed for the production of an afternoon edition, *Últimas Noticias*, which helped improve the bottom line. Other enterprises emerged in these years with similarly conservative ideological tendencies, political loyalties, and economic ambitions, including *Novedades* in 1935, and in the 1940s the García Valseca chain, which produced *El Sol de México* and other newspapers across the country.[35]

The diversity of opinions in Mexico City's industrial newspapers reflected a broader access to the public sphere since the 1920s. The revolution gave more prominence to the voices of peasants and industrial workers, not only as allies of the regime but also through their own publications representing parties, unions, civic organizations, and religious points of view. Publications in the states acquired new vitality, for example in Veracruz (*El Dictamen*), Guadalajara (*El Informador*), and Monterrey (*El Porvenir*)—all of which could be moderately critical of the central government and express local political interests.[36] The most important example of this transformation was the emergence of a Catholic press sympathetic to the Cristero cause and critical of liberalism. Besides the diplomatic pressure raised by the church's hierarchy and the armed resistance of urban middle-class and peasant or ranchero Catholics, newspapers with large printings, like *El Informador*, voiced criticisms of the educational policies of post-revolutionary governments. There had been a tradition of a Catholic press since the nineteenth century in states like Michoacán, which produced dozens of titles, many of them devotional in character but others intended to participate in political debates according to the same rules as the rest of the press. These publications were not meant to create a self-contained Catholic public sphere but to reach broader sections of the public to influence opinion. Periodicals like *Dios y Mi Derecho*, only four pages long but keen on critically engaging other newspapers, were said to print 120,000 copies. Behind these publications were Catholic civic associations similar to others that emerged during the nineteenth century, whose goal was to represent the interests of a sector of civil society in the face of the government and other groups' opinions.[37] Although Cristero resistance and the assassination of Obregón in 1928 could be construed as undermining these efforts, it is clear from the reaction of the government during the Toral trial and the attacks against *Excélsior* that the potential for Catholic opinions to reach broad audiences remained. Much of this conservative perspective was incorporated into industrial newspapers after the 1940s.

Parallel to the growth and diversification of dailies beginning in the 1920s, new titles covered less respectable themes to exploit profitable niches in the market. Publications like *Vea* and *Detectives* offered their audiences entertainment news, suggestive images of women, and stories with sexual content. While titles that the government deemed pornographic had an uncertain and marginal life (*Vea* was banned in 1937 by order of President Lázaro Cárdenas), those containing gruesome descriptions of crime and its victims turned out to be more stable and influential.[38] Echoing the tabloids from the United States and other countries, these magazines and dailies focused on crime news to reach a broad range of readers, and in doing so transformed journalism itself. Afternoon editions like *Últimas Noticias* and *El Universal Gráfico* were shorter versions of the morning editions with more crime and sports news, smaller ads, and fewer political items. They had a populist flavor, plenty of photographs, and lowbrow themes. They avoided the solemn tone that characterized the headlines and articles of their morning parents.[39]

The *nota roja*, as crime news is called because of the abundance of blood on its pages, made innovative use of narratives, interviews, photos, and other graphic resources. When a murder was gruesome enough or involved famous, wealthy, or powerful people, nota roja editors deployed a diversity of perspectives on the events and their causes over several days and many pages. On the assumption that no single actor, including the representatives of the state, had perfect knowledge about a case, articles and interviews conveyed the voices of suspects, victims, neighbors, and even passersby. The coverage often began with an incursion into the crime scene, which reporters sometimes wrote in the first person. It then followed the police investigation, with a dose of skepticism but also with the goal of helping solve the case. The involvement of readers was invoked, either by directly requesting their help or by encouraging their moral indignation. The success of these new journalistic strategies could be measured day by day through street sales. Editors aggressively competed for exclusive interviews, images, and insights into the case of the moment. As a result of their commercial success, some publications managed to limit the importance of government subsidies in their finances; this allowed them to maintain a critical attitude toward the police and judiciary, although they seldom adopted a confrontational stance toward the federal government. Since the 1960s, and clearly with the emergence of *Alarma!* and other illustrated magazines, the nota roja moved toward a greater reliance on gory images and a diminished emphasis on investigations and reporters. But sales remained strong.

La Prensa, founded in 1928 as the first newspaper to focus on crime in its main edition, was the most successful daily in the twentieth century. It had the highest circulation and from the 1940s onward enjoyed solid revenues. Despite labor conflicts early on and the aggressive conservative tendencies of its most influential editor, Miguel Ordorica, President Lázaro Cárdenas allowed the newspaper to survive with loan guarantees and the formation of a cooperative. He recognized that the nota roja reached popular audiences better than other journalistic genres. "I am interested in what *La Prensa* says, and not the other newspapers," Cárdenas told George W. Glass, the manager and president of the cooperative, in 1937.[40] Criticism or praise in its pages influenced many more readers than the government's own newspaper, *El Nacional*. By the following decade, most of *La Prensa*'s revenue came from direct sales in Mexico City and other localities in the country, and only a small percentage of its advertisements were purchased by government agencies.[41]

In the years of prosperity after the 1940s, the cooperative provided stability for workers and healthy finances, but the editors trod carefully on political matters, as did other privately owned newspapers. Thus, while *La Prensa* featured propaganda for Manuel Ávila Camacho during his campaign, tensions arose when the new president's brother, Maximino, learned that the editors had refused to publish favorable coverage for his work as governor of Puebla and that one of them had privately called him a "clown." The managing editor himself had to offer explanations to the irascible politician in order to avoid further damage.[42] In political matters, the newspaper followed the increasingly conservative tendencies of the federal governments after Cárdenas. When it came to coverage of crime, the newsroom maintained enough autonomy to denounce corruption and brutality among the police, although seldom framing it as a systemic problem that would implicate higher authorities. Letters from readers and opinion columns connected insecurity and impunity with other problems of urban governance. Rather than a form of radical opposition to the state, this critical tone was part of the pragmatic habits of reading that made the nota roja a staple of everyday life. Readers needed newspapers like *La Prensa* because they helped them navigate the dangers of urban life. They used the stories and images to make sense of reality and build what I have called elsewhere "criminal literacy," the informal and broadly shared knowledge about the practices of criminals and agents of the state.[43]

Newspapers in general stressed their practical utility as a way to reach readers who were diverse in terms of class and gender. Although there were variations in tone, none of the large post-revolutionary dailies could be accurately described as solely targeted at the elites. If there was an ideal reader for *Excélsior* or *El Universal*, it was probably a slightly conservative middle-class person, interested in public affairs and in a socially integrative modern consumer culture. In the perspective of a critic of the industry at the beginning of the 1930s, the key for newspapers to survive despite the low number of total readers was to create dailies "for all tastes and all economic means." Within newspapers, different sections had different styles and their own visual and written languages, addressing multiple parallel audiences.[44] Editors tried to offer a comprehensive picture of everyday life, including national and foreign politics, high society gossip, sports, crime, and show business. Advertisements portrayed ideals of beauty and modernity associated with a consumer culture that was receptive to imported products and models. Readers were also economic agents who bought and sold products and services through classified ads, significantly improving earnings for companies. Encouraging this active role, newspapers sponsored contests of feminine beauty, pictures of newborns, nativity arrangements, and oratory. They also increased sales through festivals, lotteries, and new occasions for consumer spending, like Mother's Day, a festivity invented in Mexico by *Excélsior*.[45] The intense activity conveyed by their pages seemed to create a space where the market operated without any intervention of the state.

In the absence of internal financial archives from the newspapers, it is challenging to measure the size and strength of that space. The number of newspapers printed and sold remains difficult to establish. Even the Secretaría de Gobernación gathered widely different numbers: 120,000 a day for *Excélsior* in a 1961 estimate, but 20,000 in another from 1966.[46] Editors tended to exaggerate the numbers, and the powerful Unión de Voceadores (Newspaper Sellers Union), which monopolized street distribution through vendors from 1923 onward, tinkered with sales. Scattered information, however, points to the strength of the nota roja. In 1923, *La Prensa* sold between 35,000 and 70,000 a day, about the same numbers it had in the 1940s, and *El Universal Gráfico* sold 20,000 copies in the afternoon, whereas the morning editions of *El Universal* and *Excélsior* sold 60,000.[47] A magazine with a police theme, *Detectives*, published since 1931, claimed to sell 42,720 copies each week.[48] In the 1960s *Alarma!*—the most popular magazine of the genre—was said to sell half a million copies during a famous case of multiple homicides in a brothel in Guanajuato.[49] Daily figures were highly variable, depending on the day's story or the price: when the administrators of *La Prensa* raised the price per copy in 1939, trying to counter losses caused by the increase in the cost of paper, daily sales dropped from 70,000 to 50,000.[50] But none of these numbers sound especially high for a city that in 1950 had a population of 3,137,600 inhabitants and a literacy rate of over 80 percent.

Given the fragmentation of the demand and the large number of titles in competition, the state's support was an important factor in the success of journalistic enterprises in the post-revolutionary period. From the government's perspective, the need to have strong industrial newspapers was never in doubt. Thus, despite episodes like the attacks against *Excélsior* in 1928 and 1976, the relationship between post-revolutionary governments and industrial newspapers was one of productive reciprocity. Beginning around 1929, there was an environment with many titles, growing circulations, and selective political control by the government. Yet even though its emergence coincided with the unification of myriad electoral parties under the Partido Nacional Revolucionario (PNR, National Revolutionary Party), this new environment reflected the continued diversity of the political landscape, in terms of both national and international politics. Primary elections, local personalist disputes, and conflicts within the ruling bloc provided for multiple ideological perspectives and enough material for informative and sometimes explosive political coverage. Fascism, the Spanish Civil War, and the alliance with the United States in World War II generated diverse opinions and attracted multiple domestic and foreign interests, as I discuss below. The economic success of the major dailies, both in Mexico City and elsewhere, and their cozy relationships with the government suggest that the dominant strategy on the latter's side was to create a stable relationship with owners and editors, rather than seek obvious subordination. Obregón, for example, promoted the unionization of journalists and street sellers. Instead of undermining employers, the goal was, as in other industries, to create unions that would be amenable to negotiations and political directives. Calles saw in a cooperative an option to tame *Excélsior* but also to prevent the Confederación Regional Obrera Mexicana (CROM, Regional Confederation of Mexican Workers) from acquiring too much power. Cárdenas used loan guarantees and subsidized paper imports to put the main dailies on a solid financial basis.[51] For smaller newspapers in the interior, the range of accommodations and disputes was broader, as new research by Benjamin Smith and others is beginning to show.

The state did not abandon the production of content and propaganda, but set it in the context of a competitive market. *El Nacional Revolucionario* had been created in 1929 to broadcast the official perspective of the PNR. *El Nacional* was first the organ of the government, but it became formally autonomous, losing the word "Revolucionario" in the title, in 1941. Journalistic value was not contradictory with this project, since the newspaper was conceived to compete with the other large dailies. There were sections on art, literature, movies, music, the military, children, women, and agrarian themes, and ads occupied considerable space. The Hermanos Mayo, a group of photographers who were republican exiles from Spain, provided photographic quality, and competent writers like José Revueltas worked in the police section. Columns reflected a diversity of views, although they tended to be more strident in their nationalism.[52] With the creation of the Productora e Importadora de Papel, SA (PIPSA, Producer and Importer of Paper Company) and the Departamento Autónomo de Prensa y Publicidad (DAPP, Autonomous Department of Press and Publicity), Cárdenas also tried to consolidate the propaganda operation while building an economically viable relationship with industrial newspapers. Like other sectors during these years, newspaper directors had formed corporative organizations to defend their interests. They had asked the government's help to undermine the monopoly of Fábrica San Rafael over the supply of newsprint, which led to the creation of PIPSA. The main newspapers owned 49 percent of the new company's stock. The government's majority control allowed the company to both pressure newspapers, by withholding supplies, or help them, by selling on credit. Cárdenas saw the DAPP as a way to centralize the production and supervision of political content for official and commercial media, as an "organ of expression for the Executive power . . . with the goal of achieving public consensus."[53] It produced copy for radio, books, newspapers, theater, movies, and postcards; sponsored El Nacional and El Popular; and bought publicity space in other newspapers. Press releases facilitated the work of reporters in conveying the government's position. They often came with a cash tip to make sure they got published.[54] The DAPP was closed in 1939, and its main functions were directly transferred to the Ministry of the Interior. Just like PIPSA, it was an early step in a process of consolidating a less intrusive but nevertheless close governmental collaboration with editors and owners.[55]

An implicit premise of this collaboration was the existence of effective means of control. Besides PIPSA there were other economic mechanisms available to the government. The Unión de Voceadores joined the CROM, offered some security to members, many of them minors, and offered massive distribution networks for several newspapers. Vendors kept a fourth of the selling price and had the power to decide what was going to be sold in the streets—or not, as was the case with *Excélsior* in 1933. By the 1950s the union was a powerful organization under the seemingly permanent leadership of Enrique Gómez Corchado.[56] New research, some of it featured in this volume, shows how violence and other means of pressure could be exercised by local actors in smaller cities, although cases of murder against journalists would remain rare until the *sexenio* (six-year term) of President Carlos Salinas.

New, more pragmatic expectations about the profession of journalism extended the control of the government and cautious owners into the news-room. Reporters no longer went into the trade hoping to create for themselves a reputation as men of honor, as in the days of periodismo de combate in the nineteenth century. They continued to have low salaries, but they could now benefit from other perks: direct cash payments from their sources (*embutes*), fictitious jobs (*aviadurías*), a percentage of the sale of advertise-ments, and, for the most profligate, alcohol, drugs, sex, and police protection. In the eyes of one observer of contemporary journalism, the typical reporter was "disrespectful, careless, undisciplined, skeptical."[57] Along with other workers associated with the industry, reporters formed unions and threat-ened strikes,[58] but it was clear that they no longer nurtured the artisanal pride that had been embraced by nineteenth-century journalists. Autonomy of conscience was not a useful commodity for journalists because the ideo-logical program of newspapers was dictated from above, and the private lives of public men were no longer a legitimate area of criticism. Personal attacks were also rare, and duels disappeared, as did the constant threat of indict-ments for libel from the government. The men in power since the 1920s shared Francisco Bulnes's thesis that the best way to deal with the "intellec-tual proletariat" was to take care of their "hunger, which agitates intellectuals the most."[59] For those at the top and the bottom of the profession, the busi-ness model established by *Excélsior* and *El Universal* implied a new relation-ship between press and political power in which economic opportunity countered reputation.

The combination of news and business at the heart of industrial newspa-pers found fertile terrain in the international section. The large newspapers acquired cable news from the Associated Press, United Press International, and Reuters and had correspondents in the United States and in Latin Amer-ican and European countries. This interest in foreign affairs began in full force with the supply of information through transatlantic cable agencies and then during World War I. In 1918, US representative Henry P. Fletcher asked Luis Cabrera to request Palavicini to please lower the hostile tone of *El Universal* toward the United States. If it was necessary, he added, he could send the newspaper money.[60] Although all newspapers fell in line with the Mexican government's 1942 decision to enter World War II on the side of the Allies, the preceding years saw public expressions of support for all the contenders, and deals between editors and representatives of foreign governments aimed at swaying national public opinion.[61] Some dailies had been expressing sympathy toward fascism since the 1920s. *El Universal* maintained a circumspect tone in the morning edition but was rabidly in favor of the *falangista* rebels led by Franco in the Spanish Civil War in the afternoon's *El Universal Gráfico*. *La Prensa* published an article by Francisco Cardona y Rosell in 1936 defending Germany's policies of "preservation of ethnic purity."[62] Just before World War II, *Excélsior* maintained a pro-Allies stance, but its *Últimas Noticias* was so openly favorable to the Nazis that it began losing advertisers.[63] The German government probably spent resources to achieve that solidarity. Its embassy financed *Timón* in 1940, under the direction of José Vasconcelos. Germany's press attaché was Arthur Dietrich, the brother of Adolf Hitler's press secretary, Otto.[64] Whether inspired by money or true ideological beliefs, these contrasting stances regarding world affairs show that the coordination of political content by the Mexican government was never completely achieved. Anticommunism was dominant among large newspapers during the Cold War, for example, but there was plenty of variation behind the rhetorical unanimity.

The ideological confluence of governments and industrial newspapers after the 1940s allowed for this loose harmony, but the new pact was ultimately based on a complex system that combined market competition with the preservation of labor and property rights. The creation of cooperatives at *Excélsior* and *La Prensa* did not translate into an editorial shift to the left. It did allow editors and a few writers to be paid well, and it provided stability for workers and their families. As with other cooperatives, these newspapers' assemblies, where major decisions had to be confirmed, including labor disputes and financial commitments, were supervised by the government. Surreptitious government intervention in general assemblies seems to have been rare until the famous dispute that led to a crisis at *Excélsior* in 1976 and the departure of Julio Scherer García from the newspaper, a result of President Luis Echeverría's meddling. Other dailies, like *Novedades* and *El Sol de México*, were privately owned, closely personal in their interactions with the government, and steadier in their adherence to the official conservative line.[65] Yet, if we consider the diversity of opinions and voices contained in post-revolutionary newspapers (especially in comparison with the strict officialism of *El Imparcial* or the economically self-destructive opposition of *El Diario del Hogar*), it does not seem too easy to classify them politically. It was clear to both editors and owners that identification with a single political faction could be dangerous. Martín Luis Guzmán's *El Mundo*, started in 1922, quickly failed because he was too close to the *sonorenses* (Sonorans), particularly to the wrong one, Adolfo de la Huerta, in 1923. The same happened to Palavicini at *El Universal*, although that newspaper had consolidated itself and provided a more comprehensive offering to readers by 1924.[66] For industrial newspapers, success was a balancing act that required fine political instincts, strong social networks, and reliable market savvy.

Legacies and New Conditions

The structure that emerged in the first decades of the twentieth century and was consolidated in the 1940s remains in place, albeit in a ruinous condition. *Excélsior* is a shadow of its former self, *El Universal* and *La Prensa* survive but have lost their authority, and *El Nacional* was a ghost of its Cardenista past when it finally closed in 1998. New and influential titles, some of which emerged after Echeverría's coup against *Excélsior*, like *Unomásuno*, *La Jornada*, and *Proceso*, and others from a more business perspective, like *El Financiero* and *Reforma*, have broadened the ideological spectrum. Web-based outlets like *Ríodoce*, *SinEmbargo*, *Animal Político*, and others have added value and quality in the twenty-first century.

The established narrative of the process that led to this present pitches a small cadre of intellectuals defending democracy against the corrupting influence of the PRI. In this historical perspective, everything that happened before Julio Scherer's *Excélsior* began to criticize the president in the 1960s was negligible from an ethical point of view. This interpretation was in the main developed by writers close to the group that left *Excélsior* in 1976, including Vicente Leñero, Miguel Ángel Granados Chapa, and Carlos

Monsiváis. They offered a powerful account of corrupt directors of newspapers who were close to the president in contrast with honest journalists struggling in precarious conditions to reach their public. The problem with this narrative is that it gives too much importance to a few dramatic moments (1968, 1976) but gives little credit to sectors of the industry that were not ideologically close to its authors. There is a tradition of critical journalism that can be detected if we read beyond, or below, the first page and editorial section of newspapers, and if we look in cities other than the capital. The trajectory of Manuel Buendía, who wrote for *La Prensa* before working for *Excélsior*, reminds us that despite the new pragmatism, the trade still involved many of the values of nineteenth-century *periodistas de combate*: integrity, concern about reputations, and a close relationship with readers. It was not a matter of being on the left or the right but of persuading every reader, every day, to purchase a copy of your newspaper.[67] Industrial newspapers expanded the business but maintained, along with their smaller competitors, the relevance of that daily transaction. The increasing violence faced by journalists today proves the continuity of that relevance, the persistence of journalistic integrity, and the complex relationships among civil society, the market, and the state in contemporary Mexico.[68]

Notes

1. Ángel Rama talks about the "writing market" in *The Lettered City*, 52, 88–89.
2. For a more detailed treatment of some of these topics, see Piccato, "Altibajos de la esfera pública," 240–91. For a general perspective, see Ruiz Castañeda et al., *El periodismo*.
3. See a similar argument from an economic perspective and on a much broader canvas in Bakker, "Trading Facts," 9–54.
4. I develop the argument in Piccato, "Public Sphere in Latin America."
5. See, for example, the third period of the *Gazeta de México* (1784), http:// hemerotecadigital.bne.es/results.vm?q=parent%3A0004520440&s=0&lang=en (accessed July 7, 2015).
6. The basic narrative is found in Castelán Rueda, *La fuerza de la palabra impresa*. Intellectual history approaches prevail in Rojas, *La escritura de la independencia*; Aguilar and Rojas, *El republicanismo*; Palti, *La invención*. For a closer look at the economics of publications and the expansion in the number of periodicals during the era, see Forment, *Democracy*. Similar approaches are in González Bernaldo, "Sociabilidad"; Uribe-Uran, "Birth of a Public Sphere."

7. Piccato, "Public Sphere and Liberalism."
8. I discuss this episode and the ideas of these two paragraphs in Piccato, *Tyranny of Opinion*. On the influence of *La Libertad*, see Hale, *Transformation of Liberalism*.
9. Sierra, *Obras completas*, 4:242.
10. Prieto, *Obras completas*, 9:296.
11. Sierra, *Evolución política*; Cosío Villegas, *Historia moderna*. A similar argument about the press as a factor of instability was also applied to the aborted presidency of Francisco I. Madero. Rodríguez Kuri, "El discurso del miedo."
12. See examples in Palti, "La Sociedad Filarmónica del Pito" and "Los diarios y el sistema."
13. Celis de la Cruz, "Vicente García Torres"; Giron Barthe, "El entorno editorial"; Guerra, "Las posibles lecturas"; Del Palacio Montiel, *Rompecabezas de papel*; Nava Martínez, "Origen y desarrollo," 130; Wright-Rios, *Searching for Madre Matiana*.
14. Treviño, "Los bandidos de río Frío."
15. Hale, *Transformation of Liberalism*.
16. *El Foro*, Aug. 13, 1885.
17. Barajas, *El país de "El Llorón de Icamole."* A fuller treatment of this change is in Piccato, *Tyranny of Opinion*, ch. 5.
18. Gamboa, *Impresiones y recuerdos*.
19. Ruiz Castañeda et al., *El periodismo*, 226, 229, 232 (for the US journalist's estimates), 233, 250.
20. Toussaint Alcaraz, *Periodismo*, 63–68.
21. Toussaint Alcaraz, *Escenario de la prensa*.
22. Rafael Reyes Spíndola to José I. Limantour, Dec. 5, 1902, CEHM/AL/Mem. 2nd ser., roll. 14.
23. Reyes Spíndola to Limantour, Dec. 5, 1902; Bazant, "Lecturas del Porfiriato"; Salado Álvarez, *Memorias*, 149; Carlos Luis de Cuenca, "El licenciado Rafael Reyes Spíndola," clipping in CEU/CL, Miscelánea de escritos, vol. 1516. His participation in enterprises with other científicos can be seen in AGN/FFB/27, 1, 92–97; Arenas Guzmán, *El periodismo*, 160, 161. A lower estimate of the paper's circulation, around 40,000 copies, is in Ochoa Campos, *Reseña histórica*, 102, 125–26.
24. On Reyes's involvement with publications, see Reyes to R. Chousal, June 4, 1897, CEU/RC/15, 174, folio 131–35; Reyes to R. Chousal, Monterrey, Oct. 18, 1904, CEU/RC/28, 249, folio 65–67; Rosendo Pineda to Limantour, Jan. 9, 1903, CEHM/AL, ser. 2, roll 18; Limantour, *Apuntes*, 133–34, 324–25; Arenas Guzmán, *El periodismo*, 123, 211.
25. Cabrera Acevedo, *Obras políticas*, 32; Arenas Guzmán, *El periodismo*, 97, 168, 175, 215–16; Gómez-Quiñones, *Porfirio Díaz*, 113–15; Cockcroft, *Precursores intelectuales*; Limantour, *Apuntes*, 154; Blanquel, "Setenta años de la entrevista Díaz-Creelman."

26. Arenas Guzmán, *El periodismo*, 182, 191, 194, 235. The extent of *Regeneración*'s impact on revolutionary mobilization has been the subject of some debate. Ruiz Castañeda et al., *El periodismo*, 229; Guerra, *México*; Knight, *Mexican Revolution*, 1:47; Katz, *Villa*, 45, 313, 800.

27. Arenas Guzmán, *El periodismo*, 2:251–52; Piccato, *Congreso y revolución*; Moheno Tabares, *¿Hacia dónde vamos?*; Enríquez, *Dictadura presidencial*, 5–6.

28. Méndez Reyes, "La prensa opositora"; Arenas Guzmán, *El periodismo*, 1:1254–64; Rodríguez Kuri, "El discurso del miedo."

29. Brunk, "Zapata and the City Boys"; Arenas Guzmán, *El periodismo*, 1:272–73.

30. Arenas Guzmán, *El periodismo*, 2:265–68.

31. "Ley sobre delitos de imprenta," https://www.juridicas.unam.mx/legislacion/ordenamiento/ley-sobre-delitos-de-imprenta (accessed Nov. 9, 2017).

32. *El Antireeleccionista*, Aug. 1909, 2; Ibarra de Anda, *El periodismo*, 74; Arenas Guzmán, *El periodismo*, 2:149, 273; Federico Campbell, quoting unpublished manuscript by Eduardo Clavé at Hora del Lobo, http://horalelobo.blogspot.com/2008/02/nuestro-hombre-en-quertaro.html (accessed Aug. 30, 2008); González Marín, *Prensa y poder político*, 22–24. On German influence, see Henry P. Fletcher to Secretary of State, June 6, 1917, NARA/RG59/M274/roll 241, 812.911/32; Katz, *La guerra secreta*, 2:153.

33. Balderas Martínez, "José de León Toral," 150; Burkholder de la Rosa, "El periódico," 1407–13; Velasco Valdés, *Historia del periodismo*, 199.

34. González Marín, *Prensa y poder político*, 25–28; Burkholder de la Rosa, *La red de los espejos*.

35. For a favorable account, see Ruiz Castañeda et al., *El periodismo*, 286.

36. Weldon, "El presidente como legislador"; Ruiz Castañeda et al., *El periodismo*, 273; Cano Andaluz, "*El Dictamen* de Veracruz," 234, 236, 239.

37. Pineda Soto, "La prensa religiosa," 74–76, 85–86, 94–95; Wright-Rios, *Searching for Madre Matiana*; Ruiz Castañeda et al., *El periodismo*, 272, 275, 284; Hernández, "Between War and Writing"; Forment, *Democracy*.

38. Sluis, *Deco Body*, 147.

39. González Marín, *Prensa y poder político*, 25–28. See Piccato, *History of Infamy*, ch. 2.

40. Report on general assembly of Aug. 14, 1937, AGN/SCEP/1, folio 1151. See also Velasco Valdés, *Historia del periodismo*, 217; George W. Glass to President Cárdenas, Feb. 4, 1936, AGN/LCR/704.1/72.

41. Sociedad Cooperativa Editora de Periódicos, "Estado de rendimientos por el periodo de 10 de enero al 31 de diciembre de 1943," AGN/SCEP/3.

42. Minutes of assembly, Nov. 11, 1942, AGN/SCEP/2.

43. Piccato, *History of Infamy*, 6.

44. Ibarra de Anda, *El periodismo*, 51. On the expansion of consumers as subjects, see Sosenski, "El niño consumidor"; Sosenski and López León, "La construcción visual"; Moreno, *Yankee Don't Go Home!*; Bunker and Macías González, "Consumption and Material Culture."

45. Macías González, "El caso de una beldad asesina"; González Marín, *Prensa y poder político*, 18; Ruiz Castañeda et al., *El periodismo*, 266.
46. Rodríguez Munguía, *La otra guerra secreta*, 90, 94, 149.
47. Report of US consulate, Mexico City, NARA/RG59/M274/roll 240, 812.91/18; Scherer García and Monsiváis, *Tiempo de saber*, 165; Rodríguez Munguía, *La otra guerra secreta*, 242; Aguilar and Terrazas, *La prensa*, 119.
48. *Detectives* 1:1 (Aug. 15, 1932); *Detectives* 1:2 (Aug. 22, 1932): 8–9.
49. Brocca, *Nota roja 60's*, 111.
50. Luis Novaro to Consejo de Administración, Feb. 2, 1939, AGN/SCEP/1, folio 1340. The Sunday edition went from 45,000 to 40,000. See the introduction to this volume.
51. See Gillingham and Smith, *Dictablanda*; Burkholder de la Rosa, *La red de los espejos*; Lempérière, *Intellectuels*.
52. González Marín, *Prensa y poder político*, 39, 40, 42.
53. González Marín, *Prensa y poder político*, 106.
54. See also González Marín, *Prensa y poder político*, 122; Scherer García and Monsiváis, *Tiempo de saber*, 149.
55. Hayes, *Radio Nation*, 66–67, 77–78; Mejía Barquera, *La industria*, 64–66, 68–69.
56. Aguilar and Terrazas, *La prensa*, 12–14, 28, 32, 39, 40; Lombardo de Ruiz, *De la opinión*, 103, 106; Ibarra de Anda, *El periodismo*, 81, 131; Burkholder de la Rosa, *La red de los espejos*.
57. Ibarra de Anda, *El periodismo*, 95, 102–10.
58. Ibarra de Anda, *El periodismo*, 83, 84, 86, 88.
59. Bulnes, *El verdadero*, 17–18.
60. Henry P. Fletcher to Secretary of State, May 1, 1918, NARA/RG59/M274/roll 241, 812.911/32.
61. Among the pro-fascist editors who would later work for government publications was Diego Arenas Guzmán. González Marín, *Prensa y poder político*, 21, 34, 62–63, 160; Ibarra de Anda, *El periodismo*, 66.
62. *La Prensa*, July 4, 1936, 11.
63. González Marín, *Prensa y poder político*, 21, 22, 24, 25, 27, 29.
64. González Marín, *Prensa y poder político*, 55, 56; Niblo, *Mexico in the 1940s*, ch. 6.
65. Ruiz Castañeda et al., *El periodismo*, 286.
66. Guzmán had worked at *El Heraldo de México*, established in 1919 with Obregón's support to compete against *El Universal and Excélsior*. Miquel, *Disolvencias*, 156–57, 169.
67. Leñero, *Los periodistas*; Scherer García and Monsiváis, *Tiempo de saber*; Freije, "Exposing Scandals"; Smith, *The Mexican Press and Civil Society*.
68. Del Palacio Montiel, *Violencia y periodismo*; Piccato, "Ya saben quién."

2 | Journalists on Trial

The Press, Censorship, and the Law,
1898–1920

ANA MARÍA SERNA RODRÍGUEZ

D uring the last decades of the nineteenth century, a structured censorship campaign directed from the top of the state emerged in Mexico. It took the form of prosecutions of journalists, editors, and newspaper owners whose writing, directly or tangentially, censured any aspect of President Porfirio Díaz's regime or issues related to the political elite. In a systematic witch hunt supported by the lower courts, whenever the public behavior of a government official was criticized or even mentioned by any journalist, the writer together with other people responsible for the publication, such as managers and editors, and even family members stood a good chance of ending up accused of libel, slander, or sedition. Nearly all journalists who claimed a modicum of independence were found guilty at some point and spent six months to four years in prison. In almost every case, the newspaper's presses were seized, the printing shops were closed, and the newspaper that contained the alleged defamatory piece was forced out of circulation.[1] Independent journalism was criminalized, and the censorship apparatus, operating within the law, crushed any opposition.

After 1910 this mechanism did not work as efficiently as it had previously. However, the study of censorship during the decade of the armed phase of the Mexican Revolution shows the limits imposed on the exercise of democracy by war, the political struggle for power, and the persistence of cultural values resistant to criticism. From the nineteenth century onward, censorship was intimately linked to the public defense of reputation and honor. Disputes calling these cultural values into question, which would have been settled by duels in the latter half of the nineteenth century, moved further into the realm of the legal system as the Porfiriato aged. Honor became a political good, and its defense in the courts turned into repression of freedom of expression. But what happened to this political-cultural apparatus when war and revolutionary discourse erupted in 1910?

Repression of the Mexican press has prospered via three routes: violence, financial inducements, and the application of criminal penalties. Among these control mechanisms, I focus on trials because they highlight the matrix of cultural values and discursive processes involved in the censoring of the press.[2] As I analyze the period from the fin de siècle until the end of the armed revolution, I suggest some potential tools for thinking about censorship in Mexico. Use of the law to repress journalism has led us to term any legal charges levied against the press "censorship," but here I attempt a more nuanced claim, or at least try to show that the censorship of the press that took place under the aegis of the legal system was more complex than outright repression. Instead, following Deborah Schuger, I suggest that censorship be considered, rather than a state-structured policy, as a cultural-political practice emerging from a multiplicity of sites, voices, and subjectivities that function to convert a published article into the instrument of a press crime.[3]

In this chapter I look at the realm of repressive censorship, that is, the regulation of written language through legal channels after an article is published. (Preventive censorship, or prior restraint, such as the registration and review of written materials for approval before publication, disappeared in Mexico in 1820—with the exception of religious texts).[4] To do so I examine a handful of amparo cases from the late nineteenth and early twentieth centuries that ended up in Mexico's Supreme Court. (The amparo is a guarantee of protection of an individual's constitutional rights to which all accused people can appeal.)[5] Such a focus generates a series of questions. How complicit was the judicial branch of government in repressing the press? How did the judiciary contribute to either strengthening or weakening the public sphere in Mexico? Did the judiciary tip the balance against journalists, or did it support their power? Furthermore, to what extent did these legal and cultural traditions shape future, post-revolutionary attitudes to journalism, writing, and censorship?

The first section of this chapter briefly explains the well-known mechanism for trying journalists under the ancien régime, and the second section presents some legal cases dealing with freedom of expression and with libel and slander, the so-called crimes against honor, in the first decade of the revolution. To analyze and understand the trials between 1910 and 1920, it is important to take into account that the structure of the judicial system was weakened during this decade.[6] With the gradual deconstruction of the repressive system of the Porfirian era, judges such as the notorious Wistano Velázquez and Juan Pérez de León, who had enjoyed a direct line to the upper echelons of the regime, lost the protective halo they had obtained from their former political sponsors. The judicial system was also weakened by the loss of financial support. The structure of the Supreme Court was maintained until 1914, when Venustiano Carranza dissolved it; it did not return until 1917.[7] Perhaps dismantling the system enabled judges and government ministers who had not benefited from the Díaz regime to promote a more liberal interpretation of press law. But the judges' poor reputation was not miraculously wiped out by revolutionary declarations or the proliferation of troops across the country.[8] Nor were the judges' working conditions or educational levels improved. Furthermore, Mexico remained poorly served by its legal infrastructure. There were few judges or courts to serve the country, and few people could afford a lawyer. Finally, though many revolutionaries made ambitious claims about press freedom, court records show that everyday understandings of the limits of open speech retained a distinct continuity with the past. This can be seen clearly in the 1911 and 1917 debates on press law reforms, which showed a trend more of imposing limits than loosening restraints on journalists. With the exception of the Zapatistas' 1916 press law proposal, the revolutionary leadership did not show themselves to be particularly open to criticism.[9] In fact, the tension between the extremes of full freedom and limiting what they termed "licentiousness," fake news, and incitements to violence and rebellion was a central current running through the history of expression during this period of open warfare.[10]

The Mechanics of Porfirian Silence

Cutting out tongues, at least metaphorically, was a common practice in Mexico during the late Porfiriato. Mexican politicians of all levels and members of the ruling and affluent elites used the courts to silence those who spoke against them. The persecution of independent journalists had risen to scandalous dimensions by the end of Díaz's rule. Even people who were once Díaz's supporters were not spared educational sojourns in the Belén Prison. In 1910, the list of incarcerated and persecuted journalists included such important names as Filomeno Mata, Rafael Martínez, Ireneo Paz, Lucio Cabrera, Diego Arenas Guzmán, Raúl Navarro, Alfonso Barrera Peniche, Crescencia Martínez, Querido Moheno Tabares, Juan Sarabia, Jesús Flores Magón, and Ricardo Arenales. But these incidents are merely the headlines. Historians have already documented the increasingly repressive nature of the Porfirian regime from the 1890s onward.[11] What is much less understood is how these prosecutions came about and what they reveal about the changing boundaries of acceptable and unacceptable writing.

In 1882, the Mexican authorities reformed the legal code and banned citizen juries from adjudicating freedom of expression trials. From then on, only judges were charged with deciding on the guilt of journalists accused of libel, slander, defamation, or sedition.[12] Reviewing these cases confirms the thesis that journalists who attempted to air the slightest criticism of public officials' behavior were met with fierce retaliation by the apparatus of power.[13] The critiquing of public officials—which had been seen, to a certain extent, during the early liberal period as a public good—became a personal offense, a slap in the face, an *injuria* (slander), *calumnia* (libel), *ultraje* (insult), or *difamación* (defamation). This was even the case if the text in question tried to avoid direct censure in favor of more general accusations. The heart of this strategy relied on judges' and lawyers' ability to link press legislation (i.e., press crimes) to libel laws. They did this by connecting the press law to the articles of the criminal code, which defined all crimes against honor. The idea that certain words could damage the honor or reputation of any person or could provoke what today is called "moral damages" was employed to halt criticism of public figures and bluntly repress any expression of political dissent against Díaz's regime.

Generally, the writer was not the only one accused. Third parties indirectly involved in the publishing of an article, such as the editor of the publication or the manager of the relevant printing shop, were often locked up too. In extreme cases so were administrative personnel and even the newspaper boys. Sometimes family members were employed at the press, which put them at risk, but all newspaper staff fell under suspicion. In 1909 Crescencia Garza de Martínez lost an appeal because her husband, Paulino Martínez, was accused of inciting rebellion when he published an article in his newspaper *El Chinaco* entitled "Where Are We Going?" "After the Attorney General denounced this crime, the First District Judge proceeded to carry out the inquiries. As he found out that Paulino Martínez, who was responsible for the publication, was out of town, he brought an action against his wife, jailed her, and initiated a trial against her."[14] She spent more than a month in jail.[15]

A trademark of this repressive legal machinery was that the printing shops where the "defamatory publication" was produced was always shut down. The machinery, including the newspaper presses, and every other material asset necessary to publish a newspaper or magazine, such as type, paper, and ink, were confiscated or locked down. For the many editors like Paulino Martínez this kind of penalty meant economic ruin because they had a variety of jobs aside from editing newspapers. The closure of their printshops paralyzed their entire business activity and deprived them and all their workers of a living. The practice of closing down the printing shops where rebellious newspapers were edited became so common that it even provoked a reaction by the judges of the Supreme Court. In 1910, at one of Filomeno Mata's many trials, his lawyers successfully argued that it was actually unlawful to confiscate printing equipment.[16]

Some judges, like Wistano Velázquez and Juan Pérez de León, became specialist prosecutors of journalistic "crimes."[17] By lodging amparos, journalists implicitly questioned the authority of the lower courts and the legal interpretation of their judges. When the trial appeared in the Supreme Court, the journalists and their lawyers (for good reason the roles often overlapped—Jesús Flores Magón, for example, was both libel lawyer and writer) reviewed, criticized, and argued against those judges' decisions, attempting to convince the Supreme Court justices that the charges against them were based on a misinterpretation of the law. Thus every case suggested a revision, a debate, a forced dialogue between writers and censors that became, as Robert Darnton terms it, a "true hermeneutic discussion."[18] Here meaningful issues were brought to the fore: What constitutes a press crime? Should freedom of expression suffer any limitation? When can a piece of written language be considered a social threat?[19]

Running parallel to these discussions over press freedom was another debate about the relative professionalization of journalism. During the late Porfiriato, the role of newspaper writers changed. What had been a group of *escritores públicos* (public writers), including private citizens given to presenting their opinions in print, evolved into a class of professional—if not yet trained—*periodistas* (journalists) with distinct roles, specializations, and even wages. What media scholars term "industrial" newspapers were born. Shifting labor practices in turn affected ethics. Unlike newspapers today, even the most modern of Porfirian newspapers was not written according to any ethical code or manual of style. As a result, many of the arguments in the Supreme Court slipped from debates over liberty to considerations of journalistic style. What was understood to be good journalism? How was good journalism to be written? What were the ethics involved? What exactly defined the concept that Jesús Flores Magón termed "journalistic integrity"?

These were difficult problems to solve, and they arose again and again. Some examples can help illuminate what was at stake in this battle of interpretations. In 1910, Filomeno Mata spent six months in prison for having printed an issue of *Regeneración* in which Guillermo Flores wrote a defamatory article entitled "Savage Instincts" criticizing the official behavior of Luis G. Córdova, political boss of Huajuapan de León, Oaxaca. The paragraph that caused the imprisonment went as follows:

> In the districts . . . certain parasites called Political Bosses thrive and prosper as they like under the shadow of obliging governments. These authorities are chosen from among the coarsest men, and once in a position of command, they bring into play a whole load of passions. . . . There must be some honest Political Bosses, though they are scarce. Like the one in Cuicatlán, the one in Huajuapan de León . . . is an arbitrary despot. It is not long since it occurred to that headstrong tyrant that the road that links Huajuapan with Tezoatlán should be diverted from its route.[20]

Undoubtedly Flores, like any journalist, provided the public with valid information: the political boss had changed the route of the road. Moreover, he denounced the wrongdoings of a public servant. However, it was the style—the string of abusive terms ("parasites," "coarsest men," "arbitrary despot,"

"headstrong tyrant")—that was used as the rationale for sending both journalist and publisher to jail.

Paulino Martínez was one of the most important newspaper editors at the
turn of the twentieth century. His publications *El Chinaco*, *El Insurgente*, and
La Voz de Juárez were very popular. He was involved in trials on several
occasions, quite possibly because he was one of the most trenchant critics of
the Porfirian regime—and even more dangerous due to his appeal to the
popular masses. In 1909, "Martínez launched a political contest in his newspaper *La Voz de Juárez*, asking the citizens of this Republic their opinion
about the current political problems."[21] When his newspaper published this
call for opinions, he offered to publish the submissions and present a prize
for the most insightful commentary. Diego A. S. Murillo's opinion was published in the June 24 edition.[22] The letter spoke of the lack of morality of
some members of the army. While Martínez declared that he did not share
the contestant's opinion and added a caveat from the editorial board, he nevertheless published it.[23] The office of the public prosecutor considered the
letter an insult against the army (*era ultrajante para el Ejército*) and demanded
an investigation.[24] Martínez's lawyer appealed to the Supreme Court for an
amparo.[25]

Perhaps because the case involved such an important institution as the
Mexican Army, the amparo was denied and Martínez spent some time in
jail. But his arguments, albeit failed, were interesting. First and foremost, the
attorney claimed that the deed attributed to his client was not a crime
because there had been no malice, which was considered the constituent element of a crime against honor; however, this argument left the door open for
another interpretive problem: How could it be assessed whether a written
text expressed malice or an intention to do damage? Did defamation imply
a moral or pecuniary damage?

Clearly, Martínez was a shrewd editor who found a way to criticize the
army's behavior without bearing the responsibility of having written the
comments. Moreover, according to his lawyer, Murillo's published opinion
did not transgress the limits of Article 7 of the Mexican Constitution: "it
respected the private life, morality, and public peace . . . of the Mexican
Army, [which] as a public institution lacks private life. Only each of its members has a private life, and none of them has accused Paulino Martínez."[26]

Martínez's appeal also included a thorough criticism of the 1882 reform of press legislation, which had criminalized and politicized press matters: "Not jurisprudence, which is inflexible . . . but political trickery, which is essentially manipulable, has claimed that the amendment to Article 7 [relating to press freedom] of the Constitution throws reporters into the grip of a reactionary criminal code unresponsive to the modern demands of civilization. . . . This constitutional amendment, improperly applied to stifle protest, has yielded much bitter fruit that often has not allowed the vigorous intervention of the Supreme Court to ripen."[27]

As Mata did, Martínez also highlighted his loss of earnings, emphasizing that the shutdown of the printing shop meant that his business was paralyzed and his family deprived of a living. Moreover, this was happening in 1909—in the midst of the intense debate over Díaz's reelection—and Martínez's defense pushed the Supreme Court judges to consider the political context: "It has been repeated in the current unusual political movement . . . that this poor nation is on a direct path to reclaiming her rights and freedoms. It may be that it is so. . . . If it were so, society itself would have an interest in the cessation of old and harmful political prosecutions of the independent press."[28] Finally, to emphasize this context and point to the hypocrisy and subjectivity of the press law, Martínez's lawyer compared his client's article with a ferocious attack on the opposition presidential candidate, Bernardo Reyes, headlined "De tal palo, tales astillas" (A chip off the old block), which was clearly written with intent to cause harm and was an example of the press allied to the regime "spewing fury against its enemies."

> Never, ever has an independent newspaper in this country under this administration been allowed to use such unrestrained language, not in reference to the governor of a state, nor even to the most insignificant political boss. This article throws mud at General Reyes, insults him, jeers at him, mocks and denigrates him (I think the basis of the attack is fair, as much as I condemn the way it is carried out), and yet the newspaper continues to publish, and in each issue continues to sling mud at its enemies.[29]

If some defendants pleaded the political context, others spoke of matters of business and economics. In 1910, Carlos R. Menéndez, chief executive, owner, and editor of *La Revista de Mérida*, applied for an amparo against the actions of the judge of the Third Criminal Court of Mérida, Yucatán. He was accused of provoking rebellion by means of print when he printed the article "El tercer alcance" in *El Sufragio*, a publication of a local opposition group called the Centro de Elecciones Independientes (Independent Elections Center). Oscar Menéndez, his defending attorney, argued that the arrest order was unjustified, illegal, and anticonstitutional and that it would inflict damages to his "person and interests" that would be difficult to repair. Menéndez's defense was based on the fact that he was completely unrelated to the deeds cited in the accusation. As in the Filomeno Mata case, he explained that while his company ran the press in question it printed much more than just *El Sufragio*. He was not the manager of the press; it had its own manager and employees. In a written personal defense, he clarified the chain of events with greater detail:

> The Independent Elections Center engaged this press to publish "El tercer alcance" in issue 8 of *El Sufragio*, the center's publication. This bulletin was nothing but a reply on a single printed sheet by the board of directors of the Independent Elections Center to the accusations made by an antagonistic political group, especially to the charge of being "revolutionary and mutinous." This bulletin contains nothing that could be considered as incitement to rebellion: a simple reading is enough to prove it. Nevertheless, it was unjustly deemed subversive by the public prosecutor, and the judge of the Third Criminal Court of Mérida prosecuted those who signed it and those whom it considered accessories for attempted rebellion. I did not agree, nor did I write, nor contribute to the writing of it. Nor was I involved in any way in the bulletin, nor did I sign it, nor am I manager of the press, nor do I have anything to do with *El Sufragio*.[30]

Despite this argument, the judge defended his decision by saying that "there was no doubt that the managing director of *La Revista de Mérida* had criminal liability for the printed bulletin, since the sheet was printed, as it said at the bottom of the page, by the press of 'La Revista de Mérida.'" He added that the directors, administrators, and managers of presses were liable as perpetrators of crimes committed in print, as clearly stated in Part VIII of Article 615 of the criminal code. Menéndez counterattacked by citing another interpretation of Article 615, which he said referred to "the prevention and ready investigation and punishment of CRIMES AGAINST REPUTATION COMMITTED BY MEANS OF PRINT and not to the crime of rebellion of which he had been accused" (capitalization per original). "Since in this case it was not a crime against reputation," he concluded, "this part of the law does not apply to me, and even less so since I am not the manager or editor of the press in question." In spite of his deft legal argument, the amparo was denied.[31]

Revolutionary Defense, Manipulation, and the Trampling of Liberal Principles

During the 1910 revolution, insurgents repeatedly called for both freedom of the press and better protection of individual rights (and, by extension, the more generous use of the amparo). Yet ongoing political conflicts militated against the immediate implementation of these changes. In fact, the cases for the period 1910–1920 demonstrate a distinct continuity with the past and underline the idea that censorship practices are less based on law or even politics but rather on the cultural support that a society, or particular groups within it, give to them. Eleven years after the armed phase of the revolution ended, Luis Cabrera—who was expelled from the country in 1931 because he "dared" to evaluate the revolution's achievements—wrote a stinging assessment of the conditions for freedom of expression: "In Mexico we are at the third level of lack of freedom of the press. The first level is persecution for what has been published. The second level is to forbid the free publication of what has been written, that is, censorship before publication. And the third level consists of not wanting to read what has been published, whatever it may be."[32]

Cabrera's assessment was probably overly bleak. Though continuities existed, the revolution did result in a transformation of the mechanisms for controlling free expression. Not only were there political adjustments, there was also a shift in mentalities, a change in the cultural understandings that underlaid Porfirian censorship. Repression never disappeared, but it could not be as flagrant as before. Instead it became less systematic, more haphazard, and violent, or what Cabrera eloquently described as *neurasténico* (neurotic). Some spaces for expression opened, and public discussion also emerged. The 1917 constitution, particularly Articles 6 and 7, did include defenses of press freedom. Furthermore, a new generation of writers with a modern view of journalism began to control newspaper production. The popular press—newspapers written under the motto "of the people and for the people"—underwent a boom. Journalists attempted to protect themselves through unions and organizations (though most of these attempts eventually failed). These elements, together with the weakness of the state that emerged after the armed conflict, did serve to strengthen the Mexican public sphere.[33]

The press freedom trials of the 1910s demonstrate an ongoing conflict among three cultural traditions: authoritarianism; the liberal right to express opinions; and implicit, often class-based concerns over discretion, morality, and social status. The weight given to each cultural tradition changed depending on the revolutionary (or counterrevolutionary) faction in charge. At first, Francisco Madero tried to be as democratic and pro–free press as possible, but he ended up creating his own newspaper, *Nueva Era*, and his brother led a campaign to repress directly critical publications (of which there were many). During the Madero regime, there were eighteen cases of journalists applying for amparo against press repression. The military dictator Victoriano Huerta violently repressed public expressions of dissent and dissolved Congress, but he also kept the judicial system's structure working. Venustiano Carranza is known for having implemented more subtle but no less violent tactics to deal with opinions that displeased him, such as financial subsidies and the notorious "rectification trips" (the forced exile of journalists).[34]

Crackdowns on press freedom, like election rigging and elite land grabs, had been one of the notorious features of political oppression during the Porfiriato. Popular reaction generated some shift in the cultural appreciation of journalism. There were also some tangible changes in legal codes. The most important were Articles 6 and 7 of the 1917 constitution, which prohibited closing, stopping, destroying, or seizing printing machinery and which stated that the author of what could be considered an incriminating piece would be the only one responsible in the event of any legal dispute, trial, or accusation against it. No other person could be found guilty.[35] Additionally, Article 20 was modified to revive trial by jury exclusively for cases that involved journalists who questioned the conduct of public officials.[36] But the constitution also retained many of the interests of the old guard: the protection of privacy and honor and the need to dampen any call to social unrest were important social values that lived on. A great majority held that society had to shield itself from the threat of newspaper writers' lack of accountability. The common feeling that it was possible and even a public good to criticize the activities of public officials had emerged, but at the same time the old regime's cultural sensitivity endured. The sentiment was that criticism of elites' behavior was risky and irresponsible and could damage a "gentleman's reputation," upset the necessary social equilibrium, and lead to disruption.

Revolutionary change also seemed to generate greater judicial autonomy. The attitude of the Supreme Court apparently changed during the period: more amparos were granted; fewer people served long sentences in jail; no printing shops were seized; the only people considered guilty of press crimes were the writers of libelous texts; and no longer were the entire staffs of periodicals, nor the families of accused writers, imprisoned indiscriminately. The standards that determined whether opinions published in newspapers were considered press crimes also became less rigid. The skins of politicians and other members of the elite were apparently thicker, perhaps because of the recent violence or perhaps because their reputation and prestige were not so important because of their social origins. Or perhaps, in the face of the disintegration of state power, they could no longer so easily restrain the press by legal means.

For example, in 1911 Ignacio Vargas brought an accusation against Enrique Villaseñor, editor of the satirical publication *El Gato* of Guadalajara, Jalisco. Vargas, who must have occupied some public office, although the record does not specify which, accused Villaseñor of slander because he had published a short poem containing a reference to one Ignacio Vargas, claiming that this person was "a long-clawed animal." Villaseñor applied for an amparo from the judge of the Second Criminal Court who had sentenced him to prison, claiming that the poem referred to a different person with the same name. To prove that the person he named in the periodical, of which he brought a copy, was not the plaintiff, he called on two witnesses. He then argued:

> In spite of having given the explanation in the inquiry that the text
> was not about the complainant but of another person with the same
> name, and that this did not constitute libel, the judge of the Second

Criminal Court ordered him imprisoned for libel; . . . the text directed
at Vargas's namesake did not constitute libel according to Article 641
of the criminal code, since in the end it would be an expression that
legally warranted an explanation according to Article 647 of the criminal
code, . . . [and] proceedings [should] not be initiated for slander, the
conditions stipulated in Article 255 of the code not having been fulfilled,
which require that for a prison sentence to be imposed, the existence of
the offense must be proved, which was not done in this case, and hence
Articles 14 and 18 of the constitution were violated against him.[37]

The Supreme Court dismissed the request for amparo because Villaseñor had
another appeal in effect. He served a prison sentence but was released on bail
after paying a 200-peso fine.[38] Villaseñor, clearly an enthusiastic satirist, figured in many other trials at various times and was well versed in defense
before the courts. A loser in this case, in numerous others he triumphed over
his opponents.

Similarly, in May 1912 Trinidad Sánchez Santos, the renowned editor of
the Catholic periodical *El País*, headed the list of President Madero's enemies
and was brought to trial on charges of insulting the president. The eighty-
two-year-old editor "was declared [a] prisoner without prejudice to the con-
ditional freedom that he had enjoyed since April."[39] Sánchez Santos applied
to the judge of the Second District Court for an amparo and was granted
protection from the ruling. Of all public insults, an insult to the president of
the country was considered the most serious. It is well known that during
Madero's presidency, the opposition press turned on him; the Trinidad Sánchez Santos case is important because it demonstrates how far those journalists thought they were allowed to go.[40] But even adulatory works on Sánchez
Santos admit that the article in question went too far: "First the adjectives,
then the weapons. First the insults, then the killing. Sánchez Santos scoffs at
the unmoving eye of Gustavo Madero; weeks later the military descends on
him [Madero] and he is tortured and killed. José María Lozano calls Zapata
a Spartan and calls loudly for him to be killed. His discourse, like the editorials of Sánchez Santos in *El País*, exemplify fear, hate, and an unrestrained
thirst for vengeance."[41]

In 1913 the country descended into another civil war. At the same time,
trials of journalists increased. Gerónimo Gorena of *El Combate* appealed for

an amparo against rulings by the judge of Nuevo León's Second District Court when he was accused by Ramón Díaz of libel for an account he had written on electoral irregularities. Gorena appealed on the basis of the guarantees granted by Articles 7, 14, and 16 of the Mexican Constitution. He also claimed that Article 134 of the criminal trials code had not been applied. This article required proof of the corpus delicti (concrete evidence) for a criminal trial. In his case, Gorena said, this was not present, since the article was merely about a political issue and did not touch on the private life of the complainant. In fact, he argued, the article clearly exculpated Díaz from any blame; a paragraph at the beginning of the El Combate piece read as follows:

> Let us permit ourselves to dedicate a few lines to the submission which, under the heading "The Truth of What Happened in the Council of Electoral Return Officers" appeared in yesterday's issue of our colleague El Noticiero. It was signed over the signatures of Edelmiro Rangel and Ramón Díaz. We address ourselves only to Mr. E. Rangel, because of the two signatories, he is the only one we consider worthy of our attention because it is our understanding that R. Díaz has had his rights as a citizen suspended for issues that are not pertinent here, and so we do not care to concern ourselves with him or his deeds in any way.[42]

Despite the argument, the Supreme Court judges were not persuaded and voted unanimously that the article had damaged Díaz's reputation; the amparo was denied.

In the same year Guillermo Enríquez Simoni, a Catholic journalist who edited the Jalisco periodical El Regional (and went on to become editor of Excélsior), applied for an amparo after a ruling by the judge of the First Criminal Court of Guadalajara. The political boss of the city held Enríquez responsible for libel and slander because of an article published in El Regional. (The title of the article is not known.)[43] The charges were eventually dismissed because they were waived by the accuser, but Enríquez was taken to Mexico City and tried for sedition. At the same time El Regional and another Catholic Party organ, El Nacional,[44] were both shut down. These acts, in effect, broke the alliance between the party and the Huerta government.[45] Yet internal political divisions and the judicial system still militated against outright repression. Enríquez was rescued from a firing squad when a sympathetic minister from Huerta's cabinet intervened. At the same time other members of the Catholic Party had lodged amparo appeals to keep Enríquez and a handful of other Catholic journalists from being taken to jail in far-off Quintana Roo.

The case of Guillermo Aguirre y Fierro, also in 1913, touched on an element that was uncommon in press trials of the period, namely the connection between politics and moral damage. Aguirre y Fierro applied for an amparo against the judge of the Fifth Correctional Court and the inspector general of the police. He was a well-known and beloved poet who had written "Brindis del Bohemio" (Toast of the Bohemian), one of the most famous examples of the bittersweet love poems dedicated to Mexico City's racy lifestyle. On this occasion Aguirre was accused of libeling Federico González Garza, the governor of the Federal District, in an article entitled "Lo que se puede decir y lo que no" (What may be said and what may not be said), which was published in issue number 32 of *El Ahuizote* under the pseudonym El Periquillo. One paragraph of the article stated that the governor had revoked an agreement to remove the brothels on the outskirts of the city in response to the "pleas of certain unrepentant Magdalenes and the influence of certain cronies of the new regime and certain [bosses]." Apparently, although no names were mentioned, this libeled not only the cronies but also the complicit governor. In response Aguirre argued that he had published the article without malicious intent since it concerned a public official and the public good. His amparo was granted, and he was released from the city jail.[46]

The following year, Carlos Valle Gagern applied for an amparo against the political leader of the port of Veracruz and its military commander. They had shut down his periodical *El Monitor* and imprisoned him in the notorious cells of San Juan de Ulúa, violating his rights under Articles 7, 16, 18, 19, and 20 of the constitution. Valle Gagern, the managing editor, claimed in his defense that he had been "fulfilling his mission as a journalist, publishing news that was entirely true, but the authorities considered it a danger for this news to enter the public domain." His attorneys, Solís y Bede, stated:

Simply for having included in his newspaper the news to which I referred, first his newspaper was shut down, and then don Carlos was arrested and . . . imprisoned in Ulúa Fort. Now then, Article 7 of the constitution guarantees the freedom to write and publish on any subject, and these freedoms may not be restricted by any law or authority; [they] may not establish any censorship whatsoever unless, in the case of the press, [published articles] constitute a crime against a person's honor [referring to his private life] or against morals or public order. . . . The violation would be less flagrant if Valle had actually committed some crime, but I challenge the court to prove the existence of the alleged deed in these issues of *El Monitor*, which are the only ones that have been published.

Again, the journalist's argument won, and the case was dismissed.[47]

Despite the implementation of the 1917 constitution, the debate between authorities keen to defend their honor and writers willing to defend the public importance of journalism continued well into the final years of the armed revolution. In 1919, for example, Nephtalí R. Soto, Absalón Herrera G., and Luis M. Flores applied for an amparo from the district judge of Tuxtla Gutiérrez, Chiapas. They claimed that the San Cristóbal Criminal Court judge had violated the guarantees of Articles 14, 16, and 18 of the constitution to their detriment. The judge had persecuted the entire staff of *El Tribuno*, without any legal grounds or reason, for the publication of an article on the aspiring federal official Genaro R. de Chávez. The paragraph to which the official objected ran as follows: "There are in Chávez's private life, in his public conduct, and [in] his professional life such blots that we dare not publish them; nevertheless, we have proofs and if he persists as a candidate, we shall find ourselves obliged to publish them."[48]

Chávez was launching his campaign to become a federal representative and considered this article to be rife with "threats, defamation, and libel."[49] According to the editors, immediately after it was published a representative of Chávez approached them and asked that they not publish the proof and instead allow him to continue his candidacy. The editors' defense was that by putting himself forth as a federal candidate, Chávez had subjected himself to public scrutiny, and undoubtedly the press was competent to point out his defects. Following the 1917 constitution's reforms, only the actual writer of the article, Soto, was held responsible for its content; the manager and secretary of the newspaper were acquitted. Eventually, the case was dismissed because the documents that would prove Soto's guilt never arrived; they were lost in the mail. This trial demonstrates three changes to press trials from the

Porfiriato. First, in the new, more democratic, revolutionary Mexico, ideas of honor now overlapped with concerns for job prospects. Critical journalism endangered not only honor but also popular election. Second, the blanket repression of the ancien régime had disappeared: writers and not their associates were judged the sole people responsible for their articles. Third, state weakness—in this case, the inefficiency of the postal system—provided space for leniency even when it was not intended.

Conclusions

By the time of the Mexican Revolution, legal cases of private people offended by a writer's work were rare. Rather, accusations against journalists tended to come from midrange politicians such as governors, army officers, and senators or from lower-range politicians like political bosses, small-town mayors, public prosecutors, and local judges. The cases I have discussed, which often implicated journalists of only minor importance, show that the drive for censorship reached far outside the traditional urban centers of journalism like Mexico City or big cities like Guadalajara and Monterrey. They demonstrate the daily struggles of journalists across the country. They also show the emerging structures of self-censorship. Few journalists (or, at least, few that were accused in court) attacked the president of the country or members of his cabinet. But they also reveal the limits of this new pattern of censorship. In only a very few instances did court cases succeed in suppressing a newspaper entirely. Instead, the cases corresponded to a meting out of discipline, punishing libel with jail terms. Violent though these admonishments were, journalists kept doing their work and, for the most part, publishing.

In this arena, where men fought over their public image, another important factor can be observed: the utilization of the legal apparatus. Did it serve as a barrier to hold back violence? Did the amparo operate as a social good, which militated against autocratic legal decisions? There is still much to find out. However, what I have shown in this chapter is that the issue of censorship was intimately linked to the development of legal culture. Thanks to the existence of the writ of amparo and the fact that ordinary citizens seized it as a defensive weapon, the trials discussed here represent an important forum where civil rights were contested.

One last set of questions is left for future inquiries. Was the public manipulation of the concepts of honor, reputation, and prestige important only to the elite? Did these concepts matter only to the social class with a high socioeconomic level and powerful political interests, or did they matter to social actors across the board? Did this nineteenth-century value survive the social upheaval of the early twentieth century? To flip that question, did a decline in concern about this value allow Mexican journalism to evolve more modern practices? Two generations after the revolution, the US scholar Charles Cumberland was less than enthusiastic. He thought that removing the legal framework and eliminating concerns over honor had been dangerous and destructive: "When Madero lifted censorship and stimulated constructive criticism by press leaders, for the first time the newspapers and periodicals felt free to express any opinion and report on any incident. But editorial responsibility, that finely-grained nuance of civic conscience that keeps freedom from degenerating into excess, barely existed among the journalists of the day, and the result was disastrous."[50]

The solution, at least in many revolutionaries' minds, was to clap the lid back onto the rubbish bin. Following 1920 it was clear that political elites had changed, and for a time the patronage that had linked elites and the lower courts was absent. Some cases surpassed the limits of regulation of language and showed a heightened degree of violence, but these were exceptions rather than the rule, and they did not go through the legal system, at least directly. The appeal to the jury (*jurado popular*) as a truly democratic court became an important part of the discussions between the 1910s and 1930s. After the revolution, the notorious Belén and Islas Marías prisons, where many journalists served their sentences during the Porfiriato, became, like the Bastille in France, symbols of an oppression now gone.

Acknowledgments

I gratefully acknowledge the help of research assistant Clara López López and Instituto Mora scholarship interns David Alfonso Bolañas López and Fausto Adriano Ramírez Arellano.

Notes

1. Cosío Villegas, *Historia moderna*, vol. 9, and 10:229–53; Gantús, *Caricatura y poder político*; Lomnitz, *The Return*; Barajas, *El país de "El Ahuizote"*; Piccato, *Tyranny of Opinion*; Paz, *Hoguera que fue.*
2. Darnton, *The Devil in the Holy Water*; Bourdieu, *Language and Symbolic Power*; Darnton, *Censors at Work.*
3. Schuger, "Civility and Censorship" and *Censorship and Cultural Sensibility.*
4. Paz, "Libertad de imprenta," 33.
5. Reich, "Recent Research."
6. Cossío, *La justicia prometida* and *La teoría constitucional*; Morales Moreno, *El poder judicial.*
7. "The Supreme Court was respected. The Declaration of Guadalupe that brought Venustiano Carranza to triumph did not recognize the three branches, and therefore the High Court was dissolved and its offices shut down on August 14, 1914." Parada Gay, *Breve reseña histórica*, 64–65. "In June 1917 the Supreme Court had its first session according to the new Constitution." Cabrera Acevedo, *La Suprema Corte de Justicia* (1991), 23–24.
8. Cárdenas Gutiérrez, *El juez.*
9. Arenas Guzmán, *Historia de la cámara de diputados*, vol. 4; Marván Laborde, *Nueva edición*; "Iniciativa de ley de imprenta presentada por la Secretaría de Gobernación, México, imprenta de la Cámara de Diputados 1912: Ley de imprenta," Jan. 8, 1916, AGN/CCGS/exp. 2, folio 1–2; Cámara de Diputados del H. Congreso de la Unión, "Ley sobre delitos de imprenta," Apr. 11, 2015, http://www.diputados.gob.mx/LeyesBiblio/pdf/40_041115.pdf.
10. Andrews, *La tradición constitucional.*
11. See Cosío Villegas, *Historia moderna*, vol. 9, and 10:229–53.
12. Gantús, *Caricatura y poder político*; Piccato, *Tyranny of Opinion*. For the legal terms, see Pascual García, *Código penal* (1906, 1907, 1910).
13. Gantús, *Caricatura y poder político*; Barajas, *El país de "El Ahuizote."*
14. Case dated Sept. 23, 1909, AHSCJN/Primera Secretaría/Toca al Juicio de Amparo/exp. 2110.
15. Crescencia Garza Viuda de Martínez to Lázaro Cárdenas, Oct. 4, 1935, AGN/LCR/704/39.
16. Case dated Apr. 26, 1910, AHSCJN/Primera Secretaría/Toca al Juicio de Amparo/exp. 1004.
17. "El proceso de La Voz de Méjico," *El Tiempo*, June 13, 1901; "El asunto Reyes Spíndola—Abregro," *El Tiempo*, June 1, 1900; "Formalmente presos," *La Patria*, July 9, 1899; "Procedimiento contra 'El Alacrán,'" *El Popular*, Sept. 2, 1899; "Sentencia contra los redactores de 'El Alacrán,'" *El Popular*, Nov. 1, 1899; "Denuncia de 'La Nación Española,'" *La Patria*, Apr. 19, 1901; "La familia de

don Paulino Martínez," *Diario del Hogar*, May 19, 1909; "Lo del Día," *El Popular*, Aug. 23, 1908; "Periodistas perseguidos," *La Iberia*, July 12, 1906; "De orden superior es clausurada la casa del Sr. Mata," *La Patria*, Jan. 17, 1910; "Don Filomeno Mata, formalmente preso," *El Tiempo*, Jan, 20, 1910; "Los redactores del 'Antireeleccionista' formalmente presos," *El Tiempo*, Mar. 10, 1909.

18. See Darnton, *Censors at Work*.
19. Serna Rodríguez, *Un análisis de los casos* and *La justicia*.
20. Case dated Apr. 26, 1910, AHSCJN/Primera Secretaría/Toca al Juicio de Amparo/exp. 1004.
21. Case dated Dec. 7, 1909, AHSCJN/Primera Secretaría/Toca al Juicio de Amparo/exp. 1447.
22. I have not been able to find a copy of the article in any newspaper collection.
23. Case dated Dec. 7, 1909, exp. 1447.
24. Article 909 of the 1910 criminal code states that anyone who "in writing, orally, or in any other manner privately harms, slanders, or insults the President in the course of the performance of his duties or by reason of them shall be punished by a fine of 100 to 1,000 pesos, by arrest for one to eleven months, or both penalties." Article 910: "Anyone who privately harms, slanders, or insults an individual of the legislature, a secretary of the office, a magistrate, judge, or member of the jury, or the governor of the district in the course of the performance of his duties or by reason of them shall be punished by arrest of fifteen days to six months, a fine of 50 to 300 pesos, or both penalties." Pascual García, *Código penal* (1910), 334.
25. Case dated Dec. 7, 1909, exp. 1447.
26. Case dated Dec. 7, 1909, exp. 1447.
27. Case dated Dec. 7, 1909, exp. 1447.
28. Case dated Dec. 7, 1909, exp. 1447.
29. Case dated Dec. 7, 1909, exp. 1447.
30. Case dated Nov. 25, 1909, AHSCJN/Primera Secretaría/Toca al Juicio de Amparo/exp. 2648.
31. Case dated Nov. 25, 1909, exp. 2648.
32. Cabrera, "El balance de la revolución," 116.
33. Serna Rodríguez, "Prensa y sociedad."
34. Baqueiro López, *La prensa*, 157.
35. Piccato, *Tyranny of Opinion*, 27–62; Cabrera Acevedo, *La Suprema Corte de Justicia* (1991), 39–44.
36. See the discussion about Articles 6, 7, and 20 in Marván Laborde, *Nueva edición*.
37. Case dated Oct. 24, 1911, AHSCJN/Primera Secretaría/Toca al Juicio de Amparo/exp. 2685.
38. Case dated Oct. 24, 1911, exp. 2685.
39. Reos, June 8, 1914, AHDF/Reos de Penitenciaría, 1.17, folio 12.

40. Cruz García, *Nueva era*.

41. García Cantú, *El pensamiento*, 238.

42. Case dated Feb. 20, 1913, AHSCJN/Primera Secretaría/Toca al Juicio de Amparo/exp. 746.

43. Case dated July 31, 1913, AHSCJN/Primera Secretaría/Toca al Juicio de Amparo/exp. 4357.

44. This *El Nacional* is a different paper than the one discussed elsewhere in this volume.

45. O'Dogherty Madrazo, *De urnas y sotanas*, 247; Burkholder de la Rosa, *La red de los espejos*.

46. Case dated Jan. 28, 1913, AHSCJN/Primera Secretaría/Toca al Juicio de Amparo/exp. 505.

47. Case dated July 3, 1914, AHSCJN/Primera Secretaría/Toca al Juicio de Amparo/exp. 1103.

48. Case dated Aug. 8, 1929, AHSCJN/Primera Secretaría/Toca al Juicio de Amparo/exp. 751.

49. Case dated Aug. 8, 1929, exp. 751.

50. Cumberland, *Madero*, 282.

3 | Changing Opinions in *La Opinión*

Maximino Ávila Camacho and the Puebla Press, 1936–1941

ANDREW PAXMAN

Carnival of Fraud

In early 1938, Puebla City witnessed a contest not seen in thirty years. Huddles of students harried passersby to sign for one candidate or another. As their booklets of signatures were notarized, the state's leading newspaper, *La Opinión*, gave a daily count of the votes. Portraits of the rivals adorned the front page in turn, and columnists wrote poems in their praise. For the first time since the Porfirian era, Puebla was to elect a carnival queen.[1]

By January 15, a week into the race, two front-runners had emerged among the six competitors: Amelia Ibañez (866 votes), the striking daughter of a lawyer and his French wife, and Martita Hill (1,477 votes), a Vivien Leigh lookalike of Spanish parentage. But that day produced a surprise late entrant: Alicia Ávila, daughter of the state's governor, Maximino Ávila Camacho. Her plain looks notwithstanding, Alicia soon had the support of the Association of Charros, which practiced the traditional horsemanship that Maximino—as he was popularly known—held dear; in fact, he was the club's president. The block vote for Alicia invested fresh momentum in the race, since various unions and societies made declarations of allegiance. Next to benefit was Lupita Chain, the candidate of the Lebanese Association. Overnight, on January 25, she zoomed from last place to first, with 10,027 ballots. This was a tally far higher than that of the city's ethnic enclave; perhaps the Lebanese mill owners had pressed a unanimous vote from their employees.

In a shock reversal two days later, Lupita Chain withdrew from the race. Textile magnate Miguel Abed wrote to *La Opinión* that he was unhappy with his community's aggressive lobbying; he feared their naked "patriotism" might backfire. No doubt, he also wished not to offend his good friend Maximino, whose daughter was trailing in fifth. But a public outcry ensued, Lupita's candidacy was reinstated, and then it was the turn of a second contestant, Amelia Puget, to face controversy, as the railroad workers declared en masse for her; this produced another resignation and another reinstatement. Clearly, Puebla's most eligible young ladies were having difficulty balancing grace and etiquette with the gloves-off realities of campaigning in the corporatist era.

By February 10, two days before the election, Puebla had a three-way race. Martita Hill still led, with 89,000 votes, Lupita Chain held 58,000, and Alicia Ávila had made up ground with a respectable 41,000. *La Opinión* remained firmly in Martita's camp: she *will* be queen, it opined on the morning of February 12. But that night's final count, held amid pomp at the city bullring, told a different tale. Her tally having mushroomed overnight—to 257,000, more than that of her two closest rivals put together—Maximino's daughter was proclaimed carnival queen. In a small act of defiance the next day, *La Opinión* ran "Homage to Martita" on page one: beneath her luminous portrait a poem exalted her "florid youth" and pledged that though she may not have triumphed, her beauty would ever reign "in the profound depths of our hearts." The front page also announced the result, but the text was a dry summary of the proceedings rather than a tribute to the governor's daughter.

Two weeks later, however, came the parade, and with it banner coverage in *La Opinión*. Her Majesty Alicia the First rode a float in the shape of a dragon, and companies sponsored barges promoting their wares. The German firm Bayer pushed its medicine for colds. Cigarrera la Moderna ("the modern cigarette maker") was there; so too was the O'Farrill auto dealership, showing off a Graham Supercharger on a float bedecked with streamers and salesgirls clad in white. Columns on subsequent days would praise Alicia for her beauty. It was as though the newspaper were stricken with amnesia.[2]

Here was Puebla under Maximino in a nutshell: a triumphal concoction of Catholic ritual, neo-Porfirian tradition, capitalistic modernity, and electoral fraud. As grand master of the pageantry, Ávila Camacho was in his populist element. When the crowds cheered his daughter they were also cheering him: the bringer of order to a long-violent state, builder of roads and schools, redistributor of land, and reviver of carnival.

The 1938 carnival queen campaign would mark the last time that *La Opinión* notably differed with the governor. Its unquestioning report of his daughter's victory parade capped a slow surrender. Two years before, it had vigorously thrown its weight behind Maximino's chief rival for the governorship, Gilberto Bosques; it had reported accusations of fraud when, with ruling-party backing, Maximino claimed victory in the crucial (and quite dirty) primary election; and it had retained an independent line for another year, including the first six months of Maximino's reign. Yet for the remainder of his term—which would see his younger brother Manuel compete for the presidency—Maximino could rest assured that any significant opinion in *La Opinión* was effectively his.

What befell this newspaper between 1936 and 1938 holds significance at both the provincial and the national levels. Locally, the governor's co-optation of *La Opinión* was part of a broader strategy of authoritarian subjugation, so as to create a univocal, laudatory press. This included his founding and subsidizing of *El Diario de Puebla*, which began life as Maximino's campaign propaganda sheet, and the murder of the publisher of a third paper, who dared to back Manuel's opponent in the presidential race.

Nationally, the co-optation might seem anomalous. The era of President Lázaro Cárdenas was one of "ample freedom of speech," in which the national press often criticized policy.[3] But many dailies evinced a reactionary quality at odds with state radicalism. The top two broadsheets, *El Universal* and *Excélsior*, along with the popular *La Prensa*, purveyed a conservative brand of *oficialismo*, while *Novedades* and the leading newsweekly *Hoy* were not only right-wing but pro-Axis. Such conservatism held in common a respect for the president and tolerance of his land redistribution program, but a skepticism toward organized labor, a sympathy for the Catholic Church and the business elite, and an admiration for Benito Mussolini and Francisco Franco.[4] In sum, while the state-backed papers *El Nacional* and *El Popular* voiced the leftist government line, most print media anticipated the right-of-center zeitgeist of the 1940s. In this context, *La Opinión* migrated from a minority position to a majority one.

There is also a useful structural dimension to this story. It shows how any critical analysis of journalism must take into account not only the state's tools of influence and a periodical's political profile but also the abilities, affective leanings, and financial strength of media owners and editors. For reasons of profit, ideology, loyalty, and even pride, power elites often diverge, even those famed for their interdependence. As Celeste González has written of the Institutional Revolutionary Party (PRI) and Telesistema Mexicano in the period 1955–1970, the ruling party and the TV monopoly "walked together, but not exactly in lockstep."[5] That *La Opinión* was able to hold out against Maximino for two years owed something to the general's initial need to tread softly in the state capital and build credibility following an election widely viewed as crooked. But it also owed much to the independent-mindedness of the paper's owners, the convictions of its staff, and relatively solid finances. Such instances of differentiation from officialdom suggest there were spaces for maneuver, if often at a risk, under the soft dictatorship of the ruling party.[6] However, the governor's eventual subjugation of Puebla's press shows what a particularly ruthless provincial boss might achieve, irrespective of a tolerant federal government.

The Electoral Contest of 1936: Bosques versus Maximino

By 1936, the Partido Nacional Revolucionario (PNR) held sufficient power in Puebla that the real contest that year would be not the gubernatorial election but the PNR primary in the spring. The paramountcy of the primary was typical in the 1930s and '40s, as the party sought to impose itself on Mexico's electoral system.[7] One candidate in the primary was Maximino, a general of dubious reputation who nonetheless had been named by Cárdenas as the state's military commander in January 1935. In September of that year, by which time he had wooed the business elite by breaking strikes and protecting haciendas from *agraristas* (radical agrarian activists), he resigned his commission to begin his campaign. Maximino was effectively the official candidate, inasmuch as he enjoyed the friendship of the president and the blessing of the PNR. Cárdenas counted on him as one of a number of military counterweights to governors aligned with former president Plutarco Elías Calles, who until April 1936 would continue to loom large in Mexican politics, coveting influence.[8] Such Callista governors included Puebla's incumbent, José Mijares Palencia.

Maximino's rival in the primary was Gilberto Bosques. Once a delegate at the Constitutional Convention of 1917, Bosques had gone on to the federal Congress, rising to preside over the Chamber of Deputies. As well as excellent credentials, Bosques had the support of the Regional Front of Workers and Peasants (FROC), the biggest labor confederation in Puebla and an affiliate of the Confederation of Mexican Workers (CTM), and of other worker and peasant associations. So great was Bosques's grassroots popularity that Maximino needed to run a vigorous campaign—a matter attested to by the number of rallies he held and by his devotion to fund-raising. William Jenkins, Puebla's richest industrialist, chipped in 40,000 pesos (equivalent to US$200,000 today). Private-sector largesse was crucial: as well as subsidizing campaign stops, it would help buy the bloc votes of municipal power brokers and pay for the busing of voters on polling day. It would also help Maximino buy good press.

Both Maximino and Bosques had the support of dedicated campaign weeklies: *El Guardián* and *La Fogata*, respectively. But more influential, with their journalistic bona fides and wide circulation, were the daily newspapers that backed them: *El Diario de Puebla* and *La Opinión*. Since most papers launched in the 1920s and early '30s had fallen victim to Puebla's political and economic turmoil, these two periodicals basically constituted the press. Not until 1944, with the launch of *El Sol de Puebla*, would the state see a major new competitor.[9]

El Diario de Puebla purportedly belonged to its editor, Julián Cacho. But its 1935 launch date, adulation of Ávila Camacho, and vilification of Bosques—along with Cacho's modest origins (a few years earlier, he was editing copy at *La Opinión*)—give credence to the rumors that Cacho was fronting for the general and that the paper's raison d'être was to hype his campaign. Marked by exaggerated reporting and low credibility, *El Diario* was likely of limited persuasive impact as propaganda.[10]

La Opinión, by contrast, was Puebla's newspaper of record. While no other post-Porfirian paper had survived to its fifth anniversary, *La Opinión* had appeared uninterrupted since 1924. While most local dailies ran to four pages (a single sheet of newsprint), *La Opinión* published six and sometimes eight pages. It carried wire stories from the United Press and the Associated Press. In a key sign of financial health, fully half of its space was given to advertising, which featured such prominent brands as Packard automobiles, Corona and Carta Blanca beer, Nestlé condensed milk, and Puebla's largest department stores. Although not alien to expedient boosterism—as during the leftist administration of Leonides Andreu Almazán (1929–1933) and again under his right-leaning successor, Mijares—the paper was of good repute. Further, it had the backing of a group of investors, rather than a single political adventurer. Among them was Sergio Guzmán, a Northwestern University graduate, dental surgeon, and former state legislator. In 1931, Guzmán had bought out one of the cofounders, who was married to his sister. Guzmán was a political moderate, and in 1935—around which time he gained prominence by buying out a second cofounder—he permitted the paper, whose employees adhered to the left-wing FROC, to back that union's candidate for Puebla City mayor. So its backing of Bosques was a continuation of staff preferences and editorial affiliation.[11]

While *La Opinión* supported Bosques with upbeat reports on his rallies and daily extracts from his manifesto, it refrained from criticizing his opponent.[12] Rather, it ignored him. There are two likely explanations. First, Guzmán and the editors may have calculated that Maximino should be treated with care. As a general during the Cristero rebellion (1926–1929) he had come to be known for mercilessness, ordering executions for minor offenses. He was widely held to be the mastermind of the Topilejo massacre of 1930, when sixty loyalists who supported the defeated presidential candidate José Vasconcelos were made to dig their own graves on Valentine's Day. As Puebla's military chief Maximino had employed utilitarian violence, arming vigilante groups to contain agraristas and brutally suppressing a general strike by the FROC. During the 1936 campaign there were various allegations of political killings (on both sides) and a reported attempt on the life of Bosques. One source claims that Maximino threatened *La Opinión*'s owners and editors.[13] Second, Guzmán faced a balancing act: on one hand, there was his loyalty to his capable employees, who had built *La Opinión* into the most successful paper in a generation; on the other, his adherence to Maximino, who had persuaded Guzmán to join him and run side by side for governor and Puebla City mayor. The surgeon had his reservations, but the general was almost family: the two had grown up together in the Puebla sierra, where Maximino's mother had worked in the Guzmán household.[14]

As of election day, April 5, the paper abandoned its reserve. It claimed that seventy buses and thirty-four trucks had arrived from the capital, bearing thousands of "political tourists" to inflate Maximino's vote; having dropped off their cargo in Puebla they proceeded to Tlaxcala and Veracruz to gather further voters. It reported that one driver, whose bus was firebombed by Bosques supporters, admitted he had been contracted by Maximino's people. To be fair, Maximino made a similar claim regarding the busing of out-of-state voters by the FROC. The day after the poll, *La Opinión* automatically proclaimed Bosques's triumph.[15]

Not until the night of April 29 did the PNR declare Maximino victorious. That the party took twenty-four days to announce the result seemed to affirm that the general had needed a massaging of the vote. On May 1, *La Opinión* led with the eight-column headline "March on Mexico City." When that march took place—some 20,000 protested in the capital on May 13—the paper's coverage unswervingly caught the mood. It cited a banner calling Maximino "the murderer of the workers." It quoted a FROC leader declaring in a speech that he would only accept a governor "who is not the enemy of the working class, who does not kill them, who does not machine-gun them, who does not limit their right to strike, who is not allied with the clergy and the business elite."[16]

A Year of Neutrality: June 1936–June 1937

Once it was clear the PNR would not reverse its ruling, *La Opinión* ceased to press the case. In June, hinting at an olive branch, it mentioned Maximino's attendance at a society wedding. Over the year that followed, the paper maintained a dignified neutrality, facilitated by the commitment of the outgoing governor Mijares to a plural press.[17]

On July 7, *La Opinión* reported the general's victory in the gubernatorial election; a handsome portrait of Maximino in military cap and collar accompanied the story. The final poll was to have been held in November, but the PNR brought it forward, presumably to forestall any attempt by Bosques to mount a new challenge with a separate party, yet the paper made no mention of that nor of the disputed primary.[18] Neutrality did not mean blandness, however. While conciliatory toward Maximino, *La Opinión* remained a feisty critic of those in his circle it deemed corrupt or irresponsible.

The balance was visible in an August editorial, "The Enemies That Gen. Maximino Ávila Camacho Still Faces." First it commended the future governor for declining either to boast of his triumph or to bully those who had opposed him. Then, at length, it assailed those "improvised journalists" who had sided with him: they churned out propaganda of the lowest order, ham-fisted and incompetent. The target here was *El Diario de Puebla*. *La Opinión* reported that its offices had been shot at by Julián Cacho and several of his staff while they were driving drunk at 5 a.m. This display of politicized machismo (a recurrent news item in postwar Puebla) may have been pro-voked by a *La Opinión* story a few weeks before, which claimed that *El Diario* had used a defamatory article to blackmail a cinema into buying advertising. But it hinted at an incipient culture of political violence and impunity that would flourish once Maximino took office: his cronies would often act as though they were above the law.[19]

November 1 brought a change of leadership, as Guzmán and his partners transferred their shareholdings so that *La Opinión* became an employee-owned cooperative. The circumstances are mysterious. While Guzmán had won the PNR primary in September, the mayoral election proper would not take place until November 29, and Guzmán's rival in the first poll, the popu-lar labor leader Manuel Rivera, had determined to stand again, as a FROC candidate. Why would Guzmán surrender control of *La Opinión* just four weeks prior to a hotly contested vote, especially given the paper's alignment with his opponent's backers? His son would later claim that Guzmán divested due to growing tensions with Maximino over the paper's reporting; Guzmán probably foresaw further friction once the general was installed as governor. *La Opinión* itself would record (three years later) that Guzmán had sold out due to financial difficulties at the paper. Still, the timing remains odd. Per-haps he received assurances from the PNR that he would be mayor whatever the vote. Perhaps he responded to the quandary facing his employees—their loyalties torn between their boss and their candidate—by making a good-faith gesture of neutrality. Whatever the case, during November, *La Opinión* switched its endorsement from Guzmán to Rivera. On December 7, contrary to the paper's claim, the PNR declared Guzmán the winner.[20]

Maximino was sworn in on February 1, 1937, and for five months *La Opin-ión* remained the fair-minded civic actor, praising the governor on some counts, criticizing him on others, and taking him at his word when he railed against those who exploited his friendship to seek employment or abuse their office.[21] It commended him for his choice of cabinet, and it trumpeted his threat to turn tax-avoiding businesses into cooperatives and his firing of a corrupt arbitration board.[22] It criticized him for raising homeowner property taxes in an "arbitrary" manner and for plotting to divide the FROC leadership.[23] Despite a notoriously short fuse, Maximino may have tolerated such criticisms as the price of restoring some democratic credibility after his dubious election; in the short run, the paper could function as a useful escape valve. A similar calculus presumably explained his early declarations against corruption. Most often, the criticisms in *La Opinión* were implicit, as though the editors feared that too much direct defiance would bring reprisals. Such cases included the reporting of a threatened strike by the FROC over Maximino's proposed education policy and the naming and shaming of certain appointees, including a covert police force made up of Lebanese immigrants.[24] Above all, *La Opinión* denounced the industrialist closest to the governor: William Jenkins.

A US expatriate, Jenkins was the state's largest private-sector employer. His giant sugar plantation, Atencingo, gave work to 5,000 people. His five or six textile mills employed another 2,000. Since the latter years of the Mexican Revolution, Jenkins had been acquiring land and mills while many who had prospered under Porfirio Díaz were losing theirs. This feat, his control of Puebla's sugar supply, and his talent for weaving rings of political protection around Atencingo to ward off agraristas, earned him a broad antipathy. Rightly or wrongly—and much of the talk about Jenkins was partial—he represented to many Pueblans the bad old values that the revolution was supposed to have defeated: monopoly, large landholding, exploitation of workers and peons, mutual favoritism between business and political elites, and US economic dominion. From the viewpoints of the Left and the nationalist Right, Jenkins's continued flourishing under Maximino, not to mention the two men's evident friendship, reflected badly on them both.[25]

To attack Jenkins was to criticize Maximino by proxy, and *La Opinión* did so often that spring and early summer.[26] In March 1937, it reported that Jenkins was setting up a regional alcohol production cartel that would undersell and eliminate rivals. The paper predicted that the move would force the federal government to quadruple its local tax inspection force, since it had long had problems taxing Atencingo's alcohol output. In April, a column assailed "the voracious octopus of sugar," claiming that the monopoly—that is, Jenkins—was helping drive up the price of staple foods. In June, as word began to filter from the capital that the irrigated heartland of Atencingo would be divvied up among the region's peasants after all, the combative column "El dedo en la llaga" (The finger on the wound) rejoiced at the news. This "feudal lord," this "great Yankee estate owner" had trampled the constitution, creating at Atencingo "almost a sovereign and independent republic." But now, "President Cárdenas has fixed his gaze on this embarrassment that for twenty years slapped the face of the fatherland." The column concluded: "Citizens, applaud!"[27]

Two weeks after the column came the presidential decree. Conspicuous in the paper's report was the absence of Maximino. Surely the governor had something to say, some role to play, regarding the most important land grant in Puebla since the revolution? According to La Opinión, he did not. All the credit went to Cárdenas.[28] In the months to follow, however, the Atencingo expropriation would become very much a story about the governor.

Co-optation Completed: July 1937 and After

As of July 1937, all criticism of Maximino—explicit or implicit—disappeared from La Opinión. Its coverage assumed the sycophantic tone that he would soon start to cultivate in the national press, as he aspired to the presidency; indeed, the flattery of officialdom would become standard practice, but the general was unusually adept at using the press to develop a personality cult.[29] At La Opinión, the change first emerged in a sequence of soft news: Maximino's inauguration of a jai alai championship; plans for a statewide tour of a film documenting his investiture; his visit to a trade fair in his hometown of Teziutlán, where at a packed bullring he received "great and lavish ovations" when showing his *fiesta brava* skills; and his birthday celebration at the Puebla bullring, where the seats in the sun were free to the public and a highlight was a procession of the general's Arab chargers.[30]

The change emerged also in reporting on the Atencingo expropriation, a story in which Maximino was now the lead actor. The new emphasis was merited, but not for the reasons the newspaper gave. No sooner had Cárdenas declared the redistribution, Maximino began to lobby in Jenkins's defense. He argued that the land should go not to the agraristas who had long sought it, but to the *peones acasillados*: the peons in Jenkins's employ who lived on his land, played in sports teams he patronized, and sent their children to schools he had built. That July, Cárdenas suspended the seizure and handed the project to the general. In the autumn, when CTM leader Vicente Lombardo Toledano advocated that the mill be expropriated too, Maximino again defended Jenkins. In the end, Jenkins retained the mill—Atencingo's profit center and hence a major Puebla tax base—along with an exclusive supply deal with the peons; he could therefore set the price of the cane. Credit for growing the crops was to come from Jenkins, rather than from the public Bank of Ejidal Credit, and the Atencingo company retained the right to name the manager of the Ejidal Cooperative Society, which oversaw work schedules and submanager appointments. What was heralded as a patriotic victory on behalf of Puebla's peasants ended up preserving Jenkins's reign.[31]

Aiding in this sleight of hand was *La Opinión*, which adorned the maneuver with glowing rhetoric. For the December hand-over event, it blazed a double banner: "The Promises Made by the Revolution to the People Were Fulfilled Yesterday in Atencingo." These were the words of Brigadier General Maximino Ávila Camacho, noted the first subhead. Added a second: "8,567 Hectares Passed into the Hands of the Proletariat." Half of the text-dense front page was taken up with the ceremony—partly rendered in the present tense to lend it a sense of the epic—and with Maximino's speech. The governor was the star: his discourse "was received with tumultuous applause and with bugle calls, and in the orator's most brilliant passages the battle bands of the unions gathered there also struck up." Cárdenas went unmentioned until the fourth paragraph. Jenkins was respectfully referred to as "don Guillermo."[32]

Since July, language about a "feudal Yankee" had disappeared from *La Opinión*. That autumn, Maximino's private-sector pal was admiringly documented winning the state's tennis doubles tournament (at age fifty-nine, no less); building another school for his sugar workers' children; and taking part in a chess championship. A few days after December's Atencingo ceremony, the columnist Luis Castro, later one of Puebla's most respected journalists, claimed that in his development of the estate Jenkins had "fulfilled, and exceeded, the work of the revolution" by avoiding strikes and paying above the minimum wage.[33]

The following month, *La Opinión*'s decision to back Martita Hill for carnival queen even after Alicia Ávila entered the race would prove the paper's last independent whisper, a pale throwback to the autonomy of 1936 and early 1937. The same day that it noted Alicia's entry, the paper also gave full and flattering coverage to her father's first state-of-the-state speech. Here the tone truly indicated what was to come. Luis Castro praised Maximino for having overcome the difficulties of his first months in office (as though those early stories criticizing him had been a tad harsh), noting his "serene voice . . . in the middle of the storm." Editorialized the banner: "A Year of Honest and Correct Activity."[34]

Veteran editor Gabriel Sánchez Guerrero must have held his nose as he wrote that line. Every journalist knew that Maximino was anything but honest. He had long exploited his military postings to hoard loot culled from Cristero sympathizers and from the hacienda owners he had protected against agraristas. In Puebla he was no different, accumulating ranches and automobiles and, it was widely rumored, helping himself to whichever teenaged daughter caught his eye. Within another year Sergio Guzmán had quit as mayor, fearing Maximino's wrath over his attempts to protect his budget; one of the general's tricks was to buy expensive jewelry for his lovers and then send the bill to City Hall.[35]

The governor's dishonesty extended to his populist gestures. Elevating the state college to university status brought fanfare but few material improvements beyond a swimming pool, a billiard room, and a drugstore. When, early in 1937, Maximino overrode Guzmán's refusal to allow the FROC to stage a rally demanding consumer-goods price cuts, he seemed a paragon of magnanimity; after all, over the previous two years he had tried to suppress the union in favor of its more pliant rival, the CROM. What the papers did not report was that Maximino had told Guzmán to prohibit the rally in the first place.[36]

La Opinión continued to champion the FROC, favorably reporting its declarations and amply covering its annual congress, May Day marches, and even the occasional strike. But that posture, less vociferous than before, barely echoed the old editorial independence. By mid-1937 the governor had co-opted several of the union's leaders, a process begun a year earlier, when in an apparent exchange for recognizing his election the FROC was allotted two seats in the state congress. One of the officials elected, Blas Chumacero, would rally the sugar-mill workers of Atencingo to support the Maximino-Jenkins plan for the estate.[37] The paper's backing of FROC activities took on a cosmetic role: it gave the impression that Maximino permitted freedom of the press. After all, everybody knew that the FROC had long been his brave opponent.

The newspaper was in thrall to officialdom. Its editorials lost their bite, preferring to focus on events in Europe and gradually shedding their advocacy for workers; a 1940 column even declared, "We are not for strikes." Elevation of Maximino became the norm, to the point of self-parody. The paper termed his governorship "revolutionary" and "progressive" and deemed the man himself "reasonable." It slobbered over his annual state addresses, calling one of them "brillantísimo." It recorded its own feting of the governor at a journalists' banquet, where the assembly lauded his respect for freedom of speech—an Orwellian routine later adopted by the national press.[38]

Most slavish of all was the annual front-page coverage of Maximino's birthday party, an established event at the city bullring, always announced on the day and written up the day after, and usually accompanied by a photographic portrait taken some ten years earlier. In 1939 Maximino again took to the ring, now on horseback as a lance-wielding *rejoneador*, and *La Opinión* praised his "art and elegance." The birthday ritual continued after he left office, and so did the front-page brownnosing. In 1941, when Maximino was out of office and as yet unnamed to his brother's cabinet, Puebla's politicians cheered him up with four days of festivities: a banquet at City Hall, a variety show at the Cine Reforma, a brass band concert and an equestrian fiesta at the Plaza del Charro, a bullfight, and finally a dinner-dance at the home of a Lebanese businessman. *La Opinión* wrote up each occasion with gusto, calling the last of them "the most notable event of our social circles in recent times."[39]

So why, back in the autumn of 1937, did *La Opinión* give up? What went on behind the scenes that bent the will of Puebla's leading newspaper to that of the governor? And what pressures kept it supine?

The paper's finances were surely one factor. During 1937 they certainly weakened. Now a cooperative, *La Opinión* lacked the wealthy backers who could dip into their pockets when times were tough, making it more vulnerable to external pressures, and it surely lost the access to bank credit it would have enjoyed as a joint-stock company. When the cooperative was set up, it did receive "an important amount of money" from the FROC, but the paper said this was merely a loan to help it pay off the buyout. Ongoing support from that union was probably limited. The FROC was already publishing its own weekly paper, *Resurgimiento*, and as noted above, by 1937 its autonomy had begun to be compromised. Second, while *La Opinión* continued to draw top-dollar advertisers, *El Diario de Puebla* saw its ad count improve. Local businesses no doubt felt compelled to please the governor by buying space in his pet paper, and this budgetary reallocation would have harmed its rival.[40]

Along with newsstand sales, subscriptions, and advertising (which included the paid insertions masquerading as news known as *gacetillas*), the fourth key revenue source for a Mexican newspaper—in some cases, the main one—was government financing. This took the form of cut-price newsprint, payments to amenable reporters, and direct but unannounced subsidies. (Official publicity would appear in later decades.) Puebla's governors had routinely granted subsidies in exchange for favorable coverage since 1917, with precedents dating from the 1830s.[41] At one point during the 1936 campaign, Congress formally asked Governor Mijares to pay *El Diario de Puebla* 200 pesos (US$1,000 today) for "diverse published items," and other transfers were presumably made informally. The FROC later attacked *El Diario* for living off state handouts, but that did not mean that *La Opinión* was not also a recipient. Its switch of allegiance to Mijares during the 1932 campaign, followed by nearly four years of flattery, indicates a mutually convenient friendship.[42] If the paper had then grown accustomed to a Mijares-approved subsidy, Maximino would have had no qualms in closing the spigot. Nor, as a regular maker of "gifts" to the press, would he have hesitated to reopen it once the paper had learned its lesson.[43]

The other factor behind the paper's submission, without any doubt, was fear. For all his public jollity and charm, Maximino's reputation for violence had never abated. Guzmán had quit as mayor—having refused to reimburse the general for a diamond necklace—after two of Maximino's pistol-toting goons showed up at his door one night. Unco-opted labor leaders were arrested or assassinated. People close to him said that Maximino had an impetuous, ferocious temper.[44]

Avante: The Paper That Wouldn't Toe the Line

The night of April 22, 1939, Trinidad Mata knew that he was going to die. The men with guns who accosted him outside the office of his weekly paper, *Avante*, had bundled him into a car. It was past midnight and they had now been driving for some time. Mata took the small crucifix that he habitually wore and clasped it—tight—in his right hand. Devout Catholic that he was, he surely began to pray. No doubt, he thought of his wife and five children. Quite possibly, he questioned the wisdom of *Avante*'s latest edition: replete with critique of the Cárdenas regime, carrying a front-page declaration of political independence, and bearing a column that called Hitler and Mussolini "political geniuses of immeasurable size." And it had led with a manifesto from the National Front of Professionals and Intellectuals, one of several parties backing Juan Andreu Almazán, chief rival in the presidential race to the soon-to-be-named official candidate: Manuel Ávila Camacho.[45]

Although the election was fifteen months away, signs already showed it would be heated. Cárdenas's radical policies, and the chain reaction of capital flight, currency devaluation, and economic slowdown they provoked, had spurred a political opening on the right. Almazán's candidacy—not yet declared but heralded by feverish groundwork—greatly troubled the Party of the Mexican Revolution (the PRM, as the PNR had recently become). And what threatened Manuel also threatened Maximino.

When the police discovered Mata the following morning, forty yards from the highway outside the town of San Martín, they found a body that was naked but for the trench coat draped over it. They found a trio of entry holes in the cranium, made point-blank by a 45-caliber pistol. They found dried streams of blood that had collected in his lap, deducing that the victim had been stripped and made to sit before his execution. And prizing back the fingers of a stiffly clenched fist, they found his small crucifix.

To the surprise of no one, Mata's murder was never solved. It would prove to be an early example of a series of political killings in Puebla in 1939–1940, and there was little doubt in the vox populi as to its mastermind. Within days, flyers appeared on walls across the city, "Who killed the journalist Mata?," on which anonymous citizens scribbled answers accusing the governor. Nor was there doubt in the mind of leading local chronicler Enrique Cordero y Torres, who after Maximino's death would devote ten pages of his history of Puebla journalism to the case.

La Opinión and *El Diario de Puebla* emitted standard expressions of horror at the killing and portrayed the police as diligently at work; they showed no investigative initiative. Four weeks later, the case long absent from its pages, *La Opinión* frothed with delight at Maximino's plan for state-subsidized life insurance for journalists. Of all of Puebla's governors, it said with no trace of irony, "none helped the profession in so trustworthy and efficient a manner as General Maximino Ávila Camacho."[46]

The national press was less cowed. *Excélsior* and *El Universal* published verbatim a telegram from Maximino to the attorney general, in which the author protested too much: "it is public and well known that my government has made efforts to solve the murder of don José Trinidad Mata, with whom I was bound in ties of open friendship." Prompting his outcry was a story in *El Universal Gráfico*, which reported the rumor that Maximino was the culprit. *Hoy* dispatched a reporter, who found all but one of Mata's friends too nervous to speak. The lone voice revealed that *Avante* had for some time drawn a subsidy from Maximino's government, although that ended after Mata, on a visit to police headquarters, lost his temper and accused the governor of embezzlement.[47]

The revelation of a subsidy is telling. It complements Cordero's report that *Avante* had belonged to Maximino's camp and matches the tenor of the paper until early 1939. Seven months before his demise, Mata had run a front-page photograph of the governor dated August 1935 and signed "For José Trinidad Mata . . . director of 'Avante.' With affection." Maximino had tolerated minor opposition organs, such as the radical labor press, and a month after Mata's killing there appeared a pro-Almazán news sheet, *Chiltipiquín*, which survived until after the election.[48] What he could not abide, it seems, was a newspaper to which he had channeled public money exercising freedom of speech.

Media Co-optation: Soft, Gradual—and Persistent

In the annals of Mexican media history, famous cases of state intrusion have been harsh and swift: Gustavo Díaz Ordaz's move to throttle *El Diario de México* in 1966, after it transposed his photograph with that of a couple of monkeys, rendering the presidential caption "The zoo is enriched"; Luis Echeverría's infamous coup against the independent leadership of *Excélsior* in 1976; José López Portillo's resentful advertising boycott of *Proceso* in 1982.[49] One might add the murder of Trinidad Mata.

Yet the experience of *La Opinión* in the late 1930s suggests that state interference, or the impact thereof, is frequently gradual. No matter how authoritarian their instincts, presidents and governors have seldom wished to be seen as suppressors of freedoms, not least because that would run contrary to their discourse of modernization. A parallel can be drawn with elections. During its long reign, wherever its candidates faced strong opposition, the PRI much preferred to work behind the scenes, using corporatist persuasion, vote buying, and electoral "alchemy" and only in the last resort making a dramatic imposition. Such suasions were necessary because Mexicans wished to exercise their electoral rights and because the PRI claimed to be democratic.[50]

The gradual nature of co-optation is also explained by the personal relationships between politicians and publishers and by media economics. Where political and business elites are on cordial terms, the latter may act as a buffer to the autocratic instincts of the former. And since print media have multiple revenue streams (and sometimes capital reserves), a newspaper or magazine may try to tough it out rather than opt for appeasement when the state removes its subsidies, as *Proceso* successfully did in 1982.

As of the early 1990s, largely liberated from a half century of indirect censorship, newspapers emerged that embraced an independent or plural posture, even in PRI-dominated Puebla.[51] But in the contemporary world of petty despotism in the provinces, concerns over media gagging have regained prominence, revealing the structural weaknesses of a sector that continues to rely greatly on government handouts.[52] Under the hard-line governor Rafael Moreno Valle Rosas (2011–2017)—a longtime *priista* with presidential ambitions, who defected to the Partido Acción Nacional in 2006 for electoral expediency—Puebla again provided a harsh example of the challenges facing provincial journalism.

By the time Moreno Valle left office, Puebla's already bloated press had expanded to some fifteen daily newspapers (five of them launched during his term, in each case somewhat dependent on the public purse) and some fifteen stand-alone websites. Local academics and journalists concur that of these thirty or so media, only a quarter managed to resist co-optation during Moreno Valle's term. At the governor's initiative, critical media all suffered a coordinated advertising boycott by Puebla's top three spenders: the state government, the city government, and the state university, a threesome termed *el tripack*. The gravity of the situation was aggravated by Moreno Valle's coziness with the main broadcasters, Televisa and TV Azteca, and with most of Puebla's radio stations. During his first year in power, *Proceso* labeled the governor "the flippant tormentor of the press." Reports of his having harassed and spied on independent journalists persisted even after he left office.[53]

Moreno Valle's actions, though differing little from those of his predecessors in their favoritism, constituted a hardening of local practice. They underscored the continued fragility of the Puebla press and its limited ability to practice critical journalism, eighty years after Maximino co-opted *La Opinión*.

Notes

1. *La Opinión*, Jan. 10–Feb. 13, 1938; Feb. 15, 1939, 2.
2. *La Opinión*, Mar. 1, 1938, 1.
3. González Marín, "La prensa y el poder político," 158. See also González Marín, *Prensa y poder político*.
4. González Marín, "La prensa y el poder político," 158. As Philip Russell succinctly puts it, *El Universal* and *Excélsior* "were more conservative than the government and criticized what were perceived as its leftist excesses." Russell, *The History of Mexico*, 380.
5. González de Bustamante, *Muy buenas noches*, xxiv.
6. For further provincial examples of this space for maneuver, see Gillingham, this volume.
7. For the 1936 primary, see Valencia Castrejón, *Poder regional*, 33–64; Quintana, *Maximino Ávila Camacho*, 64–72; Paxman, *Jenkins of Mexico*, 215–19. On primary elections as the main contest, see Gillingham, "We Don't Have Arms."
8. Hernández Chávez, *La mecánica*, 44–46.
9. Cordero y Torres, *Historia del periodismo*, 125–37, 233–35, 437–41, 454–55.
10. *El Diario de Puebla*, Jan. 4–May 1, 1936; Cordero y Torres, *Historia del periodismo*, 130, 558; Pansters, *Politics and Power*, 64; Quintana, *Maximino Ávila Camacho*, 80. *El Diario* debuted in March 1935, a few weeks after Maximino became military chief, and Cordero puts its print run at around 1,000, a third of that of *La Opinión* (*Historia del periodismo*, 129, 131).
11. Cordero y Torres, *Historia del periodismo*, 125–29, and *Diccionario biográfico de Puebla*, 318–20; *Excélsior*, June 10, 1928, 9; *La Opinión*, Feb. 24, 1931, 1, 3; Feb. 1, 1935, 1; July 31, 1935, 3; author interview with Sergio Guzmán Ramos (son of Guzmán), Puebla, May 16, 2005. Until 1937, mayoral terms were a single year; Guzmán himself would become Puebla's first two-year mayor (1937–1939).
12. *La Opinión*, Jan. 14–Apr. 4, 1936. The Bosques manifesto ran on page three from Mar. 1 to Apr. 4.

13. Valencia Castrejón, *Poder regional*, 36–37, 50–51; Pansters, *Politics and Power*, 64; Quintana, *Maximino Ávila Camacho*, 43–45, 64; *La Opinión*, Feb. 7 and Mar. 24, 1936, 1; *El Diario de Puebla*, Feb. 11 and Mar. 24, 1936, 1.

14. As it turned out, Maximino and Guzmán probably campaigned together little, for the mayoral primary was not held until September (*La Opinión*, Sept. 29, 1936, 1), five months after the gubernatorial contest.

15. *La Opinión*, Apr. 5, 1936, 1; Apr. 6, 1936, 1; Valencia Castrejón, *Poder regional*, 55.

16. *La Opinión*, Apr. 30, 1936, 1; May 1, 1936, 1; May 3, 1936, 1; May 15, 1936, 1; *New York Times*, May 14, 1936, 13.

17. *La Opinión*, June 28, 1936, 1, 4; Cordero y Torres, *Historia del periodismo*, 228–34.

18. *La Opinión*, July 7, 1936, 1.

19. *La Opinión*, July 11, 1936, 1; Aug. 8, 1936, 1, 3.

20. Cordero y Torres, *Historia del periodismo*, 127; *La Opinión*, Sept. 29, 1936, 1; Nov. 26–Dec. 7, 1936; Aug. 14, 1938, 1; July 28, 1939, 1; *Excélsior*, Dec. 7, 1936, 4; Guzmán Ramos interview, May 16, 2005. *La Opinión* renewed its loyalty upon Guzmán's investiture, complimenting him on his "competence, training, and people skills"; Feb. 16, 1937, 1.

21. *La Opinión*, Feb. 6, 1937, 1; Aug. 30, 1936, 1.

22. *La Opinión*, Mar. 1, 1937, 3; *La Opinión*, Apr. 16, 1937, 1; *La Opinión*, June, 20, 1937, 1.

23. *La Opinión*, Mar. 30, 1937, 1; *La Opinión*, Mar. 31, 1937, 1.

24. *La Opinión*, Feb. 19, 1937, 1; *La Opinión*, Apr. 6, 1937, 1.

25. On Jenkins's development of Atencingo and his assets by 1937, see Paxman, *Jenkins of Mexico*, chs. 5 and 7.

26. *La Opinión* had criticized Jenkins much less in previous years, likely owing to his close friendship with the paper's former co-owner Sergio Guzmán; Paxman, *Jenkins of Mexico*, ch. 7.

27. *La Opinión*, Mar. 16, 1937, 1; Apr. 7, 1937, 3; June 11, 1937, 1, 6.

28. *La Opinión*, June 28, 1937, 1.

29. Quintana, *Maximino Ávila Camacho*, 115–16; special section on Puebla in *Hoy*, Jan. 21, 1939, 34–46; "Maximino Ávila Camacho," *Hoy*, Mar. 9, 1940, 38–47; "No hay obra sin hombre," *Mañana*, Dec. 16, 1944, 25–40; Rodríguez Castañeda, *Prensa vendida*, ch. 1.

30. *La Opinión*, July 4, 1937, 1; July 8, 1937, 3; Aug. 14 and 17, 1937, 1; Aug. 28 and 30, 1937, 1.

31. Ronfeldt, *Atencingo*, ch. 2; Paxman, *Jenkins of Mexico*, ch. 7; *La Opinión*, July 30, 1937, 1; Aug. 13, 1937, 1; Aug. 18, 1937, 1; Aug. 19, 1937, 1.

32. *La Opinión*, Dec. 21, 1937, 1, 6.

33. *La Opinión*, Oct. 20, 1937, 6; *La Opinión*, Nov. 16, 1937, 1; *La Opinión*, Dec. 2, 1937, 1; *La Opinión*, Dec. 24, 1937, 2.

34. *La Opinión*, Jan. 16, 1938, 1, 2.

35. Valencia Castrejón, *Poder regional*, 23, 36; Henderson and LaFrance, "Maximino Ávila Camacho," 159–61; *La Opinión*, Jan. 21, 1939, 1; Guzmán Ramos interview, May 16, 2005.

36. *La Opinión*, Mar. 14, 1937, 1; *La Opinión*, May, 20, 1937, 1; interview with Sergio Guzmán Ramos, Puebla, Nov. 28, 2005. On the change in status as a ruse to bring a college known for agitation under Maximino's control, see Sotelo Mendoza, *Crónica*, 63–68.

37. See, e.g., *La Opinión*, Nov. 20, 1937, 1; Mar. 28, 1938, 1; June 11 and 12, 1938, 1; Mar. 28, 1939, 1; May 3, 1939, 1. On Maximino's weakening of the FROC: Pansters, *Politics and Power*, 57–59; Valencia Castrejón, *Poder regional*, 80–90.

38. *La Opinión*, Mar. 13, 1938, 1; May 12, 1938, 1; May, 20, 1939, 2; Jan. 16, 1940, 1; Mar. 16, 1940, 2. Note: Rodríguez Castañeda, *Prensa vendida* (op. cit.) shows such events taking place annually in Mexico City, 1951.

39. *La Opinión*, Aug. 23 & 24, 1938, 1; Aug. 23 & 24, 1939, 1; Aug. 22–26, 1941, 1. Note: Maximino continued to be feted each subsequent year; see, for example, Aug. 20–25, 1942, 1. After he died, the paper commemorated his birthday for another fifteen years.

40. Cordero y Torres, *Historia del periodismo*, 127, 131, 437–39; *La Opinión*, July 28, 1939, 1.

41. LaFrance, *Revolution in México's Heartland*, 147–50; *El Monitor* [Puebla], June 30, 1921, 4; *El Universal*, Mar. 9, 1922, 10; Calles to Gov. Manjarrez, Mexico City, Jan. 25, 1923, APEC/161, leg. 6/6, inv. 388. Note: In, 1832, Gov. Cosme Furlong funded the daily *Aurora de la Libertad*; Cordero y Torres, *Historia del periodismo*, 71–73, 537.

42. Cordero y Torres, *Historia del periodismo*, 228; Martínez Cantellano and Domínguez to Mijares, Apr. 3, 1936, ACEP/CCXCI, file 1895; *La Opinión*, Aug. 18, 1936, 1.

43. On Maximino's regular bribing of the press, see Cerwin, *These Are the Mexicans*, 79; Cordero y Bernal, *Maximino Ávila Camacho*, 54.

44. Quintana, *Maximino Ávila Camacho*, 83; Santos, *Memorias*, 646–51, 683, 754; Paxman, *Jenkins of Mexico*, 232.

45. Trinidad Mata's murder is reconstructed from Cordero y Torres, *Historia del periodismo*, 542–51; Valencia Castrejón, *Poder regional*, 143, 147; *La Opinión*, Apr. 24–26, 1939, 1; *Avante*, Apr. 6 and issues through July 1940; see also Cordero y Bernal, *Maximino Ávila Camacho*, 21, 132–53. On the Almazán campaign, see Sherman, *The Mexican Right*, ch. 8.

46. *La Opinión* and *El Diario de Puebla*, Apr. 24–30, 1939, 1; *La Opinión*, May 17, 1939, 1.

47. *Excélsior*, Apr. 28, 1939, 11; *El Universal*, Apr. 28, 1939, 1, 12; *Hoy*, May 27, 1939, 30–31. Mata took a further risk by publishing an alleged fracture between Maximino and Cárdenas; Quintana, *Maximino Ávila Camacho*, 80.

48. Cordero y Torres, *Historia del periodismo*, 235–37, 438–40; *Avante*, Sept. 1, 1938, 1.

49. Rodríguez Castañeda, *Prensa vendida*, 106, 171–75, 216–23.

50. Gillingham, "We Don't Have Arms."

51. Preston and Dillon, *Opening Mexico*, ch. 14. The era of *apertura* saw the launch in Puebla of daily papers *La Jornada del Oriente* (1990), *Síntesis* (1992) and *Intolerancia* (2001), all less monotonously *oficialista* than market leader *El Sol de Puebla*.

52. *Libertad de expresión en venta* (on such practices in Puebla, see 48–53). See also the final section of Garza Ramos, this volume.

53. *La Jornada*, June 1, 2015, 13; conversations with communications faculty at the Universidad Autónoma de Puebla (Nov. 20, 2014), Universidad Iberoamericana Puebla (Apr. 13, 2015), and Universidad Popular Autónoma del Estado de Puebla, Apr. 14, 2015; conversations with five Puebla journalists, Nov. 2016 and July 2017. On Moreno Valle, see Juan Pablo Proal, "Moreno Valle, el frívolo verdugo de la prensa," *Proceso*, Oct. 20, 2011, www.proceso.com.mx/?p=285243; Juan Pablo Proal, "Un dictador quiere ser presidente de México," *Proceso*, June 6, 2014, www.proceso.com.mx/?p=373975; Alfredo González and Gabriela Hernández, "El espía que quiere gobernarnos," *Proceso*, July 7, 2017, 6–9.

4 | The Year Mexico Stopped Laughing

The Crowd, Satire, and Censorship in Mexico City

BENJAMIN T. SMITH

On March 17, 1949, the satirical magazine *Presente* finally shut its doors. For nine months, the publication had provided what its writers called a "space for the angry voice of the people."[1] It was not alone. During that brief period, other journalists, artists, and amateur satirists had joined in, writing articles, plays, songs, and jokes that mocked the political elite. Their denunciations rocked the country's political establishment. Mexican officials confessed to the British ambassador that in the summer of 1948 "the flood gates of criticism were opened wide." There was a "tenseness in the political atmosphere, which seemed to render anything possible."[2] In the city's cantinas, barroom bookies took bets on when the Miguel Alemán government was going to fall.[3] If the magazine's brief run was a high point for satire's political potential, its closure proved a turning point for the Mexico City press. As Carlos Monsiváis argued, after *Presente* folded "what had been the critical space of Mexican journalism restricted itself in a compulsive manner."[4] Lessons were learned. Reporters were reluctant to stoke the political unrest of the capital's crowd, and political satire for a mass audience disappeared.

Gradual social changes transformed Mexicans' relationships to the written word. Broad cultural, economic, and political frameworks shaped what was written. But the history of the press is not only one of long-term structures, but also one of individual moments.[5] These were brief, intense interactions among journalists, officials, and readers; they linked to broader street protests; and they carried both short- and long-term consequences. The year 1948 was one such moment. For a few months, readers' connections to the press changed. In the second year of Alemán's presidency, the confluence of rising prices, monetary devaluation, and elite corruption generated serious disquiet. Critical publications found a real audience. *Presente*'s writers—and other journalists, playwrights, and street protesters—came together to produce a savage denunciation of the post-revolutionary regime and posit the real chance of political upheaval. The crisis also changed the state's political strategies. Forced resignations and cheap food co-opted the workers, housewives, artisans, and white-collar employees who comprised the Mexico City crowd. Attacks on the press and on satirical works were frequent.[6] The government's spin machine was in its infancy, and violence, dirty tricks, and propaganda closed down critical spaces and brought mainstream newspapers to its side. Functionaries adapted and learned; similar emergency measures would shape the management of future crises. Finally, the 1948 crisis also changed the nature of humor itself. Over the next few years, officials moved against popular satirists, co-opting the pliant and starving the more recalcitrant of space and funds. By the early 1950s, printed satire had lost its connection to popular protest; it had become the preserve of the political elite.

The Satiric Moment

The Revolution unleashed a wave of political satire throughout the Mexican capital. Freed from the constraints of Porfirian censorship, writers now lampooned the political elite in two spaces, the theater and text. For three decades music hall political skits and satirical magazines were revolutionary cultural forms on a par with muralism or corridos.[7] At first President Miguel Alemán favored the production of political humor. Like his predecessors, he thought it an escape valve and even sponsored satirical magazines. But during the first two years of his rule, political and socioeconomic changes generated serious popular unrest, especially in Mexico City. Rumors of high-level sleaze, from juicy public contracts to contraband and drug trafficking, created the perception that Alemán was running a corrupt and inefficient administration. Anti-union policies, the sidelining of the military, rising prices, and the messy peso devaluation made these accusations stick. Individual jokes, they say, are all about timing; so is effective satire. In 1948, political corruption and economic forces combined to generate what I term here a "satiric moment," a Mexican Saturnalia. During this brief period, Mexicans of all stripes put aside class rivalries and came together to criticize and lampoon the ruling elite.[8]

At first Alemán encouraged Mexican satirists to ply their trade. He was known as the smiling president—Mr. Colgate—whose broad, toothy grin was meant to indicate a sense of humor. During his campaign, he allowed playwrights to mock his riotous student days and his lack of military experience.[9] And when he came to power, he announced a new era of cultural openness by allowing the first performance of Rodolfo Usigli's righteous attack on revolutionary hypocrisy, *El gesticulador*, written a decade earlier.[10] Initially, his relations with print satirists were equally close. In 1944, as secretary of the interior, he sponsored the creation of *Don Timorato*, a cartoon-heavy humor magazine. It was edited by one of Mexico's leading columnists (and future *Presente* head), Jorge Piño Sandoval. And it was lavishly illustrated. The artistic director was *Hoy*'s star cartoonist, Antonio Arias Bernal.[11]

But such close connections did not last long. The first two years of the administration alienated writers, workers, and the Mexico City crowd. Many saw the central problem as corruption. Alemán had come to power flanked by a group of young lawyers, officials, and hangers-on known as his amigos.[12] Some held official positions. Fernando Casas Alemán was an old Veracruz ally, whom Alemán appointed as chief of Mexico City. Ramón Beteta and Antonio Ruíz Galindo were former law school classmates at the Universidad Nacional Autónoma de México.[13] Alemán made them the heads of the Mexican Treasury and the Ministry of the Economy respectively. Others simply orbited their friend and his newfound power. Enrique Parra Hernández was another law school buddy. Described as "the minister without a budget," he was in charge of Alemán's finances and, so rumor had it, his amorous affairs.[14] Jorge Pasquel was an old Veracruz friend who became an import-export merchant, baseball impresario, and media owner.[15] Others held combined roles. Carlos Serrano was an old military contact from Veracruz who not only headed the Mexican senate, but also acted as the informal chief of the secret service and as the president's collector of campaign contributions.[16]

Whatever their official roles, the amigos used their proximity to the president to line their own pockets. Some exploited their connections to gain access to public contracts. Parra specialized in deals with state companies. In 1947, he took a 30 percent commission for flogging 19 million pesos worth of tracks to the railway company. And over the next year, he used his brother's position at the Bank of Exterior Commerce to buy agricultural products on the cheap and sell them overseas.[17] So did Jorge Pasquel. In 1947 he received a contract to import all the state's construction materials through his customs houses; in 1948 he got a government concession to sell gasoline in Mexico City. The deal gave Pasquel the profits from three-quarters of the capital's petrol stations.[18] He also rented planes, launches, and his private yacht directly to Miguel Alemán, charging the president 123,000 pesos per year.[19]

The amigos also used their newfound status and consequent impunity to operate illegal enterprises. Pasquel specialized in contraband cars. This was big business since import taxes were steep. In the United States a four-door Cadillac cost US$2,485. Over the border, with import taxes added on, the same car cost around 50 percent more. Officials estimated that smugglers brought in around 4,500 illegal vehicles per year.[20] Pasquel's customs offices in Ciudad Juárez, Nuevo Laredo, and Veracruz offered a perfect cover for the trade. He would front the smugglers the money to buy the cars in the United States, collect them at the border, issue fake import duty certificates, and then flog them in Mexico at inflated prices. His ranches in San Luis Potosí doubled as upscale car lots, their rows of Cadillacs and Studebakers secured by armed guards.[21]

Others employed their status to traffic drugs. This was even bigger business, worth an annual US$20 million according to the US Treasury and US$60 million according to Alemán's private secretary.[22] At first Carlos Serrano attempted to monopolize the trade. As the campaign's fund manager, he came into contact with a range of smugglers, who agreed to make lavish contributions in return for protection.[23] He also used these new associates to move more directly into smuggling. In June 1946, immediately before Alemán's election, US customs officials in Laredo, Texas, discovered sixty-three tins of opium stashed in a secret compartment in a Cadillac. The car was Serrano's, the driver a nephew of one of his close associates, Juan Ramón Gurrola. Despite US pressure, Serrano refused to prosecute Gurrola and even rewarded him with a leading job at the Federal Office of Security (Dirección Federal de Seguridad, DFS).[24] After 1947 his effective control over the DFS strengthened these links. The two heads, Gurrola and Marcelino Inurreta, already had connections to the narcotics trade. After overhearing their plans for expanding the business, the US military attaché concluded that they were "using the organization as a front for illegal operations to amass personal fortunes" and that Serrano was "fully cognizant of these sideline operations."[25] The chiefs were not alone; lesser DFS agents also had shady pasts. In 1947 the US Federal Bureau of Narcotics speculated that "anyone with a past record as a crooked narcotics enforcement officer needs no other qualification to be accepted as an agent."[26]

In post-revolutionary Mexico, official graft was nothing new. Maximino Ávila Camacho's propensity for bribes was legendary; for good reason, he was nicknamed "Mr. 15 Percent."[27] Nor were illegal businesses. On the border, former president Abelardo Rodríguez had a hand in gambling dens, brothels, and the drug trade.[28] Mexicans often brushed off such corruption with a shrug of the shoulders or a shake of the head. They were politicians; what could one expect? Some even understood it. Wouldn't they do the same in Maximino's place? But the amigos' venality was different. It caused much more widespread protest than previous dishonesty had. In fact, it became the key trope of both written and oral satire during the 1948 crisis. The question remains: why? Why did the amigos' corruption generate such cross-class dissent?

First, the amigos rarely tried to hide their wealth. In fact, they flaunted it. Conspicuous consumption was the rule, and Pasquel was playboy in chief. He stepped out with famous beauties like María Félix. He spent months hunting wild game in Africa. He amassed huge collections of planes, boats, guns, cars, and watches. His Tlalpan residence was decorated with Diego Rivera paintings, Sèvres china, Louis XV furniture, and Florentine marble sculptures.[29] His San Luis Potosí hacienda was even grander. It had its own private airfield and was covered in murals depicting the miracle of the Virgin of Guadalupe. A visiting tourist described the bedroom as "an ornate voluptuarium somewhere between Cecil DeMille's Hollywood and the late King Farouk's Alexandria."[30] This lifestyle made him the most hated of Alemán's amigos. But he was not alone. Gossip and spreads in the social pages revealed the rapid enrichment of other functionaries close to the president. The British ambassador observed that while Beteta had once been poor, "now he is rich but has not sufficient sagacity to camouflage his sudden accretion of wealth. The mansion he is building for himself and his bejewelled American wife has not escaped the notice of either his chief or the public."[31] Parra went from a damp house in the down-at-the-heels Colonia Santa María la Ribera to a vast Polanco mansion and purchased his wife a necklace so gaudy that it "looked like a planetary system."[32]

Second, stories of high-profile corruption started to leak out in the mainstream press. For the first eighteen months of Alemán's rule, government relations with the big nationals were shaky. The government's spin machine was still solidifying, and financial incentives were irregular and weak. Many also suspected (correctly) that Alemán was behind Pasquel's 1946 takeover of the broadsheet *Novedades*.[33] In early 1948, Alemán worsened relations further by putting in place stringent new copyright legislation. The law was designed to protect the rights of authors, but also included rigid articles that seemed to infringe on the freedom of the press. One backed up the old press law, giving federal authorities "the right to restrict or prohibit the publication, production, circulation, representation or exhibition of works which are considered contrary to the respect which is due to private life, morals, and public peace." Others prohibited the publication of official documents and unauthorized photographs, effectively curtailing the press's ability to corroborate an exposé.[34]

Such tensions opened up space for criticism. In 1947, *Excélsior* reprinted Daniel Cosío Villegas's venomous condemnation of the revolutionary regime, "La crisis de México." The original piece had been published in an academic journal. *Excélsior*'s publication brought the denunciations to a broader audience. His condemnation of "general, ostentatious, and offensive administrative corruption disguised beneath a cloak of impunity" looked like an open attack on Alemán's amigos. The government quickly silenced Cosío Villegas, threatening to spill rumors about his love life over the pages of the national press.[35] These tensions also encouraged papers to pursue high-profile scandals. In the first six months of 1948, the nationals explored a dramatic daylight hit on a senator, touched on the connections between political elites and the country's drug industry, and attacked the administration for allowing US soldiers connected to the foot-and-mouth disease commission to carry arms and intimidate journalists.[36]

Third, President Alemán quickly managed to alienate three key groups—the military, the unions, and the Mexico City crowd. Scholars have written extensively about divisions between the new government and the traditional bases of official support.[37] But the growing disenfranchisement of the capital's white-collar clerks and factory workers is less well known. Housing crises, university unrest, and summer floods played a major role.[38] But the biggest problem—the one that alienated Mexico City residents from across the social spectrum, triggered the 1948 crisis, and threatened to bring down the Alemán government—was the devaluation of the peso. Within months of Alemán's election, Mexico's balance of payments started to worsen. As the United States eliminated price and export controls, the volume of US imports increased dramatically. In contrast, Mexican exports barely grew. Increased postwar competition and the lowering of demand for raw materials cut into Mexico's industrial and agricultural sectors. Foreign exchange reserves dropped. And the smart money started to leave Mexico. Large businesses, fearful of devaluation, reduced their inventories and sent their money to the United States. Foreign loans managed to keep the peso afloat during the first half of 1948. But money kept flowing out. Medium-sized enterprises started to convert their pesos into dollars as well. Finally, on July 21, 1948, the Mexican government was forced to float the peso and hence devalue. It immediately fell from its fixed exchange rate of 4.85 pesos to the dollar to around 6 or 7 pesos to the dollar before being fixed again at 8.65.[39]

The devaluation had two important secondary effects. First, it increased the price of foodstuffs and other staples. These had been on the rise since the late 1930s.[40] But the devaluation caused a rapid upsurge. The day after the devaluation, the prices of some foods, like tinned products, ham, and cooking oil, rose 40 percent; eggs and vegetables rose 20 percent. Within a week, meat was running out. Medicines, most of which were imported from the United States, also climbed in price by around 40 percent.[41] Second, the devaluation seemed to establish an explicit causal link between high-level corruption and widespread poverty. Whatever the broader economic reasons for the devaluation, many perceived the move as the fault of the new post-revolutionary bourgeoisie. They had destabilized the currency by buying expensive, foreign-made consumer goods; they had undercut the peso still further by importing contraband from the United States; they had even made fortunes from the policy by converting their pesos to dollars ahead of time. For the Mexico City crowd, Alemán's amigos triggered the devaluation, the price rises, and their consequent hunger. The smiling president was no longer laughing with them; he was laughing at them.

Satire in the Streets

In summer 1948, corruption, the shift in military power, anti-union policies, housing, floods, and price rises combined to produce serious unrest across Mexico City. Middle-class housewives, merchants, workers, and soldiers concentrated their anger against the president and his coterie of hangers-on. They used four means to express their dissatisfaction: insults, rumors, jokes, and songs. Most insults criticized those members of Alemán's administration held responsible for the current situation. They included Beteta, the secretary of the treasury; Ruíz Galindo, the secretary of the economy; Casas Alemán, the mayor of Mexico City; and Pasquel, amigo and contrabandist in chief. At the city's markets, government agents recorded "virulent attacks," "harsh commentaries," and "expressions of ill feeling and disgust" against the amigos.[42] Such verbal assaults reflected changes both in public opinion and in people's willingness to express their anger. One agent remarked that "men as well as women were more violent and less cautious and didn't hesitate to slander the government."[43] Another noticed that the invective went "beyond simple censures and arrived at personal insult."[44] Ministers were described as "merchants of hunger, bandits, and thieves"; the government was labeled a "bunch of bandits starting from the top"; and crowds shouted "death to the exploiters of the people."[45]

The president was not immune. Throughout July and early August, worried government agents repeatedly noticed that Alemán was "the target of the attacks" and that some of the most vocal street critics "arrived at a lack of respect for the president."[46] People accused him of incompetence and being incapable of "reining in the hunger merchants or the influential politicians."[47] They accused him of lacking political sense and being unable to "glean public opinion" or "read the papers."[48] And, most concerning, they started to voice the idea that he was no better than his amigos. They insulted him by whistling at his image when it appeared on cinema screens.[49] By late

August, flyers in the markets read "Death to the Spurious President Alemán, Death to the Exploiters of the People / Prepare . . . to kick the STUPID and BANDIT Alemán and his thieves from power."[50] For good reason, agents concluded that Mexico City's inhabitants were "losing respect for high office."[51]

During the summer of 1948, rumors were also rife. Some tales were explicatory. They made the direct link between the current problems and high-level corruption. They were based on selective readings of the press, and they had some factual basis. They provided comprehensible, moralistic organizing narratives for complex changes, and they exacerbated the overall dissatisfaction with the administration. For example, many Mexicans reduced the causes of the devaluation to illegal contraband. Smuggling US goods was illegal, involved the transfer of dollars to pesos, undercut Mexican businesses, and reduced tax income. One agent reported that he heard people on the buses blaming the devaluation on the government "permitting contraband on a massive scale"; they pointed to Pasquel as "the principal contrabandist."[52] Other rumors did not offer explanations. Instead, they organized people's understanding of political instability. They expanded the parameters of the conceivable, the boundaries of what people thought could happen.[53] For the government, this looked pretty bad. In early August, a rumor emerged that assassins had ambushed Alemán on the Mexico City–Cuernavaca road, killing his driver and injuring the president.[54] It may have been started deliberately. Government agents suggested that two air force pilots who were now Popular Party activists were first overheard loudly discussing the plot on a Mexico City bus; they had done so on purpose in order to generate uncertainty and instability.[55] Some whispered that it was the start of a military coup, overlaying their own prejudices atop the event. Railway workers claimed that "poor salaries" had driven soldiers to revolt.[56] The US embassy held that a dozen army generals headed by the chief of the military academy were responsible.[57] Whatever the rumors' origins, people believed them, and in a vicious circle the rumors reinforced the instability that underlaid them.

People in Mexico City also swapped jokes. Most employed a distinctly black humor and mixed frustration with rumors of official corruption. In La Merced, one woman complained to a vendor about the price of eggs: "You're robbing us. I bet you came to an agreement with the inspectors to sell at this price." Then she softened her tone and followed up with "well, the price probably covers the bribes you have to pay at least." Both vendor and customer laughed. By creating a common enemy, such jokes often deflected blame away from the stall owners and smoothed over tensions with their customers.[58] But jokes did not smooth over tensions with the leaders they named. Playing on the title of a recent US film, *Ali Baba and the Forty Thieves*, street jokers started to refer to the president and his friends as "Alemán and His Forty Lawyers." Such wags often invoked violence. One man, who was buying a knife in the Tepito street market, remarked, "Either these things go down in price or we will have to lower them with this." "Yeah, and you'll be Juan Charrasqueado [the macho hero of a 1948 film]," the stall owner replied.[59]

Finally, the capital's residents also produced a flurry of satirical songs. In a society with a large illiterate population, songs formed the key means of condensing, transmitting, and popularizing the insults, rumors, and jokes.[60] They were sung in plazas, in bars, and in apartment courtyards. The journalists and skit writers who penned them made them easy to remember, lifting the melodies from and often parodying the lyrics of popular tunes. Songs were printed on cheap paper and sold for a few cents by street sellers and newsboys; many were republished in newspapers and magazines. The most widespread of all, "Miguel," referred to the president. A parody of the popular Agustín Lara song "Madrid," it was catchy and easy to recite; it also neatly summarized the central themes of rising prices, corruption, anti-presidentialism, and threatened violence. But "Miguel" was the gentlest of the satiric songs.[61] Other tunes, dotted with sexual references and swear words, were less family-friendly. "Los Ahuehuetes" (literally, "the cypress trees" but used here to denote Alemán's amigos)[62] started as follows:

Los Ahuehuetes ladrones	The Ahuehuetes are thieves.
Parra, Pasquel, y Parada	Parra, Pasquel, and Parada
Son puritos cabrones	Are complete assholes
E hijos de la chingada.	And sons of bitches.
Roban al pueblo sufrido	They steal from the suffering people
Llevando putas al jefe	Taking whores to the chief

Quien después de haber cojido   Who after fucking
Los agredece y los proteje   Thanks them and protects
                                              them.[63]

Such songs concerned the listening agents. Their lyrics underlined popular frustrations, indicated a deep distrust of the president and his advisers,
and threatened insurrection. They were extremely popular. *La Prensa* admitted that "everyone in Mexico knows the jokes, funny stories, allusions, and
musical parodies that freely circulate from mouth to mouth."[64] The songs
forged direct links between the cultural worlds of stage, print, and the street,
and they fitted the mood of the 1948 Mexico City crowd—halfway between
carnival and revolt.

Satire and Censorship

In the summer of 1948, high-level corruption, political problems, and social
deprivation also generated an upsurge in the production of all sorts of satire
in print and theater. While *Presente* was the most notorious, there were also
plays, skits, and books, which interacted with and fed off (and fed into)
street-level humor. But they went further. They organized diffuse dissatisfaction into coherent narratives; they offered credibility to rumors; and they
popularized a cogent indictment of the Alemán administration. Like the
slander rags of eighteenth-century France, they "reduced the complex politics of the regime into a storyline that could be grasped by any reader at any
distance from the center of the action."[65] In the context of 1948's street satire,
those close to Alemán deemed productions like *Presente* to be dangerous.
And they started to combat humorous magazines and plays in a variety of
ways. Some of these reactions were aimed at the audience for satirical culture. Emergency food markets and a handful of firings bought off some.
Anticommunist rhetoric, which blamed the unions for the country's economic woes, split working-class Mexicans from their temporary middle-
class allies. Other measures were aimed at the satirists. Officials rewarded
compliant writers with well-paid sinecures. They deprived stubborn journalists of paper and funds. And they started a mainstream campaign that
attacked both professional and amateur satirists as *murmureadores* (gossip-
mongers).

The founder, director, and editor of *Presente* was the columnist Jorge Piño Sandoval. Piño was not your average Mexico City journalist. He was not middle class, university educated, or, at least initially, right-wing. He was born in San Luis Potosí in 1902. During the revolution, he was orphaned and moved to Mexico City. There, he moved in with the painter and communist David Siqueiros. First, he was employed as a delivery boy, hawking Siqueiros's paintings around town for a small commission. By the late 1920s he also distributed the radical newspaper *El Machete*. That job gave him a taste for journalism, and he started to write the occasional story for the publication.[66] Over the following decade, Piño shed his links to the Mexican Communist Party and moved into the world of journalism full time. He leveraged his friendship with another former leftist, Carlos Denegri, to gain a job at *Excélsior*. There, he gradually climbed the hierarchy, moving from the culture section to political news. But Piño's place in the newspaper establishment was always precarious. He found the social world of journalists suffocating and infuriating. Salvador Novo described him as "moody . . . always in crisis, a misfit, inflexible, always in a state of protest and rebellion." The tension between his radical past and his present role as an *oficialista* columnist often caused confrontation. He walked out of *Excélsior* twice over differences with the editor.[67]

Such tensions also shaped his brief employment by Jorge Pasquel's revamped *Novedades*. In 1947 Piño joined that newspaper and was given a front-page column entitled "Presente." In general, his articles were overtly pro-government.[68] But in May 1948 something changed. Whether Piño's conscience finally caught up with him or he fell out with Pasquel is unclear. On May 19, "Presente" was relegated to the inside pages, and the following week the column radically changed tone. In a strangely personal article, which seemed to reflect his ambiguous relationship with the role of the modern Mexican journalist, Piño interviewed himself. He explained that in order to become a columnist, he had been forced to "conquer the friendship" of "thousands of contacts." Yet, such friendships came with expectations. "Before public men, we [journalists] are little or nothing. . . . they tolerate us and nothing more." In return for friendship, the public men wanted publicity. When journalists were unwilling to provide it, they were cut off. Liberty of the press and the apparent freedom of Mexico's political columnists were a sham, invented by businessmen and politicians to secure exposure.[69] The next two columns were similarly vitriolic. Presaging his work on the magazine *Presente*, Piño employed rumors of government corruption to attack those close to the regime.[70] Inevitably, such revelations caused a confrontation with the newspaper's owner. According to Piño, Pasquel offered him a round-the-world trip, the directorship of a new magazine, and a substantial salary increase to tone down his column. Piño refused and was sacked. Later he claimed that he "could not convince them that my motive was not money but a clean Mexico."[71]

Less than six weeks later, he founded the weekly satirical magazine *Presente*. In the magazine's first editorial Piño explained the publication's aim. Building on his self-critique of a few months earlier, he claimed that he had started *Presente* to "liberate [him]self from political and commercial inducements," avoid the pro-government lies of the mainstream press, and tell the truth about what was going on in Mexico.[72] To do so, his contributors would use two approaches—critiquing unpopular official policies and tying these policies directly to Alemán's amigos. Attacks on the foot-and-mouth disease campaign, for example, were frequent.[73] But after July 22, like many Mexicans, *Presente* focused its critiques on the devaluation. Six days later, Piño's editorial mocked the government's theory that lowering the value of the currency made Mexican goods exportable. "Mexico exports nothing; in the north we are even forced to import gasoline from the US." Industry was failing, and over the previous eighteen months 300 factories had closed. In fact, Mexico only "exported braceros," and all their money "goes into the hands of Spanish contractors." In a follow-up article, one of the contributors, writing under a pen name, speculated that officials had hinted to bankers of the devaluation ahead of time. And in the next issue, writers elaborated on this, claiming that in the days before the shift, elites had moved US$70 million to the United States. When Beteta publicized the names of some people who had transferred money, *Presente*'s journalists rubbished the revelations, claiming that the treasury minister had deliberately left out the principal offenders.[74]

Such criticisms were pointed but not unusual. In the summer of 1948, mainstream newspapers published similar, if slightly toned-down, versions of these claims. *Presente*, however, went further. Rather than leaving the accusations hanging, shrouded in vague accusations against bankers, elites, or *influyentazos* (very influential people), the magazine's journalists started

to name names. Like the street satirists, they connected economic misman-
agement, poverty, and rising prices to high-profile corruption. In his column, Renato Leduc made this break with expected practice clear: "There is
a tendency in the press not to personalize issues, not to name names." In
contrast, in *Presente*, "we will name names and we will personalize problems."[75] Such an approach not only infringed on the unwritten rules of the
press, it also transformed scattered rumors and murmured disquiet into a
coherent, anti-system attack. Loose talk became coherent discourse. Mexico
City's consumers were struggling, not because of the impersonal, uncontrollable, and impenetrable shifts of the international markets but due to individual acts of fraud and private enrichment.

In July, Piño, writing under a pseudonym, exposed the extent of Treasury
Secretary Beteta's wealth. The article focused on his new house and parodied
the society pages, offering pictures of the establishment, its address, its size,
its price, and a description of its luxurious amenities.[76] But unlike the traditional society pages, the article also had bite. Piño claimed that Manuel
Suárez, a close business associate of the president, had given the house to
Beteta in a simulated sale. Suárez had also given Beteta's former boss a similar property just outside the Morelos holiday retreat of Tepoztlán. And Beteta
was now so rich that he was doing the same, offering his secretary a 70,000-
peso house in return for her silence.[77]

Investigations into the sources of the amigos' wealth culminated in an
overt attack on Piño's former boss, Jorge Pasquel. After revealing that Pasquel
had tried to bribe him to stay on at *Novedades*, Piño started to trawl through
his other business interests. He repeated rumors that Pasquel had increased
the price of food by charging high rates at his customs houses. He also
accused Pasquel of specifically pushing up the price of wheat and bread by
monopolizing their import into the country. Piño insulted Pasquel's kin,
claiming that he came from a "rancid family," a gang of Valle Nacional
tobacco plantation owners, whose repressive labor practices had "left cruel
memories in the flesh of the people." And he exposed Pasquel's properties,
including the cinemas in Veracruz, the offices on Ramón Guzmán, the "pal-
ace" in Tlalpan, and the lovers' retreat in the center of the city.[78]

At least initially, Piño and his collaborators were keen to demonstrate that
they were attacking Alemán's cronies rather than the president himself. In fact,
on August 11, *Presente*'s chiefs—Piño, Leduc, and Arias Bernal—published an

interview they had managed to secure with Alemán.[79] The article was a real coup. In Mexico one-on-one interviews with sitting presidents were extremely rare; critical, seemingly unmediated discussions about failing policies, dodgy alliances, and corruption even more so. Yet this was the format of the interview. During the talk, the three journalists threw a series of increasingly hostile accusations at the president. They attacked his economic policy, arguing that rich bankers had made fortunes out of the devaluation. They denounced his plans for Mexico City, arguing that the capital was "full of potholes, rubbish, the overcrowding of stalls," and the illegal sales of poor, underserviced lots. They pointed to the "huge, splendid residences" of his friends, which rubbed "the arrogance of those with influence" in the faces of the people, who "suffer scarcity or lack of basic foods." They followed this up by stating, "You, Mr. President, with the greatest respect, don't seem to care." They even confronted Alemán with his growing unpopularity: "They whistle when your figure crosses the cinema screen."[80]

The journalists presented Alemán as confused and weak in response. He batted away questions about the devaluation with the usual references to larger economic forces. He agreed with the journalists about the state of the city's press. And he even approved of their condemnation of his acquaintances, calling them "friends of the second or third class" and "a disgrace or a sickness that no government of any country has been able to cure completely." But as the accusations piled up, he appeared less and less in control. When they reproached him for not caring about the perception of the Mexican people, the journalists claimed that "an expression of surprise, which took the qualities of a painful rictus, crossed his face." For the remainder of the interview, he appeared to go silent, allowing the journalists to pile on more complaints with little or no riposte.[81]

Presente's exposés, bold illustrations, and critical style made the magazine extremely popular. At twenty centavos per issue, the publication was affordable, half the price of a Mexico City broadsheet and a fifth of the price of a glossy magazine. In July the US embassy estimated that the magazine sold around 30,000 copies. By late August the print run had increased to 120,000; Piño even claimed that circulation reached 182,000. Print runs ran out in a day; copies were changing hands for 1.50 pesos.[82] Such figures were ten times the sales of most magazines and double the sales of broadsheets.[83] In the streets, government agents observed that Mexico City residents were reading

Presente and weaving the printed stories into their criticisms, rumors, and jokes. In late July, one agent found that *Presente*'s piece on Beteta had generated "bitter comments" about the minister, especially among the poor.[84] *Presente*'s Parra exposé inserted the "minister without a budget" into popular comic songs.[85]

During this period, other cultural productions shared *Presente*'s satirical coverage of the government. Just two days before the devaluation, journalist Roberto Blanco Moheno attempted to put on a political revue at the Lírico theater. Entitled *El Cuarto Poder* (The Fourth Estate), no copy of the work survives. But according to Blanco Moheno, it was "written after a bottle of rum and with a guitar" and included songs, skits, and jokes on the corruption of the mainstream press and Alemán's amigos.[86] Less than a month later, Magdalena Mondragón, former editor of the humorous magazine *Chist*, published her take on political humor, *Los presidentes dan risa*. The book defended the social need for satire and offered an overview of jokes about those in power from the Mexican Revolution to the present. In the final section on Miguel Alemán, she trod lightly. She admitted that there were "many very cruel jokes about Alemán, [and] some of these [were] very vulgar and intervene[d] in the private and family life of the president." These, she refused to publish. But she did print "Miguel," the parody of the Lara song "Madrid."[87] The comic actor Palillo was also busy. His "Astillas" column in the bullfighting magazine *Redondel* made jokes at the expense of Alemán's amigos. Meanwhile his show at the Follies theater "put the government in the bin and told the truth about its worth." According to one of his fans, he said the government was "a mafia of the shameless, who if they had any shame, would have already resigned."[88]

The tone and popularity of such works worried the government, which in the summer of 1948 offered a raft of measures to end the popular dissatisfaction caused by the devaluation. Some were economic, aimed at the grumbling Mexico City consumers. They included cheap food. On August 14, the authorities rolled out two state-subsidized markets in the upper-class neighborhoods of Colonia del Ex Hipódromo de Peralvillo and Colonia del Valle. By the end of September, they had opened four others in less salubrious barrios like Colonia Bondojito and Colonia Cuauhtémoc.[89] In fact, Renato Leduc later blamed the subsequent decline in *Presente*'s popularity on what become known as the "popular markets." "The uproar ceased," he mourned, "and the people of naïve opinion dedicated themselves to eating bruised but cheap bananas."[90] Other measures were political: the uproar also ceased, or at least declined, when Alemán disposed of some of his most unpopular cronies. In mid-August 1948, the minister of the economy, Ruíz Galindo, resigned.[91] Parra left Mexico City and withdrew his candidacy for the governorship of San Luis Potosí.[92] And, perhaps most important of all, Pasquel also left the capital and (at least visible) power. On August 18, he resigned as director of *Novedades*, and within a week he had gone into self-imposed exile at his country retreat in San Luis Potosí.[93]

The government also gradually brought the capital's newspapers back to its side. Exactly why editors and journalists changed tack remains unclear. Perhaps shared concerns over social instability and increasing union power kicked in. But financial considerations also seem to have played a role. There were rumors that the government had offered to cover newspaper losses on overseas purchases in return for more cautious treatment of the devaluation's economic effects. And it seems no coincidence that Alemán donated land in Las Lomas for journalists' houses at the end of the year.[94] Whatever the reasons for the change, the pro-government press campaign started in early August 1948. Beyond highlighting and lauding Alemán's attempts to lower prices, the operation took two forms. First, writers tried to split the middle-class and working-class opposition by blaming union chiefs for street-level dissatisfaction. On August 10, *La Prensa* ran the headline "Centers of Agitation against the Government." The article declared that miners and railway men, infiltrated by "communist elements employed to create problems," were orchestrating the attacks on Alemán's cabinet members.[95] Second, editors started a campaign against *murmuración* (gossip). In mid-August the capital's newspapers started to publish a rash of paid inserts by groups variously calling themselves the National Orientation Center and the Committee for Struggle against Murmuración. These inserts were broadly similar. They defended the devaluation using official arguments about the international economic situation and falling exports. And they attacked a new figure in Mexican politics, whom they termed "El Murmurador" (The Gossip). They claimed that the gossip was taking advantage of the devaluation to "go into the street and spread slander and alarm." El Murmurador aimed not to help improve the Mexican economy, but to undermine it. "He leaves his machine to gossip. He leaves an urgent meeting to gossip. He abandons his children and prefers the streets to spread his gossip. He who gossips never works, for gossip needs leisure." Newspaper columnists adopted the trope. *La Prensa* ran an editorial entitled "Pro-Confidence and against Gossip" that lauded the goals of this hurriedly assembled group.[96]

Beyond this general campaign to control prices and co-opt the dailies, government agents also attacked the satirists. Measures against *Presente* started almost immediately. While Piño was readying the first issue of the magazine, the authorities tried to close down the venture by publishing a rival magazine with the same name. Government lawyers claimed that Piño's magazine infringed on the official journal's copyright.[97] The accusations came to nothing, but they foreshadowed the problems to come. On the publication of the magazine, the authorities used their most common strategy. They offered money for silence. The president's private secretary, Rogelio de la Selva, approached Leduc and asked him, "Hey, you bastard. . . . What do you want? It's fine that Piño and Arias Bernal are fucking around, they're not friends with the president. But you are a friend of don Miguel, and I need to know what you want to shut your mouth." Leduc replied that he wanted nothing. "So why are you shouting in that little fucking paper?" De la Selva asked again. "Because as soon as you university people got to power, people started to want the military back because they stole less," Leduc responded.[98] Government agents also harassed *Presente* staff. At the end of an August interview, the directors complained that both Jorge Pasquel and his brother had threatened them with death. Piño lived with three police guards outside and a machine gun trained on the door. His friends each carried a pistol. Arias Bernal protested that unnamed gunmen had kicked down his door and trashed his apartment, and Tomás Perrín, another *Presente* journalist, moaned that his house was being watched by "suspicious types."[99]

Presente survived these attacks relatively unscathed. Costs were low; sales were healthy; income was good; and Piño, Leduc, and Arias Bernal, at least, had expected this kind of provocation. But on August 21 an attack on the magazine's printing press threatened to close the publication for good. At 10:40 p.m. twenty *pistoleros* broke into the shop where Presente was being printed. They held the workers at gunpoint, smashed the presses, and stole copies of *Presente*, two other magazines, watches, fountain pens, and a wallet containing over a thousand pesos. Workers called the police, but the cops didn't arrive until an hour after the incident. According to the newspaper reports, the gunmen did 70,000 pesos of damage.[100]

From the beginning, theories on who ordered the attack abounded. Many, including Piño, accused Pasquel. He had a motive: the previous issue of *Presente* had attacked him directly. The piece had precipitated a further exposé in the tabloid *La Prensa* and Pasquel's hurried resignation from *Novedades*.[101] He also had the style: Pasquel's temper was an open secret. He had beaten up workers for insulting his father, and he had shot a migration officer in a firefight in Nuevo Laredo just five years earlier.[102] Circumstantial evidence was also strong. The day before the attack, Pasquel had published an interview in *Novedades*, which defended his business practices, rubbished his critics, and seemed to suggest he would not leave Mexico City without a fight. According to Piño, Pasquel had followed up this insinuation with a threatening phone call. Finally, the owner of the printshop recognized one of the gunmen as Veracruz hitman Manuel Felipe Villaverde, also known as El Asturiano. She had previously seen the man hanging around Pasquel's offices.[103]

Despite the evidence, the case against Pasquel soon started to unravel. Pasquel vehemently denied the charges, arguing that he would not have been stupid enough to destroy the press the day after his defiant interview. The potential gunman, Villaverde, was shot in mysterious circumstances in a downtown cantina.[104] Finally, government agents and policemen began claiming that the assault on *Presente* was not all it seemed. Journalists picked up on the rumors and hinted that the attack was actually an "auto-assault," planned and directed by either Piño or a shadowy cabal of politicians funding the magazine.[105] On August 27, *La Prensa* pointed out other holes in the case. The article indicated that the gunmen were clearly clueless, since despite the damage *Presente* was published two days later without a hitch. And it suggested that "it was strange that the maneuvers of the squadron of assaulters was not seen by anyone in the barrio before the attack."[106]

The same day, *El Universal* published an odd insert by a man calling himself Salvador Pérez de León. The writer did not explain his role, his interest in the case, or why he had decided to take out an expensive, full-page advertisement in the newspaper. But in his letter he suggested that the attack was either an auto-assault or a deliberate attempt to frame Pasquel. He concluded with a bizarre section on Piño's psychological well-being. He argued that Piño had dubbed his group of daring reporters "The Suicide Squad," not because they were confronting the establishment, but because Piño himself was suicidal. He claimed that Piño had tried to kill himself on previous occasions. He suggested that the magazine was an "attempt to commit suicide and leave the charge at someone else's door . . . to create the myth of a sacrificed man and make himself a martyr." Out of context, the piece seems surreal. But at the time, those in the know, including Piño, probably read between the lines. Setting up fake suicides was a specialty of the Mexican secret services. During the 1930s, they had used similar techniques to kill unwelcome criminals, and Alemán's DFS would later use the method to rid the regime of difficult politicians and journalists. The letter was actually an indirect threat.[107]

So who did order the attack? Pasquel was probably involved; Piño maintained his accusations against the playboy in the face of police denials. Yet Piño also suggested that other "fat cats" were involved. He never dropped names. However, reading between the lines of various news stories and interviews, it seems that he suspected Rogelio De la Selva, the president's private secretary. Piño had regularly mocked de la Selva in the magazine; a representative from De la Selva's sister's magazine had visited the printing shop just an hour before the attack.[108] De la Selva usually took his orders directly from Alemán. Perhaps in this case he acted alone to maintain his own reputation. But it seems unlikely that the under-fire, foreign-born bureaucrat did something so risky without some kind of presidential authorization. The interview with Alemán had appeared just before the attack. And Alemán certainly sympathized with the assault's aims. In the following months, the president publicly sought to redraw the lines of acceptable journalism. At the end of August, *Excélsior* reported that Alemán supported the anti-murmuración campaign. "While the capital gossips, the rest of the country works," he stated.[109] In his September annual report Alemán directly condemned "opportunist critics" and journalists who took advantage of the freedom of expression, "exaggerated" discontent, and disoriented public opinion.[110]

The attack on *Presente*'s printing press was the most high-profile example of the summer of 1948's top-down censorship. But there were other examples of both legal censorship and dirty tricks. The day before the devaluation, police raided the Lírico theater and banned the performance of the political revue *El Cuarto Poder*. Casas Alemán claimed the language and dancing were too risqué. Blanco Moheno responded that the Mexico City chief was trying to censor critical jokes about his own administration and that of the president. When Blanco Moheno cut the offending gags, the play went ahead—albeit with a much-reduced crowd, unexcited by the bland rewritten work.[111] Government agents and the police also bought up or simply took all of the Mexico City copies of Mondragón's *Los presidentes dan risa*. In late August, gunmen visited her house, banged on the door, and, finding no one home, shot up the outside of the building. A neighbor identified their get-away car as belonging to one of Alemán's personal bodyguards.[112] Even Palillo was gagged. His column was cut from *Redondel*; his show at the Follies theater was canceled early.[113]

Humor Post-1948

Despite the assault, *Presente* continued. The tone, however, changed. Alarmist, if stimulating, conspiracies replaced the carefully compiled indictments of official corruption. In October, for example, the magazine covered a bizarre story about big construction sites in Tacubaya. Author and poet Jorge Ferretis claimed that various women had approached the magazine to complain that their husbands, who were working at the site, had disappeared. They claimed that shadowy government forces, including Alemán, were searching for the treasure of the bloodthirsty, nineteenth-century conservative general Leonardo Márquez, known as the Tiger of Tacubaya. The women suggested that state agents had murdered their spouses in order to cover up the plan. Ferretis seemed to confirm the story, denouncing soldiers for confiscating his camera at the site.[114]

As this story suggests, after the assault *Presente*'s reporters were less cautious about implicating the president in tales of murder and corruption. In November the front page was headlined "Machiavellian Alemán Valdés." The article laid the blame for the amigos firmly on President Alemán. The author claimed that the president practiced a narrow and unpatriotic form of favoritism, taken directly from Machiavelli's instructions.[115] And in early 1949, Arias Bernal adorned the front cover with a cartoon of a buck-toothed, smiling Alemán holding the keys to a prison. Inside languished a woman, representing the Mexican Constitution. On the bars were scrawled "monopolies," "the halting of newspapers," and "zero democracy." Underneath, a peasant asked the president, "Why won't you let her free?"[116] The message was now clear. Alemán, not his amigos, was the problem.

Yet the greater bluntness failed; for the average Mexico City reader, *Presente*'s time had passed. The price rose to forty centavos a copy while circulation fell to around 25,000 per issue.[117] More important, the cross-class fury that had fueled the magazine's popularity dissipated. The provision of cheap food played a key role. So did the high-profile dismissals. So did the anticommunist and anti-murmuración campaigns, which helped destroy the unity between middle-class and working-class Mexicans. By October support for anticommunism was so great that DFS agents, supported by a pliant press, helped a government stooge gain control of the breakaway railway union without causing any fuss.[118] Public opinion had changed. In September, government agents had reported that Alemán's annual report had made a "very good impression among all the social classes." Citizens outside the Hotel Regis pharmacy "showed greater optimism" and commented that the president should "put a brake on the blackmailing journalists and punish them with an iron fist."[119] The satiric moment had gone; fearmongering and appeasement had trumped critical jokes.

As *Presente*'s journalists admitted, popular disinterest killed the magazine. But persistent government intervention didn't help. In October 1948 the government-run paper company cut the supply of paper to *Presente* by 75 percent. The magazine now only received two metric tons per week. Piño was forced to buy highly taxed Finnish paper from abroad and beg for scraps from friends in the journalism industry.[120] Over the next few months, the magazine shrunk in size, even as it increased in price. The final issue was printed on poor-quality paper and was only eight pages long.[121] Finally, there is some evidence that government agents finally made good on the surreptitious threat to attempt to kill Piño. Just before the closure of the magazine, Piño tumbled from a second-story balcony to the ground below, breaking multiple bones. He survived, but only just. Many suspected, as suggested by the shady threats of suicide, that he was pushed.[122]

The short-term effects of the authorities' campaigns were dramatic. Publications and theaters were closed; journalists were shot at and pushed from balconies. But the long-term effects were perhaps more significant. For at least two decades, Mexico City's production of political satire aimed at a mass audience disappeared. In the capital, if not in the provinces, satirical magazines declined.[123] So did political revues.[124] Only illustrative satire—in the form of cartoons—remained relatively free of self-censorship. The satirists and journalists who had used their talents to embarrass the Alemán administration became increasingly oficialista. Piño went into forced exile in Argentina. When he returned in the 1950s, he reverted to his job as a political columnist, earning a 2,000-peso monthly *iguala* (fee) for his silence.[125] Arias Bernal toned down his work and went back to producing anticommunist cartoons for overpriced full-color magazines. Even the professional comics calmed down. Cantinflas became a government shill, marching arm in arm with Alemán, acting as an electoral observer during the controversial 1952 election, and producing a series of increasingly unfunny films.[126]

Political humor did not disappear completely. But as text and stage versions declined, the audience for satire narrowed. Satirical jokes became part of elite lore, the informal system of gossip and rules, and were limited to Mexico City's ministries, administrative offices, and newsrooms.[127] According to Monsiváis, a "sense of humor" was one of the three rights that journalists now kept to themselves. In private they were "acute and destructive commentators"; in public they were "corny and oficialista."[128] To enjoy such jokes, listeners needed an intimate knowledge of leaders' personal foibles, the inner workings of the party, and the oblique language of the PRI. They also needed a shared cynicism about the actual aims of power. As a result, such gags rarely made their way onto the street. If they reached print, they were encoded in incomprehensible political columns in underread newspapers or hidden away in *cartas secretas*, limited edition political newsletters, which not coincidentally saw a rapid upsurge after 1948.[129] As a result, most Mexicans lacked the references, the context, and the values to make such jokes.[130] In fact, Samuel Schmidt goes as far as to argue that "among the non-elite groups not a single political joke seems to have been produced" after 1948. Satirizing the system was a game for the PRI's inner circle.[131]

Conclusions

This story of street jokes, satirical cultural works, and suppression helps explain the chronology of Mexican political humor, the connections between press readership and broader social and political forces, and the mechanics of state censorship. But it also suggests some more general rules governing the production and reception of political satire. In 1948, satire was not simply a release valve. It was a genuine threat. By providing a narrative that linked popular suffering to elite corruption, satire offered a comprehensible, unifying language for dissent. But the popularity and efficacy of this language—the level of this threat—depended on broader socioeconomic and political processes, including, in this case, the price of basic foods and the perceived possibility of government reform. The work also depended on satirical entrepreneurs, those inside the media who were prepared to leak the world of the elite to the public and organize these stories into wider narratives. And, temporarily at least, satire intensified the interactions between the worlds of journalists and of readers.

The story also suggests more universal understandings of censorship. Censorship involves medium-term cultural processes, including the development of broad insights into nationalism, economic progress, and the proper practice of journalism. But it also comprises moments of somewhat ad hoc, multiagency repression. In Mexico during this time, these included the use of violence. Such strategies did not only stop the immediate threat. Buttressed by the authorities' explanations in public statements and private letters, they also provided a new manual for journalists' behavior. The story of *Presente* became an instructive myth. From 1948 onward, Mexico City's reporters knew the limits of acceptable discourse, modified and coded the language of satire, rejigged the boundaries of their audience, and understood the prospective punishments for those who wandered off message.

Notes

1. *Presente*, Mar. 17, 1949.
2. Report, Aug. 29, 1950, NA/FO/AM1015/2, Mexico.
3. Informe, Aug. 4, 1948, AGN/DGIPS/112, exp. 1.
4. Monsiváis, "La crónica," 25.
5. For a theory of the importance of moments or "temporalities," see Sewell, *Logics of History*.
6. Asociación Mexicana de Periodistas to President Alemán, Oct. 12, 1948, AGN/MAV/542.1/700.
7. Wright-Rios, *Searching for Madre Matiana*; Mraz, *Looking for Mexico*, 153–200; De María y Campos, *El teatro*; Pilcher, *Cantinflas*; Ortiz Bullé Goyri, "Origines."
8. Bakhtin, *Rabelais and His World*, 8–9, 198–99.
9. De María y Campos, *El teatro*, 442.

10. Beardsell, *Theatre for Cannibals*, 56–65.

11. *Don Timorato*, June 30, 1944.

12. In Veracruz, they had been known as the *polacos*. See Gil Mendieta, Schmidt, and Ruiz León, *Estudios sobre la red política*; Alexander, "Fortunate Sons," 93, 105, 107.

13. Camp, "Education and Political Recruitment."

14. Niblo, *Mexico in the 1940s*, 216.

15. Agundis, *El verdadero*.

16. Report to Commissioner of Customs, Aug. 17, 1947, NARA/RG170/160.

17. León Ossorio, *El pantano*, 14–15.

18. Agundis, *El verdadero*, 153–58.

19. Mariano Narro to Secretario Particular, Nov. 24, 1949, AGN/MAV/568.1/5.

20. *La Nación*, May 15, 1948.

21. *Presente*, Sept. 14, 1948; *Heraldo de San Luis*, Jan. 12, 1955.

22. Report to Commissioner of Customs, Aug. 17, 1947, NARA/RG170/160.

23. Flores, "La lógica," 152–53.

24. Carlos Serrano file, NARA/RG170/160; Astorga, *Drogas*, 74–75, Niblo, *Mexico in the 1940s*, 259–61.

25. Report of Maurice Holden, July 16, 1947, NARA/RG59/22.

26. Carlos Serrano file, NARA/RG170/160. There is no doubt that the Federal Bureau of Narcotics overemphasized the DFS's links to the drug trade. Its chief, Harry Anslinger, thrived off creating new, often phantom threats. But the DFS was a strange target, given its anticommunist stance and the fact that it was created with FBI assistance. Navarro, *Political Intelligence*, 184.

27. Quintana, *Maximino Ávila Camacho*, 112.

28. Gómez Estrada, *Gobierno y casinos*.

29. Agundis, *El verdadero*, 65–69.

30. Rodman, *Mexican Journal*, 48.

31. Niblo, *Mexico in the 1940s*, 258.

32. León Ossorio, *El pantano*, 38, 41–42.

33. Report, June 3, 1946, CUSDCF/Mexico/IA/1945-9/32.

34. *La Prensa*, Aug. 21, 1948; *Novedades*, Mar. 3, 1948.

35. Niblo, *Mexico in the 1940s*, 103.

36. Rath, "Paratroopers"; Piccato, "Pistoleros," 329–34; *Novedades*, Mar. 10, 1948.

37. Rath, *Myths of Demilitarization*, 94–101; Niblo, *Mexico in the 1940s*, 176–79; Middlebrook, *Paradox of Revolution*, 107–58.

38. *La Nación*, Apr. 24, 1948; *La Nación*, May 1 and June 15, 1948.

39. Torres Ramírez, *Hacia la utopía industrial*, 119–31.

40. Bortz, *Los salarios industriales*.

41. Informe, July 25, 1948; Informe, July 28, 1948; Informe, Aug. 8, 1948, all at AGN/DGIPS/111/exp. 2 (Carestia).

42. Informe, Aug. 2, 1948, AGN/DGIPS/111/exp. 2 (Carestia).

43. Informe, Aug. 10, 1948, AGN/DGIPS/111/exp. 2 (Carestia).

44. Informe, Lamberto Ortega Peregrina, July 24, 1948, AGN/DGIPS/111/exp. 2 (Carestia).

45. Memorandum, July 28, 1948, AGN/DGIPS/111/exp. 2 (Carestia).

46. Memorandum, Jesus González Valencia, July 28, 1948, AGN/DGIPS/111/exp. 2 (Carestia).

47. Informe, Lamberto Ortega Peregrina, July 24, 1948, AGN/DGIPS/111/exp. 2 (Carestia).

48. Memorandum, Inspector SF 54, July 23, 1948, AGN/DGIPS/111/exp. 2 (Carestia).

49. Informe, Lamberto Ortega Peregrina, July 24, 1948, AGN/DGIPS/111/exp. 2 (Carestia).

50. Cadena de Liberación, AGN/DGIPS/111/exp. 2 (Carestia).

51. Memorandum, July 23, 1948, AGN/DGIPS/111/exp. 2 (Carestia).

52. Memorandum, Inspector 15 RJD, July 16, 1948, AGN/DGIPS/111/exp. 2 (Carestia).

53. White, "Telling More."

54. Informe, Aug. 12, 1948, AGN/DGIPS/111/exp. 2 (Carestia).

55. Memorandum, Aug. 13, 1948, AGN/DGIPS/111/exp. 2 (Carestia).

56. Memo, Aug. 31, 1948, AGN/DGIPS/24/exp. 3.

57. John R. Speaks to ambassador, Aug. 3, 1948, NARA/RG59.

58. Informe, Fernando Fagoaga, July 22, 1948, AGN/DGIPS/111/exp. 2 (Carestia).

59. Informe, July 23, 1948, AGN/DGIPS/111/exp. 2 (Carestia).

60. They were also ubiquitous in eighteenth-century France. Darnton, *Forbidden Best-Sellers*, 159.

61. Mondragón, *Los presidentes*, 134.

62. *La Prensa*, Aug. 19, 1948.

63. Memorandum, Cadena de Liberación, Aug. 12, 1948, AGN/DGIPS/111/exp. 2 (Carestia).

64. *La Prensa*, Aug. 19, 1948.

65. Darnton, *Forbidden Best-Sellers*, 158.

66. Martínez S., *La vieja guardia*, 89–106; Orozco and Stephenson, *José Clemente Orozco*, 114.

67. Martínez S., *La vieja guardia*, 89–106; Blanco Moheno, *Memorias*, 97; Novo, *La vida en México*, 226.

68. For example, see *Novedades*, Feb. 4 and Mar. 6, 1948.

69. *Novedades*, May 23, 1948.

70. *Novedades*, May 24, 1948.

71. *Novedades*, May 26, 1948; *Presente*, July 14, 1948.

72. *Presente*, July 14, 1948.

73. *Presente*, July 14 and 21, 1948.

74. *Presente*, July 28 and Sept. 4, 1948.

75. *Presente*, Aug. 18, 1948.

76. For the rise in society pages, see Agustín, *Tragicomedia mexicana*, 71.

77. *Presente*, July 28, 1948.

78. *Presente*, Aug. 18, 1948.

79. Renato Leduc had attended university with Alemán and seems to have arranged the interview.

80. *Presente*, Aug. 11, 1948.

81. *Presente*, Aug. 11, 1948.

82. Report on *Presente*, Sept. 10, 1948, CUSDCF/Mexico/IA/1945-49/32; *Presente*, Mar. 17, 1949.

83. Heitman, "Press of Mexico," 202.

84. Juan García Bernal to Lamberto Ortega Peregrina, July 30, 1948, AGN/DGIPS/111/exp. 2 (Carestia).

85. Cadena de Liberación, AGN/DGIPS/111/exp. 2 (Carestia).

86. Blanco Moheno, *Memorias*, 294, and *La corrupción*, 284–85; De María y Campos, *El teatro*, 423.

87. Mondragón, *Los presidentes*, 134–48; *Presente*, Sept. 14, 1948.

88. *La Prensa*, Aug. 23, 1948; PS 16, informe, Aug. 3, 1948, AGN/DGIPS/111/exp. 2 (Carestia).

89. *La Prensa*, Aug. 22 and 24, 1948.

90. *Presente*, Mar. 17, 1949.

91. *Excélsior*, Aug. 13, 1948.

92. *Presente*, Aug. 18, 1948.

93. *Novedades*, Aug. 20, 1948.

94. Underwood, "Survey," 129–30.

95. *La Prensa*, Aug. 10, 1948. For anticommunism and the press, see Servín, "Propaganda y guerra fría."

96. *La Prensa*, Aug. 14, 1948; *La Prensa*, Aug. 12, 1948; "El Murmurador," AGN/DGIPS/111/exp. 2 (Carestia); *Excélsior*, Aug. 13, 1948; *La Prensa*, Aug. 30, 1948.

97. *Presente*, July 14, 1948.

98. Ramón Garmabella and Leduc, *Renato por Leduc*, 152–53.

99. *El Universal*, Aug. 28, 1948.

100. *Presente*, Aug. 26, 1948; *La Prensa*, Aug. 23, 1948; *Excélsior*, Aug. 24, 1948.

101. *La Prensa*, Aug. 19, 1948; *Novedades*, Aug. 20, 1948.

102. Agundis, *El verdadero*, 45–50.

103. *La Prensa*, Aug. 25, 1948.

104. *La Prensa*, Aug. 30, 1948.

105. Blanco Moheno, *Memorias*, 292–93, and *La corrupción*, 246–48.

106. *La Prensa*, Aug. 27, 1948.

107. *El Universal*, Aug. 27, 1948; Monsiváis, *Los mil*, 27; *Presente*, Sept. 7, 1948; email correspondence with Paul Gillingham.

108. *La Prensa*, Aug. 30, 1948.

109. *Excélsior*, Aug. 31, 1948; *Presente*, Aug. 11, 1948.

110. See also his warning to the Asociación Mexicana de Periodistas: President Alemán to Alfonso Anaya, Oct. 27, 1948, AGN/MAV/542.1/700.

111. De María y Campos, *El teatro*, 424–25; Blanco Moheno, *Memorias*, 295–98, and *La corrupción*, 285–87.

112. Martínez S., *La vieja guardia*, 234.

113. Asociación Mexicana de Periodistas to President Alemán, Oct. 12, 1948, AGN/ MAV/542.1/700; *Presente*, Sept. 14, 1948.

114. *Presente*, Oct. 5, 1948.

115. *Presente*, Nov. 19, 1948.

116. *Presente*, Feb. 3, 1949.

117. Novo, *La vida en México*, 346.

118. Middlebrook, *Paradox of Revolution*, 140.

119. Informe, Sept. 2, 1948, AGN/DGIPS/132/exp. 33.

120. *Presente*, Oct. 12, 1948.

121. *Presente*, Mar. 17, 1949.

122. Martínez S., *La vieja guardia*, 92.

123. See the fate of *Presente*'s successor, *El Apretado*, or the 1959 left-wing satirical magazine *Rototemas*. *Rototemas*, Jan. 17, 1959; various documents, AGN/ALM, 704/211; Mraz, *Looking for Mexico*, 256. For the endurance of satirical newspapers in the provinces, see Gillingham, this volume.

124. De María y Campos, *El teatro*, 433–39.

125. Lista de subsidios, n.d., AGN/DGIPS/2953B; Manuel Alvarez to Jorge Piño Sandoval, July 17, 1950, AGN/MAV/272.2/272.

126. Pilcher, *Cantinflas*, 147.

127. Schmidt, *Seriously Funny*, 11; Schmidt, "Elite Lore."

128. Scherer García and Monsiváis, *Tiempo de saber*, 150–51.

129. The original carta secreta was the Buro de Investigaciones Políticas, established in 1948. For the coding of political columns, see Carlos Ortega, "Como se hacen las columnas politicas," *Por Que?*, Sept. 10, 1970.

130. For the common frameworks that govern humor, see Hutchinson, *A Theory of Parody*; Hutchinson, *Irony's Edge*.

131. Schmidt, *Seriously Funny*, 11. There was a resurgence of popular political satire in 1969–1970. Again, it was tied to shifts in the newspaper industry. On one level, satirical writers like Jorge Ibargüengoitia started to write about politics in mainstream newspapers like *Excélsior* (Ibargüengoitia, *Autopsias*). On another level, journalists again worked as satirical entrepreneurs, bringing covert rumors of official malfeasance into the public sphere. Journalist Manuel Buendía was even allegedly employed by the Monterrey industrial group to write jokes about Luis Echeverría. Walker, "Spying."

5 | In the Service of the *Gremio*

Bus Industry Magazines,
PRI Corporatism, and
the Politics of Trade Publications

MICHAEL LETTIERI

The first issue of *El Informador Camionero* in November 1941 opened with an editorial treatise on the moral fiber of Mexico City's bus industry entrepreneurs (*camioneros*). The essay exhorted the magazine's readers, presumably the same camioneros, to dedicate themselves to both unity and hard work. This was, perhaps, an odd way to begin a trade publication, yet given the context in which it appeared, such a tone was unsurprising. Five months earlier the organization that published the magazine and represented the interests of the transportation entrepreneurs, the Alianza de Camioneros, had been fractured by internal factionalism. The appearance of *El Informador Camionero* in November was a clear response to that infighting. Over the next thirty-eight years, apart from one six-year interruption, the alianza continually published the magazine and used it to trumpet the value of organizational unity. This message was ostensibly part of a broader mission, as *El Informador Camionero* claimed to serve the interests of the collective of transportation entrepreneurs—what the camioneros called their *gremio* (guild). As a self-congratulatory editorial in 1954 remarked, the magazine by then had provided thirteen years of "uninterrupted service to the industry and its men, carrying out a true social function . . . linking, unifying, seeking the fraternity of all the elements that make up the Alianza de Camioneros."[1] In this chapter, I examine magazines published by the bus and trucking industry—principally but not exclusively *El Informador Camionero*—in an attempt to explain the role of such trade industry publications in Mexican society and politics. I also explore how these sometimes idiosyncratic documents can be read as a source for understanding the history of the Institutional Revolutionary Party (Partido Revolucionario Institucional, PRI) regime. I ultimately suggest that these publications flourished because they were important pieces in the PRI's system of corporatist control, yet simultaneously offered a space for limited critiques of that system.

Trade publications such as *El Informador Camionero* occupied a strange place in the world of mid-twentieth-century Mexican political life. Their contents were a unique combination of *People* magazine–style social reportage, technical manuals, industry news, and editorial commentary. They were conceived of and promoted as informative outlets, yet because these trade publications were also the direct channel through which organizational leaders could communicate with their affiliates, the magazines also served a fundamentally political purpose. Informing, in this context, meant orienting. Indeed, *El Informador Camionero* was published as the official journal of the alianza and was often under the direct control of the group's executive committee. Irrespective of the industry or organization in which they operated, leaders saw the trade magazines as valuable tools for maintaining the coherence of the corporatist system. Those who attempted to control groups as dissimilar as camioneros and mill workers were quick to patronize such official magazines.

While union publications are not explored at length here, their purposes and usages bear much resemblance to trade publications. The similarities are strongest when trade magazines are compared with smaller labor publications. In the 1940s, union boss Antonio Hernández controlled sugar workers at the La Concha and El León sugar mills, though rather than challenging owner William O. Jenkins and manager Ronnie Eustace, Hernández collaborated with them. Yet this alliance needed to be veiled, and Hernández apparently used his union newspaper to present a more radical image, one that would legitimize his leadership. As Andrew Paxman writes, on one occasion Hernández's newspaper published "a cartoon of Eustace and Jenkins, drawn as beasts sucking the blood of the workers." When Eustace demanded an explanation, Hernández replied that "he had to allow such things from time to time; he had to keep up appearances."[2] Union publications also served to justify collaboration with the government. In analyzing major labor confederation magazines, Joseph Lenti observes that "they conveyed an editorial alliance with the state that promoted their mutually shared goals," and they served as a targeted vehicle for delivering the rhetoric of paternalism and collectivism.[3]

Since politically ambitious leaders needed to ensure the loyalty of their groups to the PRI, these magazines tended to promote both internal unity and political discipline. Yet these officially controlled magazines did not consist entirely of the self-serving rhetoric that might have predictably emanated from such loyal PRI actors. Rather, they were the legible texts of the corporatist system with all its tensions and disputes. They were arenas in which corporatist actors fought almost endless rhetorical struggles over the definition of legitimate leadership and the character of their relationship with the regime. The pages of *El Informador Camionero* reveal a continual renegotiation of organizational discipline and unity, and in part to retain credibility with the average camionero, the magazines contained open critiques of leaders gone awry and ill-conceived government policies.[4]

Setting aside the somewhat provincial content of *El Informador Camionero*, there are important reasons to examine small, narrow-audience publications such as trade journals and union magazines. In particular, the analysis presented here underscores their value as a source for social and political history. First, this research suggests that these periodicals were a space where censorship, if not absent, was perhaps different from that present elsewhere. Obscure enough that they almost certainly fell into the holes of the PRI's "Swiss cheese" authoritarianism, their content was limited by self-censorship and the decisions of the leadership groups that bankrolled the publications. Second, the frequently editorializing content of these publications, penned by a diverse group of political actors and specialized journalists, provides a different sort of voice than exists in other documentary records.[5] Third, the sheer volume of such publications is staggering: a list of union and worker publications compiled in 1980 by Guillermina Bringas and David Mascareño runs some thirty-five pages, and a similar list of small trade publications likely would be of similar heft.[6] Understanding the function (and functioning) of such periodicals, then, gives insights on the subtle mechanisms of the PRI's corporatist rule and the importance of a public sphere in maintaining it.

I begin with a discussion of the history of transportation industry publications, suggesting that linkages between leadership groups, internal politics, and trade publications reveal the unique motivations behind the magazines. I then discuss in detail the history of *El Informador Camionero* during the 1954–1958 period when the alianza experienced a major internal schism, showing how the publication attempted to construct the concept of legitimate leadership rhetorically. The chapter concludes with a broader discussion of how such publications offered a limited space for critiques of the corporatist system and how they thus illuminate the understandings inherent to the functioning of that system.

Organizations, Mastheads, and Political Careers

Interpreting camionero publications is not a straightforward task. This is partly because the history of the alianza and the country's bus industry is not well understood.[7] The improvised automobile transportation system that emerged after 1916 quickly grew into a flourishing bus transportation industry by the early 1930s. This was partly due to official support since various political factions saw the collective organizations of moderate owner-drivers to be a bulwark against more radical workers of the city's trolley system.[8] Indeed, Álvaro Obregón had personally backed the alianza's early commercial ventures, aiding the group in securing gasoline contracts and capital for a commercial bank. Throughout the 1930s, the alianza consolidated its preeminent position in the industry, and in 1939 entrepreneurial forces organized within the group successfully thwarted an attempt to convert the bus system into one operated by state-directed workers cooperatives, ensuring that for the following forty-three years, the city's bus transportation network would be operated by alianza-affiliated permit holders.[9] Although many of these permits were held by individuals who owned and operated single buses, perhaps a greater number were concentrated in the hands of entrepreneurs who managed small fleets of buses. Though the city government set fare rates, the combination of subsidized oil, vehicles, and parts—and the lack of competition from other modes of public transportation—ensured that most bus owners were able to turn a profit, though it was clearly harder for those with a single bus. While poor service and rumors of fabulously wealthy bus magnates led urban residents to label the system the *pulpo camionero*—the bus octopus[10]—it was in truth not a centralized monopoly but a fractious group of entrepreneurs that dominated the city's public transportation network. As the organization that represented the interests of those owners, the alianza was therefore something of a hybrid. It was equal parts classical PRI urban corporatist organization and commercial interest lobby, combining elements of groups as disparate as street vendors and hoteliers.[11]

Official publications were among the strategies employed by alianza leaders to control their fractious group. Analyzing the bus industry trade press is complicated, however, because of the sheer volume of publications that appeared during some sixty years of history. Since their content cannot be understood outside of their context—the personal feuds and political struggles that shaped camioneros' concerns—it is helpful to briefly chart a history of publishing in the transportation industry and the organizations and men (the writers were exclusively men) involved in it.

The first camionero magazine, *Movimiento*, appeared in the late 1920s and was published by a newly founded alianza that was a loose collective of bus owners and drivers. *Movimiento* was followed in 1931 by *El Heraldo Camionero*, which was published as the official journal of the Alianza de Camioneros under the direction of two longtime alianza leaders.[12] During the run of *El Heraldo Camionero* from 1931 to 1933, the alianza consolidated its position as the sole political representative of bus industry entrepreneurs, and the magazine's content reflected that sense of collective progress, emphasizing the economic achievements of the camioneros and the advancement of the organization as a whole. During its short run, *El Heraldo Camionero* presented a decidedly romantic cooperative vision of the industry, one where the leadership seemed to have much in common with the average bus owner; fraternity was the order of the day. *El Heraldo Camionero* bore much similarity to roughly contemporaneous workers publications in Monterrey. On "The Workers Page" of *Colectividad*, the "slick monthly magazine" of a company-supported steelworkers' recreational society, essayists emphasized "class harmony, work discipline, and self-improvement," and "the language of revolution and constitutional rights" was "notably absent" from the magazine's pages.[13]

When *El Informador Camionero* appeared in 1941 as the alianza's reconstituted official publication, much had changed. The organization was firmly positioned politically as the most important national representative body for camioneros, and crucially, the dynamics of leadership had undergone a dramatic shift. As the alianza's executive committee came to resemble an insular clique composed of relatively wealthy members who owned small fleets of buses, the organization lost the egalitarian aura of a society of "emancipated workers" that had characterized the years of *El Heraldo Camionero*. The rapid erosion of the romantic early structure of the industry marked a profound change in the organization's politics, and it was of no small consequence that by the 1940s a perceptible gap had opened between the alianza's leaders and its average member in terms of wealth, influence, and political aspirations. *El Informador Camionero* was, in part, an attempt to bridge that divide.

At the time of its founding, *El Informador Camionero* was placed under the direction of Narciso Contreras, the alianza's secretary of press and propaganda. The position was a new one—the alianza's committee had previously consisted only of administrative positions—and its primary responsibility seems to have been the management of the magazine. Until the mid-1960s, the organization's propaganda secretary would also appear on *El Informador Camionero*'s masthead as the magazine's managing editor. Importantly, Contreras was close to Antonio Díaz Lombardo, the organization's powerful secretary-general and the man whose leadership had been challenged in the 1941 schism described at the start of this chapter. There was little doubt at the magazine's founding, then, that its editorial voice was that of the alianza's high and mighty. Contreras controlled the magazine until 1954 when his bid to succeed Díaz Lombardo (who had resigned the secretary-generalship) failed. During that rupture, Contreras's rival and the eventual victor, José Valdovinos, installed his own adherents in the positions of editor and director and bent the magazine toward bolstering his leadership. In 1958, however, *El Informador Camionero* ceased publication. After massive protests over fares and poor service shook the capital that year, the city government intervened in the alianza, ousting Valdovinos, installing a new leadership group, and placing the entire industry under the control of a newly created administrative institution called the Unión de Permisionarios. Through the union, the city government assumed a more direct role in urban transportation policy, managing routes, loans, subsidies, and vehicular models—areas where the alianza members had previously enjoyed significant autonomy.

That *El Informador Camionero* was shuttered following the intervention reveals just how autonomous and organic trade publications were. The decision to either intentionally kill off the publication or simply let it fall into desuetude in these years indicates that the dissemination of these trade publications and the control of their content was a central concern for industry leaders, but was less of an issue for political authorities. This is somewhat surprising, but supports two conclusions. First, trade publications were indeed a somewhat unintended space where criticism could flourish; and second, the corporatist system worked through independent agents, not central control, and trade publications were an expression of that autonomy. The appearance two years later of an independent bus industry magazine—and its prompt co-optation by alianza leadership—underscores the importance of these magazines for the group's leaders.

El Informador Camionero returned to print in 1965 when government control of the alianza loosened and a group of politically and economically powerful camioneros supported by Rubén Figueroa gained control of the organization.[14] Under Figueroa, *El Informador Camionero*'s masthead was reworked, and the publication was placed under the control of the alianza's secretary-general, who now served as the magazine's director. A close Figueroa ally, Isidoro Rodríguez, became its general manager. With the modified title of *El Informador Camionero: Voz de la Transportista Nacional*,[15] the magazine acquired a new national focus as Figueroa sought to unify Mexico's camioneros into a single countrywide alianza. He exerted increasing control over the publication, and by 1970 Figueroa was included on the masthead as director-general. The revived *Informador Camionero* was published until 1979, although it slipped into obsolescence after 1975 when Figueroa abandoned the magazine following an acrimonious power struggle with Rodríguez.

Although *El Informador Camionero* was the most important, it was not the only industry publication tied to the alianza. In 1960 an independent group began publishing *Transportes y Turismo*. By 1963, the magazine had fallen under the sway of an embattled alianza leadership group, then struggling to gain legitimacy among the camioneros who resented its collaboration with the city government's intervention in the industry. From 1963 to 1965, *Transportes y Turismo* mimicked the function of *El Informador Camionero* as a communication tool for alianza leadership. When the collaborationist leaders lost power in 1965 and *El Informador Camionero* was resurrected, *Transportes y Turismo* returned to semi-independence, but remained closely tied to industry politics. The magazine did attempt to develop a market niche, focusing its content on Mexico City's transportation issues while *El Informador Camionero* aimed at a national audience. Following the Figueroa-Rodríguez schism in 1975, *Transportes y Turismo* was colonized again, this time by Figueroa's allies, who ensured it was published steadily until 1978. Elsewhere in the country, transportation entrepreneurs also published magazines, though most had much shorter lives than those of *Transportes y Turismo* and *El Informador Camionero*—for instance, the 1966–1968 run of *La Voz del Chofer*, a publication of Acapulco's bus entrepreneurs.

That the fortunes of these magazines were so closely tied to the projects and aspirations of camionero leadership groups suggests that their fundamental importance was political, not journalistic or professional, though this was not readily apparent from their authorship. Indeed, the men associated with the magazines can be classified into two categories—career journalists and political careerists. The former group comprised men who did not feature among the alianza's notable members and may not even have owned buses; they were professional camionero journalists who covered industry issues and events. These professionals occasionally editorialized and did have links to factions within the alianza, but their careers tended to survive political schisms. Enrique Aguirre Harris, for example, was one of Valdovinos's choices to lead *El Informador Camionero* in 1954, but he remained active in camionero journalism through the 1970s, when he directed *Transportes y Turismo*. Fernando Andrade Warner was a frequent columnist in *El Informador Camionero* during the 1940s and '50s and seemed to have ties to Díaz Lombardo; he later served as subdirector of *Transportes y Turismo* from 1960 to 1962 and subsequently returned to the resurrected *El Informador Camionero* in 1965.

The political careerists sometimes had equally long tenures as contributors to the magazines but were distinguished from their professional colleagues by their status as bus owners and their involvement in industry (and often national) politics. Narciso Contreras, *El Informador Camionero*'s first and long-tenured director, was a wealthy bus owner, a member of Díaz

Lombardo's inner circle, and later a national congressman. Carlos Dufoo briefly succeeded Contreras before being replaced in 1954, returned to edit *El Informador Camionero* in the late 1960s and '70s, and was a prominent industry leader who twice served as a national congressman. For careerists such as Contreras and Dufoo, involvement with the magazines had the clear goal of promoting the projects and messages of their political groups in an effort to solidify the leadership's control over the camioneros, but their messages of unity and discipline were often interchangeable and bland.

Neither was the content of the magazines wholly indicative of particular political motivations. Although the purpose of *El Informador Camionero* had been clear at its founding, articles tended to range from the overtly political to the purely social, and this mixture was central to the sui generis nature of all the publications. A typical issue might contain an editorial on the history of Labor Day celebrations, articles on fare disputes in a provincial city and on new policies for route placards in the capital, photographs from a recent banquet hosted by a bus line, a section on camionero sporting activities, information on tire maintenance, and official alianza circulars regarding taxes. Political content was sprinkled throughout, in both opening editorials and middle-page commentaries. Articles were frequently unsigned, leaving some purportedly informational columns with obviously editorial content unattributed, though their tone and messages made their nature (and likely authorship) clear. At times, the magazines engaged in a classic strategy of journalistic deflection, republishing columns from national broadsheets or foreign publications that offered more biting critiques of transportation policy than the camioneros perhaps felt comfortable advancing independently. Though the balance shifted toward this more strident political content during times of internal alianza conflict, the magazines tended to return to a state of relative equilibrium where the social and technical content offset the political messages. Indeed, the relative consistency of the magazines' blandness across some sixty years is striking. This was because the target audience for these publications was the average camionero, and for the magazines to be credible they had to appear to be serving the interests and needs of the gremio, which meant not simply serving the political objectives of leaders, but also catering to the quotidian interests of members. The relatively broad diffusion of camionero magazines—10,000 copies monthly of *Transportes y Turismo* in 1962 and 15,000 copies of *El Informador Camionero* in 1965—suggests that they were intended to reach all members of the alianza.[16]

With its content thus ranging from highly technical reports to bickering over arcane internal disputes, *El Informador Camionero* and its ilk on superficial examination hardly seem an intriguing source for the study of twentieth-century Mexican political life, and the publications' prosaic qualities hardly seem to make for exciting historical research. Yet when these magazines are properly contextualized and their messages more closely considered, they emerge as fascinating elements of the PRI corporatist system. If publications such as *El Informador Camionero* were unremarkable examples of journalism, they were nevertheless remarkable pieces of marketing and agitprop, and the resources that camionero leaders invested in them suggests their importance.

Constructing Leadership on Glossy Pages

How the editors and editorialists of *El Informador Camionero* pursued their political objectives is perhaps best illustrated by an examination of the magazine's content during the organizational rupture in 1954. That year, a dispute over the group's strategies for negotiating an increase in bus fares provoked a major schism when the leadership group tied to Narciso Contreras found itself out of political favor and stonewalled by the city government. The conflict came to a head when, with the backing of Ernesto Uruchurtu, the head of Mexico City's government, a collaborationist faction led by José Valdovinos succeeded in forcing Contreras's group from power through a series of shadowy maneuvers. Yet this story was entirely absent from the pages of *El Informador Camionero* where Valdovinos simply appeared as the group's new secretary-general—without explanation—three-quarters of the way through the magazine's May edition as if the partially completed issue had been amended shortly before press time. Sharp-eyed readers would have noticed that the following month, *El Informador Camionero* had an entirely new masthead since Valdovinos had apparently installed those loyal to him as the magazine's editor and director. Less subtle was the message splashed across the publication's cover, where Valdovinos appeared alongside Uruchurtu. This and additional interior photos where the organization's new secretary-general was captured in meetings with the mayor and the president clearly indicated to readers that the new leader of the camioneros had a degree of political access that his predecessor, Contreras—who had been shut out of the mayor's office—had lacked.

Opposition to Valdovinos was fierce, however, as some dissident members of the alianza saw him as an opportunist who, in seeking to use the group for his own political gain, had adopted an overly collaborationist stance toward the city government. In order to consolidate his leadership in the face of these challenges, Valdovinos's *El Informador Camionero* undertook a massive effort to establish his legitimacy and to promote unity in the face of dissent. The June 1954 issue featured an article entitled "A Ray of Hope," which reported on Valdovinos's meeting with the mayor—documented on the cover—and suggested that the warm relationship between the two men offered the best chance for a favorable resolution of the dispute over fares. The magazine also sought to contrast Valdovinos's rectitude, moderation, and dedication with the venality and extravagance of his predecessors and rivals: a photo of the alianza's executive committee hosting a working dinner was captioned with the comment: "Notice the sodas—the price of whiskey is sky high!"[17] These were clear efforts to persuade camioneros to line up behind Valdovinos, presenting his leadership as both effective and more legitimate than that of his opponents. By September, with the schism in the organization deepening, the alianza increased the circulation of *El Informador Camionero* by 5,000, to a total of 20,000 copies, a clear indication that the leaders saw the magazine as an important method of spreading official messages during times of conflict. That month's editorial offered a strident but hardly unique commentary, remarking that "now, more than ever, the unity of the gremio is necessary. True unity, stripped of all individual interest. Unity without sophism, demagoguery, or betrayal of our tradition of guild fraternity." The editorial asserted that "three unalterable principles . . . have permitted the survival of our dear gremio camionero: unity, discipline, and responsibility."[18] Suggesting that the camioneros rise above personal ambitions for collective gain was hardly an apolitical or altruistic message: industry schisms disrupted service and deeply concerned government officials, weakening Valdovinos's position as a leader. If Valdovinos could not unify the organization and ensure that it accepted official decisions on fares, the regime would likely force him from office just as it had his predecessor.

The 1954 episode underscores three common techniques that the trade magazines used to consolidate the authority of leadership. First, by advertising the advantageous political position of leaders through photography and reporting on meetings with officials, the magazines sought to portray leaders as working diligently and effectively to solve industry issues. Second, in their portrayals of these men as models of rectitude, the publications set the terms of debates over legitimate leadership, attempting to cast dissidents as disloyal to the interests of the gremio. Third, through the aggressive and continual rhetorical promotion of unity and discipline, the magazines argued that only through subordination to that legitimate leadership could the camioneros expect the industry to advance. Organizational unity and discipline had benefits beyond the collective interests of the camioneros, however, since those qualities also bolstered the positions of alianza leaders within the PRI's corporatist system. The mechanics of that system, well documented by the labor leaders who advanced politically by ensuring the docility of their organizational affiliates, was developed by entrepreneurial groups such as the camioneros as well.[19] Nevertheless, alianza leaders were never the authoritarian union bosses of classic *charrismo* caricature, nor were they industry caciques.[20] Political success was predicated on more than heavy-handed leadership: those who could also build some measure of "legitimate" support were the regime's preferred intermediaries, and specialized publications were a tool to construct that support.[21] In this, the careers of alianza leaders followed common patterns. Valdovinos's success in consolidating his authority resulted in his nomination to a congressional seat in 1958—though this too was scarcely mentioned in the magazine's pages.

Legible Corporatism

If the individual benefits of the alianza's collaboration with the regime were frequently elided in the pages of *El Informador Camionero*, leaders nevertheless had to defend the legitimacy of the organization's involvement in politics. *El Informador Camionero* proved a valuable tool for justifying both cooperation with official policy and participation in PRI rituals, particularly after 1946 when the camioneros began providing the party with free bus service during campaigns and when industry leaders were first nominated to political posts. As the magazine's chief editorialist wrote that year, the naming of the alianza's president to a cabinet position "represented an honor for all the camioneros of the country . . . [and] is an explicit recognition of the virtues of our gremio."[22] This rhetorical attempt to portray the advancement of the political careers of camionero leaders as a collective rather than individual gain was a typical trope in the magazine. Similarly, *El Informador Camionero* sought to justify the group's participation in electoral campaigns, which imposed significant costs on members, by suggesting that it was both a civic duty and a means to obtain policy benefits. As a May 1958 commentary observed, the group's contribution of a hundred vehicles to campaign convoys "was of such magnitude that it could go neither unnoticed nor unappreciated by our government. This effort will not be in vain, and we hope that in a not-too-distant future the industry will reap the fruits."[23] The alianza's collaboration in these mobilizations served to demonstrate leaders' control over the group but was also indispensable for the regime's political theater: the group's vehicles provided the transportation necessary to make large rallies and demonstrations possible. Alianza leaders thus had every reason to ensure that members cooperated, and they continually sought ways to reinforce the importance of the practice. In 1969, on the eve of another election, the magazine published a photographic retrospective of alianza participation in every presidential campaign since 1946, reminding readers that support for the PRI had the legitimacy of tradition and that the camioneros were the most important spokesmen of the revolution.[24] Extra copies of that edition were printed, further underscoring that leadership believed the magazine to serve an important orienting purpose.

Yet alianza leadership was careful to maintain an image of distance from the PRI, and the magazine occasionally addressed the tensions caused by the significant costs of collaboration. In one instance, *El Informador Camionero* published a commentary that criticized government ministries for misusing the buses provided free of cost by the alianza in support of demonstrations, noting that on occasion vehicles would spend six hours waiting for ralliers to board and that frequently ministries requested more buses than necessary. Such practices were deemed egregious because of their wastefulness: taking buses out of circulation both harmed the interests of the public and caused a pointless loss of income for the camioneros.[25]

Indeed, the role of camioneros in supporting *acarreo*—the PRI's practice of mobilizing ralliers[26]—seems to have been a perennial source of friction. Industry publications thus give a valuable glimpse of discontent even within the most solidly *priista* corners of the corporatist system, illuminating the way these groups viewed the terms of their participation in authoritarian politics. In one lively example from Acapulco's *La Voz del Chofer*, one faction of the port city's struggling camioneros offered a harangue against leaders arranging buses for acarreo:

> Sheep! Let us consider the matter calmly. [Head of the PRI] Dr. Lauro Ortega comes and now they [the camionero leaders] are organizing the "supposedly revolutionary masses" and are going to the capital to receive orders, and we ask: Is the secretary of the organization [Acapulco's camioneros] going to require that new recipients of operating permits be bootlickers . . . ? Isn't it true that when the president came he said beforehand that he did not want any demonstration of that sort? That he didn't want the workers to waste time, but nevertheless the bootlickers obliged all the bus owners and workers to demonstrate, and not even then were their interests considered. . . . Now it's the same thing. Are the "advisers" going to oblige the workers to go like flocks of sheep to shout and applaud a man we don't even know? What have we gained? Nothing, it is true. The poor campesinos that they bring from the villages even get a "cold drink and a taco" . . . but we who lose more than half a day of work, what do we gain? They say that all of this is to prepare the way for Juan Chueco [a local leader] to become a congressman, because that is what Rubén Figueroa desires, but what have we done to deserve such poor treatment?[27]

While the terms "bootlickers" and "sheep" clearly critiqued the practice of acarreo, this commentary aimed only at its most exaggerated expression as orchestrated by unscrupulous, self-interested local actors—which the head of the PRI and the president were both cast as opposing. This sprawling denunciation was thus hardly revolutionary. Transportation industry entrepreneurs tended to be loyal priistas, and this airing of grievances was more about internal politics than any direct challenge to the regime's core values. Obscure provincial trade publications such as this would likely have received little scrutiny from censors, and neither would it have been necessary to restrain their content since complaints would have passed more or less unnoticed except by the camionero audience for whom they were intended—and with whom this expression of naked frustration might have resonated. What ire this commentary might have raised would have come from the local politicians who staked their careers on turning out acarreados with Acapulco's buses. Indeed, the editorial's shot at Chueco and Figueroa—who was then maneuvering for the governorship of Guerrero—may have had repercussions since after that issue all political content vanished from the publication. What the episode reveals, though, is the degree to which grudging collaborators with acarreo expected their leaders to take their interests into consideration, and the internal bickering that often surrounded participation in political rituals.

When bickering escalated into leadership struggles, rivals often targeted each other with savage printed salvos. Indeed, the *Voz del Chofer* editorial was not the first time Figueroa had been criticized in industry publications. Under Valdovinos, *El Informador Camionero* had lambasted Figueroa's attempts to claim the leadership of provincial camioneros during the mid-1950s. In one instance, after Figueroa had published a newspaper advertisement attempting to take credit for obtaining subsidized chassis for Monterrey's camioneros, the magazine sniped that "the announcement was signed by someone who calls himself 'ingeniero' [engineer] and is named Rubén Figueroa. It was this 'Mister' Figueroa who had the shameful audacity to try to take advantage and capitalize on the work of the Alianza de Camioneros of Mexico. And this is not a critique of Figueroa, but a recognition of his deplorable attitude, worthy of Petronius's tirade against Nero: 'You are worthy of the spectacle, and the spectacle is worthy of you.'"[28] The mockery of Figueroa's title of ingeniero (he had received a degree in hydrological engineering from the Universidad Nacional Autónoma de México) was undoubtedly intended to suggest that he was a political opportunist, not an authentic camionero, despite the fact that by that point he had been involved in the industry for nearly a decade. On other occasions, the magazine accused rivals of engaging in "vulgar political maneuvers . . . [and] attempting at any cost to use [the camioneros] as a trampoline to obtain political office."[29] The tenor of these commentaries seems to have been calibrated to inflame the sensibilities of alianza members by suggesting that opponents were violating the moral codes of camionero leadership. That strategy could be adapted ex post facto as well, and alianza leaders occasionally shored up their position by attacking former leaders, as was the case in 1965 when *El Informador*

Camionero published a cartoon depicting the recently deposed—and much despised—secretary-general as a snake wrapped around a distraught bus owner. The caption read, "This is how that pseudo lawyer with false pretenses wanted to strangle the gremio."[30]

Open criticism of rivals was central to trade publications not only because it served the political needs of leaders, but also because it occasionally reflected the discontents of members. Similarly, in seeking to maintain unity and discipline the periodicals had to reflect the more prosaic policy concerns and complaints of their readers. Since the camioneros saw themselves as loyal collaborators of the regime, but maintained a stubborn, conservative, middle-class sense of self-sufficiency and frequently struggled with the government over transportation policy, leaders needed to appear as though they were faithful advocates of the gremio's interests. This involved not only painting rivals as self-serving or traitorous but also channeling the expression of collective grievances into the pages of the magazine. In *El Informador Camionero*, this tended to take the form of editorials that obliquely critiqued officials' decisions and lamented officials' incomprehension of the issues. Fares were a particular area of dispute, and the blunt observations of the following column are a representative example of the typical strategy for addressing uncooperative authorities:

> In a free market such as ours, despite its numerous elements of directed economy, there are inflationary tendencies in products and services that require periodic leveling of prices. . . . Transportation does not escape these phenomena. The revision, every two years, of labor contracts and the ever-increasing rate of the minimum wage, as well as the increase in prices of automotive parts, repairs, and maintenance, necessarily influence the cost of the services we provide. . . . The [government's] adjustment of fares does not coincide with these cycles, and when they are raised, it is with such delay as to cause fatal disparities in the economy of transportation.[31]

The dry tone of this introduction quickly shifted to a more plaintive voice, lamenting that whenever the issue of fare increases is raised, "from all corners emerge 'technical experts in these matters' who offer opinions that range from reasonable to the most absurd" and that almost always the conclusion blames the camioneros for failing to turn a profit even though they do not control the price of their own product. The column finished in full-throated wail, reminding camionero readers—and perhaps celebrating their abnegation—that "bus transportation in Mexico City is in the hands of more than 4,500 permit holders, Mexicans of working backgrounds who over 50 years organized and maintained the industry, making of it an honest living. . . . Their efforts and perseverance have sustained it in conditions ever less favorable. . . . We cannot ignore or avoid the solution. The raising of fares is an imperative that now more than ever is fully justified."[32] Absent from this full-page missive was any direct confrontation of those responsible for setting fares: blame was laid at the feet of false experts and a stingy public, but government officials went unmentioned. This was not unusual: low-level transit officials might come in for sharp-edged criticism, but the chief complaint against the head of Mexico City's government was never more than a vaguely blameless incomprehension of the issue. The purpose of the column, then, was less to elicit an official reaction, and much less to achieve a change in policy, but more to present to average camioneros the image of a leadership sympathetic to their struggle; it was empathetic, not proactive.

Such policy critiques, therefore, like the commentary on acarreo discussed above, were more discussions of the *terms* of political incorporation, not debates over incorporation itself. The collective of camioneros had no choice but to participate in PRI rituals, and they had little ability to alter transportation policies, which were often shaped by public protest over any fare increases rather than by economic calculations. In addressing these topics, the magazines did not aspire to change them. What the discussion in trade publications did achieve, however, was to reinforce the sense that the camioneros had a voice in the official government sphere, that policy *could* be discussed openly, and that leaders *could* challenge the government on issues of importance to the industry. It was an illusion that was useful for nearly all involved.

Conclusion

Within the PRI's corporatist system, groups like the Alianza de Camioneros offer an important explanation for the stability of the regime from the 1950s to the 1980s. If their loyalty bordered on unconditional, it was not blind, and the leaders of these organizations needed to construct the legitimacy of their cooperation with authoritarian politics. Magazines like *El Informador Camionero* not only pushed for unity and discipline, but also provided a space for hashing out the rules of corporatist politics. They were fundamentally political, conceived and purposed to support the needs of organizational leadership, but they did not consist entirely of anodyne puffery. Rather, these publications reflected the complex and difficult process of establishing authority in corporatist organizations. Precisely framed denunciations of rivals and frank discussions of policy were among the subtle techniques that successful leaders employed to bolster their moral and pragmatic legitimacy. Similarly, leaders used these publications to finesse the integration of their groups into the PRI's corporatist system, balancing the concerns of affiliates with the demands of political patrons. This often meant presenting leaders as staunch advocates for the best interests of the group while simultaneously explaining the collective benefits of collaboration and arguing for its necessity. Ultimately, these publications became the texts of the corporatist system, and as groups like the alianza negotiated their relationship with the regime, their official journals set the terms of the discussion. Between the lines of the magazines, it is possible to read the unwritten rules of the PRI.

Notes

1. *El Informador Camionero*, Apr. 1954.
2. Paxman, *Jenkins of Mexico*, 305.
3. Lenti, "Collaboration and Conflict," 21. Since leaders of the major labor confederations had a greater degree of security (enjoying careers several times longer than those of even the longest tenured alianza leaders) the need to reinforce the legitimacy of their leadership was perhaps lower. See also Gutiérrez Espíndola, *Prensa obrera*.
4. Predictably, however, what were seen as "ill-conceived government policies" were subject to rather tendentious interpretations.
5. With the exception of Salvador Novo, who famously wrote for *El Chafirete* in the early 1920s, those who contributed to *El Informador Camionero* were relatively anonymous historical actors, and their writing thus offers a fresh look at the internal workings of the corporatist system.
6. Bringas and Mascareño, "Un siglo de publicaciones."
7. A much more detailed account of the history of the alianza, its leaders, and its members can be found in my dissertation: Lettieri, "Wheels of Government."

8. For a history of the politics and emergence of the bus transportation industry in Mexico City, see Davis, *Urban Leviathan*, 58.

9. The attempt to create a system of cooperatives, pushed by Francisco Múgica, was in part a response to the alianza's alleged mistreatment and blacklisting of bus drivers.

10. The alianza was labeled a "pulpo" as early as 1934.

11. See Cross, *Informal Politics*.

12. Juan P. Morales, the director of the magazine, was a prominent member of the alianza, and Francisco Zubillaga, the publication's editor, was the alianza's recording secretary.

13. Snodgrass, *Deference and Defiance*, 92.

14. Figueroa's career and the intersection between his political aspirations and his involvement with the alianza are detailed in Lettieri, "A Model Dinosaur."

15. This rebranding notwithstanding, the post-1965 magazine was a continuation of the earlier publication, and I use the shorter, original name of *El Informador Camionero* in all cases.

16. A 1965 promotional page in *El Informador Camionero* soliciting advertisers depicted the publication's supposed national coverage with a map showing its distribution routes stretching out from Mexico City; it further claimed that "an average of four readers per copy 'see' and 'hear' our messages." That would have meant that the magazine had approximately 60,000 readers, which strains credulity. *El Informador Camionero*, Sept. 1965.

17. *El Informador Camionero*, June 1954.

18. *El Informador Camionero*, Sept. 1954.

19. Maldonado Aranda, "Between Law and Arbitrariness"; Middlebrook, *Paradox of Revolution*.

20. As Michael Snodgrass has pointed out, *charro* rule was often legitimized by the benefits delivered to affiliated workers. Snodgrass, "The Golden Age of Charrismo," 183–84.

21. Smith, "Who Governed?"

22. *El Informador Camionero*, Dec. 1946.

23. *El Informador Camionero*, May, 1958.

24. *El Informador Camionero*, Nov. 1969.

25. *El Informador Camionero*, Aug. 1967.

26. These demonstrators were minimally compensated with food, T-shirts, or the promise of future intangible benefits (electrification, a playground, jobs); they were also frequently coerced to attend with threats of blacklisting, and other repercussions, but it was never a purely monetary transaction.

27. *La Voz del Chofer*, Sept. 1966. Illustrating the importance of context and the difficulty of analyzing trade publications without it, there is little more that can be said about this commentary, which was published under a comedic alias (Agent 007). With little external information available about the politics of

buses in Acapulco, it is only possible to make the rather obvious inference that the co-opted leadership of the city's transportation industry had failed to deliver adequate benefits to the camioneros after organizing them in support of PRI activities. The leaders were thus facing a challenge from those who controlled the magazine. More substantive analysis about that struggle is elusive, as is any context for the references to Chueco and Figueroa.

28. *El Informador Camionero*, Jan. 1956.
29. *El Informador Camionero*, Sept. 1954.
30. "Así quisiera ver al gremio, ahorcado, un pseudo licenciado con título colorado"; *El Informador Camionero*, July 1965.
31. *El Informador Camionero*, Jan. 1970.
32. *El Informador Camionero*, Jan. 1970.

6

The Regional Press Boom, ca. 1945–1965

How Much News Was Fit to Print?

PAUL GILLINGHAM

M exico's regional newspapers have historically been dismissed as unfit to print much news, their comments unfree and their facts unsacred. It is a commonplace that Mexican governments smoothly and comprehensively censored the mid-twentieth-century press and that the relations between the state and journalists constitute a microcosm of state-society relations.[1] In this chapter I argue that the relationship between politicians and print journalists was indeed a microcosm of the period's political system, but one understood not as a perfect dictatorship but rather as a *dictablanda*, a state that combined authoritarian and democratic elements and that exerted tenuous control over markedly autonomous local societies. A long-standing focus on the national media has led scholars to overlook a diverse and profoundly politicized provincial press that, far from being shut down in the PRI's heyday, boomed.[2]

This boom did not come out of nowhere. There was a rich tradition of local newspapers in the second half of the nineteenth century and the early twentieth and a print culture that went far beyond engagingly eccentric almanacs.[3] At the beginning of the Porfiriato there was a robust provincial press, with titles ranging from the weighty—there were several *Regenerators*, a *Son of the Worker*, a *Friend of the People*—to the satirical (Orizaba had a *Reproducer*, Guadalajara enjoyed a *Clown* and a *Fairy*).[4] This press stretched far beyond the main cities: the readers of Isla del Carmen had *La Perla del Golfo*, while Tlacotalpan enjoyed *El Correo del Sotavento*, the forerunner to *El Dictamen*.[5] Over the next fifty years, twenty-seven dailies and sixty-seven weeklies appeared in Veracruz; the market town of San Andrés Tuxtla alone housed six. (Admittedly some were mayflies: the pragmatic burghers of San Andrés were not keen on *El Intransigente*, which ran to all of three editions.)[6] Even some of Mexico's larger villages had their own newspapers: a school-teacher in Tepoztlán published a Nahuatl-language paper, *Xocoyotzin*, in the 1880s.[7] Their autonomy declined during and after the presidency of Manuel González, with the 1882 abolition of press juries and the passage of the press law of 1885. Yet that fall from grace should not be overstated, and even at the height of Porfirian social control the papers read in the provinces were not all anodyne.[8] Assorted scurrilous tabloids endured, occasionally outraging the prim distant nationals.[9] One of Francisco Madero's first political acts was to fund two local papers, one characteristically earnest—*El Demócrata*—and the other (less characteristically) humorous, *El Mosco*.[10] Thus our contemporary assumption that "the state papers . . . have long operated as the propaganda organs of the powerful elites that dominate the political arena and the local private sectors" does not apply to the Porfirian period.[11]

Neither does it apply to the period covered in this chapter, when three phenomena interacted to produce an order-of-magnitude increase in Mexico's regional newspapers. First, these were the decades when the revolutionary governments' intense focus on primary education bore fruit in the form of mass literacy.[12] In 1950, for the first time, a majority of Mexicans were literate. The focus of education secretaries from José Vasconcelos onward on rural schools was clearly revealed in the distribution of those readers: while Mexico City remained by far the most literate part of the country, even the poorest states were averaging approximately 10 percent increases in literacy every decade.[13] Second, the urban middle classes in those states were growing rapidly, and people could spare the twenty or twenty-five centavos for a daily paper. Finally, two key technologies helped a whole new provincial media to emerge: the spread of printing presses, many cheap and second-hand, and the rapidly expanding road system, which eased the perennial problem of distribution.[14]

The takeoff began in the mid-1940s, when at least eight newspapers emerged in Oaxaca alone and some twenty in Veracruz.[15] The boom continued in the 1950s, as the number of newspapers in Mexico increased by over 500 percent. By 1958 there were nearly a thousand news publications in print.[16] Reading a paper had a certain prestige: one federal deputy, who had bucked the trend and remained illiterate, was found in Congress reading a newspaper upside down.[17] Yet habits had changed, making it a far more common practice. In Tepoztlán, for example, Oscar Lewis found a "considerable increase in the reading of newspapers in recent years." By the mid-1940s fifty-six people there bought papers at least twice a week—and not just the Mexico City press, but also *La Pluma*, a weekly from Cuernavaca, and assorted Sinarquista papers.[18] Like many other country folk, *tepoztecos* were not just a new readership, but also a distinctly politicized one.

That regional newspapers ran off—and fueled—political curiosity and engagement was evident from the mastheads down. In Chihuahua, *La Jeringa* billed itself as "independent and combative," with the titillating promise to reveal "the naked truth." Truth was always a central selling point: Tuxtla Gutiérrez's *Faraón* hawked "the truth in fun and earnest," while Uruapán's *La Palabra* was "in the service of the truth to benefit the people," and Acapulco's crusading left-wing paper ("agile, audacious, dynamic") was straightforwardly *La Verdad*. *La Verdad* also billed itself—it was a lengthy masthead—as a public service, a claim that recurred across other papers, that overlapped with the central theme of Mexican nationalism, self-sacrifice, and that was frequently further developed in manifestos and editorials. In southern Veracruz, for example, *Adelante: El Periódico de los Tuxtlas* promised that it would "express with virility this zone's free thinking, with valor, steadfastness, and an unquenchable faith in the grandeur of noble causes."[19] There was a certain macho swagger in such lines, which repeatedly linked truth telling to manliness.[20] The editor of the *Diario de Xalapa*, for example, spent much of August 1948—admittedly a frightening month, as the peso collapsed, generals plotted, and the government tottered—proclaiming his masculinity to readers. On the twelfth he promised that "we will tell the people the truth with total virility," on the eighteenth that he would denounce local profiteers "in a sincere yet virile way," and on the twentieth that his readers had sent him warm congratulations for his "virile and patriotic" reportage.[21] Such pressmen saw themselves quite clearly as a puckish, courageous, and endangered species of that universal necessity, the fourth estate.[22] The extent to which this was realistic was determined by three factors: a newspaper's

Table 1. Illiteracy Rates in Mexico, 1895–1960 (%)

	1895	1940	1950	1960
National	82	58	43	34
Guerrero	92	78	68	59
Veracruz	85	60	51	41
Jalisco	78	48	39	30
Mexico City	55	21	18	13

Source: INEGI, *Estadísticas históricas de México* (2000), CD-ROM.

Table 2. Number of Newspapers Registered with the Secretaría de Gobernación (Ministry of the Interior), 1952–1958.

Year	Number of newspapers
1952	65
1953	179
1954	197
1955	242
1956	277
1957	312
1958	321

Source: González Casanova, *La democracía*, 40.

Table 3. Number of Titles by Type of Periodical as Registered by the Secretaría de Industria y Comercio (Ministry of Industry and Commerce), 1958

Type of periodical	Number of titles
News	955
Literary	159
Entertainment	475
Religious	297
Diverse	954

Source: Ross, "El historiador," 379.

business model, the sociology of its newsroom, and the reactions of the local and, to a lesser extent, national agents of the state.

Newspaper businesses came in all shapes and sizes. At the top were the regional and national chains: the Periódicos Healy chain of the northwest, the Bercun group's Asociación de Periódicos Independientes in the center-north, and above all the Periódicos García Valseca empire. One step down, the owners of more than one newspaper still enjoyed economies of scale. When the Malpica family, owners of *El Dictamen*, set up a small tabloid they could instantly endow it with a wire service, seven reporters, three photographers, a couple of columnists, and a couple of cartoonists.[23] These were the industrial newspapers; at the other end of the market came artisanal papers like Guerrero's *Provincia Libre*, which printed plagiarized stories under fictitious bylines, or *Evolución* of Guanajuato, whose two pages, edited and printed in the same shop for over twenty years, appeared on Thursdays and Sundays, or *Adelante*, a weekly with a staff of two local intellectuals, its four pages peppered with small advertisements from local businesses—Farmacía la Cruz Roja, Vinos Finos Carlos A. Pérez—and appeals for more.[24] Despite the economic chasm separating these businesses, there was the common ground of where income originated, for both industrial and artisanal papers could—though not all did—draw on both formal, on-the-books revenues and the informal, but equally structural backhanders of the *prensa vendida*, the sellout press.

There were four publicly admissible sources of funding for newspapers: sales, advertising, credit, and charitable donations. Sales alone did not cover costs. While claims and estimates of press circulation figures vary greatly, even the nationals seem to have had relatively small sales. In 1961 *Excélsior* supposedly sold 120,000 copies a day; *Siempre!* 54,000 a week; and *Política*, the most aggressively critical of all, 21,000 a week. (The rabidly anticommunist *Selecciones del Reader's Digest*, on the other hand, sold 220,320 per issue.)[25] The papers of the García Valseca chain were the most commercially successful; a 1958 US survey of 300 households in Aguascalientes found over 70 percent of them reading *El Sol*.[26] For the rest it was a different story. In 1949 the *Diario de Xalapa*, a medium-sized paper in a prosperous town, claimed a daily print run of 10,000 copies, which at fifteen centavos a copy would have theoretically given a daily turnover of 1,500 pesos, or 319 daily minimum wages.[27] It is unlikely to have made anything near that; inflated circulation claims were common currency.[28] In a 1960 Interior Ministry sample of twenty-four regional papers from outside the major chains, none had a circulation greater than 5,000; the vast majority of independently owned papers printed fewer than that, although they often claimed substantially more.[29] (While Ben Smith argues for notarized circulation figures as proof of surprisingly high levels of production, the sociology of provincial Mexican notaries makes those figures something less than a gold standard.) There was undoubtedly a political rationale for this inflation, but the economic rationale—intertwined with the political, to be sure—was fundamental: to justify the advertising charges that paid the bills. Advertising took up half of the *Diario de Xalapa*, and local shops and national businesses such as Dos Equis, Goodyear, and Tolteca cement paid between 60 pesos for a quarter page to 200 pesos for a full page.[30] In addition to advertising, regional newspapers also relied heavily on credit, though the state paper monopoly, PIPSA, did not extend much to independent titles. Finally, the more hand-to-mouth papers had a certain charitable aspect about them, launching fundraising drives and happily boasting of popular donations.[31]

Other donations were less transparent, voluntary, or licit. Some papers were straightforwardly subsidized: in 1960 Mazatlán's *El Demócrata Sinaloense* took 400 pesos a month from the state government, while its rival *El Sinaloense* got 300 pesos from the city government.[32] Just about all accepted government funds at one time or another. For politicians, the flip side of paying literally for positive coverage was paying metaphorically for failing to subsidize the press. Pressmen were prone to extortion: it was so expected that entrepreneurial types sometimes passed themselves off as reporters to bilk the great and good.[33] The ensuing payments could be off the books—*chayotes* (squashes), *embutes* (bribes), or *igualas* (fees)—they could be regular subsidies; and they could also be laundered through advertising budgets, as politicians took out generous and frequent adverts. Between 30 and 40 percent of advertising was governmental.[34] Some newspapers were barely euphemized ransom notes. The weekly P. U. A. of Aguascalientes, for example, was not sold publicly, but rather mailed to public and government figures.[35] The visible result of these tense relationships was a periodic swinging between bitter hostility and unconditional support, and the Interior Ministry's secret policemen used such commonplace U-turns as code for venality in their briefs, noting systematically those newspapers that devoted themselves "to

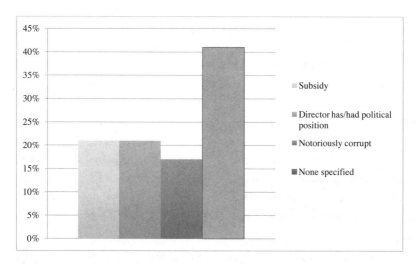

FIGURE 1. Modes of Overt Government Influence over the Regional Press, 1960. An Interior Ministry sample of twenty-four independently owned newspapers in the major cities of twelve states; government selection criteria are unspecified in the document. Source: "Relación de periódicos de las diferentes entidades federativas de la república," June 11, 1960, AGN/DGIPS/1279.

attacking those whom they subsequently adulate." At times they were more blunt: Hermosillo's *El Heraldo* was reputed to be "a blackmailer." Diplomats from the United States concurred: one prominent Sonoran publisher had "frequently been accused of having a tendency toward blackmail."[36] Such reputational extortion was held as central to the entire García Valseca chain.[37]

Since Interior Ministry agents found such cases of interest—a key part of their job was assessing the veracity of reports of provincial dirty work—we in turn enjoy detailed reports of some transactions. In Puebla, for example, the young freelancer Juan José Mayoral Repinho (a dropout from the Universidad Nacional Autónoma de México law school who wore green spectacles and was "pretty nervous") attacked the governor under compelling headlines ("Vice and Depravity Fostered in Puebla: Brothels and Cantinas in the Hands of [Governor] Moreno Valle's Cronies").[38] According to an agent, Mayoral's civic passion originated more in his own interest than in that of the public: the governor had denied him cash to found his own newspaper, after which the attacks had started on both the state and municipal administrations. They were confined, however, to tabloids and scandal rags, as "serious papers" refused to work with him due to his long-standing habit of "pursu[ing] people or functionaries who make mistakes, to obtain from them payoffs in exchange for positive coverage; otherwise . . . uncovering negative or difficult points that might damage the aforementioned functionaries in their posts."[39] Morally reprehensible, it clearly worked to inform the public, since the agent twice confirmed Mayoral's scandalmongering. The quick shifts of editorial line that indicated political bribes suggest that extortion functioned more to conceal than to reveal; that regional figures could be extorted at all, of course, suggests a certain revealing weakness in the face of the press.

As Mayoral's potted biography indicates, there was real diversity in the ranks of the pressmen of the time. The editor of *Todo*, one of the largest magazines, was a secret policeman; the editor of Baja California's *La Centinela* was—according to a different secret policeman—a convicted "pederast and a murderer."[40] Editors and journalists were often local intellectuals, such as *cronistas del pueblo* (those ubiquitous and influential town chroniclers), schoolmasters, or popular activists. Such categories often overlapped: Vicente Ramírez Sandoval of Ometepec was a schoolteacher, a communist, and a correspondent for *La Verdad de Acapulco*.[41] Revolutionary social mobility moreover meant that some of those local intellectuals, particularly in the early years, had started off in peasant or poor urban families: León Medel in San Andrés Tuxtla, who went from cane cutter through three years of primary school to the 1911 Congress and then on to decades as a regional journalist and cronista, was a striking example.[42] Some were geographically mobile, moving from state to state and paper to paper: Arturo Soleto Canett, editor of La Paz's *Últimas Noticias*, came to the state in the mid-1940s to set up the paper.[43] Other editors were businessmen on a larger scale: *La Voz de León* was owned by scions of the regional shoemaking industry, *Excélsior*'s man in northern Guerrero was a major landholder, and *Novedades*'s Acapulco correspondent was a Spanish hotelier.[44] They could be party men, such as *El Monitor* of Hermosillo's editor, Alfonso Aldama, "an old politician who [had] been part of several state governments," or they could become them through their work, as did Jesús Tapía Avilés, publisher of the Cadena Periodística del Noroeste, who became head of Sonora's peasant confederation.[45]

They could be a mixture: Vicente Villasana, the ill-fated editor of *El Mundo*, was also an entrepreneur who owned eight or nine cinemas in the Tampico area and a politician (he ran for the senate as a candidate of the Partido Acción Nacional).[46] Even soldiers made their way into newsrooms: in 1945 the grand old lady of regional journalism, *El Dictamen* of Veracruz, was invaded by the zone commander, who dispatched a man identified only as Captain Barrazas to the newsroom "to look after [the general's] interests."[47]

The papers' coverage reflects that diversity. At one supine extreme there were at least sixteen papers called *Orientación* between 1940 and 1952, which guided their readers toward fuller appreciation of the efforts of politicians, bureaucrats, peasant leaders, and union bosses on their behalf. At the other there was an opposition far more real than that of the national press. In a comparative analysis of metropolitan and regional papers stretching from 1951 to 1980, Louise Montgomery finds the regional press "dramatically more critical than the metropolitan newspapers," even *Excélsior* in its post-1968 incarnation (which was significantly less combative than generally appreciated, particularly in its coverage of student movements and the Dirty War).[48] Some 50 percent of the provincial papers sampled by the Interior Ministry in 1960 were not reliably officialist, and over 50 percent of articles on the president and his cabinet published by Guadalajara's *El Informador* in the '50s, '60s, and '70s were critical. This was a much more hostile press than that of the contemporary United States, where one study classed a mere 11 percent of articles on public figures as critical.[49]

The viability of such criticism was conditioned by the reactions of the state. Elites' first recourse was the off-the-books funding discussed above: in typical *priista* fashion local and state officials generally chose co-option before coercion. When co-option failed, they turned to economic pressure: pulling advertising (both governmental and private), cutting off newsprint from the state supplier PIPSA, and finally encouraging printers' unions to demand higher wages or strike. These tactics were often combined with violence. The editor of San Luis Potosí's *La Tribuna* was arrested and his presses smashed by soldiers before a printers' strike and a block on his PIPSA credit administered the *coup de grâce*; the governor of Tamaulipas fathered a strike against *El Mundo* and then induced the Confederation of Mexican Workers to back it up by stoning the offices and the home of the editor.[50] When that didn't work, the state police commander killed him.[51] Such violence provided

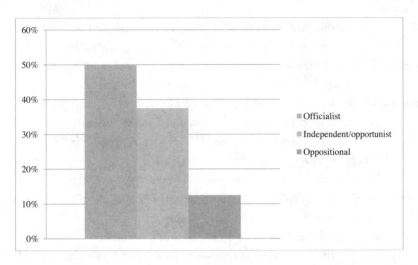

FIGURE 2. Perceived Political Positioning of Provincial Newspapers, 1960. An Interior Ministry sample of twenty-four independently owned newspapers in the major cities of twelve states; government selection criteria are unspecified in the document. Source: "Relación de periódicos de las diferentes entidades federativas de la república," June 11, 1960, AGN/DGIPS/1279.

the state with the ultimate veto on press content. Yet outright murder was a rarity, a minor subset of the three types of violence that rent-a-mobs, policemen, soldiers, and *pistoleros* exerted against journalists, namely virtual violence, material violence, and physical violence.

Virtual violence—threats—played on the violent imaginaries formed by physical violence, on journalists' often intimate knowledge of arrests or beatings and their usually more distant knowledge of murder. Reporters who delved into the murky world of municipal accounting were regularly threatened with death. When *La Voz de Sinaloa* revealed that the mayor of Culiacán was awarding himself municipal construction contracts, the editor was told to his face that "his days were numbered."[52] Material violence was more like work for its perpetrators—after all, something had to be done about it— but it was probably more effective given the shoestring budgets of provincial papers. Distribution was easily dented by chasing off the *voceadores* (sellers) whose loud mouths were critical to a newspaper's success.[53] Entire editions of newspapers could be seized.[54] More permanent damage was done by breaking the printing presses. In the summer of 1945, for example, agents of the Sinaloa and Tamaulipas state governments destroyed the presses of *El Nacional de Culiacán* and *El Mañana de Nuevo Laredo*.[55] When the threats and warning signals of material violence failed to achieve their goals, politicians resorted to physical violence: jailings, beatings, and shootings. Some journalists narrowly escaped with their lives: one editor eluded the credulous gunmen sent to kill him by claiming that he was actually his own brother.[56] Others did not: at least nineteen journalists were murdered between 1940 and 1960. Violent incidents correlated with stress points—the devaluation crisis of 1948, the antigraft campaign of 1955, the rail workers' strike of 1959— and in absolute terms rose between 1940 and 1960.[57] Relative to the numbers of either papers, pressmen, or the general population, however, state violence against the press declined appreciably in the period, reflecting the broader stabilization of the dictablanda.[58]

Operating within these constraints were three types of publication: government papers, chain newspapers, and single-owner papers, the latter a capacious category that encompassed everything from well-funded broadsheets to penurious newsletters, satirical weeklies, scandal rags, and pamphlets.

The surge in the provincial government press dates to the second half of the 1940s, when it became de rigueur for state administrations across Mexico to have their own newspapers.[59] These were directly government-sponsored, down to the purchase of equipment: the government of Guerrero, for example, spent 40,000 pesos on an electric Miller press and linotype with which to print its daily. (As in other states, officials did not publicize the link, promoting instead the equipment's use for reprinting the state constitution.)[60] These papers were also sponsored in terms of news, getting wire agency access as well as some key scoops—such as the favored candidate for the governorship—ahead of their rivals.[61] Politicians saw them as key tools (perhaps for impressing Mexico City more than their constituents); the Sonoran administration set up one in the late 1950s and a second in 1963.[62] Some were predictably scorned. *El Diario de Puebla*'s editor had been a local priista since the time of Maximino Ávila Camacho, rising through the ranks to seats in both state and federal congresses; people from Puebla, the Interior Ministry reported, gave his paper "short shrift" despite its large print run.[63] Other government newspapers were less predictable, reflecting perhaps the enforced political diversity of some state administrations or perhaps just the complexity of press-state relations in the period. Despite complete state ownership, Mérida's *Diario del Sureste* was "rather leftist," the US consul observed, and gave ample publicity to the cultural programing of the Cuban consulate.[64] *El Mexicano* of Baja California actually opposed government policy in the fraught elections of 1965. An agent there fretted that the "vague hope based on Licenciado [Carlos] Madrazo's declarations [of internal democracy] while mistrust endures makes it critical to control the press, so they can duly orient public opinion"; yet despite this "*El Mexicano*, which is federal government property and which nevertheless acts like a private enterprise, [is] being used to further the campaign of one of the pre-candidates [by] making them look 'anointed from on high.'"[65] From a reader's point of view government papers were intrinsically unreliable. Yet they were neither universally biddable nor anodyne.

Neither were the major newspaper chains. Colonel José García Valseca's press empire, founded on the back of a close relationship with Maximino Ávila Camacho and two of the extremely lucrative comics of the 1930s, comprised twenty-seven dailies by the mid-1950s; the Healy chain spread out of Sonora across the northwest; the Bercun chain had titles in Aguascalientes, San Luis Potosí, León, Irapuato, Querétaro, and Guanajuato.[66] (Assorted smaller associations and groupings emerged across the period, such as the three papers published by El Mundo Compañía Editorial, and the Pomposa Salazar bloc of Sonoran newspapers.)[67] The García Valseca newspapers enjoyed copious credit, high-level patronage, and impressive circulations. When the group was preparing to launch *El Sol de Guadalajara* in 1947, it bought a Goss cylindrical press that could print 25,000 papers an hour, 200,000 pesos of newsprint, two radio masts, a photogravure workshop, and a backup generator.[68] By 1954 its local titles sold 50,000 a day in Guadalajara, 21,000 a day in Chihuahua, and 30,000 a day in Ciudad Juárez.[69] The García Valseca journalists were fundamentally state allies: pro-government, anti-communist, respectful of national political boundaries. Yet their very favor, size, and collective sway simultaneously gave them real leverage over provincial politicians, which was commonly believed to be one of the financial guarantees of the García Valseca empire. Diplomats noted the curious rhythms of voluble support for state administrations following immediately in the wake of "bitter attacks" on municipal corruption.[70] In 1963 it was the

Healy newspapers that housed "the most avid critics of personalities in the [Sonoran] State Administration."[71] Chains did not invariably translate their links to the top levels of politics into support for politicians further down.

Finally, there were the single-owner publications of the "independent press," which constituted a large majority of the provincial papers and which covered a broad range of formats, frequencies, capacities, styles, and political opinions. By the 1950s most major cities had at least two broadsheet dailies, sometimes ordered in right-left dyads (*El Regional* and *La Voz de la Frontera* in Matamoros, *El Diario de Yucatán* and *El Diario del Sureste* in Mérida). Monterrey had four.[72] It would be a simplistic error, however, to assume that a single owner implied either independence or investigative zeal. Corruption among reporters was universal, structural in fact, and political blandness the default reporting position irrespective of business model. Of twelve regional newspapers reviewed by the US consul in Mazatlán in 1954, eight, he judged, had "no clearly defined political policy."[73] On the other side of the country the US consul in Matamoros judged that the press did "not wield much influence as none of the papers has a platform, the honesty and accuracy of the reporting is often suspect, neither the editors nor staff members can lay any claim to better than average intelligence, and poor financing cuts down on the caliber of the services rendered."[74] However this was slightly harsh, even by his own subsequent account; not all provincial papers, not even the ones listed, were toothless. The many less reputable, less frequently circulating, and less costly papers could be systematically provocative: *El Yucatanista* was "anti-government, anti-American and anti-commie," while in Ciudad Juárez *El Alacrán*'s "prime aim [was] to goad local officialdom."[75] Some dailies did likewise. *La Tribuna* of San Luis Potosí "gave a thoughtful presentation of public problems and was unceasing in its exposure of malfeasance in local government." It did them little good; the paper was closed down after a "brief and troubled two years' existence."[76] Yet others endured against the odds, such as *La Voz de la Frontera*, which focused on local news, eschewed the cost (and distraction) of a wire service, pirated whatever it felt like, and was "famed for its inaccuracy, apparent immunity to libel suits, and fearlessness."[77]

For a better look at the limits of the possible in provincial reporting, I have chosen three single-owner newspapers for a closer reading: the *Diario de Xalapa*, Guadalajara's *El Informador*, and *La Verdad de Acapulco*, selected for their range in location, size, and ideology.[78] *Diario de Xalapa* was for obvious reasons well positioned to garner political gossip for Veracruz and, with two *veracruzano* presidencies in succession, farther afield. It was midsized, comprising four pages with a claimed circulation of 10,000 in 1949, and middle-of-the-road, the most conformist of the three. The editor, Rubén Pabello Acosta, became something of a deacon of local journalists; much of his coverage was resolutely officialist, and in 1950 he was made state congressman for Misantla.[79] In 1953 he became the municipal president of Xalapa.[80] His newspaper followed a revealing parallel trajectory. It was founded in 1943, when Veracruz under Governor Jorge Cerdán was a failed state, and was at first poorly funded, with a wonky, wild-west font and happy typos (when a tailor—*un sastre*—committed murder, the headline accused Sartre).[81] This early, amateurish *Diario de Xalapa* was distinctly confrontational, tackling municipal corruption, election rigging, and regional politicians' implication in the murderous pistolerismo of the time; in 1945 it printed an open letter to the governor protesting attempted censorship.[82] The paper was increasingly tamed under the Alemán presidency, and in 1948 dropped much local reporting in favor of international wire agency news, with particular enthusiasm for the latest triumphs of British engineering (a classic means of soft censorship, as Colombian colonels knew).[83] The shift was noted and regretted by readers, and the paper published a front-page denial that it was turning away from local news.[84] This was untrue. Pabello Acosta kept, however, a taste for occasional reports on Veracruz faction fighting and corruption, for editorials that leveled systemic if unspecific political criticism, and for the sly asides, rumors, and allusive juxtapositions that comprised so much of controversial journalism in the provinces.

El Informador was quite different, one of the oldest newspapers in the provinces and one of the largest in Mexico. While its circulation was "a closely guarded secret" (it may have been as low as 12,000 in 1950), *El Informador* was the most influential newspaper in Jalisco, Colima, Nayarit, and Aguascalientes, and it was also widely read in the towns of adjacent states and along the northwestern coast.[85] Like the other two papers under consideration here, its editor across the midcentury was its founder, in this case Jesús Alvarez del Castillo, who ran the newsroom from 1917 until his death in 1966. Alvarez del Castillo was a dynasty builder who studied chemistry and accounting in California and France and who flirted with revolutionary

FIGURE 3. Front page of
the *Diario de Xalapa*,
Dec. 24, 1947.

politics (he was an also-ran for governor in 1920) and business (he ran a shoe factory) before settling on journalism.[86] His paper's editorial policy seems from the start to have been "uncompromisingly independent"; at different points in the 1930s it was proscribed by both the archbishop and the Confederación de Trabajadores de México (despite consisting largely of advertising).[87] A bitter strike in 1937–1938 made the Alvarez del Castillo family more politically cautious, while competition from a second independent broadsheet in 1942 pushed them to increase the amount of reportage. As a consequence by the late 1940s both the paper's business and its identity were firmly established: prosperous, technically advanced—two Goss cylindrical presses capable of producing 75,000 newspapers an hour, teletype, radiotelegraph, newsfeeds from Reuters, AP, UPI, and US syndicates—and broadly conservative. Editorial policy was to treat proven dangerous opponents, such as

EL INFORMADOR

DIARIO INDEPENDIENTE

MIEMBRO DE LA PRENSA ASOCIADA. · MIEMBRO DE LA UNITED PRESS.

AÑO XXXVIII — TOMO CXLIII · VALE VEINTICINCO CENTAVOS · GUADALAJARA, JAL., LUNES 4 DE JULIO DE 1955 · NUMERO 13,519

En General fue Pacífica la Votación y Hubo Calma

HAY CLAROS INDICIOS DE QUE BORLENGHI HUYO DE ARGENTINA

Prepara Rusia el Terreno

La Mujer dio la Nota de Alto Civismo en México

VARIADA Y RICA ES LA AGRICULTURA MEXICANA

Se Manejó con Orden y Compostura

Impresionante Exhibición de Aviones Soviéticos

Ningún Incidente Importante se Registró el día de Ayer

Contacto con Todo el País

Hubo más Votantes Mujeres que Hombres en el Pto. de Veracruz

Indiferencia en Zamora, Mich.

Los Primeros Resultados

El Voto de Ruiz Cortines

Hubo Chicanas en Torreón

No Hubo Desorden Alguno en Todo el Estado de Jalisco

178o. Aniversario de la Independencia de Estados Unidos

Pocos Actos de Violencia

La mujer votó por primera vez en todo el país, para elegir diputados federales

En Deplorable Abandono

Mucho Influyó el Voto de la Mujer en las Elecciones

Inauguración de una Carretera

Declaraciones de los Partidos

Salió de Manera Irregular

HOY 18 PAGINAS

FIGURE 4. Front page of *El Informador*, July 4, 1955.

labor or the church, "with a meticulous regard for accuracy and impartiality," and to avoid controversy whenever possible, preferring "coolness" or "an absolute minimum of sympathy" to confrontation. (Just in case, though, the paper kept a stockpile of two months of newsprint.) It enjoyed, the US consul wrote, "something of the semi-official status accorded newspapers such as the London *Times*."[88]

The third paper, *La Verdad de Acapulco*, did not enjoy semiofficial status or very much status at all, at least in the consul's sense. It was again largely the product of one man, in this case Ignacio de la Hoya, who from 1946 onward produced four pages daily—except when he was sick—from an office cum printer's shop in a rented apartment in downtown Acapulco.[89] De la Hoya was a nomad: he came from the north, set up his base in Acapulco, but also founded *El Diario de Morelos* and was briefly listed as director of Zacatecas's *La Hora*. He was, suitably enough for an admirer of Jean-Paul Sartre (whose writings on Cuba he published), distinctly engagé: cofounder and president of the Unión Inquilinaria de Acapulco (Acapulco Tenants Union), a leader—under the nickname "the Preacher"—of squatters' land invasions, a close ally of long-standing *guerrerense* radicals such as María de la O and Alfredo López Cisneros (whom he also published), and a recruit to causes ranging from Soviet scholarships to protests against the US president's visit.[90]

De la Hoya was not incorruptible: he was reported to have taken money from the gubernatorial campaign of Caballero Aburto and from the Acapulco town council of Canuto Nogueda Radilla, and he occasionally ran advertisements from government organizations and logging companies.[91] He was, however, aggressively and lastingly critical, dedicating the bulk of his paper to frontal attacks on the city and state powers over subjects as varied as corruption (both petty and grand), election rigging, political assassination, and the misappropriation of common goods ranging from river lands to public laundries. His was a highly readable, tabloid radicalism, epitomized in headlines such as "Grafter Taxman Goes to Jail," "[Town Councillor]—Hopeless Drunk with Don Juanesque Inclinations—Staggers Off to Jail Accused of Statutory Rape," "Utter Swinishness in the Construction of the Town Square," and "PRI Candidate Accused of 10 Murders." "Is there no one," one article demanded rhetorically, "who will cut these rapacious bureaucrats' nails?"[92] De la Hoya claimed to have trimmed some in his career.[93] In return he suffered almost the entire spectrum of repression. In

1947 the municipal president of Petatlán tried to kill one of his reporters; in 1949 de la Hoya was told that people had been trying to take out a contract on his life.[94] In 1956 he was arrested and badly beaten by the police; in 1958 he was shot in his office; in 1960 gunmen broke the press; in 1962 his workers launched a labor dispute against him, and five federal agents kidnapped him, beat him, and abandoned him in the hills; in 1969 he was arrested once more, tortured, threatened with deportation to Nicaragua, and finally released half-mad. He never recovered.[95]

These were self-evidently three very different publications. Moreover, we do not have complete print runs for the period. *El Informador*'s archive is complete; when research was conducted, that of the *Diario de Xalapa* ended in the early 1950s; that of *La Verdad* comprised all of ten months' worth of copies from 1949. These caveats noted, a generalizing, broadly synchronic analysis is possible, since samples of stress points—elections, regional and national crises—demonstrate that *El Informador*'s editorial policy was essentially constant across the period; and the same can be inferred for *La Verdad*, as we have assorted references to that paper's enduringly provocative coverage from other sources, such as the Dirección Federal de Seguridad.[96] The *Diario de Xalapa*, in short, was the only one to demonstrate a marked progression toward greater press curbs. And while both style and intensity varied greatly, all three papers reported meaningfully on national politics, provincial politics, and social questions, with particular emphasis on crime, violence, and poverty. Readers knew that a minimum of one column in every paper—"Palpitaciones" in the *Diario de Xalapa*, "Comentarios al Día" and "Charlas de Sobremesa" in *El Informador*, the lead story in *La Verdad*—would be critical.[97]

Coverage of national politics was generally columnists' domain, with their criticism tending to the systemic rather than the individualized. There were, to be sure, exceptions during crises. In August 1948 the *Diario de Xalapa* called for the resignations of the secretaries of the treasury, national economy, public education, water, and communication and public works; one year later *La Verdad* demanded the heads of the secretaries of the treasury, health, and social services and the director of the Banco de México.[98] Journalists also broke the taboo on criticizing the army. The *Diario de Xalapa* slyly attributed political killings to "people dressed as soldiers," perhaps cowed by a visit from "a commission" of officers after the paper accused the

FIGURE 5. Front page of *La Verdad*, Jan. 4, 1949.

army of kidnapping local youths for conscripts.[99] *La Verdad* was more straightforward, mining the rich vein of material offered by petty counter-insurgency along Guerrero's coasts for stories on murdered peasants, invaded ejidos, protection rackets, arms dealing, and the serial human rights abuses overseen by named officers, such as General Miguel Z. Martínez, the well-connected zone commander, or Jesús Monroy, Ometepec's reserves commander, or General Piza Martínez of Tecpan, described in one headline as "a little Führer."[100] It was not the only paper to chance military hostility: in 1963 both *El Sol* and *El Mundo* attacked the army's invasions of peasant small-holdings to secure land for a veterans' colony.[101]

The most striking criticism, however, came in all three papers' periodic and devastating condemnations of the political system as a whole, and elections in particular. Both *El Informador* and the *Diario de Xalapa* adopted what seems to have been a common strategy of juxtaposing officialist reportage on the front page with editorial radicalism.[102] *El Informador* went one better, punctuating the party line with barbed asides and poker-faced observations, often at the very end of reports, in what might be called "structural slyness." Its coverage of one of the PRI's greatest crises, the putsch against party president Carlos Madrazo, reproduced priistas' copious bland quotes (under an impeccably boring headline) before ending on page six with the Central Campesina Independiente's reaction, which deemed the event "a grave setback for the democratization of the party and Mexico," yet one foreseeable in a party "that wants to keep peasants downtrodden."[103] In covering the July 1955 elections the banner headline read "Voting in General Was Peaceful and There Was Calm." Below, interspersed with eulogies to the day's success, minor seemingly factual follow-up stories might cause attentive readers to wonder why "reports from the states indicated that the turnout was heavy, despite the apparent disinterest in the campaign"; why it should be a "miracle" that women, voting for the first time, achieved "clean and impartial elections"; why there was a separate report on the military presence in Mexico City, including a reinforced guard on the Palacio Nacional; or why a one-line article at the bottom of the page, headlined "The Parties' Declarations," should read, "The competing parties in today's elections have issued statements concerning the results, and naturally all claim to have won." Inside there was less to wonder about. The main editorial, "Sufragio efectivo y no reelección" (A real vote and no reelection), concluded that Mexico was a "directed democracy, which is the negation of democracy"; below, "Charlas de Sobremesa" pointed out that warning about the election's probity was like rediscovering the Mediterranean; next door, "Comentarios al Día" rammed home that this was the fault of the PRI, which had taught Mexicans about "chicanery, forced votes, urns with false bottoms, and the votes of the dead in place of electoral contests, with all of which [the party] ensured itself victories in the elections, which have made it invincible. [These are] lessons that the public employees and the entire people pay for heavily, so that a few can reach electoral appointments under the façade of having won them in democratic elections."[104]

Tracing specific national politicians through such philippics was like reading a roman à clef. Yet if Mexico City's great and good were generally protected species, state and municipal politicians were, in contrast, fair game for stories regarding their corruption, abuse of power, election rigging, and violent crime. Amid the *Diario de Xalapa*'s officialist hyperbole in July–August 1948—the "brilliant work" of Deputy Topete, the "magnificent initiative of Deputy Arriola Molina," the "brilliant work" of Deputy Ochoa y

Ochoa—there came the news of the mass arrest of fourteen municipal presidents for misappropriation of federal taxes and a protest against the abuses of power of the governors of Aguascalientes and Durango.[105] *El Informador* was reliably austere with egregious offenders at all levels of the Jalisco hierarchy; *La Verdad* was (often ironically) furious with everyone from the zone commander and the governor down to Jesús "El Pichón" Sánchez, a Petatlán politician who got drunk on mezcal, refused to settle his tab, and then ran to the army barracks begging for protection.[106] When an attempt was made on the editor's life in 1958, he enumerated the twelve stories that he believed had provoked the failed murderers, which included more than a thousand extrajudicial killings, the murky privatization of Acapulco's town hall and market, protection rackets by members of the governor's entourage, the disappearance of federal emergency relief funds for earthquake victims, tax farming, and the extraordinary number of relatives of the governor who had received leading government appointments.[107]

Though relatively exceptional in its intensity and constancy, *La Verdad* was far from the only provincial paper to inveigh against leading state politicians. All three of Poza Rica's papers—*La Tarde, El Porvenir,* and *El Diario*—formed a common front in October 1959 against the PEMEX (Mexican Petroleum Company) cacique Jaime Merino and his tame city government.[108] *El Diario de Michoacán* published a full-page open letter to the governor recommending that his government focus on development rather than peculation; the Saltillo press described Madero's governorship in Coahuila as "the error that was six years long"; one "middle of the road" newspaper deemed state governors in general to be "unbelievable cretins."[109] The last verdict came, admittedly, in extraordinary circumstances, after the December 30, 1960, massacre in Chilpancingo of fifteen people who were demonstrating against the incumbent governor.[110]

Lesser acts of violence, however, were also regularly reported. Stories of criminal violence often constituted, as in the Mexico City *nota roja* (crime pages), an indirect political as well as social commentary.[111] The *Diario de Xalapa*'s five-year campaign against Veracruz's endemic pistolerismo of the 1940s was generally phrased in straightforwardly criminal terms, but with enough references to the political links of the leading gunmen as to leave readers in no doubt regarding the political implications of their violence.[112] Crispín Aguilar, it was noted, was part of the agribusiness elite; Rafael

Armenta had provided a rent-a-mob of 5,000 for the Adolfo Ruiz Cortines campaign stop.[113] *La Verdad* likewise carried dense reporting of regional violence, but with the political content emphasized. Provincial papers, whether by accident or design, also carried more details about nationally sensitive violence than their metropolitan counterparts: the Mexico City coverage of the 1947 Balsas rebellion, for example, was minimal and misleading, while one of the biggest stories of the Alemán years—the nationwide rumors regarding an assassination attempt on the president in August 1948—went almost wholly unreported by the nationals. In the first case, Iguala's *El Suriano* gave the nearby rebellion detailed if speculative coverage, while in the second the *Diario de Xalapa* broke the press silence surrounding the alleged attack.[114] Military violence went underreported; violence against the press, on the other hand, ranging from raids on printing shops to out-and-out murder, was covered with detail and outrage across a wide spectrum of papers.[115]

Such collective self-defense—now decayed—was one of the reasons that the provincial press could exercise a certain qualified liberty.[116] The other was a systematic use of satire for criticism, a national tradition that stretched back to independence.[117] It was in the main a Horatian mockery that was gentle in tone while powerful in implication. The Día de Muertos (Day of the Dead), for example, was used to poke fun at figures ranging from the anonymous "Licenciado venal o ramplón / que vende sus decisiones" ("no vengo a darle razones / sino a llevarlo al panteón") to dangerous characters such as Crispín Aguilar.[118] In the midst of a deadly serious report on the transfer of municipal power in Iguala, rife with possibilities for severe violence, *La Verdad* reported how behind the machine guns and bayonets the new town council was getting drunk on cider, while the incoming mayor lamented winning.[119] De la Hoya called Guerrero's political factions the Frente Único de Lambiscones.[120] Other satire was Juvenalian, bitter, and vituperous, yet it too seemed to draw on the tolerance of the carnival or the court jester. As "Palpitaciones" put it on October 12, 1947, "Today the Día de la Raza will be celebrated, the day of this poor race so mistreated, so full of wounds, undernourished, beaten down with problems and on the verge of desperation. But its day will be celebrated!"[121] While satire retreated in the nationals after the 1948 crisis, it endured—along with the rest of the critical apparatus—in the nationally invisible inside pages of the regional press.

Given the secular history of the press in Mexico, and given what we now know of the often feeble nature of the state outside the capital, finding the qualified press explored above is no surprise. The surprise would rather be if provincial reporters were universally docile, iterations of men like Jesús M. Lozano, also known as "the Idiot" ("and you can bet he was one," wrote the local historian), who donned a uniform to pick up his payoff from Acapulco's police.[122] The articles drawn on in this chapter have often come at stress points, and one of the papers used as a case study was unusually radical. Yet anyone who reviews consular or intelligence reports from the period will not have to go far to find parallels. The booming regional print press of the mid-twentieth century was significantly more critical than the national press in relative terms in its targeting of provincial executives, deputies, bureaucrats, policemen, and soldiers, and in absolute terms in its occasionally cutting-edge treatment of national events. Regional papers from across the political spectrum covered corruption, political scandals, election rigging, malfeasance, sexual misdemeanors, extortion, and violence. Their writers were co-opted; they were also repressed by virtual, material, and physical violence. In extreme cases they were murdered. It is eloquent, however, that this was a clear breach of the unwritten rules of the dictablanda and that the politicians held responsible, including governors, risked losing their jobs. The contrast with our time is self-evident.

Acknowledgments

I thank Marcel Anduiza Pimentel, Sofia Rada Zubalieta, Ben Smith, and Jules Ottino-Loffler for their kind assistance in providing documents.

Notes

1. González Casanova, *La democracia*. One argument for this smooth control is based on comparing the inefficient press control of the Porfiriato. In two months of 1893, twenty Mexico City journalists were jailed; Filomeno Mata went to Belén Penitentiary thirty times; Inocencio Arriola went one better by losing count. Cosío Villegas, *El Porfiriato*, 1:563, 557; Knight, *Mexican Revolution*, 1:39.
2. An exception is Petra Secanella, for whom the "brave critical work" of provincial newspapers makes them "essential" to any interpretation of Mexican politics (cited in Garza Ramos, this volume). For other undervalued political

media, including crime pages, sports papers, and the rough-and-ready pamphlets and tabloids produced by factories and independent unions, see Piccato, "Murders"; Gillingham, "Maximino's Bulls"; Bringas and Mascareño, *Esbozo histórico*, 147–48. For the sparse historiography on the regional press, see Covo, "La prensa," 695; Del Palacio Montiel, *Siete regiones* and *Rompecabezas de papel*; Ríos Zúñiga, "Contención del movimiento" and "Una retórica para la movilización popular."

3. While numerous small, short-lived papers appeared beforehand, a sophisticated mass market press only emerged during the Restored Republic. Forment, *Democracy*, 192–200; Palti, "La Sociedad Filarmónica del Pito."

4. Although Guadalajara's *El Duende* was probably meant in the sense of soul/spirit rather than supernatural camp. Frutos, "Prensa lozana," 116–17.

5. Valencia Ríos, *Historia de El Dictamen*, 11–16; Frutos, "Prensa lozana," 116.

6. Medel y Alvarado, *Historia de San Andrés*, 2:18–19.

7. Lewis, *Life in a Mexican Village*, xxv.

8. Piccato, *Tyranny of Opinion*, 47–48. There was, as even Cosío Villegas notes, a continual rumble of criticism from both liberal and conservative editors. Cosío Villegas, *El Porfiriato*, 2:525–27.

9. Such papers were, Forment judges, "embedded in and constitutive of democratic life." Forment, *Democracy*, xviii.

10. Krauze, *Mexico*, 249.

11. Doyle, *Investigative Journalism*, 2.

12. Even in the penurious early 1920s, Álvaro Obregón encouraged José Vasconcelos to apply for a large education budget, and in 1920 Congress passed one larger than actually requested; the 1923 education allotment, at 17 percent of the total budget, went unsurpassed until 1953. Vasconcelos, *El desastre*, 1228, 1321; INEGI, *Estadísticas históricas de México* (2000), CD-ROM.

13. Census data in INEGI, *Estadísticas históricas*.

14. The radical *La Verdad de Acapulco*, for example, was produced on printing machines bought as scrap. See http://periodistasdeacapulco.blogspot.com/2009/02/breve-cronologia-del-periodismo-de.html (accessed Sept. 4, 2017). Meanwhile, the Miguel Alemán administration invested 2.3 billion pesos in road construction, fundamentally changing provincial life; highways aside, networks of feeder and local roads doubled between 1945 and 1955. INEGI, *Estadísticas históricas*.

15. Smith, *Pistoleros and Popular Movements*, 345–46; catalog of the Hemeroteca Nacional de México, http://www.unamenlinea.unam.mx/recurso/hemeroteca-nacional-digital-de-mexico (accessed Nov. 30, 2017). This expansion went across media and borders: in these years the first Spanish-language radio station appeared in Tucson, Arizona. Cadava, *Standing on Common Ground*, 52.

16. It is worth noting the disparity between the number of newspapers that existed according to the Ministry of Industry and Commerce and the (significantly

lower) number registered with the Ministry of the Interior. González Casanova, *Democracy in Mexico*, 40; Ross, "El historiador," 379.

17. Author interview, Vicente Ramírez Sandoval, Ometepec, Mar. 9, 2002.

18. Lewis, *Life in a Mexican Village*, 34.

19. *Adelante*, Dec. 2, 1945.

20. The public sphere is traditionally seen as a "male" space. Landes, *Women and the Public Sphere*.

21. *Diario de Xalapa*, Aug. 12, 18, and 20, 1948.

22. Several papers actually called themselves "el cuarto poder," and the reporter Roberto Blanco Moheno used it as the title of his satirical play attacking corruption. Blanco Moheno, *Memorias*, 294–95. Journalists' concern for reputation, honor, and *hombría* (manliness) is a constant across the history of the Mexican press, from the "combat journalists" of the Porfiriato—and their opponents, such as Justo Sierra, who claimed that he used *La Voz de México* for wiping his bottom—to *columnistas* such as Manuel Buendía, who asked one critic whether he was "man enough" to face him. Piccato, *Tyranny of Opinion*, 63–95; Dumas and Vega, "El discurso de oposición," 246; Freije, "Exposing Scandals"; Smith, *The Mexican Press and Civil Society*, ch. 5

23. Valencia Ríos, *Historia de El Dictamen*, 136, 139.

24. Media historians such as John Nerone portray artisanal papers as easy victims of the industrial press, which can outcompete them with technology and division of labor. As Mexico makes clear, however, the two modes of production can coexist for some time. Nerone, *The Media*. The examples are drawn from author interviews, Hermilo Castorena Noriega, Chilpancingo, Nov. 18, 1997, and Adalberto Toto Linares, San Andrés Tuxtla, Dec. 28, 2002; "Relación de periódicos de las diferentes entidades federativas," June 11, 1960, AGN/DGIPS/1279.

25. Piccato, "Murders"; González Casanova, *La democracía*, table 13.

26. International Research Associates, "A Study of Newspaper Readership in Aguascalientes and Reader Attitudes toward 'Suplemento Semanal,'" June–July 1958, NARA/RG306/IRI Mex 17.

27. *Diario de Xalapa*, Nov. 2, 1949; INEGI, *Estadísticas históricas*.

28. Covo, "La prensa," 698.

29. Although in 1950 *El Sol de Guadalajara* claimed to sell 32,000 copies per day, the US consul estimated 12,000 to be the real figure. "Relación de periódicos de las diferentes entidades federativas"; T. J. Hohenthal, Guadalajara, to State Department, June 26, 1950, NARA/RG59/912.61/6-2650.

30. *Diario de Xalapa*, Dec. 17, 1947.

31. *La Verdad*, Jan. 27, 1949, was happy to report an anonymous donation of 200 pesos.

32. "Relación de periódicos de las diferentes entidades federativas."

33. *Diario de Xalapa*, Sept. 7, 1949.

34. Montgomery, "Stress on Government," 7.
35. "Relación de periódicos de las diferentes entidades federativas."
36. "Relación de periódicos de las diferentes entidades federativas"; US consul, Nogales, to State Department, Feb. 9, 1954, NARA/RG59/912.61/2-454.
37. Monsiváis, *A ustedes*.
38. "Información de Puebla," Sept. 12, 1969, AGN/DGIPS/1461A; *Prensa Americana Continental*, Aug. 15, 1969.
39. "Información de Puebla."
40. *Todo* claimed a circulation of 20,000 in the 1940s. Personnel files, AGN/DGIPS/80/1, 2, IPS-7; Agent IPS-7 to Gobernación, Oct. 31, 1955, AGN/DGIPS/2014B; Niblo, *Mexico in the 1940s*, 349.
41. Author interview, Vicente Ramírez Sandoval, Ometepec, Apr. 9, 2002.
42. Medel y Alvarado, *Historia de San Andrés*, 1:viii–ix; Notkin, "History Unheard."
43. "Relación de periódicos de las diferentes entidades federativas."
44. Newcomer, *Modernity*, 92, 147; *Últimas Noticias de Excélsior*, June 5, 1964.
45. "Relación de periódicos de las diferentes entidades federativas"; A. John Cope Jr., Nogales, to State Department, Feb. 4, 1963, NARA/RG59/IA/1963-66/roll 3.
46. Paxman, *Jenkins of Mexico*, ch. 7.
47. Gonzalo I. Migoni to Gobernación, June 15, 1945, AGN/DGIPS/787/2-1/45/282.
48. *Excélsior*'s editorial of October 3, 1968, continued the paper's skeptical line toward the student movement before describing the government's response as "neither prudent nor appropriate." Julio Scherer later regretted the paper's coverage of the Dirty War, which included editorials deeming Génaro Vázquez and Lucio Cabañas—on the occasions of their deaths—misguided and criminal. Burkholder de la Rosa, "El olimpo fracturado," 1361–62; Rodríguez Munguía, this volume.
49. The study sampled 152 articles over thirty years; Montgomery, "Stress on Government," 8, 151. See also Miller, Goldenburg, and Erbring, "Type-Set Politics." I thank Ben Smith for the reference.
50. *Excélsior*, Mar. 6, 1947.
51. Memos, Apr. 2 and 3, 1947, AGN/DGIPS/794/2-1/47/398; Charles Bateman to Ernest Bevin, Apr. 11, 1947, NA/FO371/60940/AN1478.
52. Ortega Romero [full name unknown] to Gobernación, Oct. 30, 1947, AGN/DGIPS/794/2-1/47/396.
53. Telegram, Rafael Solano Cancino, *La Voz de Orizaba*, to Alemán, Sept. 26, 1948, AGN/MAV/704/492; *La Verdad*, June 8, 1949. For more on voceadores, see Aguilar and Terrazas, *La prensa*.
54. *La Prensa*, Aug. 5, 1954.
55. *Diario de Xalapa*, July 1, 1945.
56. Telegram, director, *La Crítica*, Orizaba, to Alemán, Sept. 9, 1948, AGN/DGIPS/802/2-1/49/546; telegram, Ignacio de la Hoya to Alemán, Oct. 2, 1947, AGN/MAV-542.1/404.

57. While the average number of recorded attacks on the press more than doubled from six to thirteen a year between the Alemán and Ruiz Cortines *sexenios* (six-year terms), the number of papers increased by nearly 500 percent. González Casanova, *La democracía*, 40; Benjamin T. Smith, "Censorship and the Regional Press in Mexico, 1940–1970," talk at University of California, San Diego, 2014.

58. Press violence was moreover strongly concentrated in three states: Baja California, Tamaulipas, and Veracruz. The average of approximately one journalist a year murdered pales when compared to the approximately eighty murdered between 2005 and 2015. Smith, "Censorship and the Regional Press"; Matloff, this volume.

59. Some started earlier: Maximino Ávila Camacho led the way in Puebla in the late 1930s. Paxman, this volume.

60. Informe del gobernador del estado de Guerrero, 1948, AHEG/Archivo-Paucic/175/AP352.072.73 ETN.

61. *Diario de Guerrero*, June 27, 1950.

62. Cope, Nogales, to State Department, Oct. 31, 1963, NARA/RG59/IA/1963-66/roll 3.

63. "Relación de periódicos de las diferentes entidades federativas."

64. Paul S. Dwyer to State Department, Feb. 28, 1963, NARA/RG59/IA/1963-66/roll 3.

65. "Baja California, situación política," 1965, AGN/DGIPS/1303.

66. Cope, Nogales, to State Department, May 1963, NARA/RG59/IA/1963-66/roll 3; Hohenthal, Guadalajara, to State Department, June 26, 1950, NARA/RG59/912.61/6-2650.

67. Kennedy M. Crockett, Tampico, to State Department, Feb. 12, 1954, NARA/RG59/912.61/2-1254; Russell B. Jordan, Nogales, to State Department, Feb. 9, 1954, NARA/RG59/912.61/2-954.

68. Fregoso Peralta and Sánchez Ruiz, *Prensa y poder*, 58–59.

69. F. R. Lineaweaver, Guadalajara, to State Department, Feb. 25, 1954, NARA/RG59/912.61/2-2554; Edward S. Benet, Chihuahua, to State Department, Mar. 1, 1954, NARA/RG59/912.61/3-154; Robert Y. Brown, Ciudad Juárez, to State Department, Apr. 9, 1954, NARA/RG59/912-61/4-954.

70. US consul, Tampico, to State Department, Aug. 1963, NARA/RG59/Mexico/IA/1963-66/roll 3.

71. Cope, Nogales, to State Department, May 31, 1963, NARA/RG59/Mexico/IA/1963-66/roll 3.

72. Culver E. Gidden, Matamoros, to State Department, Jan. 28, 1954, NARA/RG59/912.61/1-2854; Arthur V. Metcalfe, Mérida, to State Department, Feb. 4, 1954, NARA-912.61/2-454; Gerald A. Mokma, Monterrey, to State Department, Jan. 22, 1954, NARA-912.61/1-2254.

73. Charley L. Rice, Mazatlán, to State Department, June 15, 1954, NARA-912.61/6-1554.

74. Gidden, Matamoros, to State Department, Jan. 28, 1954, NARA-912-61/1-2854.

75. Metcalfe, Mérida, to State Department, NARA-912.61/2-454; Brown, Ciudad Juárez, to State Department, Apr. 9, 1954, NARA-912.61/4-954.

76. Richard A. Johnson, Monterrey, to State Department, Aug. 4, 1963, NARA/RG59/Mexico/IA/1963-66/roll 3.

77. The editor boasted that the paper had brought down one municipal administration and posed a threat to the governor. Gidden, Matamoros, to State Department, Jan. 28, 1954, NARA.912-61/1-2854.

78. Unfortunately as with most provincial papers their collections are, with the exception of *El Informador*, incomplete.

79. *Diario de Xalapa*, Nov. 2, 1949, Sept. 13, 1950.

80. *Jarocho* (veracruzano) presidencies were good times for jarocho journalists: in 1955 Juan Malpica Mimendi of *El Dictamen* was given the federal congressional seat for the port of Veracruz. *El Informador*, July 4, 1955.

81. *Diario de Xalapa*, July 14, 1947.

82. See, for example, *Diario de Xalapa*, Mar. 23 and 28, May 23, and July 23, 1945, on pistolerismo; Dec. 24, 1947, on corruption; Sept. 13, 1947, and Jan. 3, 1948, on election rigging; July 7, 1945, on protest of censorship.

83. García Márquez, *El coronel no tiene quien le escriba*, 21.

84. *Diario de Xalapa*, Jan. 9, 1948.

85. Hohenthal, Guadalajara, to State Department, June 26, 1950, NARA/RG59/912.61/6-2650.

86. Fregoso Peralta and Sánchez Ruiz, *Prensa y poder*, 39.

87. Hohenthal, Guadalajara, to State Department, June 26, 1950, NARA-912.61/6-2650; Fregoso Peralta and Sánchez Ruiz, *Prensa y poder*, 31.

88. Hohenthal, Guadalajara, to State Department, June 26, 1950, NARA-912.61/6-2650.

89. "Historia de *La Verdad*," *La Verdad de Guerrero*, May 26, 2013, https://issuu.com/libertadguerrero/docs/la_verdad_de_guerrero_no._2.

90. Anduiza Pimentel, "Squatter Movements"; memo, Miguel Rangel Escamilla, director, DFS, Oct. 4, 1961, AGN/DGIPS-1475A/19.

91. Rangel Escamilla, Oct. 4, 1961, AGN/DGIPS-1475A/19; "Historia de La Verdad," *La Verdad de Guerrero*, May 26, 2013; *La Verdad*, Jan. 1 and Feb. 29, 1949.

92. *La Verdad*, June 10, 1949.

93. One of his targets was the labor cacique Alfredo Córdoba Lara, whose chance for a deputyship de la Hoya boasted he had ended, reporting that the PRI secretary-general had brandished *La Verdad* and said, "We don't want the party to back individuals about whom the press expresses itself like this Acapulco newspaper does." *La Verdad*, Mar. 31, 1949.

94. Telegram, Ignacio de la Hoya to Alemán, Oct. 2, 1947, AGN/MAV-542.1/404; *La Verdad*, Apr. 3, 1949.

95. Ignacio de la Hoya to Adolfo Ruiz Cortines, Aug. 20, 1956; Fidel Gallardo to Adolfo López Mateos, Dec. 19, 1958; Francisco Rodríguez to Adolfo López Mateos, Feb. 26, 1960; and Pablo Rosete del Razo to Adolfo López Mateos, Apr. 26, 1962, all in AGN/DGIPS, de la Hoya file; editor, *El Sol*, to Donato Miranda Fonseca, Feb. 6, 1962; Marco Antonio Vargas, "La muerte de un periodista," *Por Qué?*, Nov. 13, 1969, 21–23; Ignacio de la Hoya, amparo request, Sept. 5, 1969, Suprema Corte de Justicia de Guerrero, file 85, case file 511.

96. Montgomery, "Stress on Government," 82, 151,

97. On the later impact of *columnismo*, see Freije, "Exposing Scandals," 377–409.

98. *Diario de Xalapa*, Aug. 16, 1948; *La Verdad*, Aug. 2, 1949.

99. *Diario de Xalapa*, June 25 and 26 and July 18, 1945.

100. *La Verdad*, Jan. 4 and 23, Mar. 5, 9, 15, 23, and 25, June 4, 8, 15, and 27, July 29, Aug. 2, and Oct. 11, 1949.

101. Leland W. Warner, Tampico, to State Department, June 6, 1963, NARA/RG59/Mexico/IA/1963-66/roll 3.

102. *Diario de Xalapa*, July 1, 1945, Aug. 25, 1949, July 7, 1952.

103. *El Informador*, Nov. 19, 1965.

104. *El Informador*, July 4, 1955.

105. *Diario de Xalapa*, July 16, 19, and 20, Aug. 7 and 11, 1948. Even though the paper became more officialist, stories of corruption in particular endured; see *Diario de Xalapa*, June 21, 1952.

106. *La Verdad*, Mar. 5, May 11, and Sept. 27, 1949.

107. De la Hoya to Gustavo Díaz Ordaz, Jan. 16, 1959, AGN/DGIPS, de la Hoya file, 12–13. This list was no one-off; a similar one for six months in 1949 contains extended investigations into two particularly high-profile political murders: a scion of *El Dictamen*'s Malpica family, committed by one of Acapulco's regidores, and a state union boss, committed by the state's longtime éminence grise.

108. Del Palacio Langer, "Agrarian Reform," ch. 5.

109. *El Diario de Michoacán*, Apr. 7, 1946; Johnson, Monterrey, to State Department, July 14, 1963, NARA/RG59/Mexico/IA/1963-66/roll 3; British embassy to London, Apr. 27, 1961, NA/FO371/156281/AM1015/5.

110. Peter Garran to Henry Hankey, Jan. 5, 1961, NA/FO371/156281/AM1015/1.

111. Piccato, *History of Infamy*, ch. 5.

112. In a single month the paper published four articles on violence committed by state agents. *Diario de Xalapa*, Mar. 15, 19, 23, and 28, 1945.

113. *Diario de Xalapa*, July 1, 1952.

114. *El Suriano*, Sept. 23, 1947, *Diario de Xalapa*, Aug. 15, 1948.

115. In a revealing exception to this solidarity, national and local Acapulco journalists wrote to Mexico City praising their town's press freedoms after *La Verdad* complained of violent censorship. AGN/DGIPS, de la Hoya file, 37–41.

116. Such defense was also economic. *El Informador* only survived a year-long strike at the end of the 1930s with the "physical and economic" aid of the Asociación de Editores de los Estados, a group that brought together regional heavyweights such as *El Siglo de Torreón*, *El Dictamen*, *El Imparcial de Hermosillo*, *El Mundo de Tampico*, *El Heraldo de San Luis Potosí*, *El Diario de Yucatán*, and *El Porvenir de Monterrey*. Fregoso Peralta and Sánchez Ruiz, *Prensa y poder*, 31–32.

117. This was reflected in mastheads like that of *El Diablo Rojo*: "Semanario Joco-Serio Independiente y Feroz" (An Independent and Ferocious Half-Serious Weekly). Buffington, *Sentimental Education*, 4; Covo, "La prensa," 14; Frutos, "Prensa lozana," 114; Cosío Villegas, *El Porfiriato*, 2:573.

118. "The coarse or venal bureaucrat / who rips us off with his diktat" ("I don't come to be explanatory / but to carry him off to the cemetery").

119. *La Verdad*, Jan. 1, 1949.

120. The most polite translation is "United Arselickers Front," a formulation in widespread use at the time. *La Verdad*, Mar. 30, 1949.

121. *Diario de Xalapa*, Oct. 12, 1947.

122. Fuentes Díaz, *Guerrero*, 25.

7 | "The Invisible Tyranny"; or, The Origin of the "Perfect Dictatorship"

JACINTO RODRÍGUEZ MUNGUÍA

As a complement to this chapter, and to stress the necessity that the PRI has at its disposal a professionally organized unit that might develop programmatic rather than haphazard propaganda, the following idea is advanced: through the effect of political propaganda we might conceive of a world dominated by an Invisible Tyranny that adopts the outward form of a democratic government.

—"THE INVISIBLE TYRANNY," ARCHIVO GENERAL DE LA NACIÓN

This chapter has as its starting point a forty-one-page document found in 2002 in the archives of the Dirección General de Investigaciones Políticas y Sociales (DGIPS), the Mexican state's secret police. The text, which for practical reasons I will denominate "The Invisible Tyranny," is essentially a long essay concerning how such agencies used (or conceived of using) the media as an effective propaganda tool for consolidating the grasp of the Partido Revolucionario Institucional (PRI) on the presidency, a power that it enjoyed for over seven decades (1929–2000) and that, after losing and being sidelined for a mere twelve years (2000–2012), it managed to recover. This is a peculiar, distinctive, unique power. Neither the most authoritarian politburos of the Soviet era nor the military dictatorships of Latin America managed to achieve such political "success."

This chapter describes some of the most obvious effects of that careful strategy, which political scientists such as Norberto Bobbio have called the "invisible power" working inside autocratic states.[1] It also reveals the extent to which many journalists and media outlets were influential in allowing the PRI to flourish in this period, while on the other hand allowing the very nature of their profession and its duty to society to wither. Of course a single text cannot map out all the complexities of the relations among journalists, public relations specialists, and state officials.[2] Some of the plan's objectives were achieved; others were not. But such a focus can clarify and map the range of some bureaucrats' authoritarian dreams.

The Invisible Level of the Implied: What the Text Does Not Say

One of the fundamental characteristics of the Mexican political system during the first tenure of the PRI, which gave both foundation and form to the exercise of power, was secrecy. Both large and small decisions were made, and continue to be made, not so much in the corridors as in the cellars of power.[3] Hence, on a first reading, the style of "The Invisible Tyranny" reveals the enduring logic of secrecy as a form of power. The author(s) are perpetually alert to avoid leaking contextual specifics. There are no dates that might situate the reader in a given political or social moment; there are no precise facts that might shed light on which political season or which national problems might have led to the production of this text and the goals that it outlined. This is a power without a defined time or space.

There are no public figures, journalists, media outlets, real businessmen, or any specific chronology in "The Invisible Tyranny." The document refers instead to abstract categories of media, such as newspapers, magazines, radio, television, cinema, and posters, through which it is necessary to transmit the message of power. Media and journalists are tools for the transmission of ideology. Most important of all, it should not be known who made this and other documents. Essays, ideological plans, and other texts had to be thought up and produced by nameless and *invisible* beings. The moment that a name was linked to these essays, the power of the Mexican governments of the era would have lost the virtue of omnipresence. They wanted the general public to know and feel that the state (the government, president, army, intelligence apparatus, etc.) was everywhere. These entities were watching the people; they were observing them. It was power as the great panopticon, as Big Brother. Let no one know where it is, but let them feel its presence.

Yet inside this labyrinth of obsession over detail, over eliminating all tracks, something escaped them. It is only a number, a year: 1965. This is the only crack through which we might descry the place in which this plan was drawn up and enter into the quest for explanations and the paths that it may have followed in subsequent years.

I am, of course, talking about a time when extreme ideological polarization between capitalism and communism gave rise to the social tensions that were subsequently expressed in popular uprisings, guerrillas, and dictatorships. In this Cold War world, Mexico was inevitably, due to its proximity to the United States, one of the domains most sought after by the superpowers. An entire universe of spies had its meeting place there. In several countries the shattering experiences of 1968 and its overwhelming student movements were, with the benefit of hindsight at least, clearly on their way when this text was apparently written. In 1965, the only tangible specific that this document offers the reader, the conditions for student rebellion were also brewing in Mexico.[4] But 1968's student movement and its final massacre of students were yet to come. So too were the years of the Dirty War, when the state arrested, tortured, and disappeared hundreds of people whom it considered subversives.[5]

Seen with the perspective and distance of decades, "The Invisible Tyranny" was probably ahead of its time. It was a public relations man's fantasy—a forecast of what was to come and what would be done with newspapers, radio stations, television programs, and their journalists. Both what reporters did and what they omitted had clear consequences. In this lies another important facet of the document. The strategies proposed in "The Invisible Tyranny" were intended to attract and train the majority of media workers and journalists without worrying too much about ways or means. Without this social group it would have been impossible for the state to make its decisions, its actions, and its whole exercise of power invisible in one of its darkest periods. Journalists were not the only group seduced by power (or pressured by it, if necessary), but they were one of the most important pieces in order for the state to reach the levels of what Mario Vargas Llosa once termed the "perfect dictatorship."[6]

This document also squares with the integrated plans for military dictatorship in the Southern Cone countries: "the perfect triangle of dictatorship," as the journalist Miguel Bonasso, a survivor of the Argentine military dictatorship, put it. According to Bonasso, to exercise power, dictators need three elements or social components: a natural aptitude for dictatorial power; a legal structure (constitution, laws, judges, etc.) that lends legal backing to their decisions and actions; and media outlets and journalists willing to transmit the decisions of the military power as "good and noble actions." When the three components are perfectly aligned, one attains the power of a dictatorship.[7]

Priista Mexico was no military dictatorship, but it shared some of such regimes' key strategies. In the absence of either a military head of state or a completely cowed and compliant legal structure, the authors of the text believed that the third element of authoritarianism—the manipulation of the media—was even more crucial. In fact, by controlling the media Mexico might function like a military dictatorship but with neither the international opprobrium nor the popular opposition that dictatorships may attract. As the authors wrote, "Under these conditions, a democracy such as Mexico's can achieve levels of popular control equivalent to those that a dictatorship, which could only offer its citizens illusions and abstractions, might only achieve through violence and terror."[8]

The Explicit Level: What the Text Actually Says about Ideas, Programs, and Strategies

I will not linger long over all of the politico-ideological arguments of the document. But to gauge the explicit purpose of the writing, it is important to mention some central ideas that in the final analysis fed into the official machinery of media control in the following decade. In so doing, the state managed to regulate—if not entirely manipulate—popular reception of the suppression of both the 1968 student movement and the longer and bloodier Dirty War of 1970–1980.[9]

Here is a selection of the proposals that are advanced in concrete and explicit fashion in "The Invisible Tyranny." They are straightforward statements, and I have retained the original capitalization:

Making propaganda is in reality creating and guiding public opinion; getting past the indifference of the subject and stimulating convenient reactions; leading them to adopt the projected behavior without searching within themselves for any reason why they should act IN THIS WAY. . . .

It is, then, a way of leading rationally, of bringing into a common line a society's political thought. (The adjective is utilized because the dictatorship of the masses happens when they get aggrieved and transgress the habitual norms of the community. Revolts or revolutions, riots, disturbances of various magnitudes cannot be understood as rational leadership, but rather obedience to the majority will and as such slavery and subjection to its order.) . . .

Of all the forms that propaganda adopts in the modern world, the most important from a historical perspective is POLITICAL PROPAGANDA, as its use makes it possible to "fabricate" generations obedient to a style, a philosophy, and a morality appropriate for the interests of the State. . . .

In order for political propaganda to be lodged permanently in the citizen's subconscious and there to acquire the status of mental habit, it is essential that nothing and no one contradicts it. Propaganda that is discussed is half as effective. If it is accepted by some and rejected by others it will be more fruitless than fruitful. Hence an integrated approach demands control of the press, radio, TV, and cinema so that none of these means of communication should register any discrepancies with the line that has been imposed. If a political idea provokes the criticism of any of the mentioned instruments, no propaganda will be able to become a norm or an idea accepted by everybody. . . .

To be effective, propaganda must adopt "the language" of the group over which control is sought. It is not possible that A SINGLE TYPE of political propaganda should affect all social groups equally. . . .

Control of public opinion in a totalitarian regime is rudimentary. A democracy's political propaganda cannot and should not imitate that of a dictatorial state but it can learn much from it: faith in its abilities; persistence in action; speed in dealing with conflicts; interest in all political problems, be they minor or gigantic. . . .

Dictatorships repress ideas and popular expression by force. Under a democratic government this control should take on the level of art, given that it is free citizens who are to be directed. . . .

Political propaganda should adopt as a proposition—in the case of Mexican democracy—the use of truth. The PRI has an abundance of principles to deploy in order to generate excitement, liking, understanding . . . the promise of truth. . . .

The transmission of news by word of mouth—the phenomenon of rumor—is the best means of public dissemination, because of all the tools of propaganda it is the one that best sparks the individual imagination and gives [the news item] an exaggerated importance. In addition, the idea is sown and no one manages to track down from whence it sprang. . . .

Political propaganda is a sort of faith that should be propagated: a faith, of course, of this earth but one whose expression and dissemination have much of the psychology and technique of religions.[10]

It seems that politicians always desire and intend to control the flow of information through the media and journalists. This has, for many years, been a commonplace that applies as much to other countries as it does to Mexico.[11] But until recently in the Mexican case, the story of how this relationship came to be was something utterly out of reach of historians or any other investigators. Instead, researchers were forced to rely on a blend of anecdotes, testimonies, and autobiographies, which by their very nature are limited and subjective even if crucial.[12]

A testament to the problems with investigating these issues is the following exchange between Julio Scherer García—probably the most influential journalist of the last fifty years—and President Carlos Salinas de Gortari (1988–1994):

I asked him for documents that might attest to the marriage of politicians and journalists, the accounts in the press offices reserved for reporters and columnists, the low-interest loans to keep up the façades of businesses with financial difficulties, the hidden deals between presidents and media magnates. I argued that whether Mexicans could observe the country with a sure eye in large part depended on his will. . . . As the end of the meeting approached I asked the president once more if he could get *Excélsior*'s file to us.[13]

In the end, the president refused to comply. Neither the *Excélsior* file nor broader documents on press control were handed over. If it turned out to be impossible for the most influential journalist to get access to specific information concerning the mechanisms with which the state exerted control over the media, the possibility of getting hold of the plans, strategies, and ideological schemes for making the media into an effective tool of power was even more distant. Furthermore, one could not imagine that documents revealing the intentions and plans of the powerful would have survived the purges and cleansing of the archives. When secrecy was part of the exercise of power, obtaining evidence of it or documenting its acts was a vain aspiration.

However, an unexpected decision by one of Mexico's less imaginative presidents changed the unwritten rules concerning at least some state secrets. Vicente Fox (2000–2006) was the first president of Mexico in seventy-one years who did not come from the PRI. His executive order to unseal the archives of the DGIPS and the Dirección Federal de Seguridad (DFS) opened up hitherto unimaginable pathways into the country's recent history. When these lines were first written in 2012, it had been twelve years since that opening, and researchers were only just profiting from the documents that populate the Archivo General de la Nación (AGN).[14] As these lines go to press in 2018, new regulations and practices at the AGN have brought to an end that period of transparency.

This was the route taken by the document that forms the focus of this chapter. Both the DFS and the DGIPS were part of the Ministry of the Interior. There, at least since the 1940s, by custom if not by law, the most important political decisions were made.[15] In the more than 3,000 boxes in gallery 2 of the AGN, this and other documents live jumbled together in something that seems, as Arthur Koestler might have put it, more like the wanderings of an insomniac than the recent past of Mexico.[16] Perhaps that is how it all happened. Yet the document survives and thus brings us closer to the thoughts and intentions of the politically powerful as regards the media. It gives us the coveted opportunity to enter into the minds of those who thought about the concrete exercise of power and to get at the origins of what would become decisions, actions, and palpable realities. Engaging with this document is a journey through the dark and invisible side of power. It is, in itself, a source of reflection and analysis.

As a result, I have decided to place the document at the center of this chapter. But this is insufficient if I do not attempt to explain what happened between the state and the media in the years after the date of its apparent composition. Certain questions inevitably come up: If the document was produced sometime around 1964 or 1965, what happened to all its ideas, proposals, and recommendations in the ensuing years? Was any of this put into practice? Did these ideas work, or did they remain nothing more than the exercise of some office-bound intellectuals?

To provide some answers, I draw on the thesis of Robert Darnton, who in *Censors at Work* proposes that "no historian can get inside the heads of the dead—or, for that matter, the living, even if they can be interviewed for studies of contemporary history. But with sufficient documentation, we can detect patterns of thought and action. Only rarely are the archives adequate, because censoring took place in secret, and the secrets usually remained hidden or were destroyed."[17] In my book *La otra guerra secreta: Los archivos prohibidos de la prensa y el poder*, I used the documents of the DGIPS to lay out the broad array of government censorship mechanisms in the period 1960–1980. In many instances they seemed to follow the programs proposed by "The Invisible Tyranny." Here I only refer to a handful of cases.

When the student movement of 1968 escaped government control, bureaucrats in assorted press offices drew up strategies of information and disinformation in order to attack the leaders and the wider social movement.[18] In the first place the use of terms such as "students" and "student conflict" were to be avoided in all media outlets. Instead they applied terms such as "plotters," "terrorists," "guerrillas," "agitators," "anarchists," "those without patriotism," "mercenaries," "traitors," "foreigners," and "delinquents." Such epithets delegitimized and even dehumanized the students. They were not protesters; they were "the enemy."[19] As a complement, a strategy of exhorting parents through the country's educational institutions was deployed, asking them to control their children to avoid their manipulation for illegal ends.

This way of reinventing reality through conceptual distortion was a common model on which governments of a similar nature drew in these years. Again, parallels from the Southern Cone dictatorships are pertinent. The journalist Sergio Marelli tells how before the coup that led to Argentina's dictatorship, a pamphlet circulated with the words that the military considered inappropriate. In Argentina there were to be no "guerrillas," just "subversives" and "delinquents." Conflicts were to be described as "encounters" and never "fights." Whatever the story, the national media never covered the "war" that was taking place under their noses. The list of prohibited and unacceptable terms was a long one. As Marelli says, "We learned ingenious euphemistic juggling acts to neither betray ourselves too much nor to offend the delicate sensibilities of our assiduous readers in the intelligence services. It was a very tight bind."[20]

Inside Gustavo Díaz Ordaz's government and in particular inside Luis Echeverría's Ministry of the Interior, it was clear that the bad impressions Mexicans got from student critiques of the omissions or failures of the government had to be counteracted. "Government reports are forgotten. It is easier to forget benefits than hardships, and these are exploited by the agitators," reads another of the declassified texts drawn up in the ministry in 1968.[21] Thus the government ordered a media counter-campaign, with the aim of taking on and minimizing what criticism its opponents did manage to publish or disseminate in paid inserts and reports at the outset of the student conflict. "The statements mentioned are drawn up with the obvious intention of smearing the federal government and seeking followers or recruits to their protests. In the last few days, such publications have become even more numerous, and they are signed by individuals who claim to belong to assorted scientific, cultural, and artistic groups."[22] As laid out in "The Invisible Tyranny," during these conflicts it was thought indispensable to create a permanent information campaign regarding the achievements and successes of the regime.

By the 1970s, Mexico's Cold War had warmed up. Urban and rural guerrillas had taken up arms, and campaigns against "subversives" were more overt and violent. There were not just media campaigns, but also military campaigns. This is a part of history that still awaits a more detailed analysis.[23] There is already enough evidence, however, concerning the role of the media and its silence in the face of what was going on or, worse yet, its complicity as a docile vehicle for the plans of the powerful.[24]

For obvious reasons, we might cite the case of *Excélsior*, the newspaper that historically confronted Echeverría's power, which—according to the best-known version—led the president to intervene and topple Julio Scherer in 1976.[25] Yet there are some who raise doubts whether Scherer's *Excélsior* confronted Echeverría's government in the decisive moments of the Mexican Dirty War.[26] In summing up Scherer's legacy, Sergio Aguayo comments that he once heard Scherer criticize the journalism of his own paper in those years: "He had already published the book *Parte de guerra* with Carlos Monsiváis, that extraordinary document with the political testament of Díaz Ordaz's Secretary of Defense, Marcelino García Barragán, and he complained that he had not taken account of the importance of the Dirty War, of the repression that was under way.... 'I did not accord it the importance that it demanded, and I believe that in that sense *Excélsior* did not fulfill the role that it should have fulfilled.'"[27]

There are two striking examples that are directly linked with this mea culpa. On February 2, 1972, Génaro Vázquez, one of the guerrilla leaders of the state of Guerrero, died. *Excélsior*'s editorial explained the death under the following headline: "Vázquez Rojas: The Wrong Path." "The critiques," Scherer's paper editorialized, "that advocate changes in the country, changes that are truly necessary to achieve in order to correct economic and social inequality and to attain more just living conditions, must be channeled along democratic lines."[28] Something similar happened with the death of Lucio Cabañas. Cabañas was a perpetual thorn in the side of the Echeverría government, and the president sent a disproportionately large military force to do away with his movement.[29] When he died, *Excélsior*'s headline repeated the official version: "Lucio Cabañas Was 'Killed in a Skirmish': The Ministry of Defense." The editorial was damning: "The list of people whose kidnapping or murder is attributed to Cabañas's group is extremely long, as is also the catalog of crimes that he committed in the name of a political ideal inconsonant with such acts."[30]

In an informal conversation with Fausto Zapata Loredo, Luis Echeverría's director of press relations, he assured me—as if distancing himself from that time—that the president told the heads of the media about everything that was going on, and during the years of the Dirty War the directors of the media were well informed. Speaking vehemently, gesturing carefully, he asserted: "I, I, I myself took charge of getting them together almost every week to have breakfast with the bureaucrats that they wanted, with the secretary of defense so that he could tell them what was happening in Guerrero, in other states.... They were up to speed on everything, in detail.... We never told them what they could or couldn't publish. That was their decision." When I questioned the statement, he continued but changed the emphasis of his previous approach. "Explicit threats weren't necessary....

They knew what could happen. . . . But we never told them whether to publish or not."[31] To put it another way, the government didn't need to dictate how to approach stories; mainstream newspapers already knew the limits of their remit.

Excélsior's capitulation to state propaganda might be the most egregious, given its quite different reputation. But other newspapers were equally compliant, including the sensationalist tabloid *La Prensa*. Until recently no one paid much attention to this publication despite the fact that it has been the country's highest-selling newspaper for decades. It still reaches more of the population than any other newspaper, and it touches what political commentators call the "green circle," the people who eventually determine the results of elections.[32] As Pablo Piccato has argued, during its early days *La Prensa* did provide some space for communication between civil society and the state, especially in the crime pages.[33] But by the 1970s it was firmly in hock to the state. For *La Prensa*'s journalists, guerrillas had no political program, they were simple criminals; the Liga Comunista 23 de Septiembre was nothing more than a gang dedicated to "robberies, assaults on Baja California businesses, murders, and the elimination of police and those deemed traitors."[34]

Visible and Invisible Effects

The most important aspect of "The Invisible Tyranny" is the purposeful, carefully thought-out nature of its content. At its heart, this text is a set of strategic principles aimed at reinforcing the relationship between the state and the media and generating the conditions, through either negotiation or pressure, for a long-term alliance. To some extent this type of document allows glimpses of power's near-infinite aspirations. There is no suggestion of democracy, of the possibility of ceding power as part of the push and pull of democratic exchange. In fact, what is dealt with explicitly is how to stop that.

This shared effort in the shadows of press and power, whether licit or not, sowed multiple negative impressions in the public's perception of contemporary newspapers. Whether public or private, open or secret, the proximity between media leaders and the men in power planted in society's collective consciousness the idea of a press that was distant from them and always hand-in-hand with the state. Such strategies damaged the press as an institution and pressmen as a social group. Society coined a cutting phrase to describe this type of journalism, which, up until today, we have been unable to lose: *la prensa vendida*, the sellout press.[35]

Nothing can or should wound a journalist's dignity more than being deemed a sellout. It is the antithesis of journalism. It means that the truth—the raw material of reporting—has been changed into a currency for the economic benefit of media businessmen and journalists; and those who put a price on the truth—its purchasers, if you will—are the leaders of the state. Yet that must be accepted because it is part of reality. Whether or not the state fulfilled its plans precisely as they were set forth in "The Invisible Tyranny" is still the object of some doubt. Spaces for contention and debate existed even during the worst years of the Dirty War. Yet it cannot be denied that the state ended up converting important parts of the media and many journalists into its allies and accomplices during this period. In the thousands of boxes deposited in the AGN, there are enough documents describing that alliance between press and state to permit us, as Darnton puts it, to "detect patterns of thought and action."[36] There is evidence of the funds that the president dispensed on a discretionary basis to the media, which formed part of the government's "expenses." The long lists of reporters and media outlets with their respective payments remain for posterity. These and other documents surrounding the text I am analyzing demolish one of the perspectives that many in the press have upheld—namely that their complicit actions were forced on them by pressure from the state.

For years the common account of the period's leading media companies and reporters was that the state blocked any possibility of press freedom. Such a proposition is acceptable if we believe that those in power basically did everything they could—both legal and illegal—to control the flow of information. Up until the opening of the archives, this account worked. Yet the documents that have emerged from the archives of the Ministry of the Interior have raised profound doubts concerning that argument. These discoveries have raised the question of whether state pressure was really all that complete and whether there were journalists who, either by conviction or convenience—or both at once—allied themselves with those in power. In the final analysis, many in the press joined in the state's plans. They became a de facto branch of the government, and they did so willingly.

The story of how that relationship came to fruition is increasingly being documented and narrated.[37] Today we understand more and more about the pacts, the state's means of control, the way that radio and television stations obtained their concessions, the government's control of paper supplies that affected newspapers and magazines, and the meetings between media owners and cabinet secretaries or presidents of the republic. There are plenty of confessions in autobiographies and anecdotes. But previously there was no documentary evidence: the letters, the gifts from the powerful, the records of trips, or the receipts of the payments that were made to media outlets and journalists as if they were state employees. With the document "The Invisible Tyranny" in hand, we can grasp how critical is the role of the press in a society, how what it does or fails to do intersects with and influences all other components of a society, including culture, science, and education.

The student movement of 1968, for example, takes on a different reading in the light of these intelligence documents; the Dirty War becomes dirtier. Much of the current state of the Mexican press has, without a doubt, its origin in these years. There are the props, the letters, the accords, how much silence cost, and how much it cost to say certain things, and above all, there are the protagonists. History is written by flesh-and-blood people, and this is not a history of heroes and villains, but rather of people in whom there are all the shades of gray. At present in Mexico, there are multiple media outlets but—with some exceptions—they are the same as before. That is to say, the origins and part of the power of press conglomerates, print media, radio, and television are the same. They are the continuations of dynasties.

Among the papers in the archive of the DGIPS is the text of a 1966 article by Francisco Martínez de la Vega, one of the most famous veteran reporters in the country, which expertly sums up the nature of journalism in Mexico. He writes:

Our profession is neither peaceful nor easy. Journalism undeniably suffers from a bad public image. When a journalist attacks, it is customarily thought that he is looking for a payoff; when he applauds, it is said that he has got one; and if he neither praises nor censures, his lukewarm approach will submerge him in anonymity. . . . But it is necessary to think that in our country, on the road to development, we need a journalism that is technically competent and noble in its aims.

The sort of journalism that the young generation that replaces us will exercise will have, additionally, the task of cleaning up the mess that our generation will leave them and restoring the profession's former roles in the service of the highest causes of the city, country, and world in which we live.[38]

In the tangible and visible practice of journalism, the pretense of high-mindedness is one of the worst legacies of this scheme for state-media relations. That which has emerged from or was added to the journalistic tradition is a sort of discourse that has nothing to do with our reality; it says what we are not.

In the late 1980s Jean Baudrillard launched an interesting debate on the cultural vacuum of the United States. In brief, he asserted that this vacuum was an effect of the fact that as a nation the United States lacked a primitive, ancestral past in the symbolic realm. Lacking this, the country instead inhabited a sort of fiction, which gave it the external appearance of reality.[39] If we adopt (in a somewhat arbitrary way) Baudrillard's model as a starting point for digging into how deep the ethical roots of Mexican journalism lie, it seems to me that these roots lack a symbolic and conceptual past and thus lack a practice that might sustain them as an example and reference.

In the matter of media ethics, we journalists have constructed a discursive realm divorced from our practices because it does not form part of our long-term habits and customs. Memoirs that discuss journalists' practices leads to another sort of story, closer to a simulacrum of ethics than to a genuine set of ethics.[40] Returning to Baudrillard, I see us in the stage of constructing our symbolic-conceptual field and at the beginnings of a practice that would lend us a new legitimacy in the future. In short, at present ethical journalism does not exist; it simply pretends to. A truly ethical journalism, much like democracy, is a work in progress.

Such is the historical path that we journalists tread in Mexico. We have greater space, greater possibilities, and so it is to a great extent up to us to become media that inform and generate discussion. Even if we assume that the press is not a fourth estate, then at least it should not be an extension of the regime in power. This requires reflection on what the function of journalism is and for whom it is made. What would journalists have to do to try to modify the far from encouraging future that is in the offing? I am convinced that the main tool that we have as a profession is critical reflection on our role in this drawn-out and troubled democratic transition. As the above article shows, this is something that Francisco Martínez de_la Vega saw as essential as far back as 1966.

I suggest we should take Janus as our model, facing forward while also facing our past. It would be a mistake to affirm that nothing has changed and that the priista political system that clambered back into the presidency in 2012 is the same as it was back in its golden years. A key difference is that the PRI only coexisted with a rudimentary version of the internet at the very end of its previous rule. The internet has disrupted all the old logics of communication and power. It is no longer so easy to control the market of truth, and neither is it in the hands of a few media outlets and journalists. One of the democratic transition's clearest flaws has been the press's evasion of its responsibility to Mexico's past and the past of the media themselves. In the final analysis the priista governments did not just draw on the "best" of other dictatorships; they surpassed them. The PRI elevated the crude and even grotesque practices of military dictatorships to an art form.

By Way of Conclusion to an Ongoing Story

It is roughly five decades since "The Invisible Tyranny" was written and since the cases and histories briefly documented in this chapter. Some fifty years after the fateful day of October 2, 1968, and the outbreak of the Dirty War, we are only just now beginning to measure their true dimensions and impact. In the end, those responsible for the hundreds of arrested, tortured, and disappeared people, for all their broken stories, will remain unpunished. Many are already dead. For others, old age and "failing memory," the convenience of "I can't remember," as well as a made-to-measure judicial system will guarantee them a happy end to their lives, ensconced in their deep armchairs telling happy stories to their grandchildren.

Even today ex-president Luis Echeverría remembers those days he held power. He might persuade himself he aimed to seek a bright future. And he might remind himself of the colorful garlands, the pine branches, and the red and white carnations with which they decorated the façade of Chapultepec Castle on the day of his inauguration. Through the twists and turns of his memory, distant and perhaps hazy now, his steps may still wander up the red carpet toward the podium of the National Auditorium, and toward that photo that he wanted to last forever: himself with the presidential sash crossing his chest and, at his side, gray-faced, walking away from the lights and from history, his predecessor, Gustavo Díaz Ordaz.

All of it: the embraces, the congratulations, the smiles. All of it: the fear, the torture, the dead, the disappeared. All of it stayed in the Archivo General de la Nación. But now in the hands of historians and investigators is one trial, at least, that cannot be evaded.

On July 2, 2000, I was in the PRI's headquarters and watching, minute by minute, a myth built over seventy years falling to pieces. I had the good fortune to witness the grief that they were trying to hide in the directors' offices and to watch it spread to the faces of many of my colleagues in the national press. When the PRI fell, an entire generation of journalists fell too, ending, at least for the time being, an entire way of seeing and doing journalism. With every clip from Televisa, the most powerful media corporation in Latin America, backed up by the reports, surveys, and polls of that election day, their faces fell further. Ironies were plentiful. One was that the very television channel that for decades had faithfully served the PRI had, just before seven o'clock in the evening on July 2, 2000, the task of proclaiming the end of an era.

This time around the manuals of political propaganda weren't enough. That evening the terror that had made their skin crawl for decades caught up with them at last. The journalists felt that their time had come; they glimpsed that the eternity to which they had aspired had an expiration date and that it had passed. On July 2, 2000, the Dirty War and 1968 were already far off. Yet the majority of the media who that very night began to make the necessary adjustments to adapt to a *panista* government had the same DNA, the same genes as those who decades before didn't even try to influence the course of events. They were invisible, and they made tragedies invisible. Perhaps they consoled themselves that they had struggled against, or at least modified, the impact of a state with aspirations of absolute power. But such consolations don't ring true. The idea that Mexican journalists were victims, ever repressed by a devious and powerful state, was not reflected in the dejected faces on that July morning. They mourned the PRI's loss for a reason. The journalists of those years, some unconsciously, others by omission, others through conviction, had collaborated in weaving a cloak of invisibility that has covered a part of Mexico's history up to the present. The perspective and goals of "The Invisible Tyranny" were possible thanks to them. They too exercised an invisible tyranny.

Eighteen years later, new questions arise: To what extent did the seeds sown by that document nourish the resurgent PRI under President Enrique Peña Nieto? Will neo-priistas' dreams of permanence succeed where those of their predecessors eventually failed? Only time will tell.

Notes

1. Bobbio, "La democracía."
2. For these variations, see the other chapters in this volume; Rodríguez Munguía, *La otra guerra secreta*; Del Palacio Montiel, *Siete regiones* and *Rompecabezas de papel*.
3. See, for example, the establishment and work of the Dirección Federal de Seguridad. Aguayo, *La charola*.
4. For these Cold War divisions and the role of secrecy and spy agencies, see Pensado, *Rebel Mexico*; Keller, *Mexico's Cold War*; Morley, *Our Man in Mexico*; Iber, *Neither Peace nor Freedom*; Condés Lara, *Represión y rebelión*.
5. "What distinguishes the Dirty War is precisely the state's rejection of the rule of law. It was the job of President Luis Echeverría's government to respond to armed insurgency, but within the rule of law, without torturing, murdering, or disappearing. Instead guerrillas were subjected to endless torments, their corpses were thrown into the sea, and the unspeakable was done when all they deserved was the application of justice. If guerrillas committed acts of barbarism it was not the state's right to exact revenge without scruple. Priista governments decided to throw themselves into the extremes [of violence]." Carlos Monsiváis, *La Jornada*, June 14, 2004.
6. Vargas Llosa, *Desafíos a la libertad*.
7. Author's conversation with Miguel Bonasso, May 2005, Mexico City. Bonasso was a journalist, editor of *La Opinión*, and founder of the daily *Noticias*. He was press secretary to the peronista election campaign, and subsequently an aide to President Héctor José Cámpora, and a member of the guerrilla group the Montoneros. He lived in hiding until, 1977, the year of his exile, part of which he spent in Mexico.
8. AGN/DGIPS, Caja 2998/A, folio 3.
9. A handful of national organs did attempt to shine a light on state violence in both these periods, such as *Por Qué?* and other "marginal" journals. See Del Castillo Troncoso, *Ensayo*; Trejo Delarbre, *La prensa marginal*; Smith, *The Mexican Press and Civil Society*, ch. 4; Sánchez Sierra, "Periodismo heróico." But the state attempted to have these papers closed down. Rodríguez Munguía, *La otra guerra secreta*, 207–19.

10. AGN/DGIPS, Caja 2998/A, folios 14.
11. Classic texts on the United States include Herman and Chomsky, *Manufacturing Consent*; Gitlin, *The Whole World Is Watching*.
12. In fact, most analyses of the Mexican press in the second half of the twentieth century are based on a handful of key texts, such as Scherer García, *La tercer memoria*; Scherer García and Monsiváis, *Tiempo de saber*; Riva Palacio, "Culture of Collusion"; Leñero, *Los periodistas*.
13. Scherer García, *Estos años*, 62.
14. One of the first works that examined these documents was Aguayo, *La charola*. Since then, they have become crucial instruments for uncovering the political history of Mexico. See Navarro, *Political Intelligence*; Padilla, *Rural Resistance*; Herrera Calderón and Cedillo, *Challenging Authoritarianism*; a special issue of *Journal of Iberian and Latin American Research* (2013); Gillingham and Smith, *Dictablanda*.
15. Debate over the relative power of the Ministry of the Interior and its chronology is still ongoing. However, it seems incontestable that it was during the Second World War, under future president Miguel Alemán, that the office grew in size and importance.
16. Koestler, *Los somnámbulos*.
17. Darnton, *Censors at Work*, 14.
18. Jacinto Rodríguez Munguía, "Llámenles terroristas," *El Universal*, Sept. 29, 2003. For media control of the movement, see also Del Castillo Troncoso, *Ensayo* and "Fotoperiodismo y representaciones"; Aguayo, *1968*; Sánchez Rivera, Cano Andaluz, and Martínez Nateras, "Los libros y la prensa"; Serna Rodríguez, "La vida periodística mexicana."
19. As Carlos Monsiváis writes, "The apogee of directed disinformation came dramatically in 1968. The majority of the print press, in happy and automatic parallel with radio and television, silenced itself, libeled, and confused on principle. In an almost unanimous fashion the student movement was denounced as without patriotism, factionalist, communist, and an enemy of family and religion." Monsiváis, *A ustedes*, 89.
20. Sergio Marelli, "Medios cómplices," *Etcétera*, Mar. 2004, 5.
21. AGN/DGIPS/Caja 2876, memorandum, 1968.
22. AGN/DGIPS/Caja 2876, memorandum, 1968.
23. For an introduction to the Dirty War, see Herrera Calderón and Cedillo, *Challenging Authoritarianism*; Aguayo, *La charola*; Condés Lara, *Represión y rebelión*.
24. For an excellent introduction, see Gamiño Muñoz, *Guerrilla*.
25. The classic account is Leñero, *Los periodistas*.
26. See Burkholder de la Rosa, "El olimpo fracturado"; Gamiño Muñoz, *Guerrilla*.
27. Scherer, "Una vida intervenida por el espionaje," *Revista Emeequis*, June 18, 2015.

28. *Excélsior*, Feb. 3, 1972.

29. "La masacre desconocida de Guerrero: El informe oficial sin censura sobre la Guerra Sucia e Luis Echeverría," *Revista Emeequis*, Feb. 27, 2006.

30. *Excélsior*, Dec. 3, 1974.

31. Conversation with Fausto Zapata Loredo, Oct. 2007.

32. Rodríguez Munguía, *La otra guerra secreta*, 149–61.

33. Piccato, "Murders."

34. *La Prensa*, May 7, 1974; Gamiño Muñoz, *Guerrilla*, 84.

35. Students openly shouted this insult as they passed by the offices of the major newspapers in 1968. Serna Rodríguez, "La vida," 133.

36. While Darnton's case studies of ancien régime France, British India, and East Germany parallel the self-censorship I have described, they do not closely parallel the half-masked, transactional nature of the Mexican censorship regime; there was less *pan* (bread) to be had in Mexico. Even East Germany did not rely on violence alone, and faithful authors might enjoy privileged access to visas, cars, university positions, and even the West German press. Darnton, *Censors at Work*, 14, 172–73.

37. Works that touch on the subject include Keller, *Mexico's Cold War*, 47, 48, 50, 58–60; Pensado, *Rebel Mexico*, 152–55, 228–31; Gamiño Muñoz, *Guerrilla*; Pozas Horcasitas, *La democracía*, 204–6.

38. This article was included in Martínez de la Vega, *Aliento*.

39. Baudrillard, *En América*.

40. For example, see Scherer García, *La tercer memoria*; Mejido, *Con la maquina*.

8 | The Cartoons of Abel Quezada

RODERIC AI CAMP

Cartoonists have had a long and notable history in Mexican popular culture. Students of the medium attribute considerable influence to cartoonists at various periods in Mexican politics, especially immediately preceding the Mexican Revolution of 1910. The cartoon as a visual medium can be particularly influential on a population where literacy is not widespread. Its impact is enhanced by the fact that it is rarely an objective analysis of an event; rather, it is usually an incomplete, one-sided interpretation of a subject.[1]

As the publishing industry in Mexico expanded in the 1950s, opportunities for cartoonists increased. Mexico produced a generation of prominent illustrators who made their careers in journalism. Over the following decades competition became fierce for positions with major newspapers, most of which were located in the capital. Cartoonists, like other cultural leaders (poets, novelists, essayists, musicians, artists), were drawn to Mexico City, where they were most likely to be recognized and ultimately employed. Regionalism played a very small role in the intellectual life of Mexico, and its impact on the cartoon was negligible. Mexican cartoons are a cosmopolitan, nationally oriented medium, appealing to all population sectors.[2]

No Mexican cartoonist reflects this sophisticated cosmopolitan flavor in their art better than Abel Quezada, whose work mixes Mexican and universal themes. Quezada was born in the thriving industrial capital of the

northern border state of Nuevo León in 1920, the year that marked the end
of the violent phase of the Mexican Revolution. As a young man, his personal
experiences and philosophy were centered around family life in Comales, a
small Mexican community close to McAllen, Texas, where his father was the
mechanical superintendent in the construction of the Azúcar Dam. Quezada's boyhood proximity to the United States undoubtedly influenced his attitudes toward other countries and his belief in working toward one world of
nations living peacefully with each other.

Quezada's middle-class social origins were typical of the larger Mexican
literary community. He studied at a series of educational institutions, mostly
private schools, including the School of Commerce and Business in Mexico
City. Quezada, like his father, first pursued training in mechanical and elec-
trical engineering. But as is true of many Mexican journalists, he abandoned
his studies for a different path. Before pursuing his career as a full-time cartoonist, he illustrated books for the Public Works Secretariat and contributed
to the opposition magazines *El Mañana* and *Presente*. Quezada's political
cartoons began to appear regularly in 1950, first in the sports paper *Ovaciones* and subsequently in several major Mexican dailies, including *Últimas
Noticias* (1956–1959), *Excélsior* (1959–1976), and *Novedades* (1977–1989). From
the early 1970s onward he published several books, including *The Mexican
and Other Problems* (1976) and culminating in the retrospective *The Best of
Impossible Worlds* (1999). He was also one of the few Mexican cartoonists to
publish his work in the United States, working for Kennedy Associated in
New York and illustrating, among other things, several covers of the *New
Yorker*.

Quezada's work, as the examples in this chapter demonstrate, is profoundly political, yet at the same time it goes beyond politics to cover a wide
variety of subjects. His cartoons incorporate perceptions from his travels
abroad, a wide range of social and political issues, and commentaries on the
day-to-day life of the individual Mexican. Quezada's work is unique among
Mexican cartoons and cartoons more generally. Visually, Quezada rarely
uses his space to focus on a central illustration. Instead, the vast majority of
his work subdivides the standard cartoon space into a series of illustrations,
most commonly half the normal size, but in many cases the space is divided
in fourths or fifths. Thus, whereas the typical cartoonist relies on a single
large image to make the point simply and abruptly, Quezada's work is more

complex. Compared to the usual cartoon, his illustrations often seem busy, similar to the works of North American satirist Jules Feiffer. In fact, without the benefit of a caption, they would almost seem like doodles.

Each cartoonist has a unique style, but Quezada's use of visual space is unlike that of any other Mexican cartoonist in the nineteenth or twentieth centuries.[3] When I asked about influences on his work, he readily admitted his susceptibility to foreign ideas: "I suppose that a human being cannot live without knowing something of his past. To do this you have to read, and therefore, all of us, to some degree or another, have been influenced by written sources. Certain European currents, especially French, have been important to us, and it is legitimate to recognize these influences. I have been influenced personally by writers, painters, cartoonists, and politicians, because of my political content. In drawing, I have my favorites: [Saul] Steinberg from the United States, [André] François from France, and Lowell from the United Kingdom."[4]

The complexity of his visual style suggests at first glance a comic strip in miniature. Thus, Quezada made more than one point visually in a single illustration. Although the cartoon in general and his own work truly belong to the genre of popular culture, it would be fair to say that Quezada—as is the case for Rius (Eduardo del Río), El Fisgón (Rafael Barajas), and Antonio Helguera—was an intellectual among other cartoonists. His captions are more detailed and cover more visual space than those of any of his predecessors. The text of the captions dominates the illustrations; at times they are footnoted. The effect of this may be seen in two opposing lights. A less persevering reader may find too much text in a Quezada cartoon and pass it by. On the other hand, if Quezada properly judged his target reader—and his popularity over more than four decades suggests that he did—he was able to make multiple points in a single cartoon. In fact, he sometimes carried this technique even further by publishing a short series of cartoons over a period of three or four days. As a cartoonist, Quezada pursued his educational task with a determination and commitment stronger than that of his peers. The depth of his ideas gives his cartoons their intellectual quality.

The seriousness of Quezada's ideas brought him such respect from the cultural community in Mexico City that his work was exhibited twice in the prestigious Rufino Tamayo Museum in Chapultepec Park, in 1984 and again in 1999–2000. He was the first contemporary Mexican cartoonist to have his

La Madre Tierra (I)

— FOR ABEL QUEZADA —

DICEN LOS CLÁSICOS QUE LOS PUEBLOS SÓLO TIENEN UNA RIQUEZA: LA TIERRA QUE LIMITA SUS FRONTERAS.

TODO LO DEMÁS LO DA ESA TIERRA.

SI LA TIERRA ES BIEN TRABAJADA Y PROTEGIDA, DA TODO LO QUE EL HOMBRE NECESITA PARA VIVIR.

SI ES DESCUIDADA, MAL CULTIVADA Y SOBREPASTOREADA, SE EROSIONA Y MUERE. NO DA NADA.

ENTONCES, LA TIERRA DEBE SER DEL QUE LA TRABAJE — BIEN.

FIGURE 6. Abel Quezada, "La Madre Tierra (I)"
Mother Earth (I)
The classics say that a people have a single source of wealth: the land within their
   borders.
That land gives everything else.
If land is looked after and well worked, it provides everything man needs to survive.
If it is ill treated, badly farmed and overgrazed, it erodes and dies. It doesn't give any-
   thing.
So, the land should belong to he who works it—well.

work presented in such a setting. He was not, however, an armchair intellectual. As already mentioned, his illustrations and captions cover a broad range of topics. Most important, unlike many Mexico City intellectuals, he focused on serious social and economic problems, including those found in rural areas. He considered the lack of exchange among intellectuals, and their ignorance of Mexican reality, to be an undesirable form of "intellectual elegance."[5] In this chapter, I examine some of his cartoons in detail to show the range of his subject matter and his peculiar style.

In "La Madre Tierra (I)" (Mother Earth), the first in a series, Quezada comments on several problems crucial to Mexico's rural development. Land distribution had long been a major social and political problem in Mexico, especially after government legislation in the 1850s that forced the sale of church-owned property. Scholars agree that one of the major causes of the 1910 revolution was the peasants' desire for their own land, which was incorporated in the 1917 Mexican Constitution and which endured until the agrarian reform of 1992. However, since the revolution, despite the millions of acres of land that were distributed to peasants, serious problems continued, and by the 1980s Mexico was meeting fewer of its agricultural needs than it had twenty years earlier.

In this context, Quezada introduces a universal truth about land use in "La Madre Tierra (I)." As is typical of his work, he starts out with a general statement whose source is non-Mexican, in this case the classical tradition: the land is the wealth of nations. His next statements, which emphasize that abused land produces nothing, seem obvious, but they related to the real and terrible problem Mexico was having with erosion. Finally, moving from the universal truths of the first statements to the line at the bottom of the cartoon, Quezada leaves the reader with the thought that the land should belong to those who work it, a cry of the peasant revolutionaries that was incorporated into the rhetoric of the Mexican Revolution. His perspective is particularly important and definitely informative in a culture that valued landholding for the prestige attributed to being a landowner, but that had never placed any importance on the individuals who made the land productive.

Another common subject in Quezada's work was class attitudes and their consequences for Mexico. Much of the discussion that took place about these issues occurred within the peculiarly Mexican environment of the country's revolutionary heritage, that is, the rhetoric and history of the Mexican

Posible Revolución de Casimir

—POR ABEL QUEZADA—

NOVIEMBRE, MES DE LA REVOLUCIÓN.— BULNES DECÍA QUE CADA CINCUENTA AÑOS LOS INDIOS DE MÉXICO SE ENOJAN Y ARMAN UNA REVOLUCIÓN.

ESTA VEZ NO PARECEN LOS INDIOS TAN ENOJADOS COMO LOS QUE SE VISTEN DE CASIMIR.

LOS REVOLUCIONÓLOGOS CREEN QUE AHORA LOS QUE SE VAN A ENOJAR SON ELLOS, LOS PEQUEÑO BURGUESES DE LA CIUDAD. RAZÓN: ESTÁN MEJOR INFORMADOS; SABEN MÁS.

TODOS LOS DÍAS VEN EL DERROCHE DE LOS QUE HACEN GRANDES NEGOCIOTES: LA FUERZA OSTENSIBLE DE LOS RICOS, DE LOS POLÍTICOS, DE LOS OLIGARCAS.— CONTRA ELLOS SERÁ LA REVOLUCIÓN DE CASIMIR

PARA QUE ESTALLE SÓLO FALTA QUE ENCUENTREN UNA COSA: IDEOLOGÍA.

FIGURE 7. Abel Quezada, "Posible Revolución de Casimir"

Possible Cashmere Revolution

November, month of the Revolution. Bulnes used to say that every fifty years the Indians of Mexico get angry and launch a revolution.

This time it seems like the Indians aren't as angry as those who wear cashmere.

Revolutionologists believe that this time the ones who are going to get angry are these ones, the petit bourgeois of the city. The reason: they're better informed; they know more.

Every day they see the waste of big business: the apparent power of the rich, the politicians, the oligarchs—it's these who will be the targets of the cashmere revolution.

They only need one thing for it to explode: ideology.

Revolution, the most widely discussed social topic in Mexico. Because politicians constantly refer to the revolution and because the anniversaries of important dates occur frequently, the subject is rarely far from the minds of journalists and public figures. An example of a class theme in such a context can be seen in "Possible Cashmere Revolution." Quezada begins with an authoritative statement by an author of a classic work analyzing the causes of the Mexican Revolution: the nation's indigenous people periodically become angry enough to revolt against their condition. But this time, according to Quezada, it is the people wearing cashmere—the middle classes—who are angry. Citing the students of revolution, whom he calls "revolutionologists," Quezada argues that the middle classes are potential revolutionaries because they are better educated and therefore understand their exploitation. However, he predicts that such a revolt will not take place because the middle classes share no coherent ideology.

Of the social themes Quezada frequently developed, perhaps the most important was his humorous but scathing portrayal of the rich, whom he often depicted unflatteringly as a class without comparing them with other, less fortunate social groups. From the 1950s on, the issue of social class was much sharper in Mexico than in the United States, and inequality was more widespread. Although Mexico had received notoriety for a development model that brought it high levels of growth from the late 1940s to 1970, most economic analyses showed that this growth neither reduced inequality nor improved the distribution of income to the working classes. In the 1970s, as Mexico's economic situation worsened, Quezada used his cartoons to provide simple economic lessons.

In "More against More; More, More, More," he joins five sequential illustrations and six captions to make a point. Quoting the private sector, he provides his typical introductory statement, in this case that rising gas prices will force an increase in the prices of consumer goods and services. The consequence of increased prices, according to his next statement, will be an increase in salaries. Increased salaries, of course, increase prices, and so on. But Quezada is not content with a simple lesson in inflation; rather, he leaves the reader with his own moral conclusion: none of this changes anything, and Mexico will continue to have a maldistribution of wealth and the same rich and poor.

The cartoons that most delighted foreign readers of the Mexican press

FIGURE 8. Abel Quezada, "Más contra Más; Más, Más, Más"
More against More; More, More, More
The merchants, truckers and industrialists said that the rise in the cost of gas will
    force them to raise their own prices.
When prices go up salaries go up.
When salaries go up prices go up once more.
When prices go up gas will have to go up once more.
And when gas goes up, businessmen, merchants and truckers will raise their prices.
Thus, with this system, Mexico will keep on having the same rich and the same poor.

were those dealing with politics. Quezada was deeply interested in the political scene, and his work consistently touched on three aspects of that arena: policy questions, political events, and the nature of the political system itself. One of the policy questions with serious social and economic consequences for Mexico was the ability of the government to expand the primary education system. At the time of the Mexican Revolution, only 10 percent of all Mexicans could read and write. In absolute numbers, however, there were more Mexicans in 1970 without a primary education than there were in 1910. An important contributor to illiteracy rates was the country's incredible demographic growth.

"With No Solution in Sight" first presents in a simple drawing style three little children, who are symbolic of the three million children without primary education because of a classroom shortage. The shortage, Quezada suggests, is growing, symbolized in the next image by a longer line of children. However, Quezada does not merely generalize about the problem, he uses very precise figures. Again, scholarly studies are cited to bolster his point and to reach a sophisticated audience.

Following his description of the educational problem in the first two sections, Quezada describes the government's action to correct it through assistance from the private sector, quoting a government official of the federal school construction program. In a humorous aside, he says good-bye to Article 3, a reference to the constitutional provision stating that each child should have access to and be required to attend free public schools. As if the lack of classrooms were not serious enough, Quezada introduces an entirely separate statistical conclusion that 20 percent of Mexican children (portrayed as flowers) will die before their first year. Thus, the cartoonist leaves the reader with a duality: Mexico has insufficient educational facilities, a growing problem, and this is occurring in spite of a sizable mortality rate among children. To make the reader contemplate these questions further, Quezada invites a response at the bottom of the illustration.

The most common subject of political cartoons is day-to-day politics, which dominates journalism in general. Quezada, like other Mexican cartoonists, often used a particular event to illustrate a broader characteristic of the system. For example, during the controversial presidency of Luis Echeverría, many cabinet changes took place. In Mexico, it was rare for a minister who resigned or was fired by the president to give the true reason to the

FIGURE 9. Abel Quezada, "Sin Solución en el Frente"

With No Solution in Sight

In Mexico there are three million children of school age who do not get any education at all because of the shortage of classrooms.

The problem is growing. There is a shortfall of 35 to 40 thousand classrooms each year.

The government can't sort it out on its own and seeks (good-bye Article 3) the "help of the private sector."

On the other hand, according to the WHO 20% of children born in poor countries (like Mexico) will die before the age of one.

(Insert here the solution to these problems.)

press. During the Echeverría administration, one of the most notable resignations was that of Hugo B. Margáin in May 1973. Margáin, who was the secretary of the treasury, resigned because he found the president's economic policies unacceptable. But on the day he left office, Margáin told the press, as have many public officials before and since, that he had tendered his resignation for reasons of health.

In "Dr. Strangelove," Quezada dresses up Margáin as ambassador to England, a position he received less than three weeks after his resignation. Quezada was pleased with the appointment, but he facetiously asks Margáin, in the name of his readers, if he could provide the name of the physician who cured him so quickly. But he is also suggesting a more important, unspoken issue: Mexicans deserve to know the real reason behind the resignation of their leaders. Again, the cosmopolitan, internationalist flavor in his work is displayed in the cartoon's title, "Dr. Strangelove," referencing a film many Mexicans undoubtedly saw.

Quezada also used events to make broader statements about political beliefs in general. Unlike many other parts of Latin America, political terrorism, especially assassination, was uncommon in Mexico. An exception to this, and an event with serious repercussions for the relationship between the private sector and the state, was the murder on September 17, 1973, of Eugenio Garza Sada, the leader of the Monterrey industrial group, the most powerful influence in the private sector. Instead of concentrating on the narrow impact of the death of Garza Sada as an individual, Quezada encompasses a much broader philosophical issue in his cartoon "A Crime against Us All." The images are blunt—just two black squares. Quezada suggests to his reader that one man's murder is not only a personal crime; it is a crime against an intangible that Mexico, relative to most other Latin American countries, has ably retained: liberty. He emphasizes this point by comparing Mexico's record on liberty to that of other Latin American nations. The cartoon moves from an interpretation to an impassioned plea for all Mexicans to condemn violence as a road to a dictatorship of the right or the left.

Political jokes in Mexico abounded during Quezada's time. While the print media rarely discussed the personal qualities of an incumbent president, Mexicans did circulate orally many uncomplimentary stories about their leaders and the political system. Traditionally, cartoonists had much more freedom to criticize than the press did, and they frequently made use

FIGURE 10. Abel Quezada, "El Dr. Strangelove"
Dr. Strangelove
Lic[enciado] Hugo Margaín, ambassador to England.
In great health!—but . . .
Could Lic. Margaín recommend to us the doctor who cured him so quickly of his
    woes?

Crimen Contra Todos

———POR ABEL QUEZADA———

INDUSTRIAL EUGENIO GARZA SADA FUE COBARDEMENTE ASESINADO. EN MONTERREY.

LOS AUTORES DE ESTE CRIMEN NO ERAN ENEMIGOS DE GARZA SADA. SON LOS MISMOS QUE PUSIERON BOMBAS EN OAXACA Y EN GUADALAJARA. SON LOS ENEMIGOS DE LO ÚNICO QUE TIENE MÉXICO: LA LIBERTAD.

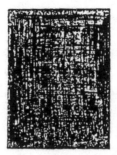

MIRE USTED: DE TODOS LOS PAÍSES DE AMÉRICA LATINA, SÓLO QUEDAN CUATRO CON GOBIERNOS CIVILES; UNO DE ESTOS ES EL NUESTRO.— LOS DEMÁS SON DICTADURAS, COLONIAS O CAOS.

EL CAMINO A LAS DICTADURAS DE IZQUIERDA O DE DERECHA FUE SIEMPRE LA INJUSTICIA SEGUIDA DEL TERRORISMO Y EL CRIMEN.

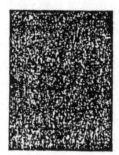

LOS MEXICANOS DEBEMOS DEFENDER LO QUE TENEMOS: NO PERMITAMOS NUNCA QUE LOS ASESINOS NOS QUITEN LA LIBERTAD.

FIGURE 11. Abel Quezada, "Crimen contra Todos"

A Crime against Us All

The industrialist Eugenio Garza Sada was murdered by cowards in Monterrey.

The perpetrators of this crime weren't enemies of Garza Sada. They were the same ones who put bombs in Oaxaca and Guadalajara. They are the enemies of the only thing Mexico has: liberty.

Look: Of all the countries in Latin America, only four still have civilian governments: one of those is ours.—The rest are dictatorships, colonies or chaos.

The path to dictatorships of the right or left was always injustice followed by terrorism and crime.

We Mexicans must defend what we have: we will never allow murderers to take away our liberty.

of it. Quezada suggested that he was given complete freedom by his publishers but that he took into account the limitations all publishers were subjected to when creating his cartoons.[6] Thus, Quezada functioned as his own censor. While maintaining some restrictions, he believed fervently in freedom of the press and pushed for an expansion of those boundaries in Mexico. In 1977, he briefly directed the government television channel before being fired for his criticism of ex-president Echeverría.[7]

In his cartoons, Quezada treated the political system with sarcasm, poking fun at its notorious weaknesses. For example, every six years, at the time of the presidential election, a list of pre-candidates to be senators and federal deputies was drawn up. Once a Mexican was selected as the official candidate of the Institutional Revolutionary Party (PRI), that was tantamount to being elected since the opposition parties never won senate seats and rarely defeated PRI candidates for seats in the Chamber of Deputies.

Quezada's cartoon "De Todas Todas" (Every Single One of Them) deals with the candidate selection process in Mexico. He reminds his readers that some unpatriotic Mexicans might recall that during the dictatorship of Francisco Franco in Spain (a much-criticized figure in Mexico for historical reasons), 80 percent of the Spanish legislature was handpicked by the government and another 20 percent elected at large. Quezada contrasts Mexico's democracy with fascist Spain, stating sarcastically that things work differently in their country. This leads the reader to expect more competition in the Mexican system. Instead, the punch line is that in Mexico 100 percent of the deputies and senators are handpicked. Thus, Quezada criticized the Mexican system for claiming to be a democracy when, at least on the level of its elected officials, there was more control of candidate designations than in a fascist dictatorship.

Any observer of the Mexican scene watched its president, and his immediate retinue, for indications of change in the political winds. Sometimes these changes could be detected in the oddest places. Fashion was just one of the interesting subjects political weather watchers inspected. In the fifth cartoon of a series done in 1973, entitled "The Necktie," Quezada discusses political fashions. He tells the reader that in Mexico there have been famous neckties, referring to the prominent bowties worn by ex-president Adolfo Ruiz Cortines. In 1971, however, soon after Echeverría was inaugurated, the president introduced two informal fashions: the guayabera, a tropical shirt

FIGURE 12. Abel Quezada, "De Todas Todas"
Every Single One of Them
Regarding the PRI's lists of senators and deputies, some unpatriotic sorts remember that . . .
In the times of the much-criticized fascist dictator Francisco Franco . . .
The Spanish parliaments were made up of 80 percent members who were designated by the government; the other 20 percent were elected.
In our democracy, things are different.
100 percent of the deputies and senators are designated.

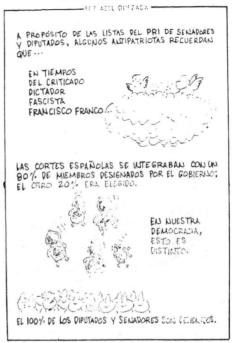

De Todas Todas

A PROPÓSITO DE LAS LISTAS DEL PRI DE SENADORES Y DIPUTADOS, ALGUNOS ANTIPATRIOTAS RECUERDAN QUE ...

EN TIEMPOS DEL CRITICADO DICTADOR FASCISTA FRANCISCO FRANCO ...

LAS CORTES ESPAÑOLAS SE INTEGRABAN CON UN 80% DE MIEMBROS DESIGNADOS POR EL GOBIERNO; EL OTRO 20% ERA ELEGIDO.

EN NUESTRA DEMOCRACIA, ESTO ES DISTINTO.

EL 100% DE LOS DIPUTADOS Y SENADORES SON ELEGIDOS.

from Yucatán worn untucked, and the leather jacket. Quezada expresses surprise at how political fashions changed as the necktie fell into disgrace. But, he asks, has the informality of the fashion changed the formality in the public official's behavior? He answers no, clothes do not make the person, and the behavior remains unchanged. The cartoon leaves unsaid another element of the political system reflected in fashion changes: the importance of the Mexican president and the subordination of his collaborators. Once President Echeverría began to wear casual outfits, so did most cabinet ministers. (In contrast, in the United States, President Jimmy Carter's predilection for cardigan sweaters did not result in a single cabinet secretary copying his dress.) In the Mexican political system, even presidential fashions could be a bellwether of a subordinate's loyalty to a superior, and few politicians had the independence to determine their own taste in dress and not subordinate their choice to their boss's.

At that stage in his career, Quezada and his work had become an

FIGURE 13. Abel Quezada, "La Corbata (V)"

The Necktie

In Mexico there have been some famous ties: the bowtie of Don Adolfo, that of the "Man with the Big Tie," the impeccable knot of the boxer "El Caballero Guaracha"—and others.

Those were days when solemnity reigned in all social circles and the tie was a mark of prestige.

But my, how things change; the tie fell into political disgrace—who would have thought?—and the ash-colored guayabera rose in its place.

But did this mean that solemnity was set aside? Did stiff formality end? Did important bureaucrats become human?

No: they all kept on as solemn as ever, but without ties.

institution in Mexico. His success was unusual. Although he moved across national boundaries, and by choice was an internationalist, he never forgot his origins and the importance of Mexican problems. His combination of a distinctive intellectual style in content and design, and his incorporation of universal and Mexican themes, made him unique among cartoonists.[8]

It is only natural to speculate about what Quezada's contribution to Mexican journalism might have been in the twenty-first century. It seems ironic to argue that since Mexico became an electoral democracy, the contemporary press workers who are heirs to Quezada face many more difficulties in presenting their views, whether through cartoons, investigative reporting, or editorials. Instead of confronting the monolithic control by a single political party, Mexicans in the journalism profession have, for more than a decade, confronted serious violence from drug cartels that have morphed into broader criminal organizations. At the state level, there are several governors who are deeply involved in illegal activities, often associated with organized crime. Mexico, unfortunately, measured by the number of journalists who have been murdered, has become one of the most dangerous countries in the world for their profession. The inability of the federal government or private security to protect journalists and their families is a commonplace. Consequently, one can only speculate about the degree to which cartoonists, like journalists, are willing to risk their lives to express criticism of organized crime or collusion between public officials and criminal elements. Twenty-first-century studies have demonstrated the extent to which these conditions seriously impinge on journalists professionally and psychologically.[9]

Acknowledgments

A special thanks to William B. Taylor, who made available his collection of Abel Quezada cartoons and translations of their captions.

Notes

1. Johnson, *Latin America*.
2. *Fuentes para la historia*, vol. 2.
3. See, for example, Pruneda, *La caricatura*; Velarde, *Siete dibujantes*; Williford, *It's the Image That Counts*.
4. Author interview with Quezada, Mexico City, Aug. 4, 1978.
5. Author interview with Quezada, Mexico City, Aug. 4, 1978.
6. Camp, *Intellectuals and the State*.
7. *Economist*, Apr. 23, 1977, 75.
8. The following sources provide further insights into the role of cartoonists in contemporary times: Acevedo Valdés, *Historia de la caricatura*; Barajas, "Transformative Power of Art"; "Mexican Cartoonists Launch Campaign against Violence," EFE World News Service, Jan. 11, 2011; Sánchez González, *Diccionario biográfico*. Quezada's memoir is *Antes y después*.
9. See Hughes and Márquez Ramírez, "Examining the Practices"; González de Bustamante and Relly, "Professionalism under Threat of Violence"; González de Bustamante and Relly, "Silencing Mexico."

9 | # Testing the Limits of Censorship?

Política *Magazine and the "Perfect Dictatorship," 1960–1967*

RENATA KELLER

According to most histories of Mexico, the mid-twentieth century was the golden age of the Partido Revolucionario Institucional (PRI), the period of the government's greatest strength, until the 1968 student movement and the Tlatelolco massacre marked the beginning of the end of the "perfect dictatorship."[1] The 1960s, specifically, were the era of Gustavo Díaz Ordaz, minister of the interior from 1958 to 1964 and then president until 1970; Díaz Ordaz has become known as one of Mexico's most repressive leaders, with a heavy hand and a thin skin.[2] According to scholars such as Roderic Camp and Chappell Lawson and journalists like Julio Scherer, Carlos Monsiváis, and Jacinto Rodríguez Munguía, one of the keys to the government's power in this period was its control over the press.[3] They depict the relationship between the PRI and the press as consisting mostly of subtle, behind-the-scenes collaboration and co-optation.

The story of *Política* magazine and its controversial director, Manuel Marcué Pardiñas, provides a stark exception that reveals a more fraught, combative relationship between the press and power in 1960s Mexico. From the very first issue, the creators of *Política* devoted their energies to exposing the shortcomings of the Mexican government. Volume 1,

El Presidente Adolfo López Mateos

FIGURE 14. Cover of *Política*'s first issue with a photograph of President Adolfo López Mateos, May 1, 1960. Source: Biblioteca Lerdo de Tejada and the US Library of Congress Historical Newspapers Collection.

number 1, appeared on May 1, 1960—Workers Day—and its lead article criticized the way that President Adolfo López Mateos (1958–1964) had repressed recent workers movements.[4] In the same issue, another article denounced the corrupt administration of the Ejidal Bank, which denied credit to campesinos, and an editorial by Carlos Fuentes chastised the nation's leaders for holding political prisoners.[5]

The first issue foreshadowed the multiple ways that *Política* broke what scholars have described as the unwritten rules of Mexican journalism. According to Camp and Lawson, even the most outspoken writers avoided directly criticizing the president.[6] Lawson also identifies other "touchy" issues that journalists supposedly ignored or downplayed, including economic and electoral fraud, corruption, political opposition, and governmental repression. But instead of being seen as a list of topics to avoid, these subjects served as a list of issues to pursue for the editors and writers of

Política. Instead of cowering in fear of the government or kowtowing to unwritten rules of self-censorship, *Política*'s creators exposed the dirtiest secrets of Mexican politics and dared its readers to do the same.

Política was perhaps the most influential magazine in Mexico in the 1960s, and it embodied the renaissance of the Mexican Left that took place in the wake of the Cuban Revolution. Twice every month, 25,000 copies streamed from the magazine's headquarters in Mexico City to readers across the country and throughout the world.[7] In *Política*'s pages, the intellectual leaders of both the Old Left of the Communist Party and the Popular Front and the radical, revolutionary New Left of the 1960s came together to discuss national politics, world events, and culture.[8] Vicente Lombardo Toledano, Carlos Fuentes, Víctor Rico Galán, Jorge Carrión, Raquel Tibol, Eduardo del Río (Rius), Alonso Aguilar Monteverde, Narciso Bassols Batalla, Eli de Gortari, Renato Leduc, and José Santos Valdés were among the magazine's many contributors. Political prisoners, including David Alfaro Siqueiros, Demetrio Vallejo, Valentín Campa, and Othón Salazar, wrote articles and letters from their cells in Lecumberri Prison.[9] In addition to news, political cartoons, and editorials, *Política* also published the full texts of important documents and speeches, such as Che Guevara's guide to guerrilla warfare; the full proceedings of the 1961 Latin American Conference for National Sovereignty, Economic Emancipation, and Peace in Mexico City; and Fidel Castro's "Declaration of Santiago de Cuba."[10] The magazine's goals ran the gamut from the local to the global: revive the Mexican Revolution, support workers and social movements, defend the Cuban Revolution, and resist US imperialism.

Política influenced the new generation of intellectuals and activists who came of age in 1960s Mexico. One participant in the 1968 student movement later recalled that the magazine was among the "required readings for all student activists."[11] Another young political leader, Paquita Calvo Zapata, who organized one of Mexico's first urban guerrilla groups after the Tlatelolco massacre, was a close friend of Marcué Pardiñas during and after her years as a student at the Universidad Nacional Autónoma de México.[12] Ramón Sosamontes, who joined the Communist Youth Party in the 1960s and would go on to help found Cuauhtémoc Cárdenas's Party of the Democratic Revolution in the late 1980s, described *Política* as "the foundation for the formation of hundreds of leftist political leaders as well as for those that joined the PRI because its pages contained the real history of our country in the years in which it was published."[13]

Política found an equally enthusiastic audience abroad. Readers from the United States, Canada, Cuba, Peru, El Salvador, Chile, Puerto Rico, Dominican Republic, Honduras, Guatemala, Brazil, Chile, Argentina, Colombia, Uruguay, Panama, Algeria, Guinea, France, East Germany, Spain, and Israel wrote letters to the editors to express their support for the magazine.[14] A Mexican visiting Volgograd, Russia, wrote the editors to say that he had heard Radio Moscow describe *Política* as the most important magazine in Latin America. "The only Mexican publication that is known in Europe and the socialist world is *Política*," he reported. "People ask for the magazine; in the schools and the factories, workers and students talk to me about it."[15] The US embassy in Mexico City collected *Política* and translated some articles, and officials in the Argentine, Ecuadorian, and Bolivian embassies cared enough about the magazine's coverage of their countries to write in with corrections.[16] Influential leftist journalist and author Carleton Beals was a fan of *Política*; in 1963, he wrote an open letter to the head of the US postal service denouncing the delays in the delivery of his subscription. He described the magazine as "superior to anything that is published in the United States. About Mexican matters it is superb and fearless. . . . for me, it is indispensable."[17]

Unlike most Mexican press, *Política* did not shy away from criticizing President López Mateos, and it waged an open war against his successor, Gustavo Díaz Ordaz. As one of the editors recalled, "Marcué assigned a great deal of importance to the political battle against . . . President Díaz Ordaz in particular."[18] A May 1963 editorial called Díaz Ordaz, who was then minister of the interior, a "reactionary" and declared that he "should not and cannot become president."[19] The cover of the magazine a few months later declared: "He Will Not Be President!"[20] The November 1, 1963, cover contained a cartoon of Díaz Ordaz wearing Catholic vestments with a Nazi swastika, carrying a bludgeon in one hand and stone tablets in the other. The tablets contained a quote from the *Wall Street Journal* that described him as "a vehement anti-communist who commands the powerful support of ex-president Miguel Alemán and of the Catholic Church." *Política* also created pamphlets containing a copy of the cartoon and the accompanying article protesting Díaz Ordaz's candidacy, which made their way into the files of the Mexican government's intelligence agencies.[21]

FIGURE 15. Cover of *Política* magazine with a cartoon by Rius of Secretary of the Interior Gustavo Díaz Ordaz wearing Catholic vestments with Nazi swastikas, Nov. 1, 1963. He carries tablets that quote a *Wall Street Journal* description of him as "a vehement anticommunist who commands the powerful support of ex-president Miguel Alemán and of the Catholic Church." Source: Biblioteca Lerdo de Tejada and the US Library of Congress Historical Newspapers Collection.

Política was one of the most outspoken critics of governmental corruption, especially when it came to the question of freedom of the press. For the June 1961 anniversary of the Day of Freedom of the Press, the magazine ran an article titled "Corruption, More than Freedom." It described recent occasions in which government officials had harassed or imprisoned journalists, but argued, "in general, the procedures [for limiting press freedom] have been indirect control and bribery more than frontal assault." According to *Política*, the debts that most major newspapers owed to Productora e Importadora de Papel, SA (PIPSA) and the Nacional Financiera,[22] as well as the fact that much of their earnings came from official sources in the form of ads, planted articles known as *gacetillas*, and bribes (*embutes*), compelled the press to follow the government's political orientation. "This, then, is the panorama as we celebrate once again the Day of Freedom of the Press: generalized corruption that extends to every level of journalism," *Política* concluded.[23]

Política also challenged the government's claim that Mexico was a democracy. A year before the elections of 1964, an editorial on the back cover of the

May 15, 1963, edition discussed why there was so much public anxiety surrounding the event and why most people referred to it as the *sucesión presidencial* (presidential succession) rather than the presidential election. The editorial denounced the practice known as *tapadismo*, in which Mexican presidents chose their successors by designating the PRI's next candidate: "The successor, chosen by the president and his close circle, who represents the interests of the oligarchy in power with its electoral apparatus, the PRI, is the future president. This antidemocratic system of cabals requires secrecy and bribery, and eliminates the participation of the masses."[24] A few months later, Ermilo Abreu Gómez published another article on the subject titled "Electoral Fraud and Civic Conscience," in which he also decried the lack of democracy in Mexican elections. He recalled for readers the era of the Porfirian dictatorship, the subsequent Mexican Revolution, and its noble goals of *sufragio efectivo y no reelección* (effective suffrage and no reelection). "But what has happened?" Abreu Gómez asked. "Something monstrous with grave consequences. Now, the vote is only free in appearance."[25]

One of the characteristics that most distinguished *Política* from the rest of the Mexican press was its coverage of the government's violent repression of opposition. In August 1960, one of the magazine's earliest issues contained a detailed description and two full pages of images of police with batons attacking a demonstration in support of striking teachers.[26] *Política* also provided extensive coverage of the assassination of agrarian leader Rubén Jaramillo and four members of his family in May 1962. The cover of the June 1, 1962, edition bore a photo of Jaramillo and President López Mateos hugging each other; the intentionally incongruous caption below read: "The Five Bodies Were Found Together." An editorial about the assassination called it "terrorism from above" and observed: "This sort of terrorism indicates that those at the height of public power do not consider themselves strong, but weak and afraid, impotent and incapable."[27]

Política's coverage of state repression called into question the government's attempts to portray Mexico as more democratic or peaceful than the rest of Latin America. The magazine published a declaration by the Mexican Communist Party about the army's occupation of the University of Sonora and the city of Hermosillo in May 1967 that warned that Mexico was veering dangerously close to the military dictatorships of Argentina, Brazil, and Bolivia. "With Methods Employed by the 'Gorillas,' Díaz Ordaz Is Heading

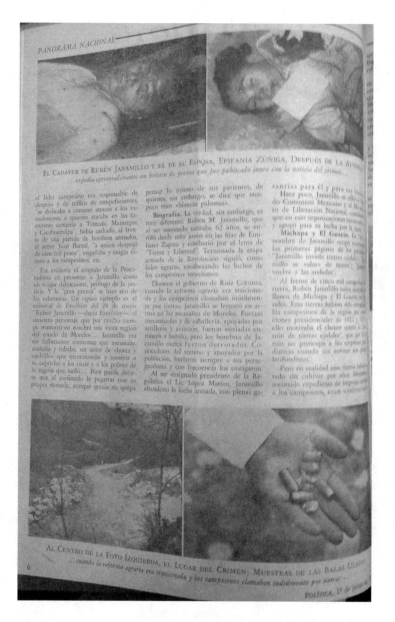

FIGURE 16. Issue of *Política* with photographs of the bodies of Rubén Jaramillo and his wife, June 1, 1962. Source: Biblioteca Lerdo de Tejada and the US Library of Congress Historical Newspapers Collection.

FIGURE 17. *Política* cartoon by Rius asking whether Mexico's self-proclaimed democratic government was actually run by military "gorillas," May 1–14, 1967. Source: Biblioteca Lerdo de Tejada and the US Library of Congress Historical Newspapers Collection.

toward a Military and Police Dictatorship," the title predicted.[28] The same issue of the magazine contained a political cartoon by Rius of a gorilla wearing an officer's cap and holding a lit match. The title of the cartoon seemed to ask readers whether Mexico's "democracy" was also run by warmongering beasts playing with fire.

But *Política*'s favorite motif for criticizing Mexico's leaders hit closer to home: comparing the self-styled revolutionary government to the dictatorial rule of Porfirio Díaz in the late nineteenth and early twentieth century, which had sparked the Mexican Revolution of 1910. An article in September 1963 about the murders of seven campesinos in Guerrero by police and members of the military called the operation "worthy of the best times of the Porfirian dictatorship."[29] Coverage of the repression of students in Sonora in 1967 compared the government's violent tactics to those practiced during the prerevolutionary era of "Porfirian peace."[30] A subsequent article about the same events in Sonora described the violence as "institutionalized terrorism"—a thinly veiled play on the PRI's claim to an "institutionalized revolution." The images accompanying that article were side-by-side photographs of Gustavo Díaz Ordaz and Porfirio Díaz.[31]

Mexico's leaders, including Díaz Ordaz, were well aware of this combative, critical magazine. Reports about *Política* and its director, Manuel Marcué Pardiñas, filled the intelligence records of both the Dirección Federal de Seguridad (DFS) and the Dirección General de Investigaciones Políticas y Sociales.[32] Agents clipped copies of articles, tapped the phone lines at the magazine's offices and at Marcué Pardiñas's home, and reported on all activity connected to the magazine. In 1966, the head of the DFS compiled a twenty-one-page report about Marcué Pardiñas and *Política*. "One of the characteristics of the magazine is the constant and systematic attack on the president of the republic," he contended. The head of intelligence described Marcué Pardiñas as "a radical communist . . . a violent and temperamental individual . . . with an irascible character." The report claimed that he was "an immoral person, especially in his intimate life," who tried to seduce the wives of his best friends and business partners.[33] The author described how Marcué Pardiñas organized and helped print propaganda for demonstrations in favor of Cuba, Dominican Republic, Vietnam, workers, students, political prisoners, and the Mexican Communist Party. The head of intelligence reported that Marcué Pardiñas made eleven trips to Cuba in the years following Castro's triumph and claimed that he received money from the Cuban and Soviet embassies to cover *Política*'s expenses.[34]

Mexican leaders responded to *Política*'s challenge using a variety of tactics. The most constant source of pressure that the government applied was financial. Unlike most magazines and newspapers in Mexico at the time, *Política* did not receive any money from the government to publish its advertisements and announcements. Indeed, after the first few issues, the magazine stopped running ads almost entirely. *Política*'s sole sources of financial support were its readers and a few generous patrons, including the painter David Alfaro Siqueiros and, if the rumors were true, Fidel Castro and Carlos A. Madrazo.[35] Additional financial strain came from the fact that *Política* had to pay a high price for newsprint since the state-run PIPSA frequently refused to sell the magazine any paper.[36] On numerous occasions, *Política* denounced PIPSA for withholding supplies from the magazine and apologized to loyal readers for having to skip issues and use inferior paper as a result.[37]

Mexican officials also resorted to intimidation in their attempts to curb Marcué Pardiñas's activities. Police arrested and fined *Política*'s director in January 1961 for his participation in a pro-Cuba demonstration, they raided the magazine's offices in search of propaganda prior to US president John F. Kennedy's visit to Mexico in the summer of 1962, and in August 1963 members of a different police force assaulted and beat Marcué Pardiñas after he spoke at a meeting on behalf of political prisoners.[38] In April 1966, the subdirector of the police of the Federal District rounded up *Política*'s director and other leftist leaders and warned them not to create any trouble during President Lyndon Johnson's visit to Mexico.[39]

When threats and paper shortages failed to silence *Política*, the Mexican government physically removed especially offensive issues from circulation. In 1966, the head of the DFS reported that approximately 1,500 copies of the March 1 edition of the magazine had been prevented from leaving the country to their intended destinations in Cuba, Puerto Rico, Colombia, and Panama.[40] The intelligence report specified that this issue contained an open letter from Marcué Pardiñas to President Díaz Ordaz and an invitation to a demonstration in support of the people of Vietnam. In the unacceptable letter, *Política* denounced the presence of illegal police groups and foreign infiltration by the CIA and FBI and warned the president that these groups were working to carry out a bloodless coup in order to impose an ultrareactionary government in Mexico.[41] Government functionaries also sometimes prevented the circulation of *Política* within the country; in November 1966, the Dirección General de Correos removed 1,000 copies of the magazine, which contained articles "offensive to the regime," that were supposed to be sent to subscribers in Michoacán.[42]

By the end of 1967, the financial burden of publishing *Política* had become too much for Marcué Pardiñas. Years later, he told his nephew and biographer, Carlos Perzabal, that he lost foreign support for the magazine after refusing to favor the Cuban line in his coverage of the debates at the Tricontinental Conference of 1966 and the Organization of Latin American Solidarity Conference of 1967.[43] Other members of the editorial staff also recalled that tight finances, rather than political pressure or intimidation, ultimately drove the magazine out of business.[44] Marcué Pardiñas had to resort to combining various issues throughout the last year of *Política*'s existence, resulting in the magazine appearing with less regularity. In his farewell letter in the last issue, Marcué Pardiñas explained that even though "all the weight of the governmental machinery and its deceptive conception of freedom of the press bore down on *Política*," it was ultimately economic conditions that silenced the magazine.[45]

Política magazine provided detailed coverage and analysis of the most controversial subjects of its day and directly challenged some of the most powerful people in Mexico, including the president. In doing so, the magazine flaunted many of the so-called unwritten rules of Mexican journalism. The story of *Política* suggests that the subjugation of the press to the government during this time was not as complete as it has appeared.

The fact that Manuel Marcué Pardiñas was able to keep publishing his combative, critical, and frequently offensive magazine for seven and a half years raises questions about the relationship between the press and the government in 1960s Mexico. How did this happen, at a time when the PRI was supposedly at the height of its control and when one of the most repressive leaders in modern Mexican history sat at the apex of national power? Gustavo Díaz Ordaz cared enough about *Política* to have his top agents follow the director's every move, and would have known about the magazine's popularity and intellectual influence. So why didn't he shut it down?

There are two likely explanations: either Díaz Ordaz couldn't shut down

Política magazine, or he didn't want to. Perhaps Díaz Ordaz was uncertain about what to do, or not confident enough in his own strength to fight *Política* head-on, and thus had to settle for a slower process of financial strangulation. This would suggest that the Mexican government and its president were not as all-powerful as they appeared. Or maybe Díaz Ordaz tolerated *Política* because the existence of the magazine contributed to the illusion that Mexico was a democracy with a free press. This tolerance of criticism and insult would suggest that Díaz Ordaz was not as thin-skinned and repressive as most accounts claim.

But if Díaz Ordaz did indeed use *Política* as a fig leaf to hide media censorship, the gamble cost him dearly. The magazine turned out to be more than just a symbolic concession or diversion. It exposed the government's shortcomings, its lies, and its crimes, and laid them bare for the entire world to see. *Política* served as a formative source of information and ideas, especially for the members of a younger generation who carried the magazine's ideas forward and went on to challenge Díaz Ordaz, the PRI, and the rest of Mexico's "perfect dictatorship."

Notes

1. Vargas Llosa, *Desafíos a la libertad*, 121. For discussions on the tendency in the literature to exaggerate the government's power in this period, see Rubin, *Decentering the Regime*; Padilla, *Rural Resistance*, 7–15; Walker, *Waking from the Dream*, 4–9.
2. Loaeza, "Gustavo Díaz Ordaz"; Krauze, *Mexico*, 665–731.
3. Camp, *Intellectuals and the State*, 177–204; Lawson, *Building the Fourth Estate*, 13–58; Scherer García and Monsiváis, *Tiempo de saber*, 163; Rodríguez Munguía, *La otra guerra secreta*, 21–45.
4. "ALM y los obreros," *Política*, May 1, 1960, 3–7. On the most important of these movements—the railroad workers—see Alegre, *Railroad Radicals*.
5. "Ni agua ni créditos," *Política*, May 1, 1960, 14–15; Carlos Fuentes, "Revolución sin brújula," *Política*, May 1, 1960, 16. On Mexico's law against social dissolution and the creation of political prisoners, see Stevens, "Legality."
6. Camp, *Intellectuals and the State*, 194; Lawson, *Building the Fourth Estate*, 50.
7. According to Mexican intelligence agents, 15,000 copies were sold in Mexico City by sidewalk vendors, 5,000 were sold in the rest of Mexico, and the remaining 5,000 were sent to subscribers in Mexico and abroad. Fernando Gutiérrez Barrios, "Antecedentes y actividades de Manuel Marcué Pardiñas," Oct. 24, 1966, AGN/DFS/11-109-1966, file 1, 158.

8. On the New Left, see Gosse, *Where the Boys Are*. On the differences between the Old and New Left in Mexico, see Zolov, "Expanding Our Conceptual Horizons." On the impact of the Cuban Revolution in Mexico, see Keller, *Mexico's Cold War*.

9. The famous Mexican painter David Alfaro Siqueiros was imprisoned in 1960 for criticizing the Mexican government during a tour of Cuba and Venezuela and supposedly supporting rioting students, teachers, and workers; Demetrio Vallejo and Valentín Campa were jailed in 1959 after leading the railroad workers movement; and Othón Salazar landed in prison in 1958 after organizing a movement of teachers that demanded a salary increase and new union leadership beginning in 1956. See White, *Siqueiros*; Alegre, *Railroad Radicals*; Pellicer de Brody and Reyna, *Historia*.

10. On the Latin American Conference for National Sovereignty, Economic Emancipation, and Peace (also known as the Latin American Peace Conference), see Keller, "Don Lázaro Rises Again"; Iber, *Neither Peace nor Freedom*, 161–62.

11. Pensado, *Rebel Mexico*, 168. On *Política*'s influence on young leftists, see also Sánchez Sierra, "Crisis mística."

12. Perzabal, *De las memorias*, 23; Daniel Molina Álvarez, "La revista *Política*: Un proyecto periodístico y político," *Siempre!*, Oct. 22, 2011, http://www.siempre.mx/2011/10/la-revista-politica-un-proyecto-periodistico-y-politico.

13. Perzabal, *De las memorias*, 132.

14. For examples of letters to the editors from readers in other countries, see "Del APRA rebelde," *Política*, Mar. 1, 1961, 3; "Aclaración salvadoreña," *Política*, Apr. 15, 1961, 2; "Desde Chile," *Política*, June 15, 1961, 3; "Voz puertorriqueña," *Política*, July 1, 1961, 1; "Inquisición hondureña," *Política*, July 1, 1961, 3; "Desde argelia," *Política*, Sept. 1, 1961, 1; "Mexicano en Chicago," *Política*, Oct. 1, 1961, 3; "Canadiense," *Política*, Nov. 15, 1961, 3.

15. "*Política* en Europa," *Política*, Dec. 1, 1961, 1.

16. The collection of *Política* magazines in the Library of Congress has US State Department stamps on various issues, as well as English translations of some articles related to the United States. For examples of letters to *Política*'s editors from other embassies, see "Afirmación diplomática," *Política*, Mar. 1, 1961, 1; "Aclaración ecuatoriana," *Política*, Sept. 15, 1961, 1–2; "Aclaración boliviana," *Política*, Mar. 15, 1966, 2–3.

17. Carleton Beals, "Al director de Correos: ¡Quite usted sus sucias manos!," *Política*, Dec. 1, 1963, B. On Beals's political and cultural importance as a leftist commentator on Latin America, see Gosse, *Where the Boys Are*, 18–19.

18. Perzabal, *De las memorias*, 106.

19. José Felipe Pardiñas, "'Política' y la sucesión presidencial," *Política*, May 15, 1963, back cover.

20. *Política*, Aug. 15, 1963.

21. *Política* pamphlet, Nov. 1, 1963, AGN/DGIPS/2851 A.

22. PIPSA was the state-run company that sold newsprint to the Mexican press. PIPSA would unofficially manipulate the price and supply of paper in order to reward or punish different publishers. See Rodríguez Munguía, *La otra guerra secreta*, 182. The Nacional Financiera was a state-run development bank that made loans to Mexican businesses. See Moreno, *Yankee Don't Go Home!*, 31.

23. "Corrupción, más que libertad," *Política*, June 15, 1961, 51.

24. On tapadismo, see Cosío Villegas, *El sistema político*; Narváez, *La sucesión presidencial*; Manuel Marcué Pardiñas, "*Política* y la sucesión presidencial," *Política*, May 15, 1963.

25. Ermilo Abreu Gómez, "El fraude electoral y la conciencia cívica," *Política*, Aug. 1, 1963, 26.

26. "Jueves trágico," *Política*, Aug. 15, 1960, 12.

27. "Un crimen del régimen," *Política*, June 1, 1962, 4. On Jaramillo's assassination, see Padilla, *Rural Resistance*.

28. Arnoldo Martínez Verdugo, "Con métodos empleados por los 'gorilas,' Díaz Ordaz camina rumbo a una dictadura militar y policiaca," *Política*, May 1–14, 1967, 3.

29. "Terror en el campo," *Política*, Sept. 15, 1963, 9.

30. "Sonora: Paz porfiriana," *Política*, May 15–31, 1967, 5.

31. "Sonora: Terrorismo institucionalizado," *Política*, June 1–July 14, 1967, 28.

32. On Mexico's intelligence services, see Navarro, *Political Intelligence*; and a special issue of *Journal of Iberian and Latin American Research* 19, no. 1 (July 2013): 1–103.

33. Gutiérrez Barrios, "Antecedentes y actividades," file 1, 158. While Marcué Pardiñas did little to hide his amorous dalliances, including an affair with actress Beatriz Baz, he never admitted to seducing his friends' wives. Perzabal, *De las memorias*, 22–25.

34. Members of the *Política* staff also speculated that a significant amount of the magazine's funding came from Cuba and the Soviet Union. Marcué Pardiñas confessed to having an account for the magazine in the National Bank of Cuba, and *Política* frequently printed Cuban, Soviet, and Chinese government documents as well as small ads for Radio Havana. Perzabal, *De las memorias*, 109, 130; Comité 68 Pro Libertadores Democráticas, *Los procesos de México*, 358.

35. Rumors also circulated that Ernesto P. Uruchurtu and Alfonso Corona del Rosal financed *Política*. Perzabal, *De las memorias*, 50, 109–10; Rodríguez Munguía, *La otra guerra secreta*, 206.

36. Telephone surveillance of magazine "Política," Oct. 18, 1965, AGN/DGIPS/2959A.

37. "Intervención contra '*Política*,'" Oct. 15, 1960, inside cover; Manuel Marcué Pardiñas and Jorge Carrión, "La maniobra continúa," *Política*, Nov. 1, 1960, inside cover; Manuel Marcué Pardiñas and Jorge Carrión, "A nuestros

lectores," Nov. 15, 1960, inside cover; "PIPSA y 'BIPSA,'" *Política*, Dec. 15, 1960, 63; "La PIPSA contra *Política*," *Política*, Mar. 15, 1966, 1.

38. "Régimen policiaco?," *Política*, Feb. 1, 1961; "Asalto a *Política*," July 1, 1962, 12; Gutiérrez Barrios, "Antecedentes y actividades."

39. Policia Judicial Federal, untitled report [Communists Warned Not to Protest Johnson's Visit], Apr. 14, 1966, AGN/GDO/205, 124.

40. Fernando Gutiérrez Barrios, "Revista '*Política*,'" Mar. 11, 1966, AGN/DGIPS/2959A.

41. Manuel Marcué Pardiñas, "Carta al presidente de la república," *Política*, Mar. 1, 1966.

42. Subdirección de la Dirección General de Correos, untitled report [Magazine "Política" Removed from Mail], Nov. 8, 1966, AGN/DGIPS/2959A.

43. Perzabal, *De las memorias*, 48. On the Tricontinental and OLAS conferences, see Keller, *Mexico's Cold War*, 182–90; Anderson, *Che Guevara*, 643–44; Domínguez, *To Make a World*, 69–70.

44. Perzabal, *De las memorias*, 109.

45. Manuel Marcué Pardiñas, "Un alto para hacer un balance de la tarea política," *Política*, Dec. 1–31, 1967, 4.

10 | Censorship in the Headlines

National News and the Contradictions of Mexico City's Press Opening in the 1970s

VANESSA FREIJE

In the early hours of March 6, 1981, local authorities removed national periodicals from Baja California newsstands. Four days later, a headline in *Zeta*, Tijuana's only investigative news publication, announced, "Mexico City Newspapers Were Confiscated on Friday."[1] The anonymous staff writer revealed that a single article, which had reported on Mexico City protests against Baja California governor Roberto de la Madrid, had prompted the seizure. *Zeta* republished the prohibited news item under a flashy headline and denounced censorship. Rather than successfully suppressing the article, officials had inadvertently drawn greater attention to the piece in question.

Studies of Mexico City's late twentieth-century press have tended to describe a gradual opening that slowly freed reporters from the structural constraints that encouraged self-censorship.[2] However, stories such as the one above point to a more complicated process in which myriad forms of censorship persisted (and at times failed) even as more publications became willing to print controversial material. This could lead, paradoxically, to the open discussion of government interventions. Few scholars have examined the consequences of making censorship visible to Mexican readers, leaving unexplored the ways in which reporters have politicized censorship. During the 1970s, some journalists flouted attempts to restrict press content, openly challenging ad hoc interventions. While these moments of contestation were not exceedingly common, they nonetheless highlight the fact that even moments of overt censorship did not always successfully silence criticism.

In this chapter, I analyze three frustrated attempts at censorship. They range from the implicit encouragement of self-censorship to the firing of individual reporters. In the first case, I examine opinion writing at *Excélsior*, one of the nation's oldest dailies. In the early 1970s, editorial writers not only challenged government statements on armed leftist groups, which reduced guerrillas to common criminals, but also contradicted the front pages of their own newspaper. This case shows, however, that even while *Excélsior* opened spaces for dissent, subtle self-censorship persisted. The second episode I revisit is the 1976 removal of *Excélsior*'s editorial staff, an action orchestrated by President Luis Echeverría (1970–1976). This case demonstrates how publicizing censorship created a powerful and lasting mythology about the former independence of *Excélsior* and its directors. In the final section, I explore the connections between local and national censorship, analyzing a 1979 intervention in a Baja California newspaper and local attempts to silence a nationally syndicated column in 1981. This case highlights that the interrelationship between local and national news could facilitate the circumvention of censorship, while also bringing syndicated Mexico City columnists face-to-face with heavy-handed tactics that were more common outside the capital.

In this chapter, I adopt contemporary journalists' definition of censorship, which they understood to be action taken by power holders to prevent the publication or dissemination of ideas.[3] Unlike the myriad forms of social control that limit speech, blatant interventions by government authorities in the late twentieth century redrew the lines of political disagreement and sparked public debate. Exploring the experience of overt censorship shows how attacks on the press were politicized during the 1970s. Journalists invoked these episodes to undergird their own reputations for independence and to appeal to a readership that distrusted official information. The exposure of censorship often called attention to the suppressed content and, in some cases, engendered international outrage against the responsible officials. Such reportage brought different publics into conversation with one another, as readers were united by their shared sense of being in the know. By publicizing censorship, journalists acknowledged persistent repression while suggesting the impossibility of fully controlling criticism.

The Opening of the Public Sphere

Since the early twentieth century, Mexico's national newspaper industry thrived with government support. Periodicals multiplied with the help of state-subsidized newsprint, advertising, and loans. Government labor authorities also oversaw newspaper cooperatives and unions, which cemented a symbiotic state-press relationship. In this context, Mexico City newspaper owners and directors generally avoided direct criticism of high-ranking public officials or the ruling party, knowing that it could spell financial ruin. Economic factors similarly encouraged journalists to self-censor. Reporters earned meager salaries and depended on the notorious *embutes* (regular cash payments) to supplement their incomes. Journalism also offered the possibility of upward mobility. Those with talent and the right connections could rise to powerful positions in the newsroom and government. Media, in short, functioned as part of the massive corporatist structure that supported the ruling Partido Revolucionario Institucional (PRI), which had held power since 1929.[4]

Beginning in the 1960s, Mexico City witnessed an expansion of the public sphere. The state's midcentury investment in public universities allowed art collectives and cultural organizations to flourish.[5] Leftist magazines, cultural supplements, and new dailies emerged and supported labor and peasant movements in a generally anticommunist political climate. Crime tabloids, meanwhile, articulated strident critiques of injustice.[6] At the same time, politicians jealously policed Mexico City broadsheets with national circulations. However, after the violent attacks against student protesters in October 1968, President Echeverría decided to allow greater criticism in *Excélsior*, which had historically served as a conservative government mouthpiece.[7] This was part of the president's "democratic opening," which he declared to appease a discontented, urban middle class.[8] Echeverría made *Excélsior*'s new, democratically minded director, Julio Scherer García, a close ally and regularly invited him to Los Pinos to discuss national problems.[9] With the president's explicit blessing, *Excélsior* became the most prominent example of critical news commentary.[10]

Even as the spaces for debate expanded, the boundaries of acceptable speech remained unpredictable. At times, confrontational pieces were printed with no government response, while at other times officials demanded that newspaper directors withhold seemingly toothless articles.[11] In the absence of a censorship agency, officials often relied on newspaper directors and journalists to internalize the norms of coverage and write their copy accordingly. When reporters did not self-censor, however, the government's mechanism for preventing critical coverage in Mexico City was relatively ineffective. By the 1970s, the limits of these policies were becoming apparent, particularly given the open criticism of the PRI after the 1968 student massacre. With the growing density of muckraking outlets and the national syndication of popular columns, Mexico City reporters could easily find an outlet for critical articles.[12] Journalists soon tested the limits of tolerance when they challenged official explanations for political kidnappings.

The Two Faces of *Excélsior*

On May 5, 1973, *Excélsior*'s front page reported that the Fuerzas Revolucionarias Armadas del Pueblo (FRAP) had kidnapped US consul general Terrence George Leonhardy in Guadalajara.[13] The abduction was the work of a leftist guerrilla group, one of a handful that had become increasingly active in Mexico since the late 1960s.[14] The previous day, sixty-year-old Leonhardy was driving alone in the early evening when two vehicles intercepted him and armed individuals forced him out of his car. Guerrilla groups had previously targeted Mexican public officials, but Leonhardy's kidnapping was the first action against a US citizen, let alone a foreign diplomat.[15]

In its list of demands, the FRAP mandated that all major Mexico City newspapers and broadcasters disseminate the group's manifesto and communiqués the following day.[16] On May 6, the guerrillas related their political agenda to a national audience, figuratively holding the country's news media hostage. The FRAP's communiqué challenged government characterizations of the group as "common criminals, paid assassins, [and] cattle robbers" and unequivocally identified their actions as a political response to wealth inequality and state repression.[17] However, the president refused to acknowledge these ideological underpinnings. To admit the existence of violent leftism, he feared, would spark concerns about Mexico's political instability and could provoke US intervention.[18] Echeverría thus quickly acceded to the kidnappers' demands, and in accordance with their specifications, he arranged to transport thirty political prisoners to Havana, Cuba, on May 6.[19]

Like governing officials, the national broadsheets generally referred to guerrillas as "delinquents" and "deranged."[20] The criminalization of leftists was not new, and examples from the early 1960s show that officials depoliticized and smeared peasant leaders and communists as drug traffickers.[21] In its coverage of Leonhardy's kidnapping, *Excélsior* split the difference: the front pages reproduced the official claims of criminality while the opinion pages challenged them. This contradictory self-presentation was apparent in the May 7 issue. Three days after Leonhardy's abduction, the periodical gave front-page coverage to an interview with the president, in which Echeverría defined the kidnapping as "the work of common criminals."[22] The article offered no alternative information that might undermine the claim that the FRAP was an apolitical organization.

On the same day that Echeverría's interview appeared, multiple opinion pieces rejected the depiction of the kidnappers as criminals, contradicting the acquiescent front-page coverage. Instead, they argued that leftist groups recurred to violence because democratic and legal channels for political change were closed.[23] Opinion writers thus held the Mexican government responsible for radicalizing guerrilla groups. Since Scherer García assumed the *Excélsior* directorship in 1968, the editorial pages gradually had become a well-regarded space for debate, modeled on the French journalistic tradition.[24] The divisions between opinion and hard news were not as starkly drawn in Mexico as in the Anglo-American tradition.[25] Commentary and literary journalism were historically revered news genres, and the editorial articles on the kidnapping could carry significant weight for the reading public. Prominently placed on the sixth and seventh pages of the first section, the opinion articles were easily located by *Excélsior* readers alongside cartoons, notorious for satirizing Mexican politics.

Excélsior's editorial writers argued that violent leftist groups grew out of state repression. For example, an Universidad Nacional Autónoma de México (UNAM) professor, Abelardo Villegas, challenged the president's neat separation between crime and politics. In a piece entitled "Crime as a Political Solution," Villegas argued that the government used extralegal violence to resolve political problems.[26] To undergird his point, Villegas referenced the continued police violence against protesters, citing recent attacks at the Ben-emérita Universidad Autónoma de Puebla, which had left five students dead. By placing the kidnapping in this context, Villegas challenged Echeverría's claims that the group was apolitical. Reminding readers of the 1968 and 1971 attacks against student protesters, Villegas pointed out that "the accumulation of victims clearly demonstrates that Mexican politics is incapable of peacefully and institutionally resolving conflicts."[27] Villegas implicitly compared two forms of civic engagement—street protests and violent direct action. He suggested that the FRAP's methods were the most successful because the government only listened to citizens' demands when it was held hostage.

Deviations from the front pages grew more pointed when *Excélsior* opinion editor Miguel Ángel Granados Chapa wrote an editorial on May 8.[28] At age thirty-two, he represented some of the young talent that Scherer García had recruited to revitalize the newspaper. Granados Chapa urged readers to consider the political significance of Leonhardy's kidnapping. In an explicit challenge to the president's statements, he opened by asserting, "No, they are not common criminals." While he disapproved of their methods, he argued that the kidnappers "acted with clear political intentions. They have questioned the system, and it is important to understand their behavior."[29] Not only did Granados Chapa take issue with the president's characterization of the kidnappers, he also implicitly contested the front page of *Excélsior* that day, which had abandoned the kidnapping for apparently more pressing issues. Indeed, the banner below the masthead announced, "Free at 10 PM in Guadalajara: A Crowd Welcomed Him," indicating that Leonhardy's safe return effectively closed the case.

Granados Chapa emphasized that the distinction between political and criminal violence was not merely semantic. Discerning the difference, he explained, "requires a conscious assessment of what the country truly is." He underscored that leaders must acknowledge deep structural problems, such as inequality and poverty, and not fixate solely on their manifestations in violence. Granados Chapa also implied that state violence produced political violence. Referencing the assassination of five protesting students in Puebla one week earlier, he asserted that "it should not be forgotten that if Guadalajara exists, so does Puebla." By invoking state violence, Granados Chapa suggested that if the kidnappers were criminals, then governing officials were as well.[30]

Yet the opinion editor simultaneously engaged in a subtle form of self-censorship. While he implicitly challenged the president, he never explicitly named Echeverría. In doing so, Granados Chapa softened his criticism, making it less likely to invite official scrutiny. This was apparent, for example, when he compared the current administration with that of the reviled dictator Porfirio Díaz, whose thirty-year rule was ended by the 1910 revolution. The journalist reminded readers, "Emiliano Zapata, idolized today as an architect of our political and social foundation, was nothing more than a 'cattle robber' for the Porfirian 'establishment' and even for the rulers of the first revolution." Connecting Echeverría's position toward the FRAP with Díaz's toward Zapata, Granados Chapa argued that the president was engaging in a long-standing strategy of undermining revolutionaries. The comparison also implicitly called into question Echeverría's promises to revive leftism. At the same time, however, Granados Chapa avoided any direct mention of him and thus adhered to the journalistic norm of showing deference for the president.[31]

To today's reader, Granados Chapa's piece may not appear to directly challenge Echeverría. Yet at the time, one reader from Acapulco interpreted the editorial as doing just that. Granados Chapa made the target of his criticism intelligible to his audience, while remaining within the norms of acceptable discourse. On the day following his editorial, a woman named Leonor sent him a two-page handwritten letter. She thanked him for his column and noted that "if you had not written it, I would have struggled to write the same thing and sent it to President Luis Echeverría, who in my opinion, committed a very serious mistake by saying that the kidnappers were nothing more than common criminals." Like Granados Chapa, Leonor saw guerrilla violence as a response to the lack of democratic avenues for change. She opined that politicians, including the president, were out of touch with the poverty that most Mexicans faced. Referencing the FRAP, she lamented, "As soon as a person or a group tries to bring [these realities] to light and change them, they are branded as 'communists.'"[32] For this *Excélsior* reader, the depoliticization of the FRAP signaled Echeverría's unwillingness to listen to dissenting opinions.

In the early 1970s, *Excélsior*'s opinion pages provided a conspicuous counterweight to the newspaper's front pages, where official viewpoints prevailed. *Excélsior*'s editorial contributors became increasingly vocal on controversial topics, such as the waning power and popularity of the PRI, and administration officials at times responded by insisting that editorialists moderate their tone to take the bite out of criticism.[33] Yet at the same time, national broadsheets, including *Excélsior*, reinforced the official position on leftist guerrillas over the following years. Periodicals dutifully reported each new arrest and, most important, concealed critical information regarding the repressive strategies being used by state security forces to quash the leftist threat.[34] Scherer García ultimately viewed Echeverría as an ally in a shared democratizing project, and thus the inconsistencies between the two faces of *Excélsior*—let alone the issue of self-censorship—were never explicitly addressed for readers.

Commemorating Censorship: The 1976 Coup at *Excélsior*

Eventually, Echeverría grew intolerant of the *Excélsior* leadership. On July 8, 1976, he surreptitiously orchestrated a coup in the newspaper cooperative, leading to the dismissal of Scherer García and his editorial team. However, the ousting of the *Excélsior* editors produced unintended consequences. More than 200 journalists and printers resigned in solidarity. And while domestic news outlets remained silent on the issue, the action was immediately met with opprobrium abroad. In light of the coup, foreign correspondents questioned the quality of the free press and democracy in Mexico.[35] Their reportage stained Echeverría's image abroad while bolstering the editors' reputations for independence at home. Finally, the removal of Scherer García did not prevent him from founding a highly critical newsmagazine, *Proceso*, which became a platform for attacking the outgoing president. In short, Echeverría miscalculated by escalating to overt censorship.

The creation of *Excélsior*'s cooperative in 1932 foreshadowed the intervention in 1976. With the newspaper facing bankruptcy, the still-powerful former president Plutarco Elías Calles had acted to keep *Excélsior*'s doors open. He calculated that the prevailing cooperative laws would allow the government to intervene if the newspaper became a political problem.[36] The 1976 intervention was also the logical outgrowth of a contradictory policy toward the press. Echeverría believed that allowing critical perspectives in a major broadsheet would both win over Mexican intellectuals and allow him to anticipate and co-opt oppositional currents.[37] Since the early 1970s, he had publicly maintained his support for the newspaper while secretly undermining it. He encouraged advertising boycotts, published defamatory leaflets, and conspired with discontented cooperative members.[38] Following the change of editorial leadership in 1976, Echeverría expected that he would be able to hide his instigating role by forbidding Mexico City news outlets from covering the episode. However, he discounted the political cost of censoring the editors.

Scholars now consider the *Excélsior* intervention to be one of the most iconic breaches of press freedom in Mexico. Indeed, one would be hard pressed to find a history of twentieth-century Mexican journalism that does not include some description of the coup and the president's responsibility.[39] This legacy endures because Mexico City writers continually have reminded readers of the episode and its significance. Beginning with roundtable discussions and continuing with speeches, articles, anniversary commemorations, memoirs, and novels, the ousted journalists upheld the intervention as an outrageous political transgression.[40] However, the memorialization of the *Excélsior* coup also served a purpose beyond political denunciation. Doing so united a public of intellectuals, journalists, and informed readers who identified with a liberal democratic ideology of speech rights. This public shared both a critical understanding of the episode and a distrust of official information.

After the intervention, Echeverría denied any involvement, publicly maintaining that *Excélsior* cooperative members had voiced their preference through a democratic vote.[41] With the exception of *Excélsior* and *Siempre!*, Mexican print media did not discuss the episode.[42] However, foreign coverage generated widespread skepticism about Echeverría abroad, and this proved critical to the initial circumvention of censorship in Mexico City. Foreign reporters did not need to worry about explicitly identifying the president's responsibility. The day after the intervention, *New York Times* correspondent Alan Riding acknowledged long-standing divisions in the *Excélsior* cooperative but pronounced that "behind the internal dispute . . . is an apparent effort by the Government of President Luis Echeverría Álvarez to silence the country's only out-spokenly critical newspaper."[43] For Riding, the removal of Scherer García signified a reversal of press opening, motivated by critical pieces published over the previous year. Riding's unquestioning assertion that Echeverría was behind the coup represented a public relations victory for the ousted editors. In his article the next day, Riding reasserted that "evidence of the government's involvement appears to be overwhelming."[44]

One week later, on July 13, a *New York Times* editorial drew even broader conclusions and argued that the intervention undermined Mexico's pretensions to democracy and press freedom. Representing the official opinion of the *New York Times*, the piece publicly shamed Echeverría for his instigating role and characterized the intervention as an "act of totalitarian suppression that discredits those who now boast of Mexico's stability and democracy."[45] Echeverría surely had not anticipated the international outrage that his actions would inspire, and he issued a vehement denial of the allegations.[46] The *Times*'s commentary not only purported to expose Echeverría's culpability but also delegitimized his democratic opening. Throughout his presidency, Echeverría had positioned himself to become a Third World leader, hoping to succeed Kurt Waldheim as the United Nations secretary-general.[47] For the lame duck, the critical foreign coverage foiled his future plans.

Governing officials prohibited Mexican newspapers from reprinting the *Times* article, but the ousted editors circumvented restrictions by reading the material aloud at public events. To this end, they organized multiple conferences and roundtables across the country to diffuse the article, denounce Echeverría, and raise support for a new magazine.[48] They also used photocopying technologies to continue the discussion of the articles. More than forty days after the *Excélsior* coup, *Times* correspondent Riding observed that "photocopies of articles about the affair published in the United States have circulated widely, even appearing mysteriously on the desks of bureaucrats."[49] The presentation of these documents to public officials both assigned blame and challenged attempts to cover up the president's role.

Organized gatherings also created a public that would follow the ousted editors in their new ventures. During a UNAM roundtable held on July 13, Granados Chapa read aloud Riding's translated articles to some 1,300 attendees.[50] The speaker called attention to a news item that would otherwise have gone unnoticed, using emphasis and elaboration to highlight the portions he found to be particularly urgent. Indeed, after reading the piece, Granados Chapa stressed that "public opinion is not aware of this document." These gatherings offered the opportunity for collective discussion and encouraged attendees to share what they heard by word of mouth. The editors upheld the articles as proof that they had been targeted for their critical journalism. This did not escape the attention of intelligence agents, who lurked in the audience and reported that the *New York Times* blamed the Mexican government for the *Excélsior* intervention.[51]

The ousted editors made a spectacle of their censorship. The overt intervention sharpened the lines of disagreement and transformed the reform-minded editors into oppositional figures. When *Excélsior* contributor Froylán López Narváez rose to speak after Granados Chapa, he characterized the intervention as an act of political repression that should be memorialized like the 1968 massacre. Rousing the crowd, he emphasized that "they did not defeat them in 1968 nor will they in 1976."[52] By rhetorically linking the students' massacre to the *Excélsior* intervention, López Narváez updated the periodization of regime delegitimation to include the action against the newspaper. At a fund-raising meeting for their new magazine venture, Granados Chapa similarly argued that "what happened on July 8, 1976, can never be forgotten. That day, an experiment of independent and critical journalism was terminated."[53] However, these discursive connections obscured the fact that *Excélsior*, like other national broadsheets, had followed government dictates in covering the Tlatelolco massacre.[54] Despite this, the intervention of 1976 gave rise to the myth that *Excélsior*'s independence began in 1968.

Journalists who had been forced out of the newspaper wanted to punish the president. Aware of the political cost of the intervention, president-elect José López Portillo (1976–1982) pledged to support the creation of the editors' new magazine, *Proceso*, which first appeared on November 6, 1976.[55] Only three weeks before Echeverría left office, *Proceso*'s inaugural issue indicted the departing president as a megalomaniac.[56] Scherer García introduced the magazine by connecting *Proceso*'s emergence with the *Excélsior* intervention four months earlier. He wrote, "This publication emerges . . . in the heat of a fight for free expression—the perennial struggle between the press, which seeks to be responsible, and power, which does not adhere to the law."[57] Scherer García upheld the government intervention as evidence of *Proceso*'s independence and appealed to readers for their support. The idealization of the prototypical liberal journalist echoed calls from both the right and left for civil society's independence from state control.

The feature article, entitled "From *Excélsior* to *Proceso*: The Struggle for the Public Voice," made the coup the central news story, while leaving unexplored the precise coverage that had motivated the intervention.[58] Offering detailed updates on the post-coup *Excélsior* and the charges brought against Scherer by the district attorney, the article presupposed insider knowledge and catered to an audience that had followed the fate of the ousted editors since July. The visual presentation of the article drew clear lines between co-opted and independent journalism. Accompanying the title page was a large black-and-white image of a dilapidated billboard for *Excélsior*. The advertisement had fallen into disrepair, and the paint was visibly peeling, blurring some of the words. The image suggested that *Excélsior* was a thing of the past. Beside the article were boldface statements from the *Guardian*, the *New York Times*, *Le Monde*, and the *Washington Post*.[59] Framed by a large box to attract readers' attention, these quotes suggested that an avalanche of international censure had followed the coup. The *Proceso* journalist used foreign coverage to underscore the magazine's independence, seeking to win over a readership that distrusted the Mexican press.

Ultimately, the coup incurred an unexpectedly high political cost. The removal of a newspaper director was not a new occurrence in Mexico City, but the Scherer García case generated a unique amount of public outcry.[60] Beginning the following year, multiple news publications commemorated the *Excélsior* intervention, solidifying a public of readers united every year by the memorialization.[61] By permitting a moderate press opening, Echeverría had invited new normative expectations of the acceptable limits on speech. The attempt to control this aperture had backfired, and the coup became a source of delegitimation for his presidency. The lame-duck president could not prevent the ousted editors from creating a new magazine, and thus his efforts to silence them were in vain. Echeverría had unwittingly created the conditions for more pointed press criticism. Indeed, two years after the intervention, Granados Chapa observed: "It seems like a joke, but it has been said to be true: don Luis Echeverría will reclaim for himself the title of benefactor of the Mexican press. Because of his actions, *Proceso*, *Unomásuno*, *Vuelta* and other [news publications] have emerged."[62]

The editors who left *Excélsior* went on to found a handful of news publications and marketed these ventures as imposing transparency on a nontransparent government. These outlets would stretch stories of censorship for days and engage a public that craved access to privileged information and that delighted in catching public officials in acts of wrongdoing.[63] However, the benefits conferred by the promise of transparency are not immediately apparent. Though press scandals increasingly led to politicians' resignations or even imprisonment, it was more often the case that nothing happened when reporters exposed wrongdoing. Editors nonetheless presented openness as a value in and of itself, regardless of whether it elicited greater government accountability. The niche but solid market for these publications also indicated that readers valued being in the know, regardless of whether exposés did more than shame offending elites.

Geographies of Censorship

The final case highlights the tensions between local and national censorship patterns. In 1979, the closure of the Baja California newspaper *ABC* attracted the attention of Mexico City reporters, who were both increasingly interested in covering local events and saw echoes of the *Excélsior* intervention. As Mexico City journalists commented on repression in Baja California, they at times found themselves the targets of local regulatory censorship. Baja California officials removed national periodicals from local newsstands and demanded that offending syndicated columns be withheld from regional publications. Regulatory censorship was the norm at the local level, and self-censorship generally predominated in the capital. However, national syndication brought local, targeted censorship to the center of the country.

On November 2, 1979, Governor Roberto de la Madrid shuttered the *ABC* newspaper under the guise of a labor dispute.[64] That day, around 300 members of the Confederación de Trabajadores de México (CTM), a powerful PRI labor organization, stormed the building and declared a strike, despite the fact that only one *ABC* employee belonged to the union.[65] One week later, the board of directors voted out Jesús Blancornelas, the editor in chief since 1977.[66] During his two years at the newspaper, Blancornelas had published scandalous exposés on gubernatorial corruption and nepotism. *ABC* appeared incendiary compared to the politesse of Mexico City journalism, even while local journalists faced a greater risk of violence.[67] Perhaps most troubling for the Baja California governor was that over the previous year, the *San Diego Union-Tribune* and the *Los Angeles Times* had translated and published the critical stories for a US readership.

Despite the relatively small circulation of *ABC*, the intervention drew international attention.[68] Journalists in the United States offered sympathetic coverage and contrasted Blancornelas against caricatures of corrupt Mexican politicians and reporters.[69] *Washington Post* reporter Carl Cannon reminded readers that, one year prior, Governor de la Madrid had referred to Blancornelas as an "insect" and had ominously pronounced, "We all know how to get rid of insects—with insecticide."[70] Many US reporters repeated the quote to suggest the governor's role in the strike.[71] For more than a week, the *San Diego Union-Tribune* devoted its second and third pages to the events in Tijuana. Mexico City journalists also took notice, lauding Blancornelas as "a young director of a young Baja California newspaper that bravely confronted Governor Roberto de la Madrid."[72]

The *ABC* intervention also struck a nerve in the Tijuana community, standing in for larger labor and political grievances. While foreign media covered the episode as a violation against free speech, an eclectic base of Tijuana supporters converged to decry the heavy-handed tactics exercised by the CTM and the governor. Around 50 maquiladora workers, mostly women, were among the first to show their solidarity, and they appeared at the *ABC* offices on the day after the closure.[73] Meanwhile, around 1,000 protesters marched on November 4. Conservative Partido Acción Nacional (PAN) sympathizers and leftist party members united with students and peasants to oppose de la Madrid, whom they burned in effigy while shouting "Death to the Governor!"[74] By November 9, a coordinating meeting attracted more than 6,000 attendees, including members of the Baja California and Sonora Telephone Workers Union, which had successfully broken from the CTM in 1976.[75] The *ABC* intervention thus galvanized local interest among groups that opposed the governor and wanted union independence.

Baja California journalists, however, argued that speech violations were more egregious than other forms of state abuse, suggesting that the repression of *ABC* would have society-wide effects. At the protest march, they circulated leaflets with declarations that the intervention was "without a doubt the most scandalous demonstration of arbitrary politics realized by Gov. Roberto de la Madrid."[76] Through the distribution of printed ephemera, the ousted editors brought issues of the press into a broader public discourse. Blancornelas and his allies also printed 10,000 flyers, which promised that they would continue to "practice honest journalism."[77] Being censored functioned as a form of intellectual currency, which journalists could mobilize to raise their profile among like-minded peers and readers.

The intervention in *ABC* stoked international criticisms of the governor, rather than silencing them. Almost immediately after Blancornelas was removed, the San Diego chapter of the Society of Professional Journalists issued a statement demanding that de la Madrid reinstate him as editor in chief.[78] Journalists in the United States also drew more attention to the allegations of nepotism and corruption against the governor by discussing the accusations made by *ABC*—the same ones that initially drew the ire of de la Madrid.[79] As in the *Excélsior* case, the change in directorship also prompted US reporters to question Mexico's pretensions to a free press. *San Diego Union-Tribune* reporter Alex Drehsler accused the Mexican national media of being complicit with the repressive PRI regime. He argued that "with the majority of Mexico's newspapers, television and radio networks unwilling to criticize a government that has killed thousands of peasants, workers and students who dared to ask for democracy . . . the prospect for a free press looks bleak."[80] Mexico City reporters also pressured President López Portillo to intervene by implying that he was partially responsible, if only because of his failure to act. Forty-two Mexico City newspaper directors signed a petition—ironically, spearheaded by *Excélsior*—asking the president to act.[81]

The proximity of the border and the collaboration between San Diego and Tijuana journalists made it possible for Blancornelas to continue criticizing the governor. After his firing, he left Tijuana for San Diego in what some referred to as "self-imposed exile."[82] There, Blancornelas and former *ABC* columnist Héctor "El Gato" Félix founded a muckraking newspaper, *Zeta*, in April 1980.[83] They decided to use US presses to print the periodical, which would allow them to avoid the censorship often imposed by the withholding of newsprint or the destruction of printing presses. Blancornelas and Félix also took charge of *Zeta*'s distribution to circumvent the influence of the Expendedores y Voceadores de los Periódicos union, and they delivered the newspaper in unmarked vans to avoid detection. Finally, Blancornelas's wife, Genoveva Villalón de Blanco, crossed the border multiple times each day with article drafts for her husband to edit.[84]

The closure of *ABC* attracted more attention to repression in Baja California, and national news on the topic was not exempt from local censorship. This was evident on February 25, 1981, when a Mexico City column was notably absent from its syndicated spot in the Baja California newspaper *El Mexicano*. Granados Chapa's Plaza Pública column appeared six days each week in the investigative Mexico City daily *Unomásuno*.[85] Though often critical, Plaza Pública was syndicated in dozens of local publications, like *El Mexicano*, that were known to toe the government line. As was the case for a handful of well-known Mexico City columnists, syndication offered Granados Chapa the opportunity to reach a readership that was distinct from *Unomásuno*'s highbrow, left-leaning audience. *Unomásuno* was formed in November 1977 by a segment of the deposed *Excélsior* editors.[86] The tabloid-size publication curated a forum for debate among Mexico's leading luminaries, reported issues of official corruption, and offered sophisticated cultural and international reportage. By contrast, *El Mexicano* was created in 1958 to fight against the growing appeal of the conservative PAN and to win back support for the PRI in Baja California.[87] Some twenty years later, *El Mexicano* continued as a mouthpiece for state officials and the federal government.

In the offending column, Granados Chapa discussed the recent violence against striking university employees at the Universidad Autónoma de Baja California (UABC). State authorities had attacked and arrested independent union leaders and then illegally expelled them from the state. Granados Chapa accused the governor of committing human rights abuses and asserted that "a long-standing sign of dictators has been the escalation that first begins with locking up, then exiling, and finally burying their opposition. The Baja California governor already has practiced the first two. He must not reach the third." While Granados Chapa held the governor personally responsible, he also called on President López Portillo, a close friend of de la Madrid, to intervene, warning of the political costs if he failed to do so.[88] Despite this confrontational position, *Unomásuno* encountered no official opposition to the piece in Mexico City.

This was not the case in Baja California, however. A public indictment in a national newspaper could encourage and legitimate university protesters, and the comparison of de la Madrid with a dictator would no doubt anger the governor. State officials ensured that Tijuana readers would not be able to find the column in *Unomásuno* that morning. Authorities purchased all available copies from newsstands, and they alerted the *El Mexicano* director that Plaza Pública should not appear that day. Since it had a limited circulation of around 25,000 copies per day, officials may have worried less about *El Mexicano* readers accessing the article than about the governor seeing it.[89]

Two days later, the editors of *Zeta* manipulated the censorship episode to their advantage, turning it into a spectacle. The front page teased "A New Criticism of the Governor in the National Press." On page five, *Zeta* reprinted the Plaza Pública column with an editor's note, which described official attempts to prevent the column's publication.[90] This not only aggrandized *Zeta*'s reputation for independence among its Mexico City and Baja California counterparts, but also underscored the importance of the information being published. The editor claimed that "under the control of the state government, *El Mexicano* censors, distorts, and refuses to publish any information dealing with the state government." Underscoring the importance of the column, the editor boasted that "despite official censorship, *Zeta* reproduces it—as more than thirty different state publications in the republic have likewise done—because it is of public interest."[91] The fact of censorship made the article appear more pressing and appealed to curious readers.

Blancornelas seized on the national attention to seek out collaborations with capital city reporters, knowing that such cooperation could raise the profile and extend the life-span of a story while punishing public officials for trying to restrict content. A few days later, he wrote a letter to Granados Chapa, informing him that Baja California authorities had tried to prevent the publication and distribution of Plaza Pública.[92] Recognizing that Mexico City reportage could elevate local issues to national problems, Blancornelas related the censorship attempt in the hope that Granados Chapa would respond with additional coverage against the Baja California governor. Blancornelas insinuated de la Madrid's responsibility, noting that "the motives are obvious," and he reported that the governor's son-in-law and public relations director, Raúl Zavala, had ordered the removal of *Unomásuno* issues from newsstands, implying an additional reason to suspect de la Madrid's culpability.[93]

With the help of Mexico City newspapers and travelers, local journalists could both circumvent and expose censorship attempts. Blancornelas explained that resourceful journalists had obtained the original Plaza Pública column by going to the airport and searching for the discarded copies of *Unomásuno* left by Mexico City travelers. The quick execution of this strategy suggests that it was one that local reporters regularly employed when authorities removed national periodicals from corner newsstands. With the copy in hand, *Zeta* journalists transcribed Plaza Pública for Tijuana readers.[94]

In the weeks that followed, *Zeta* notified readers every time Mexico City print media covered the UABC strikes.[95] On March 5, 1981, *Zeta* reprinted a *Proceso* article to suggest that national news outlets supported the independent union's cause.[96] The title, "The Mexico City Press Continues Criticizing the UABC–Roberto Case," was slightly misleading since the article had been originally published two months earlier. The piece nonetheless remained relevant in light of the ongoing conflicts at the Mexicali university. In the transcribed article, *Proceso* journalist Guillermo Villaseñor reported the nullification of workers' contracts and the repression and imprisonment of protesters. He also affirmed that the Baja California press had collaborated with authorities to marginalize the opposition.[97]

Five days later, a *Zeta* headline announced, "They Confiscated Mexico City Newspapers on Friday."[98] In this instance, state authorities had scooped up copies of national periodicals that detailed a Mexico City protest against repression in Baja California.[99] The *Zeta* article proclaimed that "thanks to the power granted him by his personal friendship with the president of the republic, state governor Roberto de la Madrid continues making a mockery of Freedom of Expression."[100] The author also reminded readers of the censorship of Plaza Pública that had occurred ten days earlier. However, the Baja California government appeared impervious to such denunciations, and authorities continued to interfere with the statewide publication and circulation of Plaza Pública and *Unomásuno*.

By devoting entire columns to foiled censorship, *Zeta* journalists challenged de la Madrid and highlighted the ineffectiveness of such restrictions. Not only did such measures fail, reporters suggested, they achieved the opposite effect. Overt censorship at times inspired additional articles on the prohibited material and placed offending public officials under greater scrutiny. Exactly one month after Granados Chapa wrote his original article, he revisited the situation in his column.[101] Signaling the interrelationship between local and national news gathering, he used the earlier letter from Blancornelas to make his own censorship the focus of the story. Granados Chapa began by reproducing the editor's note that had preceded his column's republication in *Zeta* the previous month. He also transcribed the letter from Blancornelas, which blamed the column's censorship on Governor de la Madrid.[102] In Baja California, *El Mexicano* again withheld the syndicated column from publication, and two days later, *Zeta* reprinted Granados Chapa's piece. The editor's note stated that "for the same obvious reasons that the newspaper censored the column . . . *Zeta*, independent, reveals it today."[103] The intent to limit coverage actually heightened journalists' interest in further exploring the issue. They presented themselves as engaged in a battle with public officials to expose the truth. In doing so, they appealed to readers by underscoring the independence and urgency of their news publications.

Correspondence from one reader allows us to speculate about the public forged through these publications. In April 1981, Mexico City reader Elena Salazar wrote to Granados Chapa and expressed her enthusiasm for *Unomásuno*. Salazar not only spoke of her own encounter with the periodical, but felt confident that she shared something with other readers. "For these unknown people and for me, your articles represent, along with the other collaborators of the newspaper, pieces that day by day construct a path that supports our feet to guide our steps." She particularly valued the privileged information *Unomásuno* provided. She described the articles as offering "proof" of official wrongdoing and bringing to light "many issues that are often concealed."[104] Salazar felt like she was part of a public of readers that was united by their shared knowledge.

Conclusion

For decades, the one-party regime excelled at encouraging Mexico City journalists to self-censor. In the 1970s, however, the government tried to allow a greater space for criticism while confronting the impossibility of controlling the shape that press opening assumed. Censorship was often orchestrated by prominent individuals to defend their reputations, rather than by centralized offices combing through newspapers to identify a few prohibited topics. The geographic unevenness of censorship and the national syndication of columns, in particular, made press regulation always incomplete. When reporters were willing to report on political wrongdoing, officials could find censorship efforts to be counterproductive.

Many historians have examined the ways in which clever writers circumvented censorship under oppressive governments in various countries. Aesopian literature and underground presses are only two of many well-known techniques writers deployed to avoid the scrutiny of censors in, for example, czarist Russia or Pinochet's Chile.[105] In 1970s Mexico City, by contrast, the circumvention of censorship occurred in plain sight. Journalists challenged public officials by denouncing censorship in reputable news publications underwritten by government loans or subsidies. And when they did so, they made individual officials politically vulnerable to criticism.

Exploring the on-the-ground experience of censorship during this time demonstrates the ways in which journalism, narrowly defined, articulated with different mediums of exchange and communication. The circulation and discussion of news items thrived through photocopying, oral repetition at roundtables and fund-raising events, air travel, personal correspondence, public protests, and printed broadsides. Popular and international solidarity with the targeted reporters thus depended on journalists' resourcefulness, personal relationships, and access to international borders. Circumventing and publicizing censorship required that journalists create a spectacle out of the attempts to limit their coverage. They fashioned themselves as champions of free speech, appealing to a readership that wanted access to the "real story." In so doing, they divided Mexican journalism between those who kowtowed to power and those who resisted it. They defined their readership as a public that was in the know about Mexican politics and corruption, even if their exposés failed to generate structural change.

If failed censorship was a problem for the central government, it was one of its own making. To quell dissent and court intellectuals, Echeverría allowed the gradual opening of one major daily, while leftist magazines continued the more critical coverage they had been publishing since mid-century. The establishment of muckraking publications offered journalists the opportunity to skirt efforts to control content and find alternative outlets for censored articles. The publication of criticism was sometimes met with disgruntled toleration and at other moments with aggressive or even violent measures. The story of censorship in late twentieth-century Mexico is thus not one of a linear loosening of restrictions but of increased pluralism and availability of outlets. For this reason, overt efforts to censor reporters could be met with denunciations in the headlines.

Notes

1. "Confiscaron los periódicos del DF el viernes," *Zeta*, Mar. 10, 1981, 2. This and all subsequent *Zeta* articles were found in the AHT, Hemeroteca.

2. See, for example, Lawson, *Building the Fourth Estate*.

3. Scholars refer to this as a traditional, or "regulatory," definition of censorship. This framing has primarily focused on the ways in which power holders—as opposed to peers—restrict speech. The "structuralist" approach, by contrast, focuses on internalized speech regulation that responds to social norms. See Müller, "Censorship and Cultural Regulation," 2–5, 11.

4. Scherer García, *Los presidentes*, 159; Rodríguez Munguía, *La otra guerra secreta*, 22–23.

5. See, for example, Vaughan, *Portrait of a Young Painter*.

6. On crime news, see, for example, Piccato, "Murders." On leftist publications, cultural magazines, and student newspapers, see Zolov, *Refried Elvis*; Pensado, *Rebel Mexico*; and Keller, "A Foreign Policy for Domestic Consumption." On local journalism, see Gillingham, "Who Killed Crispín Aguilar?"; Smith, *The Mexican Press and Civil Society*.

7. Burkholder de la Rosa, *La red de los espejos*, ch. 2.

8. Cabrera López, *Una inquietud de amanecer*, 37; and Walker, *Waking from the Dream*, 30. There were serious contradictions in Echeverría's policies. For example, while his government courted intellectuals in the capital city, it waged a dirty war in the countryside.

9. Becerra Acosta, *Dos poderes*, 15–17; and Scherer García, *Los presidentes*, 51–53.

10. Burkholder de la Rosa, "El olimpo fracturado," 1369.

11. Leñero, *Los periodistas*, 83–84; and Aguilar Camín, *Los días de Manuel Buendía*, 185.

12. However, only the journalists with a degree of financial freedom could afford to take such risks. Journalist Manuel Becerra Acosta described witnessing his colleague Julio Scherer García refuse a public official's bribe in the late 1960s. Becerra Acosta offered a class-based explanation for this choice, arguing that Scherer García hailed from a wealthy family, which gave him the economic freedom to risk losing his job. Becerra Acosta, *Dos poderes*, 67.

13. "Tiene 60 años, está enfermo," *Excélsior*, May 5, 1973, 1, 18.

14. Aviña, *Specters of Revolution*, 5.

15. US Embassy in Mexico, "Defense Secretary Denies Existence of Guerrillas in Mexico," May 27, 1971, NARA/RG59/1970-73/Pol 23-8 Mex, box 2476; and US State Department, Bureau of Intelligence and Research, "Mexico: An Emerging Internal Security Problem?," Sept. 23, 1971, NARA/RG59/1970-73/Pol 15 Mex, box 2475.

16. "Manifiesto de los secuestradores," *Excélsior*, May 6, 1973, 1, 19; and "Comunicado número 3: Al proletariado mexicano," *El Universal*, May 6, 1973, 1, 8.

17. "Manifiesto de los secuestradores," 19.

18. See, for example, Carey, *Plaza of Sacrifices*, 174.

19. Juan González, "Concentraron a los reos en el aeropuerto," *El Universal*, May 6, 1973, 1, 12; and "Ninguna pesquisa para no arriesgar la vida del cónsul," *El Universal*, May 6, 1973, 1, 7.

20. Gamiño Muñoz, "Prensa oficialista y acción guerrillera," 118–19.

21. See, for example, *Política*, Nov. 15, 1961, and June 1, 1962.

22. Jaime Durán, "El secuestro, obra de delincuentes comunes, dijo L[uis] E[cheverría]," *Excélsior*, May 7, 1973, 1, 9.

23. Ramón de Ertze Garamendi, "Suma y resta: Violencia," *Excélsior*, May 7, 1973, 6; and Froylán M. López Narváez, "Violencia mutua," *Excélsior*, May 7, 1973, 7.

24. See, for example, Agustín, *Tragicomedia mexicana*, 19.

25. Hallin and Mancini, *Comparing Media Systems*, 98–99.

26. Abelardo Villegas, "El crimen como solución política," *Excélsior*, May 7, 1973, 6.

27. Villegas, "El crimen," 6.

28. Miguel Ángel Granados Chapa, "No olvidar a Puebla: Delincuencia no común," *Excélsior*, May 8, 1973, 7.

29. Granados Chapa, "No olvidar a Puebla."

30. Granados Chapa, "No olvidar a Puebla."

31. Granados Chapa, "No olvidar a Puebla."

32. The writer shortened her last name when signing the letter. Leonor L. de B. to Miguel Ángel Granados Chapa, May 9, 1973, MAGC. When I consulted this collection, it was still unorganized and in the care of Granados Chapa's son Luis Fernando Granados in Mexico City. The family is planning to donate these materials to the Universidad Autónoma Metropolitana Cuajimalpa.

33. See, for example, Miguel Ángel Granados Chapa, "PRI en el DF: Vencer y convencer," *Excélsior*, Oct. 16, 1975, 6; and Leñero, *Los periodistas*, 80–81, 120.

34. Gamiño Muñoz, *Guerrilla*, 163.

35. See, for example, Marlise Simons, "Mexican Newspaper Threatened," *Washington Post*, July 8, 1976, A20; Alan Riding, "Mexican Editor Ousted by Rebels," *New York Times*, July 9, 1976, A5; Alan Riding, "Paper in Mexico Ends Liberal Tone: Conservative View Appears after Ouster of Editor and 200 on Staff," *New York Times*, July 10, 1976, 10A; "The Man Who Killed *Excelsior*," *Washington Post*, July 14, 1976, A16; and Richard Gott, "Editor Is Regime's First Victim," *Guardian*, July 15, 1976, 3.

36. Burkholder de la Rosa, "Forging a New Relationship," 89.

37. Burkholder de la Rosa, "El olimpo fracturado," 1369.

38. Burkholder de la Rosa, "El olimpo fracturado," 1381–82.

39. See, for example, Rodríguez Castañeda, *Prensa vendida*, 173–76; Lawson, *Building the Fourth Estate*, 44; Hughes, *Newsrooms in Conflict*, 83, 106, 113, 136; and Rodríguez Munguía, *La otra guerra secreta*, 145.

40. See, for example, Leñero, *Los periodistas*; Granados Chapa, *Excélsior*, 11–17; and Scherer García, *Vivir*, 35, 66. The events were also re-created in Aguilar Camín's

novel *La guerra de Galio*. Even those who remained at *Excélsior* after the coup wrote memoirs in defense of their decisions. See Díaz Redondo, *La gran mentira*.

41. "Gobierno, ajeno a lo ocurrido en Excélsior: Echeverría," *Excélsior*, July 13, 1976, 1; and Alejandro Iñigo, "Decisión de los cooperativistas," *Excélsior*, July 13, 1976, 1.

42. "*Excélsior* Leadership Ousted," July 9, 1976, WikiLeaks, https://www.wikileaks.org/plusd/cables/1976MEXICO08820_b.html.

43. Riding, "Mexican Editor Ousted."

44. Riding, "Paper in Mexico."

45. "Loses a Free Press," *New York Times*, July 13, 1976, 31.

46. "Mexico Denies Role in Editor's Ouster," *New York Times*, July 16, 1976, 5A.

47. Alan Riding, "Retiring Is Not So Retiring," *New York Times*, May 16, 1976, 17A. Echeverría also spearheaded UN advocacy for the New International Economic Order, which promoted economic protection and collaboration among non-aligned nations. See Olcott, "Empires of Information," 27.

48. "Excélsior Compañía Editorial, S.C.L.," July 19, 1976, AGN/DFS/VP/Manuel Becerra Acosta; "Problema estudiantil," July 29, 1976, AGN/DFS/VP/Excélsior, file 3; and "Conferencia 'Asunto de Excélsior' en Oaxaca," Aug. 6, 1976, AGN/DFS/VP/Excélsior, file 3.

49. Alan Riding, "Mexican Editor Plans Comeback: Ousted Editor of *Excelsior* Hopes to Start Magazine and Newspaper Soon," *New York Times*, Aug. 22, 1976, 17A.

50. "Asunto estudiantil," July 13, 1976, AGN/DFS/VP/Excélsior, file 3.

51. "Asunto estudiantil," 1.

52. "Asunto estudiantil," 3.

53. "Notas leídas en el Salón del Ángel del Hotel María Isabel," July 19, 1976, in Granados Chapa, *Excélsior*, 46.

54. Sánchez Ruíz, "Los medios de comunicación," 409–10.

55. According to Leñero, this was a promise of moral, not financial, support. Leñero, *Los periodistas*, 313.

56. "1970–1976: Consolidación del poder personal," *Proceso*, Nov. 6, 1976, 6–11.

57. "Editorial," *Proceso*, Nov. 6, 1976, 5.

58. "De *Excélsior* a *Proceso*: Lucha por la voz pública," *Proceso*, Nov. 6, 1976, 12–15. While the article was unsigned, it was likely authored by Granados Chapa, who reprinted it in an anthology of his articles. Granados Chapa, *Excélsior*, 53.

59. "De *Excélsior* a *Proceso*," 12.

60. In 1961, Fernando Benítez had been famously forced to resign from *México en la Cultura*. Interventions such as these often had the effect of inspiring editors to found new publications. This was the case with Benítez, who created *La Cultura en México*, a cultural supplement for the political magazine *Siempre!* two months later. In other instances, newspapers were punished for errant coverage

through the withholding of newsprint or the removal of government advertising. This happened to *Diario de México* in 1966. The editors publicly denounced President Gustavo Díaz Ordaz for censoring the paper. See Rodríguez Castañeda, *Prensa vendida*, 22, 107.

61. See, for example, Vicente Leñero, "Lo que ha ocurrido en *Excélsior* desde el 8 de julio de 1976," *Proceso*, Nov. 7, 1977, 7; and Miguel Ángel Granados Chapa, "*Excélsior*, un año después," *Siempre!*, Aug. 4, 1977, in Granados Chapa, *Excélsior*, 66–70.

62. Granados Chapa, "Plaza Pública," *Cine Mundial*, Nov. 6, 1978, in Granados Chapa, *Excélsior*, 79.

63. For other examples of reporting on censorship in *Excélsior* and *Proceso*, see Freije, "Exposing Scandals," 394.

64. Michael D. Lopez, Ricardo Chavira, and Alex Drehsler, "Federally Controlled Union Invades Tijuana Newspaper, Forces Closing," *San Diego Union-Tribune*, Nov. 3, 1979, A1, 3, 15; and Ricardo Chavira, "Blancornelas Ousted as Chairman of *ABC* despite Federal Injunction," *San Diego Union-Tribune*, Nov. 10, 1979, A3.

65. Trejo Delarbre, *Crónica del sindicalismo*, 341.

66. This was not the first time a governor had orchestrated the firing of Blancornelas. In December 1973, then-governor Milton Castellanos Everardo removed him from the directorship of *La Voz de la Frontera*, the newspaper with the largest circulation in Baja California. Ortiz Marín, *Los medios de comunicación*, 71.

67. José Carreño Carlón, "Literatura, periodismo y realidad," *Nexos*, Dec. 1979, 43; Smith, *Stories from the Newsroom*, ch. 5.

68. Circulation ranged from 35,000 to 45,000 issues per day. See Roberto Vizcaino, "El conflicto *ABC* vs. de la Madrid," *Proceso*, Nov. 26, 1979, 28–29; and Lopez, Chavira, and Drehsler, "Federally Controlled Union," A15.

69. Carl Cannon, "Progovernment Union Storms Outspoken Mexican Daily," *Washington Post*, Nov. 3, 1979, A13. Blancornelas was similarly described in Carl Cannon, "Papers Spar with Mexican Officials over Corruption Exposes," *Washington Post*, Feb. 17, 1980, A11; and Jack Anderson, "A Tough Editor and a Gang of Toughs," *Washington Post*, Feb. 17, 1980, C7. Governor de la Madrid responded with broadsides. Ortiz Marín, *Los medios de comunicación*, 73.

70. Cannon, "Progovernment Union."

71. See, for example, Lopez, Chavira, and Drehsler, "Federally Controlled Union," A15; and Alex Drehsler, "Ousted Baja Journalists Plan Paper," *San Diego Union-Tribune*, Nov. 7, 1979, A2.

72. Carreño Carlón, "Literatura, periodismo y realidad," 43. On Mexico City coverage, see Ricardo Garibay, "Tijuana III, indocumentados: La terca esperanza de sobrevivir," *Proceso*, Nov. 12, 1979, 16–18; Vizcaino, "El conflicto *ABC*"; and Trujillo Muñoz, *La canción del progreso*, 368.

73. Lopez, Chavira, and Drehsler, "Federally Controlled Union," A15.

74. The effigy bore the name "Bob," a reference to the fact that de la Madrid was born in the United States. Alex Drehsler, "Besieged Baja Newspaper Gets Bad Press," *San Diego Union-Tribune*, Nov. 4, 1979, A3; and Alex Drehsler, "Tijuana Marchers Protest Paper's Closing," *San Diego Union-Tribune*, Nov. 5, 1979, A3.

75. Ricardo Chavira, "Groups Protest Shutdown of Tijuana Paper," *San Diego Union-Tribune*, Nov. 9, 1979, A3; and De la Garza Toledo, *La democracía*, 19.

76. Drehsler, "Tijuana Marchers Protest."

77. Ricardo Chavira, "*ABC* Workers Print Flier in Freedom Fight," *San Diego Union-Tribune*, Nov. 8, 1979, A2.

78. Chavira, "Groups Protest Shutdown."

79. "The Tolling Bell: A Tocsin," *San Diego Union-Tribune*, Nov. 7, 1979, B8.

80. Alex Drehsler, "Fear, Bribes Stifle Free Press in Mexico," *San Diego Union-Tribune*, Nov. 5, 1979, A3.

81. "The Tolling Bell: A Tocsin."

82. Anderson, "A Tough Editor."

83. "Blancornelas: Una vida de encierro," *Proceso*, Nov. 24, 2006, 30; "Del *ABC* a la Z," *Proceso*, May 12, 1980, 28; Trujillo Muñoz, *La canción del progreso*, 379.

84. These anecdotes were told by the son of Blancornelas, who is the current co-director of *Zeta*, César René Blanco Villalón, in *Reportero*, a documentary film directed by Bernardo Ruiz (SubCine, 2012).

85. In 1981, *Unomásuno* reported a circulation of 70,000 copies per day. *Editor and Publisher International Yearbook*, 41.

86. Alan Riding, "Ousted Mexican Journalists Start a Liberal Paper," *New York Times*, Nov. 24, 1977, 7.

87. Trujillo Muñoz, *La canción del progreso*, 265, 267.

88. Miguel Ángel Granados Chapa, "Plaza Pública: Deportaciones en B[aja] C[alifornia], encierro, destierro, entierro?," *Unomásuno*, Feb. 25, 1981, 4.

89. Tijuana's estimated population at the time was 610,000. Population and *El Mexicano* circulation figures come from *Editor and Publisher International Yearbook*, 43.

90. Miguel Ángel Granados Chapa, "Plaza Pública," *Zeta*, Feb. 27, 1981, 5.

91. Granados Chapa, "Plaza Pública."

92. Jesús Blancornelas to Miguel Ángel Granados Chapa, Mar. 2, 1981, MAGC.

93. Blancornelas to Granados Chapa, Mar. 2, 1981.

94. Blancornelas to Granados Chapa, Mar. 2, 1981.

95. "Censura nacional a de la Madrid," *Zeta*, Mar. 6, 1981, 3.

96. "Sigue la prensa del D.F. criticando el caso UABC–Roberto," *Zeta*, Mar. 5, 1981, 3. An editor's note clarified that the article was originally published in *Proceso*, Jan. 12, 1981.

97. "Sigue la prensa."

98. "Confiscaron los periódicos del DF el viernes," *Zeta*, Mar. 10, 1981, 2.

99. "Censura nacional a de la Madrid," 3.

100. "Censura nacional a de la Madrid," 3, capitalization of "Freedom of Expression" per original.
101. Miguel Ángel Granados Chapa, "Plaza Pública: Carta de Blancornelas, exilio involuntario," *Unomásuno*, Mar. 25, 1981, 4. This article was collected by state spies and can be found in AGN/DGIPS/VP/Jesús Blancornelas.
102. "Plaza Pública: Carta de Blancornelas," Mar. 25, 1981.
103. Miguel Ángel Granados Chapa, "Plaza Pública: Carta de Blancornelas, exilio involuntario," *Zeta*, Mar. 27, 1981, 6.
104. Elena Salazar Mallen to Miguel Ángel Granados Chapa, Apr. 26, 1981, MAGC.
105. See, for example, Loseff, *On the Beneficence of Censorship*; Bates, "From State Monopoly," 145–46; and Bresnahan, "Reclaiming the Public Sphere."

11 | Democratization and the Regional Press

JAVIER GARZA RAMOS

The morning of Tuesday, December 5, 1978, the editors of *La Opinión*, a daily newspaper in the city of Torreón, Coahuila, were celebrating. They had just been told that the day's edition was completely sold out. "There isn't a city in the world where a newspaper is sold out by ten in the morning," said Velia Guerrero, the paper's publisher at the time, recalling her skepticism at the report.[1] But there was reason to believe it: *La Opinión* had just published on its front page the news that Edmundo Gurza, the Partido Acción Nacional (PAN) candidate for mayor of Torreón, had won the close election held two days before.

"Gurza Won, According to Count" read the story detailing the records delivered by polling stations to the local electoral authorities.[2] The vote on Sunday, December 3, had been too close to call for the next day's newspapers, so the two largest dailies in the city, *La Opinión* and *El Siglo de Torreón*, had not published any definitive result, only assertions from the Partido Revolucionario Institucional (PRI) and the PAN, both claiming victory. But after a day of vote counting, the outcome was clear: the PAN had ousted the ruling PRI from city hall for the first time in history.

In the 1970s, reports from polling stations were not immediately available to the public, but were closely guarded by government-controlled electoral authorities, especially in very close races. But *La Opinión*'s reporters had managed to get their hands on the documents, and they had the scoop.

But on that Tuesday, if Guerrero and her staff thought that thousands were reading about the election in their newspaper, they were mistaken. The state governor, Óscar Flores Tapia, had ordered that the whole edition be bought and destroyed. The news that his party, the PRI, had lost the election had to be censored. Only subscribers and those who bought the paper early that morning had read anything about it. "We were furious," recalled Guerrero. "So the next day we ran the exact same story with the exact same headline."[3] Indeed, anyone looking at *La Opinión*'s archive would be surprised to see the same story printed two days in a row. But this was no typesetter's mistake; it was a defiant act in the face of a common tactic during Mexico's pre-internet days.

For *El Siglo* and *La Opinión*, what happened next would further test their independence. Gurza launched a protest movement calling on citizens to denounce what he called a "stolen election." He had claimed a 1,600-vote margin of victory over PRI candidate Homero del Bosque, but the official count published days later had him losing by some 500 votes. In the following days, the PAN held rallies and marches, and Gurza gave press conferences and even took his case to the federal government, meeting with President José López Portillo. But to no avail. Del Bosque was declared mayor and took office on December 31 in a heavily guarded ceremony.

This was not the first time that the PAN, the main opposition party in Torreón, had held post-election protests. They were a regular feature of the 1960s and '70s. But this case would be different; a seed had been planted, and it would bear fruit less than a year later. In the 1979 elections for the Chamber of Deputies, the PAN won a congressional district in Torreón, and the government had no choice but to recognize the victory. The PAN candidate, Juan Antonio García Villa, became the first non-PRI elected legislator in the state; it was, in fact, the first election the opposition had ever won in Coahuila.

The seed was planted not only because of Gurza's protests in those cold December days, but also thanks to the coverage that his campaign and post-election rallies had received in the local press. Both *El Siglo* and *La Opinión* aggressively followed the candidate's movements and publicized his campaign events in their pages. After the election, the protests and Gurza's attacks on the state legislature (which was responsible for certifying elections at that time) featured prominently in both newspapers, whose publishers decided not to toe the official line set by the PRI and the state government, and refused to dismiss the accusations of fraud.

A review of *El Siglo's* archives (one of the few digitized newspaper archives in Mexico) produced these headlines from the end of 1978:

November 3:   "Gurza Charges That All Is Ready for a Fraud to Favor the PRI."

December 5:   "PAN Trusts Legislature Will Recognize Victory."

December 10:   "Gurza Believes Legislature Has Perpetrated a Fraud in Torreón."

December 11:   "PAN Held Packed Rally Yesterday."

December 21:   "PAN Vows to Block Del Bosque's Inauguration."[4]

The protests also provoked sympathetic editorials from both newspapers criticizing the election results. Del Bosque managed to take office, but the PAN protest spilled into 1979, and when the elections for the Chamber of Deputies were held that summer both *El Siglo* and *La Opinión* offered newly balanced coverage between the PRI and PAN candidates.

The Coahuila contest became an important part of the larger history of 1979, a pivotal year in Mexico's transition to democracy. That year's federal elections were the first following the political reform of 1977, in which the government legalized the Communist Party, and leftist parties organized new coalitions to compete formally for the first time. The reform also opened more spaces of representation for minority parties in the federal Congress. One of the new deputies elected under the proportional representation method was Edmundo Gurza. In 1981 he became the first legislator in modern Mexico to interrupt the president at the yearly State of the Union address, a quasi-sacred ceremony sarcastically dubbed "President's Day."

The 1990s are widely recognized as the decade when Mexico made its transition to democracy and the system of one-party rule came to an end. But before the PRI lost the presidency in 2000, before it lost its majority in the Chamber of Deputies in 1997, and even before it lost its first governorship in Baja California in 1989, opposition mayors and legislators were being elected all over the country. The 1977 political reform had not completely cleaned up the electoral process, but in its wake opposition candidates won mayoral races in important midsized cities, such as Tijuana, León, Durango,

Mérida, Mazatlán, Hermosillo, Ciudad Juárez, and Chihuahua. The PAN contested several competitive gubernatorial elections during the 1980s, probably winning in Nuevo León and Sonora in 1985 and Chihuahua in 1986, though fraud denied the party's victory in all three. Despite such fraud, the PAN made important gains, down payments on their series of negotiated gubernatorial wins under Carlos Salinas.

Many factors contributed to this trend, but one stands out: opposition candidates began winning elections in cities with a vigorous local press, especially in places where "civic-oriented" journalism occurred. Just as *La Opinión* and *El Siglo* were key factors in leveling the playing field in Torreón in the late 1970s, so newspapers such as *El Norte* in Monterrey, *El Diario de Yucatán* in Mérida, *AM de León* in Guanajuato, *El Diario de Chihuahua* and *El Diario de Juárez* in Chihuahua, and *El Imparcial* in Sonora all resisted pressure from state governments and opened their pages to candidates challenging the PRI's hegemony.

In the 1985 gubernatorial election in Nuevo León, *El Norte* pioneered the system of placing observers in polling stations. By deploying reporters and volunteers, it managed to prove that the election results were closer than the margin that the state legislature officially certified when it declared PRI candidate Jorge Treviño the winner. The newspaper, led by Alejandro Junco de la Vega, also gave wide coverage to the post-election protest headed by the PAN candidate, Fernando Canales Clariond.

Eight years later, Junco de la Vega arrived in Mexico City and launched the newspaper *Reforma*, which revolutionized Mexican journalism in the 1990s and became one of the country's leading news organizations pushing for a transition to democracy. But while studies of the media's influence in Mexico's democratic opening have focused on national news organizations based in Mexico City, such as the newspapers *Reforma*, *El Universal*, or *La Jornada* or the newsmagazine *Proceso*, there is something missing: the regional press is often overlooked when scholars write the history of Mexican journalism.

Local newspapers (and almost exclusively newspapers, since TV and radio stations were subjected to tighter political control) have been a powerful force in Mexico's transition from one-party rule to a democratic system during the last four decades. The regional press was among the first to report on opposition candidates, electoral fraud, and post-election protests, and it was a key player in political transitions at the local level as the PRI started losing elections in major population centers. Before 1997, when the PRI lost its majority in Congress, four states (Baja California, Chihuahua, Jalisco, and Guanajuato) elected *panista* governors, while scores of city halls and seats in federal and state legislatures were taken by opposition candidates. Many of them were able to win elections because of critical local media coverage. However, since 2005, the local press has been threatened by several forces pulling in different directions: declining circulations and falling revenues from commercial advertising, increasing reliance on government advertising, changes in ownership structure, and attacks from organized crime or political actors. All these issues pose a serious threat to the health of the regional press as a force to sustain the type of watchdog journalism needed to keep democracy vibrant at the local level.

The Cities and Their Newspapers

Prensa provinciana (provincial press) is the (pejorative) term used to describe the regional news organizations in Mexico, a description that reflects a Mexico City–centric attitude that also dominates other aspects of the country's political, economic, and cultural life. For decades, journalists based in the capital saw the "prensa provinciana" as a backwater. The few newspapers that stood out were exceptions.

Carlos Monsiváis demolished the regional press in an essay introducing his book *A ustedes les consta*, a collection of classic chronicles from Mexican journalists in the twentieth century. "In the institutionalized revolution, provincial journalism became a hunting ground: why inform when you can choose the opposite, the news quarantines that isolate the people in the states? An assignment for the provincial press: First, don't take yourself too seriously, because the national press already exists; second, keep control: don't let news of massacres, student protests, corruption reports, or the different varieties of civil resistance leak out into the public. Instead, [offer] flattery and complacency, [and a] prominent display of official statements," wrote Monsiváis in 1980.[5] He added: "In the last decades, exceptions have not amounted to much: banality, adulation, local credulity, and parochial anticommunism are still the rule." If the local press, as seen from Mexico City, looked as Monsiváis described, it is clear why nobody seemed to be paying attention. As he pointed out, centralist attitudes made Mexico City journalists look to the "provincial" only when there were "mutinies, scandals, or presidential trips."[6]

However, these opinions about the "prensa provinciana" did have challengers. Around the same time as Monsiváis delivered his devastating critique, others were beginning to take the regional press seriously. In a column in the October 1979 issue of *Nexos* magazine, journalist and academic José Carreño Carlón wrote about how *El Diario de Yucatán* had covered a riot at the local penitentiary. Carreño Carlón praised the coverage of *El Diario*, the state's largest newspaper, which proved that the mutinous inmates had surrendered but that three of them had been killed in cold blood by state police officers in an operation supported by Miguel Nazar Haro, the head of Mexico's feared political police, the infamous Dirección Federal de Seguridad (DFS). "The professional quality of Yucatán's press provides an important element to characterize the barbaric structures that have coalesced around the Mexican state's repressive role and gives a slap (with a white glove) to the ethnocentrism that, from Mexico City, pretends to ignore the cultural features—including civic life and journalistic work—of the inner country," wrote Carreño, who would later be director of communications for President Carlos Salinas from 1992 to 1994.[7]

A few years later, Petra Secanella described the regional press as "essential" to understanding Mexican public life. In the provincial press, she wrote, "there are newspapers whose brave critical work cannot be underestimated."[8] Although an independent regional press was more the exception than the rule (most news organizations still followed the official line), several political shocks during the 1980s confirmed Carreño Carlón's warning and showed that those who ignored the prensa provinciana did so at their peril.

Chihuahua and *El Diario*

In 1983 the state of Chihuahua experienced a political earthquake when the PRI lost the mayoral races of the two most important cities: Ciudad Juárez, the largest metropolitan area in the state, and Chihuahua, the capital city. Luis H. Alvarez, a legendary PAN figure who had been the party's presidential candidate in 1958, was elected mayor of the city of Chihuahua, while

Francisco Barrio, a local businessman active in political circles, won the election in Ciudad Juárez.

The cities had something in common—independent newspapers. *El Diario de Juárez* and *El Diario de Chihuahua* were founded in 1976 by the Rodríguez Borunda family and quickly established themselves as important voices in their communities. In Ciudad Juárez, it was telling that only three years after it hit the streets, *El Diario de Juárez* was commended by all but one of the state's political parties for opening its pages to opposition voices.[9] The only party that did not join the recognition was the PRI.

In 1986 the PAN recognized that conditions were favorable for a challenge in Chihuahua's gubernatorial election. Barrio, the charismatic business leader who just three years earlier had been elected mayor of Ciudad Juárez, was nominated as the PAN candidate to run against the PRI's Fernando Baeza. Officially, Baeza beat Barrio by 25 percentage points, but the PAN cried foul and began a national protest movement to challenge the election results. The protest galvanized voters all over Chihuahua, and thousands flocked to the streets to support Barrio in civil resistance actions such as blocking highways and bridges at the border with the United States. Even the Catholic Church joined the protest, with priests talking about fraud from their pulpits and the bishops announcing the suspension of masses, a move that the Vatican eventually blocked at the request of the Mexican government.

Most of the news media in Mexico City ignored the events in Chihuahua or supported the government's denial of electoral fraud. Only magazines such as *Proceso*, *Vuelta*, and *Nexos* covered Barrio's protest and documented the fraud. Some PAN leaders traveled to Washington, DC, to denounce the Mexican government in the US Congress, something that was roundly criticized by newspapers and TV newscasts in Mexico City. But in Chihuahua, *El Diario* newspapers gave wide coverage to the protest, and their stories were picked up by other regional newspapers thanks to information-sharing agreements between publishers, allowing people in other parts of the country to learn about the events. The Chihuahua election of 1986 was later viewed as a watershed in Mexico's transition to democracy, a harbinger of the disputed 1988 presidential election.

How did local newspapers get their independence? For decades, regional newspapers were profitable businesses. Even as local TV and radio stations spread around the country, newspapers managed to grab a large share of commercial advertising budgets. A look at the largest newspapers in Mexico's main cities shows that most of the advertising came from local private businesses, so the local governments could not exercise control by applying economic pressure. Mayors and governors needed the newspapers more than the newspapers needed the advertising revenue from mayors and governors. And a growing civil society recognized the value of an independent press.

Sonora and *El Imparcial*

"We did not depend on the government," recalled José Santiago Healy, the publisher of *El Imparcial*, the largest daily in the state of Sonora, from 1982 to 2003. "Government ads represented about 5 percent of our income, at most. Advertisements came from other sources and that kept us strong."[10] *El Imparcial* was strong enough to devote widespread coverage to political opposition movements from when they started gaining strength in Sonora in the 1960s. Healy's earliest memory of that time dates to 1967, when his father, José Santiago Healy Brenan, ran the paper. In that year, the capital city of Hermosillo elected its first opposition mayor, PAN candidate Jorge Valdez.

"*El Imparcial* had very critical coverage of the government at that time, and it gave the paper a lot of credibility," said Healy. In fact, the more *El Imparcial* opened its pages to opposition voices, the more its audience grew. "People wanted to know what was going on in other parties, especially the PAN," said Healy. And his newspaper was the best source for independent news. "Only we and a handful of small radio stations covered the opposition. The rest of the newspapers and TV stations were under [government] control." Healy recalled the pressure the newspaper received from the government to follow the official line: "We would get tax audits, telephone calls with death threats, or bomb scares. At least twice we had to evacuate the building because of bomb threats."[11]

Hermosillo elected another mayor from the PAN in 1982, and in the middle of an economic crisis, with the federal government's credibility plummeting, the PAN projected that it could win the governorship in 1985. Its candidate was Adalberto Rosas López, a popular politician who had been mayor of Ciudad Obregón, the state's second-largest city. The PRI nominated Rodolfo Félix

Valdés, then secretary of communication and transportation in the federal government.

El Imparcial's coverage of Félix was critical even before he was a candidate. In a front-page story on November 19, 1984, days before the PRI named Félix as its candidate, the paper advocated for a governor with a career made in Sonora and deep roots in the state, a direct reference to Félix, who was born in Sonora but left when he was twelve years old and made his home in Mexico City.

Félix won the election and immediately faced accusations of fraud, which were promptly covered by *El Imparcial*. "We were seeing what other newspapers were doing across the country," said Healy in an interview. "How *El Diario de Yucatán* did political coverage, how *El Norte* started doing polls. We were part of that movement."

Eventually, proof of the electoral fraud would emerge, again in the pages of *El Imparcial*. In 2001 the paper published declassified documents from the DFS concluding that Félix "will have to be imposed [as governor] because he will not win democratically." This document is dated September 1984, two months before Félix's nomination.[12]

As Sallie Hughes observes, *El Imparcial* was part of a trend in Mexican newspapers that had generational shifts in their leadership with the arrival of new publishers who had a more cosmopolitan outlook and had observed other forms of journalism while studying abroad. Hughes mentions Healy, who was educated in Mexico City but furthered his studies in Spain and the United States. About the Sonoran publisher, Hughes writes: "His free-market values which put him at odds with the regime made him question Mexico's brand of subordinate journalism."[13]

Nuevo León and *El Norte*

The best-known case of a publisher who kicked old journalistic habits and instilled a new culture in the newsroom based on what he had learned abroad is Alejandro Junco de la Vega, who took the helm of *El Norte* in Monterrey after graduating from the University of Texas at Austin. He immediately applied what he had learned. Junco de la Vega has been principally acclaimed for his innovation in national newspapers with the launch of *Reforma* in Mexico City in 1993, but the changes in his approach actually began years before in Monterrey, hundreds of miles away from the capital. With its coverage of elections in Nuevo León in the 1980s, *El Norte* pioneered a form of watchdog journalism previously unknown in Mexico.

El Norte reporters quickly caught on to the PRI's dirty tricks and came up with ingenious ways to expose electoral fraud. Before election day, reporters would infiltrate the party's structure by posing as volunteers and learning the names of the people organizing campaign rallies and voter mobilization. They then checked those names against judicial databases and exposed anyone with a criminal background.

On election day *El Norte* deployed poll watchers to document any irregularities, especially in polling places that had a history of conflict in previous elections, places that had been mapped in advance. Reporters also monitored voter coercion, intimidation, and other tactics, such as *el ratón loco* (crazy mouse), which involved blocking opposition votes by sending voters to several polling stations across the city and telling them at each one that their names were not registered, or its mirror image, *el carrusel* (carousel), which involved ferrying PRI voters to multiple polling stations and having them cast votes at each one.

El Norte also used aerial photography of political rallies to count the real numbers of people attending and compare those figures to the candidates' claims. Homero Hinojosa, an editor at *El Norte* during the 1980s, recalled that this was first used in the presidential election of 1988 when the newspaper refuted PAN candidate Manuel Clouthier's claim that 100,000 people had attended his rally in Monterrey's Macroplaza. "It was actually 15,000," said Hinojosa, who described this type of reporting as Operation Pinhead because pins were placed over every head in the picture and then counted before a public notary. "The smart thing was that we [first] did it with the PAN candidate so nobody would say we were supporting the PAN. When this happened, PRI officials praised us, so when we did the same thing to PRI candidates, they could not object," recalled Hinojosa.[14]

Another innovation that came from *El Norte* in the coverage of elections during the 1980s was a primitive form of press agency called Bufete Informativo, which pooled daily stories from several newspapers across the country and then distributed them. The members of Bufete Informativo were some of the publications most associated with independent journalism in Mexico: *Zeta* in Tijuana, *AM de León*, *El Diario de Chihuahua*, *El Diario de Juárez*, *El*

Mañana in Nuevo Laredo, *El Imparcial* in Hermosillo, *La Crónica de Mexicali*, and *Noroeste* in Sinaloa.

Hinojosa, who was the project's first editor, remembers that it pioneered the use of computers for transmitting stories to various newsrooms, which now had information about other regions in the country from the best sources. "For example, when the elections were held in Chihuahua in 1986, *El Diario* in Juárez and Chihuahua provided first-rate stories," said Hinojosa. These initiatives positioned *El Norte* as one of the most important regional newspapers in Mexico. According to Hinojosa, "Alejandro Junco's message was that *El Norte* was a defender of democracy and that we had an opportunity to make a difference in the country."[15]

The newspaper also stood out because it did not hesitate to put resources into journalistic projects. Another innovation that Junco brought to Mexican journalism was the position of "newsroom manager" whose task was to handle a budget set aside to cover editorial expenses. "We never had to go to the business managers to beg for money," said Hinojosa in an interview. "It was a combination of idealism with pragmatism." It was also part of the lucky combination that would transform Mexican journalism. Young publishers with international exposure who put emphasis on training, codes of ethics, and a commitment to democracy and who were willing to invest in good journalists were the common denominator in what Sallie Hughes calls the "change processes in civic newspapers."[16]

Local newspapers had to fight hard to gain and preserve their independence in the face of authoritarian mayors or governors. Occasionally, the federal government would also set its sights on the local press, using paper as its censorship tool. Until the late 1980s the Mexican government owned the only newsprint provider in the country, the Productora e Importadora de Papel, SA (PIPSA), which had a monopoly on the paper supply and which would delay shipments of paper to rebellious publishers, or even cut the supply altogether. "We had independence, but we also had this huge sword of Damocles hanging over us with PIPSA, so we had to be careful because we would then get a call from Mexico City telling us there was no paper," said Velia Guerrero, the former publisher of *La Opinión*.[17]

But PIPSA's intervention was mostly related to how the local newspapers covered the federal government. The state-owned company never intervened on behalf of governors, mayors, or local political bosses, so newspapers could assert their independence at the local level. Furthermore, in the late 1980s PIPSA was privatized, and subsequently the Mexican government allowed the free importation of paper. As *El Imparcial*'s José Santiago Healy recalled, this gave a big boost to the local press, especially in the northern cities, because publishers there could buy newsprint from the United States at cheaper prices.

The end of that government monopoly allowed newspapers to thrive in the last two decades of the twentieth century, just as the Mexican political system was opening up. Transparent and balanced coverage of civic life across the country made a major contribution to the end of one-party rule and the transition to democracy. Newspapers still had a large share of commercial advertising budgets, which meant growing profits that were invested in technological improvements and higher salaries. But the age of greater freedom and commercial success was short-lived. Numerous threats from sources as diverse as technology, business, politics, and crime soon emerged.

The Future of the Local Press

After decades of commercial success, local newspapers in twenty-first-century Mexico are struggling. Some reasons are widely known and apply all over the world: digital technologies have changed reading habits; advertising budgets are being allocated in other media; and newspapers have not found a way to monetize their websites and digital products. In Mexico, declining circulations and shrinking revenues mean that newspapers have to rely on other sources of income, and the largest sources now available are national and state governments. Increasing reliance on government advertising means newspapers have to change their editorial views again and decrease critical coverage of the governments that decide where to advertise.

Government propaganda in Mexican media is nothing new. For years, newspapers and radio and TV stations have featured government ads as well as paid inserts about the activities of high-level officials; these are written in government press offices and printed or broadcast as regular news stories without any input from reporters or editors. The problem comes when government propaganda provides too large a share of a news organization's funding.

Editorial independence has always derived from the strength of a news organization's income from circulation and commercial, as opposed to government, advertising. As I have shown, local newspapers could resist advertising blockades from the government as long as their commercial revenues kept them in business. But this independence is less common today than it was a decade or two ago. And the discretionary manner in which governments place their advertising (usually biased toward more compliant media outlets) makes it harder for independent media to get government ads even if they have greater audiences.

A 2014 report on "soft censorship" pointed out the growing influence exercised by different levels of government over the editorial policies of Mexican media. According to the study done by the World Association of Newspapers and News Publishers (WAN-IFRA), the NGO Artículo 19, and the research center Fundar: "Opaque and arbitrary allocation of official advertising constrains pluralism and a diversity of voices by selectively funding media outlets that support officials and their policies."[18]

At the regional level, local governments can exercise different types of pressure on independent media, the report added, "including tax audits, intimidation by police and statements by officials to discredit the media. But most common is still the threat to withhold government advertising. Some media outlets are willing players in this game."[19]

The discretionary selection of news outlets to receive government advertising was once a feature in PRI-dominated governments, back when the party controlled the Mexican political system. But even as the country transitioned to democracy, the opposition parties that began controlling city and state governments did not kick the habit of favoring the compliant press or silencing critical journalism. Even when PAN or Partido de la Revolución Democrática (PRD) candidates benefited from independent media to win elections, once in power they could not stomach criticism.

A case in point is *AM de León*, the largest newspaper in the state of Guanajuato. It was an important voice during the 1980s and 1990s when the PAN began to win significant political positions. In 1991 it covered the post-election protest launched by Vicente Fox, who had been the PAN candidate for governor and who was denouncing fraud. The future president eventually won the governorship of Guanajuato in 1995, and the PAN has not lost control of the state since. But once in government, the PAN could not tolerate *AM de León*'s independence. During the term of Governor

Juan Manuel Oliva, the newspaper "was denied government advertising for many years because of disagreements with the state governor, despite having one of the highest circulations in the state."[20]

The lack of transparency in government advertising works to the advantage of public officials, who do not have an obligation to disclose the use of public funds for propaganda. Not a single government in Mexico at the municipal, state, or federal level regulates the manner in which official advertising is allocated. President Enrique Peña Nieto included this as a campaign promise but has not followed up. Thirteen bills presented in the federal Congress since 2002 have been stalled.

Thanks to freedom-of-information laws, the federal government's expenditures are available, although they have to be gathered from different sources. The latest reports show that the administration of President Enrique Peña Nieto spent more than 36 billion pesos for advertising from 2013 to 2016, but nothing forces the government to allocate that money according to the penetration the advertisement could have.[21]

Since there are no regulations, municipal, state, and federal governments can place their advertisements without regard for the size of the audience in the news outlets where they buy space. In some cities, the largest newspapers are deprived of advertising because they are the most independent, while compliant publications get government money even if their audience is negligible.

Numbers for the share of government advertising in a local news organization's income are not available. Media owners do not disclose their companies' balance sheets, and practically every local government keeps secret how much money it spends in each news outlet, and so the public does not know if the budget is allocated according to audience penetration or malleability. In a 2015 update to their soft censorship report, WAN-IFRA, Article 19, and Fundar pointed out that the Oaxaca state government "halted development of a web platform for advertising transparency that was being created in cooperation with civil society." The government of Coahuila did publish its media expenditures report but without the salient details.[22]

If increasing government advertising means less editorial independence, the decline of commercial advertising means weaker journalism. Shrinking revenues result in shrinking newsrooms and layoffs at local newspapers that affect editorial quality. Newsrooms have to produce more stories than before—for print, web, and mobile editions—with fewer reporters and editors. The first victim of this trend is investigative journalism. If a reporter has to produce half a dozen stories every day, a regular occurrence at regional newspapers, devoting several days to a single story is impossible. Reading the financial reports of government agencies to find misuses of public money, examining the fine print of government contracts looking for signs of corruption, crisscrossing the cities documenting failures in public services, to name but a few routine duties of local investigative reporting, all take time that is not available for overworked journalists.[23]

The decline in commercial advertising is also tied to a fall in circulation, a trend seen around the world. But this does not mean that newspapers are read by fewer people. With most of the audience moving to the internet, some newspapers get a web readership that is up to five or six times larger than their printed edition. Since launching websites in the 1990s, local news organizations have taken advantage of the trust already placed by the public in their brands and established themselves as the prime source of news in their communities.[24] This means that local newspapers still matter. The problem is that the lack of a successful business model for web editions makes the internet a weak source of income.

As belts are tightening at newspapers all over the country, employees are not the only ones feeling the impact. Owners are also struggling because while profits decrease, the number of shareholders getting a piece of the shrinking pie is growing. Most local newspapers in Mexico are family owned, and for decades they were owned by one person, usually the family patriarch. But as the families have grown with siblings, children, nieces, and nephews, many want jobs at these newspapers, while others have begun other businesses but rely on the newspapers' influence to get ahead. No newspaper-owning family would admit it, but the changes in the ownership structure and the increasing number of family members holding shares in each company is putting them under strain because of competing political, commercial, or financial interests.

La Opinión in Torreón is a good example of a local newspaper that could not resist the pressures of a growing family. The newspaper was founded in 1917 by Rosendo Guerrero, who had four children. Two of his sons, Salvador and Edmundo, were publishers in different eras. By the 1970s control was shared between Margarita Guerrero, the only surviving child of the founder, and Velia Guerrero, Edmundo's daughter. In the 1970s and '80s, Margarita chaired the company's board while Velia acted as publisher and general manager. By the mid-1980s other members of the third generation began to work at the newspaper and fight for control of the company. The family conflicts left *La Opinión* without clear business and editorial guidelines and with financial struggles that forced the Guerrero cousins to sell the newspaper in 1993. Multimedios Estrellas de Oro, a Monterrey-based media company, bought *La Opinión* and folded it into the newspaper chain that would eventually become *Milenio*.

In the twenty-first century, threats to regional news organizations also come from organized crime groups that fight turf wars all over the country to gain control of drug trafficking, extortion, kidnapping, and other criminal enterprises. In this war, the so-called cartels have attempted to control what is said about them in local media, resorting to violent tactics such as armed attacks on the offices of newspapers and radio and TV stations, killing or kidnapping reporters and editors, and delivering threats. Many local news organizations have lost credibility because they have not reported events like shootouts, homicides, raids by security forces against drug cartels, or the presence of criminal groups in their cities. "Zones of silence" have spread in regions with high levels of violence related to organized crime.

Meanwhile the violence unleashed by drug cartels against the media has been met with impotence from the local and federal governments. Even worse, at times public officials, politicians, and police officers have threatened or attacked journalists using methods attributed to criminal groups so the violence would not be traced back to them. In other instances they have relied on criminals to carry out attacks against the press. In a high-profile case from early 2015, the homicide of Moisés Sánchez, a journalist in the city of Medellín, Veracruz, was attributed to the city's mayor, who allegedly hired a local criminal group to carry out the hit.[25]

The intimidation of the press goes on in many different ways, from the violent to the verbal, and often comes from the highest levels of government. The state of Veracruz is the most notorious example because of the vast diversity of aggressions and aggressors. A risk evaluation carried out by the International Center for Journalists and Freedom House in May 2015 showed that potential aggressors against local journalists (based on the suspected authors of prior attacks) included state and federal government officials;

members of the army and navy; police officers and commanders at the federal, state, and municipal levels; organized crime; labor unions; peasant groups; and private companies.[26]

Most of the attacks against journalists have occurred since 2010, after the drug war intensified in Mexico, and some of the most important local news organizations have been affected. Grupo Reforma's *El Norte* in Monterrey and *Mural* in Guadalajara experienced several armed attacks against their offices. *El Imparcial* in Hermosillo suffered the disappearance of reporter Alfredo Jiménez Mota in 2005. In Torreón, Eliseo Barrón, a reporter at *La Opinión*, was killed in 2009, and *El Siglo* endured armed attacks in 2009 and 2011 and the kidnapping of five workers in 2013. *El Diario de Juárez* lost two reporters, one in 2008 and the other in 2010. The newspaper ran a dramatic front-page editorial addressed to criminal bosses in the city: "What Do You Want from Us?" Local authorities could not do anything to stop the aggressions. *El Mañana* in Nuevo Laredo has had four of its staffers killed or disappeared and editors and publishers kidnapped. And that is just the physical violence: the number of threats is impossible to determine since not every journalist reports them.

Article19's yearly reports show that during the term of Peña Nieto, each year has seen more journalists killed than the one before: four in 2013, six in 2014, seven in 2015, twelve in 2016, and twelve in 2017. Victims have ranged from part-time journalists who publish small magazines unknown outside their towns, like Moisés Sánchez in Veracruz, to the most celebrated reporter in México and abroad: Javier Valdez Cárdenas, the cofounder of *Ríodoce* in Sinaloa.[27]

These and other attacks mean that local journalists still matter and news organizations remain important forces in their communities. Even as print readership is down, visitors to websites and users of mobile apps are increasing. The public is still hungry for information about their cities and regions, and they seek out trusted brands, the legacy of newspapers that refused to yield to political pressures. Snatching all the copies of a print edition off the streets in order to silence critical coverage might seem a silly thing of the past, but the current methods of controlling the local press can be as total in their ambition. They are, moreover, more ruthless and efficient. The future of local media depends on the ability of media owners and journalists to resist them.

Notes

1. Author interview with Velia Margarita Guerrero, July 2015.
2. *La Opinión*, Dec. 5, 1978, 1B.
3. Author interview with Velia Margarita Guerrero, July 2015.
4. *El Siglo de Torreón*, digital archives, https://www.elsiglodetorreon.com.mx/hd (accessed Nov. 9, 2017).
5. Monsiváis, *A ustedes*, 59.
6. Monsiváis, *A ustedes*, 60.
7. José Carreño Carlón, "Información-desinformación-reglamentación," *Nexos*, Oct. 1, 1979, http://www.nexos.com.mx/?p=3454.
8. Secanella, *El periodismo político*, 58.
9. See http://diario.mx/nosotros (accessed Jan. 18, 2018).
10. Author interview with José Santiago Healy, Oct. 2015.
11. Author interview with Healy.
12. A series of stories detailed the federal government's intervention in the Sonora gubernatorial election of 1985. Juan Carlos Zúñiga, "Cometen fraude electoral contra Rosas López en 1985," *El Imparcial*, http://www.periodismo.org.mx/assets/reportaje_2002.pdf (accessed Sept. 7, 2017). *El Imparcial* won a National Journalism Award for this work.
13. Hughes, *Newsrooms in Conflict*, 114.
14. Author interview with Homero Hinojosa, Oct. 2015.
15. Author interview with Hinojosa.
16. Hughes, *Newsrooms in Conflict*, 110–11.
17. Author interview with Guerrero.
18. World Association of Newspapers and News Publishers (WAN-IFRA), Artículo 19, and Fundar, "Buying Compliance: Governmental Advertising and Soft Censorship in Mexico" (2014), 7, https://www.cima.ned.org/resource/buying-compliance-governmental-advertising-and-soft-censorship-in-mexico.
19. WAN-IFRA et al., "Buying Compliance," 25.
20. WAN-IFRA et al., "Buying Compliance," 27.
21. Fundar, "El gasto en publicidad oficial del gobierno federal de 2013 a 2016" (Sept. 2017), 12, http://fundar.org.mx/mexico/pdf/P.O.2013-2016OK2.pdf.
22. WAN-IFRA, Article 19, and Fundar, "Breaking Promises, Blocking Reform: Soft Censorship in Mexico" (2015), 9, https://www.cima.ned.org/resource/breaking-promises-blocking-reform-soft-censorship-in-mexico.
23. Naturally, there are exceptions, and local news organizations still manage to produce quality journalism. Since 2001, local newspapers and TV stations have won sixteen National Journalism Awards for breaking news, investigative reporting, interviews, features, and other stories based on open government records. However, while this is important recognition of the work done by the local press, it represents only one-fifth of all the awards given in these categories since 2001. This year is taken as a baseline because it was when the prize

began to be awarded by an independent committee of journalists and academics. Before 2000, the federal government decided the award winners.

24. Johnson and Kaye, "Cruising Is Believing?" The study includes a survey that found a high correlation between assessments of credibility in newspapers' printed editions and their websites.

25. "El alcalde de Medellín nos pidió desaparecer a Moisés (Sánchez) porque le estorbaba," *Animal Politico* (Jan. 26, 2015), http://www.animalpolitico. com/2015/01/ el-alcalde-de-medellin-nos-pidio-desaparecer-moises-sanchez-porque-le- estorbaba.

26. Freedom House, the International Center for Journalists, and the MacArthur Foundation, "Evaluación de riesgos de periodistas de Veracruz," May 15, 2015, https://www.periodistasenriesgo.com/?s=Evaluación+de+Riesgos+de+Periodis tas+en+Veracruz.

27. Article 19, Mexico Office, "Libertades en resistencia," https://articulo19.org/ informe2016.

12 | Between the Imperius Curse and *The Matrix*

Attacks on Journalists in Mexico

RAFAEL BARAJAS

Beyond Basic Logic

According to the Committee to Protect Journalists, between 2006 and 2017 twenty-nine journalists were murdered in Mexico, making the country one of the most dangerous in the world for the press. The common assumption is that in the majority of these cases the journalists were attacked by organized crime groups, but according to the international organization Article 19, in 2014 59 percent of all attacks on the press were committed by public officials and only 7 percent by organized crime. It is not that easy to tell the difference: over three-quarters of those journalists' murders were committed with impunity.[1]

Explaining this violence against journalists is no easy task. The Mexican reality has become increasingly complex; it seems to move ever further from rational, logical explanation. To understand the underlying mechanisms that move Mexican society and media conglomerates, and to comprehend the forces and logics that are behind violence against the press, we must look beyond, examining which calculations and forces drive that press. We must even wander into the realm of magic.

The Imperius Curse; or, The Importance of Controlling the Will

In the magical world of Harry Potter, there are three unforgivable curses: the

Crucio, which tortures the victim; the Avada Kedavra, which kills; and the Imperius, through which one gains control over the actions of another. The Death Eaters freely use these spells. It seems that their master, Lord Voldemort, read Gramsci. As the Italian philosopher argued, dictatorships not only kill and torture, they also seek to control people's minds and wills.

Those in power have always sought mechanisms to dominate the thoughts of the masses. To do so they construct complex ideological apparatuses. In particular, the powerful often cultivate lies and myths, instill fanaticism, and exploit irrational fears. For centuries, religious institutions in league with secular authorities used these means to organize and control the ideas and lives of the population. In response, eighteenth-century thinkers, social reformers, and scientists promoted freedom of thought. Their greatest weapon, the bulwark of this essential freedom, was freedom of the press. Despite these advances, those in power have continually sought to control the press and convert it into an apparatus of ideological control. With the arrival of radio and television, the power of the media grew exponentially. Now the owners of those outlets, like the popes and bishops of yesteryear, have acquired a tremendous influence over public opinion.

Media moguls are aided by theorists and publicists, who defend a free market (read: capitalist) model of media control. These mouthpieces of the modern press claim that a free market system guarantees freedom of expression better than any other. This is not true.

The Dark Magic behind the Large Media Consortia

In the twenty-first century, global wealth has become concentrated in the hands of the few. Economists estimate that in 2017 a mere eight people owned as much wealth as the poorest half of the world's population.[2] We have reentered a feudal era of unequal wealth distribution. One of the principal businesses of this new oligarchy is the media. These private monopolies, which often incorporate television, print, radio, and internet outlets, have the capacity to set the agenda for vast sectors of public opinion. Today, a handful of families own the principal media consortia in all the countries of Latin America, including Grupo Globo in Brazil; El Clarín in Argentina; Grupo Cisneros in Venezuela; El Tiempo publishing house in Colombia; and Televisa and TV Azteca in Mexico.

The large media consortia have always claimed to be impartial, truthful, and objective. Nevertheless, they remain prisoners of very palpable interests, as demonstrated by the case of Televisa. The directors of that company are Mexico's main business people: Emilio Azcárraga, Roberto Hernández, Pedro Aspe, Claudio X. González, María Asunción Aramburuzabala, Carlos Slim Domit, Germán Larrea, Alberto Bailleres, Fernando Senderos, and Lorenzo Zambrano. The invariable consequence of this alignment is that the broadcaster defends the interests of the captains of industry. Rarely will it denounce their labor abuses, their financial and tax frauds, or their environmental crimes, and when a piece of information that could be damaging to these individuals is leaked to the press, the broadcaster can use its power to undertake damage control.

Televisa also defends the economic model, the political project, and the system of ideas and values that permit these important business people to concentrate their wealth and power. The company, like other large media consortia in the modern world, imposes an agenda that obscures themes affecting the interests of the majority and highlights those that matter to the wealthy. As a result, in the news there is little information about workers' salaries but a great deal about the stock market.

Mexican media consortia claim to defend the freedom of the press and the right to information, but rarely do they open spaces for dissidents or for ideas that are contrary to the interests of their owners. They claim to be a plural space for reflection and debate, but they only give real space to voices that are aligned with the regime (e.g., important government functionaries, intellectuals who defend free markets like Enrique Krauze and Hector Aguilar Camín, and business people). The dissidents are marginalized, and when an independent journalist opens a space within a media outlet, they always end up expelled, as shown by the case of Carmen Aristegui. The opposition is often the victim of ferocious campaigns of defamation, and the right of reply is nonexistent.

Psychological Operations

As a general rule, large media consortia concentrate their efforts on implanting in the majority the values and ideas that matter to wealthy business people. They operate as ideological apparatuses at the service of very concrete interests, and most of the time they use complex psychological operations to make their messages more efficient. In Mexico, like everywhere else in the world, the large media companies invest millions in researching how to manipulate public opinion. In August 2009, the journalist Eva Golinger of the Agencia Bolivariana de Noticias documented how the Rendon Group, an expert in psy-ops for the Pentagon, had invested US$3.4 million to lend "communications support" to Plan Colombia.[3] That same year, Mexican president Felipe Calderón spent nearly half a billion pesos promoting his unpopular energy reforms.[4] The high cost of this marketing can only be explained as an investment in focus groups and other psychological operations. Psy-ops are aimed at the unconscious part of the brain, at our mind's most irrational fears and aspirations. They do not seek to make us reflect on the information that we are given, but rather seek to manipulate our feelings and affections. Psychological operations are an insidious form of propaganda that does not appear to be propaganda.

The psychologist Blanca Montoya describes the most common aims of psy-ops as follows:

1. *Provoke fear.* This is the oldest psychological operation and is most efficient when it is used by those in power. Fear paralyzes, inhibits protest, and divides communities. Those who are fearful seek the protection of the powerful—generally meaning the state.
2. *Establish a "danger" that threatens the collective.* The invention of a common enemy tends to produce cohesion in society (curiously, the "common enemy" is often an obstacle for the interests of the oligarchy). This strategy was put into action to great effect by Joseph Goebbels in Nazi Germany and has not lost effectiveness.
3. *Promote hate.* This strategy seeks to create distrust and to divide society. Once a danger is established, it is destroyed without mercy.
4. *Exacerbate violence.* Once fear, danger, and hate are created, violence against the "evil object" is not simply justified but deemed "necessary."
5. *Exacerbate despondency.* Promote the idea that struggle is senseless, that there are no valid causes, and that every struggle is lost before it begins. For example, the idea that all politicians are corrupt is of great service to corrupt politicians.
6. *Utilize the shock doctrine* (described by Naomi Klein). To impose unpopular measures, those in power issue alarmist announcements. Some regimes even provoke events that destabilize the society. In

this way a crisis is created, and the desired measure is presented as a remedy.

7. *Eliminate collective identity.* This mechanism consists of erasing bit by bit the history of the people and degrading the things that give them pride and cohesion.

8. *Hide and deny the existence of conflict between social classes.* The realities of the unjust regime are systematically denied and hidden, and a fictitious idea of peace and harmony is promoted.[5]

Many of these operations are more efficient when they are presented in a coordinated way by both the media and the political institutions.

Psychological and media operations like these serve the interests of both national oligarchies and Washington, DC. They have been key in the defeat of progressive and popular leaders, such as Mohammad Mosaddegh (Iran), Jacobo Árbenz (Guatemala), Jorge Eliécer Gaitán (Colombia), Salvador Allende (Chile), and Omar Torrijos (Panama). They have also been used against opposition candidates in presidential campaigns.

The control exercised by media outlets contributes greatly to maintaining a system that benefits only a few (among them, the owners of the media).

The Matrix

Thanks to these operations, the masses are connected to a system of artificial intelligence that isolates individuals and makes them live in a virtual reality that has little to do with the real world. This sophisticated ideological apparatus uses precise information technologies to keep society disorganized and to facilitate exploitation.

The Greek economist Yanis Varoufakis is correct when he claims that the movie *The Matrix* (1999) is more documentary than science fiction.[6] The universe of *The Matrix*, in which millions of people are cultivated and enslaved, with their brains plugged into a huge machine that sucks out their life and makes them live in a fictitious world, is a very realistic metaphor for what is occurring in the twenty-first century. In this system, the hackers—like Julian Assange—who reveal the truth are a great threat.

Save for a few honorable exceptions, the large modern media consortia share the same political and economic project. Neoliberal discourse has become hegemonic around the world. This ideology does not allow for a different view of the world. It speaks of democracy, but does not allow changes. Much information that affects vast groups of citizens is hidden or dispatched to the back page. Campaigns designed to defame and discredit dissidents are common practice. The victims are rarely allowed to defend themselves.

Fourth-Generation Wars

From 1932 onward, Adolf Hitler spoke of strategies for the manipulation of public opinion and cultivated the idea of making psychological warfare and propaganda into major weapons. In 1991, the Israeli military theorist Martin van Creveld published a book entitled *The Transformation of War,* in which he posited that in a world dominated by a single power, conventional wars between large armies would no longer be possible. Van Creveld developed a theory of wars that would alternate between massive military propaganda and violent events, calling them "wars without guns" or "fourth-generation wars." In these struggles, also called "asymmetrical wars," military maneuvers are replaced by media operations and psy-ops, directed by experts in communication and mass psychology. (And, one might add in the aftermath of the 2016 US presidential election, experts in hacking and social media.) Their objective: controlling society through a constant media bombardment. In a fourth-generation war, there are no battlefronts or large combat armies. There are only small albeit very violent conflicts with little apparent interrelationship.

This type of war has been put into practice on various occasions by the US government over the past two decades. The war against drugs, declared by Felipe Calderón in 2006, seems to fit perfectly the model of a fourth-generation war. It is in the context of the war against drugs that violence against the citizenry and against journalists has grown. This helps explain why working as a reporter has become so dangerous in Mexico.

During the Calderón administration, fourteen journalists were killed. During the first two years of the administration of Enrique Peña Nieto, December 2012–December 2014, twenty-two journalists were killed.[7] Since 2006, fifty-two media outlets have been attacked with firearms or explosives.

According to the international organization Article 19, in Mexico in 2014 alone there were more than 200 attacks against journalists.

This is the logic of violence in a war without armies.

LA GUERRA QUE NOS HACEN LOS MEDIOS por El Fisgón*

* Historieta realizada a partir de conceptos de Manuel Freytas, Blanca Montoya, Noam Chomsky, Naomi Klein...

FIGURE 18. El Fisgón, "La Guerra que Nos Hacen los Medios" (The War the Media Wages on Us).

FIGURE 19. El Fisgón, "La Guerra que Nos Hacen los Medios" (The War the Media Wages on Us).

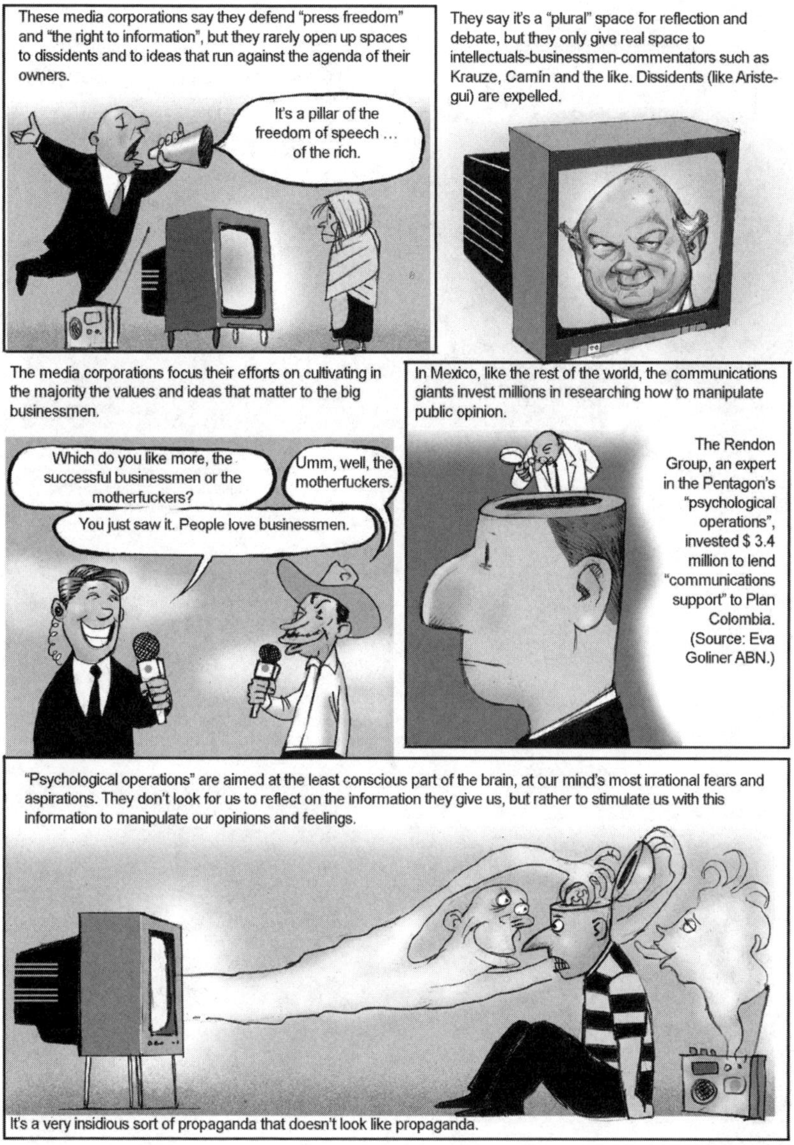

FIGURE 20. El Fisgón, "La Guerra que Nos Hacen los Medios" (The War the Media Wages on Us).

FIGURE 21. El Fisgón, "La Guerra que Nos Hacen los Medios" (The War the Media Wages on Us).

FIGURE 22. El Fisgón, "La Guerra que Nos Hacen los Medios" (The War the Media Wages on Us).

According to Blanca Montoya, among the basic techniques of psychological operations we find:

1. Massive and incessant repetition.
Repeating a lie a thousand times in the end makes many people believe that it is true.

2. The construcation of "media realities".
A world that is imaginary, idyllic and false is shared by millions through soap operas, the cinema and TV and radio series .

How kind the rich and Peña Nieto are!

ES UN PELIG... RO, ES UN PELIGRO...

It must be.

3. The selection of an entire agenda.
Due to their power to disseminate, the large conglomerates can define which issues are news and which are not. So only matters that interest the big conglomerates are news.

No es tema… Not news… Not news…

No es tema… nipulando.

Hugo Chávez went mad with joy when he saw that…

HUGO CHAVEZ SE VOLVIÓ LOCO

5. Censorship.
A very old technique for control that consists in not disclosing certain information. Once censorship was exerted by authoritarian governments; today media owners are the ones who define what will be disseminated and what will not.

6. Smokescreens.
Consist of disseminating fake news, inflating minor news or giving confused accounts to the end of diverting attention from news that might affect the groups in power.

Did you see that a nutter hijacked a plane armed only with two cans of juice?

Anónimo francés, siglo XIX.

REFORMA FISCAL

FIGURE 23. El Fisgón, "La Guerra que Nos Hacen los Medios" (The War the Media Wages on Us).

FIGURE 24. El Fisgón, "La Guerra que Nos Hacen los Medios" (The War the Media Wages on Us).

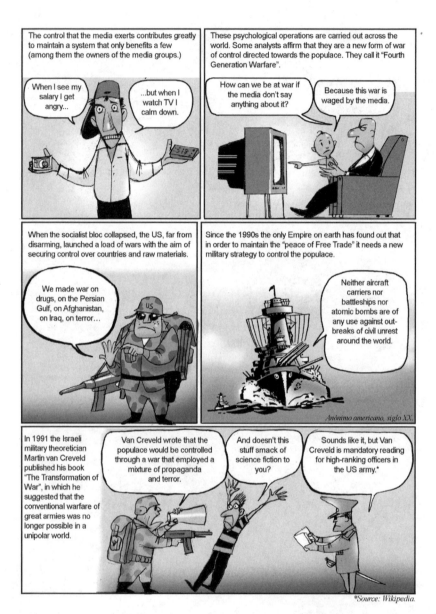

FIGURE 25. El Fisgón, "La Guerra que Nos Hacen los Medios" (The War the Media Wages on Us).

FIGURE 26. El Fisgón, "La Guerra que Nos Hacen los Medios" (The War the Media Wages on Us).

Acknowledgments

This chapter was translated by Michael Lettieri.

Notes

1. Committee to Protect Journalists, "Journalists Killed in Mexico since 1992," https://cpj.org/americas/mexico (accessed Aug. 1, 2017); "El 59 por ciento de las agresiones que recibe la prensa en México provienen de los servidores públicos: Artículo 19," *La Jornada*, Apr. 23, 2014, http://www.lajornadadeoriente.com.mx/2014/04/23/59-por-ciento-de-las-agresiones-que-recibe-la-prensa-en-mexico-provienen-de-los-servidores-publicos-articulo-19.
2. Oxfam, "Just Eight Men Own Same Wealth as Half the World" (Jan. 16, 2017), https://www.oxfam.org/en/pressroom/pressreleases/2017-01-16/just-8-men-own-same-wealth-half-world.
3. "Eva Golinger: EEUU privatiza guerra colombiana con sus transnacionales mercenarias," Aporrea, Oct. 8, 2009, https://www.aporrea.org/actualidad/n140293.html.
4. *Diario Reforma*, Jan. 5, 2009.
5. Blanca Montoya, *El dominio mediático* (2010), http://www.cronicon.net/paginas/Documentos/No.40.pdf (accessed Sept. 5, 2017).
6. Charles Mudede, "What The Matrix Tells Us about the Crisis in Greece," Stranger (July 29, 2015), https://www.thestranger.com/film/feature/2015/07/29/22612202/what-the-matrix-tells-us-about-the-crisis-in-greeceby-charles-mudede.
7. Carolina Gómez Mena, "Asesinados, 22 periodistas en lo que va de este sexenio, acusa el gremio," *La Jornada*, Dec. 11, 2014, http://www.jornada.unam.mx/2014/12/11/politica/012n2pol.

13 | The Plaza Is for the *Populacho*, the Desert Is for Deep-Sea Fish

Lessons from la Nota Roja

EVERARD MEADE

Living in the desert, thought Lalo Cura . . . is like living at sea. The border between Sonora and Arizona is a chain of haunted or enchanted islands. The cities and towns are boats. The desert is an endless sea. This is a good place for fish, especially deep-sea fish, not men.

—ROBERTO BOLAÑO, *2666*

I n his attempt to explain the murder of women in contemporary Ciudad Juárez, Roberto Bolaño eschews a master narrative in favor of lavish, tactile descriptions of the victims' bodies. These traces of larger histories reinforce the atomized ways in which his characters probe their existential insecurities (along with the rest of us). The most ethical of these characters is literally named after madness—Lalo Cura. He sees the desert all around him as a space unfit for civil society, government, or a public sphere. It's a space for predation, plain and simple. The moral desert to which Bolaño alludes and which threatens the vibrant female characters he creates has become an increasingly relevant metaphor as the violence of the "drug war" has spread from regional hotspots throughout Mexico and from the usual suspects to ordinary citizens. The characters in the novel feel helpless in the face of the desert's seemingly primordial power of physical and moral corrosion. But Bolaño shows that this desert is in fact man-made. It's a product of a larger process of turning people into things and communities into obstacles to progress. He doesn't accomplish this through some kind of simplistic Marxian calculus, but rather by showing the nexus between plausible human lives and broader historical forces, by showing violence that is under- rather than overdetermined.

What's the relevance of this novel to a critical understanding of the Mexican press and the public sphere as we confront more than a decade of chronic violence that has dwarfed the dead women of Juárez? Something about its messy humanity and underdetermined arguments resonates ten years into a "drug war" that's not really about drugs. Since its original publication in 2004, *2666* has reached a broader audience and provided greater insight into the Juárez femicides than has any long-form journalism or scholarly treatment available to a nonspecialist audience, particularly outside of Mexico. There are important exceptions, like Sandra Rodríguez Nieto's *La fábrica del crimen* (discussed in detail below), but it didn't come out until 2012 and wasn't available in English translation until 2015, more than twenty years after women's bodies started to appear in the desert.[1] For a long time, much of the available analysis of the Juárez femicides was either crying out for recognition of the victims and survivors, or tracking (and trying to preempt) the authorities in their search to identify and prosecute the culprits. Professional journalists, citizen journalists, and local activists alike produced excellent examples of both, often at considerable personal risk, and they brought significant attention to the murdered women.[2] Their work was fundamental to the 2009 Cotton Field decision by the Inter-American Court of Human Rights and to the creation of the "gender alert" system for crimes against women, which is in place today.[3] A subsequent generation of scholarship added empirical and theoretical depth and sophistication.[4] But those desiring to diagnose Juárez and define a singular cause or culprit for the femicides often fell into the same traps as the official investigations.[5] In search of a coherent whole, they often skipped the messy fragments around the edges. As each theory of the case collapsed, the horror and tragedy of the killings stood increasingly nameless and aimless, cues for apathy rather than empathy.

Internationally, the use of the murdered women to validate other theories—from radical critiques of neoliberalism and patriarchy to the US-based origins of the drug war and the political history of the Juárez cartel—closed off inconvenient avenues of inquiry and opened the door to claims that the femicides were a myth, disprovable by facile statistical comparisons with the United States.[6] Overdetermination also left the underlying story vulnerable to changes in the news cycle. When the overall level of violence in Mexico shot up in 2007, tens of thousands of new murders, forced disappearances, and bloody spectacles crowded out the Juárez femicides as a discrete phenomenon. The consequences were tangible and terrible. Outside of the spotlight and yet stuck in what became a global murder capital by 2010, local activists and outspoken members of victims' families became much more vulnerable to persecution than ever before.[7]

How do we step back from the specific incidents defining a wave of violence and offer some kind of broader historical perspective without abandoning the people sucked into the vortex? How do we bring together a community of conscience rather than mere spectators?

This is where Bolaño is most instructive, albeit in a counterintuitive fashion. Despite being an utterly impenetrable 900-page novel, which doesn't get to the chapter called "The Part about the Crimes" until 300 pages in, which has sentences and physical descriptions that go on for pages with little punctuation, and which invents an utterly byzantine intellectual history complete with a library full of fictitious books, fake authors, and their asinine disputes—his novel has reached an audience of hundreds of thousands and inspired dissertations, books, feature films, and documentaries about Ciudad Juárez on multiple continents.[8] Bolaño succeeds by avoiding the standard modus operandi of murder-in-the-desert reporting and analysis. He doesn't try to come up with a definitive narrative of the phenomenon, treat it as a whodunit, or develop a theory of a primary cause derived from quantitative data or a collection of anecdotes. Nor does he engage in wanton melodrama. Instead, he offers rich descriptions of the experience of living in and around this violence (many ripped from local headlines), a sense of how its madness becomes normal (which doesn't minimize the underlying human suffering), and an outline of the politics of how real people see some things and willfully don't see others, at particular moments, in particular places.

Journalists like Marcela Turati and Sandra Rodríguez Nieto have achieved this kind of empathetic, ethnographic perspective in much more approachable formats (and both have roots in and around Juárez). They focus on the experiences of survivors and on the broader milieu in which particular acts of violence unfold. In her reporting for *El Diario de Juárez* (and now for *SinEmbargo*) and her long-form investigative work, Rodríguez Nieto reconstructs the social universe in which the femicides take place by getting the people of Juárez right, by understanding how they see the world around them and what they perceive to be possible (or just normal), over and above the details of particular crimes or acts of violence. In *The Story of Vicente*, her masterful exploration of how and why sixteen-year-old Vicente León Chávez and two high school friends murdered his parents and sister in 2004, she reconstructs his childhood in a decadent and dysfunctional place. Rodríguez Nieto reveals a Juárez pervaded by political corruption, where criminal activity was normal and out in the open, where hundreds of disappearances in the late 1990s never made the news, where a global race to the bottom squeezed the middle classes, and where city planners subsidized industrial parks and strip malls without providing housing, transportation, or basic municipal services for the people who worked in them.

Social pathos alone didn't determine the murder, and Rodríguez reveals plenty of personal pathology and teenage angst in Vicente's story. Describing him cleaning up the crime scene after the murders, she writes: "Along with the stains, he washed away all of his parents' unjustified reprimands, the promises they took back without explanation, the constant pressure to obey rules he didn't understand, the feeling of having to belong to a group of people with which he couldn't communicate."[9] This might apply to any teenage killer (or teenager, period). But the specific outlet for this angst, the ease with which the method of its expression comes to the boys and they assume their roles in its bloody script is all about Juárez. The city where hundreds of women's bodies have been discarded in trash dumps and vacant lots for all to see is the same city where three teenagers in school uniforms could procure weapons, murder the parents and sister of one of them, and choose a vacant lot in which to burn the bodies; the same city where they would remember to scrub down the crime scene with hydrochloric acid and comfort the baby brother whom they left alive, before heading to their own beds, as if they had stayed up late working on a school project. One phenomenon isn't a necessary precursor to the other, but they are clearly related.

Rodríguez Nieto shows that individual murders in Juárez may have highly contingent origins, but they are also part of a larger self-reinforcing environment.

Marcela Turati specializes in capturing these environments in which violence seems to flourish. She was one of the first journalists in the national media to abandon the *ejecutómetro*—the running tally of organized crime assassinations after 2006—in favor of smaller, more impressionistic stories about ordinary life and survival in the places most affected by the violence. As she tells it, over and above the human suffering it masked, the body count couldn't capture the almost surreal quality of the carnage she encountered in Ciudad Juárez: "Violence in this city has spawned all kinds of sordid tales, but all of them are true. There is the story of a man from the Champotón neighborhood who, tired of finding bodies thrown outside his business every morning, put up a sign reading 'It is prohibited to dump bodies or trash.' In November, one of the bodies found there was that of his daughter. He did not see her, because he too had been murdered."[10]

Like that of Rodríguez Nieto, Turati's reporting in *Proceso* re-creates the contexts in which the violence unfolds, how ordinary people make sense of it, and in which direction the moral arc of the local universe bends. She has followed police reporters, coroners, morticians, human rights activists, and, above all, family members of the murdered and disappeared, in search of an intimacy with something more than a series of crimes. Turati's reporting on the 2010 murder of seventy-two undocumented migrants at a ranch in San Fernando, Tamaulipas, and the subsequent revelation of hundreds more victims in mass graves throughout the area shows a touch of Bolaño. She uses physical descriptions of the bodies and accounts of the suffering of the family members who arrive at the morgues in search of their loved ones in place of a linear narrative of what happened and why. She doesn't avoid reconstructing the murders or probing why they happened. Instead she shows that none of the plausible explanations of the particular incidents satisfy the broader need for truth and reconciliation amid an epic and gruesome wave of violence (whether the individual explanations are true or not).[11] Like many of the bloody events that constitute the "drug war," the San Fernando massacres defy a simple causal explanation, at least in the narrow terms of maintaining and protecting a black market. As a US intelligence official put it: "It remains to be seen how these deaths benefit the Zetas."[12] Explaining why a drug cartel that trafficks in billions of dollars' worth of illicit goods would bother to kidnap, extort, and murder a bunch of impoverished migrants on northbound passenger buses leads almost inevitably to conspiracy theories and exotic speculation on the dark and twisted logic of the cartels extrapolated from rumor and anecdote. Turati finds instead an environment in which such violence has become utterly banal, something much more like a pattern of wartime atrocities than a series of murders, or a crime to be solved. Recovering the most important truths in such a scenario requires the reporter or historian to play less of the role of prosecutor or interrogator, and more that of anthropologist and active listener.

Insufficient Independence versus the Insufficiency of Independence

How can we incorporate these insights into the critical frameworks we use as scholars and practitioners of journalism? How should they shape our understanding of the historical trajectory of the Mexican press, as it confronts a wave of violence with multiple causes? Whether from Habermas or classical liberals, most definitions of the "public sphere" place a premium on the relative independence of the press in terms of ownership, sponsorship, and censorship.[13] There are obviously good uses of this perspective for assessing the basic freedom of the press, and there has been commendable activism along these lines. A principled defense of the independence of the press fueled public indignation when respected commentator and news anchor Carmen Aristegui was fired from MVS Radio in 2015, after she demanded the reinstatement of two staffers fired for blowing the lid off the Casa Blanca scandal (the mansion gifted to President Enrique Peña Nieto's wife by a prominent government contractor).[14] Three years earlier, the lack of media independence in presidential politics was laid bare when *Reforma* revealed hundreds of thousands of dollars in direct payments from then-candidate Peña Nieto to Televisa reporter Joaquín López Dóriga (among others) in exchange for favorable coverage.[15] The same principle was at stake when media watchdogs revealed that the pro-government Televisa network was granted exclusive access to video footage of the dramatic raid in which Mexican marines captured Joaquín "El Chapo" Guzmán, boss of the Sinaloa cartel. Televisa only released the video in heavily redacted form and after adding several staged elements, designed to lionize the Mexican marines and obscure the presence of foreign military personnel.[16] The June 2017 revelation by researchers at the University of Toronto that Mexican security agencies had been using sophisticated malware to spy on prominent anti-corruption activists and journalists, including some who had been kidnapped or killed for their work, underscores the multifarious nature of the threat.[17] Media independence matters. But when the metrics of independence are too rigidly defined, they fail to properly account for the role of government ads and subsidies, self-censorship, and other practices that place the Mexican press (historically anyway) somewhere uncomfortably between authoritarian and democratic, a space that the liberal model of a public sphere isn't equipped to handle.

Social scientists have created a variety of hybrid models to explain the structure of the press during the one-party regime that controlled the Mexican state from 1929 until 2000, which remains integral to the relationships that particular government agencies and officeholders share with the media that cover them to this day. Early histories of the Mexican press emphasized its co-opted, colluded, and bought-off quality. There's plenty of evidence to support this view, and most of it remains nearly as true today as it was in the 1950s. In addition to direct payments or bribes to individual journalists in exchange for favorable coverage—known as *chayotes* or *embutes*—there were government monopolies on paper and ink; indirect control over the unions and trade associations that operate newsstands and distribution networks; large-scale government subsidies in the form of *gacetillas* (infomercials and press releases that often look like actual news stories) or advertisements for government agencies and officeholders; and shady, clientelistic practices of issuing (or denying) press credentials.[18] The opening of the one-party system to electoral competition (after 1976) and the PRI's loss of its monopoly in Congress (1997) and the presidency (2000) decentralized this system, but did not destroy it. More recently, the rapid decline of private advertising revenues has made government subsidies more important than ever to the survival of Mexican newspapers and other media outlets. Mexico is left with a "captured liberal" model of the press.[19] Overt censorship is illegal and market-based private interests dominate media ownership. But media and political elites collude to advance their parochial interests, and they use considerable state resources to "recapture" the autonomy of the press by selectively sparing it the full brunt of market forces.[20]

The compulsory coziness of the press with those in power mirrors a broader pattern among Mexican intellectuals and cultural elites under the "perfect dictatorship." The most strident critics of Diego Rivera, Octavio Paz, Carlos Fuentes, and many others point to the state dinners, funding of their pet projects, plum positions, and other perks that they enjoyed in an implicit exchange with the government (particularly individual presidents) for focusing their criticism elsewhere. In doing so, they followed the classic compromise modeled by Pablo González Casanova. Furthermore, it was compromise that contemporaries like José Revueltas and David Alfaro Siqueiros refused at the cost of their freedom.[21] These critics have a point when it comes to specific moments of decadence or blindness in the careers of certain public intellectuals—including prominent journalists—and the institutions they founded. But they can miss the content of the work and the fact that it often provided a powerful critical counterbalance to other forces in Mexican and global society.

Take the weekly *Proceso*, for example. Founded by Julio Scherer García in the aftermath of a 1976 editorial coup at *Excélsior*, which was designed to punish its most important journalists for being overly critical of the Gustavo Díaz Ordaz and Luis Echeverría administrations, *Proceso* aspired to a fierce and critical independence. But it could not survive without significant government subsidies, as was painfully revealed in a famous spat with disgraced president José López Portillo. In a testy press conference, the president declared: "A commercial enterprise organized as a professional business has the right to demand that the [political] system pay for publicity so that it can systematically oppose it? This is, gentlemen, a perverse relationship, a morbid relationship, a sadomasochistic relationship that approximates many perversions that I won't mention here out of respect for the audience: I pay you so that you can hit me. Well, no, gentlemen!"[22]

The boycott López Portillo announced faded in a matter of months, as federal and state agencies gradually began to purchase ad space once again. Civil servants, moreover, have always made up one of the largest segments of *Proceso*'s readership. And yet *Proceso*'s coverage—of everything from civil wars in Central America and the hemispheric drug war, through corruption scandals at the state-run oil company, to political assassinations during the democratic transition—set the gold standard for investigative journalism in Mexico. It has long been widely regarded as the most critical mainstream journalism outlet in the country (although perhaps surpassed recently by some online outlets).[23] Indeed, observers of *Proceso* are much more likely to criticize its tendency to see conspiracies around every corner and to reproduce every potentially incriminating government document leaked to its reporters than to claim that it soft-pedals accusations of malfeasance or gives the powerful a pass. At this point, there's also a pretty good argument that the arc of influence has shifted, such that government agencies place ads in *Proceso* because they covet the attention of its readership, rather than as an official gesture of sponsorship or patronage.

The stakes behind the liberal critique are arguably much higher now that the system has fragmented and state resources are less centralized. Fetishizing public intellectuals' or journalists' independence from the formal apparatus of the state gives an implicit pass to public intellectuals backed by private economic interests, and these networks form and dissolve more easily and are much harder to track than they were under the one-party monolith. The overemphasis on media independence also validates fatalistic elite narratives about corruption, authoritarianism, and the ignorance of the masses, whether from neoliberals or their radical critics. These days such critiques are more common with reference to state and local actors in places dominated by regional political machines. University administrators, the heads of museums and archives, the leaders of local social service providers, journalists and columnists, and other public intellectuals depend on the support of state governors, municipal presidents, and the agencies they control. This makes them soft targets for cosmopolitan critics, who can plug them into facile teleologies of democratization and howl about provincial corruption. Critics on the right see Chavista militarism and tyrannofilia in any kind of publicly subsidized progressive media,[24] and they ignore the fact that otherwise serious regional news outlets have to publish swimsuit photographs and other exploitative click bait just to keep the lights on. Meanwhile, critics on the left imagine Rupert Murdoch, Emilio Azcárraga, and the CIA behind all private media, and they ignore the fact that these outlets have exposed some of the worst political corruption scandals and human rights abuses in contemporary Latin America, or that journalists who work for private and independent media companies have been behind groundbreaking investigations, such as the Panama Papers story.[25]

Of course provincial political corruption is very real, and it has sticks as well as carrots. Consider the violence and intimidation directed at journalists. Mexico is currently one of the most dangerous places in the world for reporters—more than a hundred have been killed or disappeared since 2000.[26] Journalists in rural areas are more vulnerable to attack, as are those who work for smaller papers or otherwise enjoy less name recognition. The pattern of attacks strongly suggests that old-fashioned political repression rather than organized crime is responsible for the majority of the killings.[27] Veracruz, for example, where a dozen journalists were murdered under the governorship of Javier Duarte (2010–2016; he is now awaiting trial for corruption on a massive scale), has the lowest rate of organized-crime assassination in the country and some of the lowest overall crime rates. While many of the journalists who have been targeted in Veracruz covered the crime beat, those who reveal the nexus between criminal activity and politicians are the ones most likely to find themselves in the cross hairs.[28]

This is conventional wisdom among Mexican journalists, borne out by cases going back to the 1980s. The syndicated columnist Manuel Buendía had covered gangsters and drug traffickers for years without incident. But within weeks of implicating the defense minister, other national politicians, and the CIA in a criminal conspiracy in 1984, he was dead, assassinated by a lone gunman on his way home from work.[29] The journalist Alfredo Jiménez Mota was disappeared and apparently assassinated in Sonora in 2005. Jiménez Mota had covered drug trafficking and organized crime in Culiacán, Sinaloa, for years. He had been threatened and forced to self-censor before, and indeed he left Culiacán for Hermosillo, Sonora, in part to give some local disputes time and space to cool off. In Sonora, Jiménez Mota uncovered a considerable criminal conspiracy, tying the local affiliates of the Sinaloa cartel to municipal officials in Ciudad Obregón, statewide officeholders in Sonora, and the federal judicial police, among others. Soon after he published these revelations in *Zeta Tijuana* (his own paper was afraid to run them), Jiménez Mota disappeared.[30] The categories of crime and political corruption, of course, are not neatly divided, and there are many unknowns even in the best-documented and most-publicized cases. In Casas Grandes, Chihuahua, journalist Luis Cardona had meticulously documented and written about fifteen local disappearances in 2012. He became the sixteenth. For some reason, his captors left him alive, although badly beaten. In the documentary film he made about his ordeal, Cardona admits that he will probably never know exactly why he was taken.[31]

The same pervasive uncertainty has shrouded the 2015 murder of photo-journalist Rubén Espinosa. His body was found alongside those of activist Nadia Vera and her three roommates in her apartment in the Narvarte neighborhood of Mexico City. All five had been shot in the head with a 9mm pistol, execution-style. Espinosa and Vera were both outspoken critics of the Duarte regime in Veracruz; both had been threatened and then taken refuge in the capital; and most observers believe that the roommates were collateral damage in a political assassination. But there's just enough crime and impunity in Mexico to allow for other interpretations—a drug cartel vendetta (perhaps from Veracruz, perhaps from elsewhere), a robbery gone wrong, a crime of passion, and so on. Two years later, the investigation had turned up few leads, and hopes of justice were fading.[32]

On May 15, 2017, when Javier Valdez Cárdenas was taken out of his car and executed in broad daylight in the middle of the street, not far from the Culiacán weekly *Ríodoce* he cofounded, the organized crime connection seemed clear enough. Earlier that spring, Valdez had published an interview with an emissary from the faction of the Sinaloa cartel run by Dámaso López, also known as El Licenciado, which had incensed Los Menores, a rival faction headed by El Chapo's brash and volatile sons. They had even sent gunmen around the city to buy up all available copies of *Ríodoce*.[33] (Dámaso was subsequently arrested and his son turned himself in at the US border, effectively conceding defeat to Los Menores.)[34] But even in this case, assuming that the basic theory of the motive is correct, the possible modalities of the assassination are multiple and complex. Did Los Menores order Valdez to be killed by their own forces or by off-duty police or soldiers (in order to complicate the investigation and incriminate the authorities)? Or did they merely let it be known that Valdez was an enemy, so that those seeking to curry favor with them would act on their own? Given that the assassination seemed to validate Dámaso's characterization of Los Menores as lacking restraint or respect for civilians, is it possible that he set up the killing in order to incriminate Los Menores? Or did he merely bait them into it? Or perhaps it was powerful political actors with a stake in how the factional struggle in the cartel would shake out, who took advantage of the seemingly obvious motive in order to play a card of their own? Or perhaps the same opportunity presented itself to corrupt officials who bristled at the increasing attention that Valdez directed toward murdered journalists and the blame he leveled at Mexican officials for their deaths (the subject of a book he published the previous fall)?

Valdez seemed to outline precisely the latter scenario in the last of his *Malayerba* (Bad Weed) columns. "They Are Going to Kill You" tells the story of an unnamed journalist whose family and friends warn him that his increasingly critical coverage of political corruption is going to get him killed; he's shot on the orders of an ambitious legislator.[35] Valdez certainly had become a more strident critic of the Mexican state. He blamed politicians for the murder of journalists, especially after the killing of his friend and fellow *La Jornada* correspondent Miroslava Breach on March 23, 2017. And he claimed very publicly that he was more afraid of politicians than narcos. But Javier Valdez Cárdenas wasn't really a crime reporter or even an investigative journalist, nor was he primarily an expert on drug trafficking. He was a *cronista* (chronicler), who wrote about what it's like to live under a persistent cloud of violence. He spent most of his time with people who are not well known—the survivors and victims' families. Their trials and tribulations are the inconvenient truths he brought to light, not some trove of compromising information on powerful politicians or gangsters. His murder, like that of other journalists, cannot be reduced to either silencing coverage of illicit activities or maintaining an authoritarian regime.

The vestigial structure of the contemporary Mexican press fits well within the carrot-and-stick model of the old one-party regime. But the recent wave of violence against journalists seems to be more about the breakdown, or at least the decentralization, of that model than its perpetuation. As peace scholar Pietro Ameglio Patella explains, since 2000 there has been a "dual process" of the "widening of civic spaces" alongside "the selective restriction and elimination of social activists," most of them "local opposition leaders who are poor, unarmed, and ambushed." In 1998–1999, for example, 402 social activists were murdered in Mexico, 72 percent in southern Mexico (104 in Chiapas alone). Of these, 70 percent were members of the political opposition to the state government in the places where they were targeted, and 85 percent of the incidents in which they were killed were ambushes; federal human rights investigators found that "there was no armed confrontation." Ameglio Patella attributes a marked decline in the intensity of nonviolent protest movements in the twenty-first century to this wave of assassinations.[36]

The liberal model often involves an implicit comparison in the guise of an ideal type. Most analysis of the historical press in Mexico implicitly compares it to the contemporary US and European press, or a Whiggish historical proxy, rather than to the press that celebrated lynching and protected its perpetrators in the South during the Porfiriato and revolutionary periods, or that aided and abetted McCarthyism throughout the United States during the heyday of the PRI (Partido Revolucionario Institucional), or that characterized unarmed African American and Chicano antiwar protesters killed by police as "rioters" during the 1968 crackdown against student movements in Mexico. Particularly when it comes from abroad, this perspective lends itself to rather hollow failure and corruption narratives, which diffuse responsibility rather than assigning it—witness Julia Preston and Sam Dillon's summary of the history of democratic institutions in Mexico as "from dictatorship to despotism." An uncritical caricature of historical corruption, it leads them to a rather tragic assertion that Mexicans were "culturally unprepared for democracy" in 2000 (in a book otherwise full of good reporting).[37]

The dominant critique of this perspective in Latin American studies at the moment—the Gramscian turn—conceives of media independence only within the narrow confines of resistance to domination and the asymmetrical negotiated settlements reached in the process. In addition to the McLuhanesque biases for media over content, mass over new media, and stylized fatalism over agency or process, this imported analytic almost inevitably leads scholars to overestimate the strength, coherence, and modernity of the Mexican state and the importance of self-conscious revolutionary groups on the radical fringe, at the expense of a more nuanced understanding of the broader mediascape and spaces for democratic participation.[38] As Nick Henck shows, for example, overreading the Gramscian influence on Subcomandante Marcos and the Ejército Zapatista de Liberación Nacional in Chiapas came at the expense of a deeper understanding of the movement's indigenous cultural influences.[39]

Both perspectives—liberal and Gramscian—suffer from shortcomings that remain particularly relevant to understanding the press in contemporary Mexico. The first is an excessive nominalism and a reliance on rigid categories. If you're covering contemporary Guerrero, what counts as "the state" and who counts as its agents? Is there a difference between monetary and physical coercion—*plata o plomo* (literally, silver or lead)—or between either of these and more conventional forms of political and economic coercion (some of them formally legal)? Is it really accurate to blame the drug war for the current dearth of investigative journalism in Mexico, given that there wasn't much to begin with and that it's been the first on the chopping block in a global journalism recession that is totally unrelated to the drug war? This kind of rigidity and the apparent failure of the Mexican state to do what a state is "supposed to do" and of Mexican civil society to do what it's "supposed to do" have led to unfortunate conclusions—witness Ioan Grillo's assertion that drug cartels constitute an "insurgency" in some way comparable to the Mexican Revolution of 1910, a plainly specious and degraded understanding of both insurgency and revolution (again, in a book otherwise full of excellent reporting).[40]

The second shortcoming is a pervasive iconophobia, especially when it comes to coverage of crime and violence. Critics of the *nota roja* (crime pages) and of foreign journalists for supposedly overemphasizing violence and crime in their coverage of Mexico have long argued that bloody images or the intensive focus on particular crimes and criminals turns them into evil stereotypes or even a kind of popular fetish that breeds bloodlust, moral lassitude, and, ultimately, further crime. The Mexican criminologist José Ángel Ceniceros famously called for the abolition of the nota roja as a new form of reactionary "pornography" in 1933.[41] This perspective is relevant to certain kinds of cable news coverage or particular media campaigns that have self-consciously sought to bolster support for a *mano dura* (iron fist) approach to crime in various Latin American contexts. But this critique misses the many social and cultural issues that are examined through the prism of violence and crime and the fact that they disproportionately affect the poor and the marginal. It also ignores the fact that images can be more democratic than text, and the same goes for richly described biographical sketches when compared to data-driven policy analysis. They can lower barriers to entry in public discourse; they can invite empathy; and they can create spaces for readers to make their own sense out of the news in ways that elite political commentary and social analysis generally cannot. Of course, there can be excesses here too.

La Nota Roja as National History

There's another analytical strain, very popular in Mexico, which claims the nota roja as a unique national tradition. As Carlos Monsiváis puts it, in the heyday of the one-party regime, the crime pages turned "tragedy into spectacle, spectacle into moralistic warning, warning into fun, and fun into the stories of a collectivity."[42] Vicente Leñero and Gerardo Villadelangel's revival of *El Libro Rojo* is a perfect contemporary example. Leñero writes:

> It might seem crazy to throw it out there suddenly, but through the recounting of crimes and murders—as much the "classic individual" kinds as the collective kind that have shaken us in waves—it is possible to narrate a chronicle of the country. Writing it like a textbook makes our skin crawl while making us open our eyes to the fateful reality. Murder is like a diabolical dynamo behind our course through time. Murder is like a beautiful literary expression of the tragedies of the past and the present and, without a doubt, of the future as well.[43]

But in practice, this textbook conflates acts of extreme repression and active resistance with acts of idiosyncratic deviance and passive consumption (and not just by conflating criminal with political violence). The result is a hodgepodge that follows the whims of celebrity, rather than a coherent social theory or ethical commitment, and it totally ignores the reception of both these stories and the other stories that they may have crowded out, perhaps stories more relevant to the experience of injustice or the travails of everyday life.

There's a great bit in John Dickey's 2008 documentary about the crime pages in Oaxaca, *El diablo y la nota roja*, in which he asks a variety of people what they think of the nota roja, and then he secretly films them buying and reading newspapers around the same plaza later that day. Facing the camera, to a person, they condemn the crime pages, denouncing the base emotions crime stories provoke and the celebration of violence and scandal they promote. When they buy their papers later in the day, however, Dickey catches the same people flipping directly to the crime pages and ogling the pictures and headlines with rapt attention. One of them even tosses the other sections in the trash. A similar conceit courses through Bernardo Ruiz's 2012 documentary *Reportero*. The editors and reporters of the independent Tijuana weekly *Zeta* explain how they guard their independence and objectivity to the extent of having the paper printed in the United States to avoid the government paper monopoly and exclude the publisher from editorial meetings. Shortly thereafter, the same writers and editors admit that they sell far more

papers when they run cover stories about spectacular crimes or fatuous political scandals; in effect, they have to find and run enough of these stories in
order to keep the paper afloat.

There's a certain universalism to this guilty pleasure narrative. One can
imagine similar reluctant admissions with regard to soap operas, reality television, or even pornography in different settings. But there is something distinctive about the crime pages in Mexico that is not necessarily about their
unique prominence or quality. Crime and tabloid journalism have played an
outsized role in several key moments in the history of democracy in Mexico,
particularly when it comes to popular responses to violence or injustice in
moments of dramatic modernization. Indeed, the presumption that the
crime pages represent "public opinion"—and represent it as a passionate
mob, unable to control its emotions in the face of suggestive images—has
served as a convenient pretext for restricting popular democratic expression
and insulting an enlightened political elite.

Modern crime coverage began in Mexico City in the 1890s, and it was
closely tied to the expansion of literacy and the development of faster and
cheaper printing methods. Under Rafael Reyes Spíndola, *El Imparcial*
(founded in 1896) emphasized the capturing of "fresh" news, like "a hunter"
who tracks down his prey "while the event is still throbbing." Thanks to the
inclusion of modern crime stories and photographs, daily circulation jumped
to over 100,000 at a time when classic nineteenth-century papers with their
political debates and literary essays, like *El Monitor Republicano* and *El Siglo
XIX*, never had more than 20,000.[44] On September 7, 1907, journalist Agustín
Victor Casasola mounted a wooden platform he had nailed to a telegraph
pole more than ten meters above the street in order to photograph the execution of Florencio Morales and Bernardo Mora behind the walls of the Belén
jail. The two young Guatemalans faced the firing squad for assassinating
former Guatemalan president Manuel Lisandro Barillas in a bloody knife
attack on a crowded streetcar earlier in the year. The photographs appeared
on the front page of *El Imparcial* on September 10, helping to sell thousands
of extra copies (Casasola's name didn't appear in the credits, because the
authorities had banned photographers from the execution). Many liberal
critics of the death penalty at the time claimed that the birth of modern
crime journalism, particularly when accompanied by photographs, shored
up support for the death penalty and other regressive causes in Mexico and

reversed a long-term trend toward abolition.[45] For its part, *El Imparcial* fanned these flames, printing essays by positivist thinkers and using openly racist language at times. But the death penalty continued its long-term decline in practice, as the vast majority of the condemned were quietly given indefinite reprieves or pardons, despite the spectacle of a handful of cases in Porfirian Mexico City. In an undemocratic system, perceived popular support for the crime pages had little impact on public policy and in fact served as a convenient pretext for the continued exclusion of most of the populace from the political process.

Indeed, the prolific printmaker José Guadalupe Posada illustrated the two Guatemalan killers as *calaveras* (skeletons) alongside a satirical corrido. The corrido warned Mexicans of different social classes that these "Guatemalan shin bones" (*canillas*) would come back from their graves to haunt the selfish and the wicked. The double meaning of the corrido—the idea that these fierce calaveras would be the conscience nipping at the heels of sinful Mexicans, but also reminders of the shortcuts that broke up their daily travail—mirrored the double meaning of crime stories for the contemporary public.[46] They could be revolting and terrifying, but also fascinating, and they united the community like little else. The same mix of outrage and titillation fueled a massive expansion of crime journalism in the 1930s.

Mexico's first tabloid, *La Prensa*, was founded in 1929 and quickly became a prime source of both crime journalism and the production of "public opinion" about crime and violence. Crime stories that headlined the second section of the major dailies *Excélsior* and *El Universal* made the front page of *La Prensa* with large-format photographs and suggestive captions. In addition to the stories and photographs, *La Prensa* featured jailhouse interviews with articulate and charismatic criminals—including the famous murderers Luis Romero Carrasco and Pedro Alberto Gallegos—and lots of interviews with people on the street about the impact of their crimes, who often expressed outrage and a desire for vengeance, and the big dailies quickly followed suit.[47] The 1929 elimination of the death penalty and the jury trial from the penal code for the Federal District and all federal territories galvanized the nota roja. After Romero Carrasco and Gallegos suffered *la ley fuga* (literally, the law of flight, the term used for extrajudicial execution) in successive years and nearly identical rituals and in the aftermath of the brutal murder of an entire family at a tannery in

Mexico City in the summer of 1933, the editorial page in *La Prensa* claimed a desperate need for the reestablishment of the death penalty and its use "on a greater scale than ever." The editors described Romero Carrasco as "the founder" of a new wave of criminals, defined by their "ferocity and shamelessness." As long as he is alive, the criminal "thinks about an escape, a change of government, a miracle of the goddess of crookedness; neither jail nor penal colonies are enough of a threat to passionate beings who decide on vengeance, much less for the born criminal." *La Prensa* pledged to open "a kind of survey that will reveal to the nation the public feeling about this problem."[48] Over the next few weeks, the paper reprinted quotes from 149 individual letters and interviews—118–31 in favor of reinstatement of the death penalty—and declared it had received hundreds more. The editors claimed that these results represented "all social classes," "people on the street" as well as "experts," the veritable "pulse of the nation."[49]

The particular *vis vitalis* (vital force) behind this pulse, however, flew in the face of the radical social reforms at the core of the post-revolutionary state-building project. The elimination of the death penalty and the jury trial was part of the same campaign to bring literacy, secular education, public health, and modernity more broadly to the masses. It was a kind of prophylaxis—using experts and well-designed bureaucracies to insulate the masses from the retrograde passions, spectacles, and superstitions that had held the country back for centuries. And to the elite social engineers who masterminded the revolutionary education effort in particular, the efflorescence of popular media like comic books and crime journalism was not just an unintended consequence, but a bastardization of the project. Reading the gory details of crime scenes, treating criminals like celebrities, cheering extrajudicial executions, and calling for murderers to be burned, hanged, and shot in the public square were not what education reformers had in mind. The first issue of the specialized criminological journal *Criminalia* in 1933 included several tirades against the nota roja. And the Mexican Congress discussed measures to ban or suppress the crime pages in 1933, 1934, and again in 1942. While these efforts did not bear fruit in terms of overt censorship, crime coverage moved back into secondary sections of the big daily papers by the mid-1940s, and there were no comparable national debates spurred by the nota roja over the next couple of decades.[50]

In the 1970s, crime-only tabloids like *Alerta* and *Alarma!* gained a certain popularity by providing graphic coverage of the daily crime blotters, complete with bloody photographs and blaring headlines. These tabloids also amplified the updates to big national crime dramas, like the 1973 botched kidnapping and murder of businessman Eugenio Garza Sada in Monterrey or the 1978 murder of the Flores Muñoz couple in the swanky Lomas de Chapultepec neighborhood of Mexico City. Crime tabloids have also proved invaluable to historians and human rights investigators trying to piece together the events of the Dirty War. As Jorge Luis Sierra Guzmán explains in *El enemigo interno*, many of the disappeared showed up as murder victims in the nota roja, in ways that skirted the censorship of the rest of the press. The stories don't provide a lot of context nor do they directly indicate political persecution, but they do provide names, descriptions of wounds, signs of torture, evidence of execution, and other critical details.[51] Their focus on the bloody results of crime rather than their causes or context allowed the crime pages to slip past the censors (whether external or internal) and between the nets of liberal and Gramscian critiques alike as pure spectacle, the distraction and dulling of the masses.

The spectacle certainly got bigger with the arrival of the war on drugs and a new generation of drug lords. Froylán Enciso periodizes the birth of sensational coverage of narcos in Mexico beginning with the arrest of Cuban trafficker Alberto Sicilia Falcón: "His arrest on July 2, 1975, generated media coverage without precedent. The dailies published dozens of articles about the moment of his capture, the torture to which he was subjected, his attempted suicide in Lecumberri Prison, the arguments in his defense, the relationship he maintained with La Tigresa [The Tigress, the nickname of his society girlfriend, Irma Serrano], and finally, his successful escape from the penitentiary."[52]

Sicilia's lawyer, Roberto Sánchez Juárez, made sure that his client's letters and descriptions of his trials and tribulations received ample media coverage. Through his intimate first-person reflections, readers and viewers could explore his suffering and desperation at the hands of the authorities, but also his charisma and ingenuity, not unlike the jailhouse interviews with Luis Romero Carrasco, Pedro Alberto Gallegos, and other celebrity murderers of the early 1930s. The key difference was Sicilia's apparent wealth and connections. He consorted with movie stars and spies, and his commercial network reportedly included prominent businessmen and politicians, from rough-and-tumble caciques like Arturo Durazo to members of President Luis Echeverría's family. The involvement of a cross-section of the Mexican elite in this crime drama offered a new twist on the picaresque social critique that charismatic criminals could offer: the idea that they revealed the dysfunction of post-revolutionary progress and the hypocrisy of its boosters. Celebrating the exploits of powerful drug traffickers offered a much sharper indictment of the political class as a whole and sustained a cultural narrative of elite avarice and corruption that has only gotten stronger over the last 40 years. The possibility of this critique in the late 1970s was, however, extremely limited. As crime stories were relegated to specialized publications and as mainstream print media were dwarfed by the growing television behemoth, the depth and breadth of the crime stories that reached a mass audience declined dramatically, and the politics of capturing a mass audience shifted from crime to other spectacles. Images of criminal violence didn't disappear, but they became stylized, fictionalized, and globalized.

Television claimed the mantle of the most popular medium and guilty pleasure of choice in the 1970s. It was on the small screen that mass audiences consumed both the films of the (now-passed) golden age of Mexico's national cinema and the explosion of commercial thrillers from Hollywood, many of which featured new stereotypes of the drug trafficker, nameless and faceless victims, and the ketchup-spattered moral calculus of a zombie flick. These stereotypes, in turn, helped to shape the self-fashioning of actual narcos. As Carlos Monsiváis explains: "The movies became the arbiter of style for the criminal minority."[53] There's a little Scarface in every narco who came of age in the 1980s. Political elites once again used the popularity of this lowbrow fare as evidence of the dangerous and irresponsible character of the masses and the need for enlightened mediators of popular democracy. But the preferred medium for reaching the masses with didactic and picturesque messages of a grand national tradition and a collective journey to progress—the national cinema—had fallen into a steep decline. Echeverría pumped some money into the national cinema in the early 1970s, but most of the resulting films were either too critical or too artsy to achieve a mass audience (and they were not televised). By the early 1980s, Emilio "El Indio" Fernández, who had directed epic historical melodramas like *María Candelaria*—winner of the Cannes Film Festival in 1946—found himself doing bit parts in films like

Lola la Trailera, the first in a series of commercial adventure films featuring a sexpot female truck driver up against corrupt cops, cross-border drug traffickers in cowboy kit firing off machine guns, and *buchonas* (scantily clad girlfriends of the narcos) galore. There had been violence in the national cinema—*María Candelaria* culminates in the stoning to death of the title character by a mob—but it had been accompanied by communal acknowledgment, grief, and redemption, not the elimination of bad guys in a narrowing sieve of prefabricated drama.

In a satirical essay published in the second issue of *Proceso*, Carlos Monsiváis recounts the naming of the streets in Ciudad Nezahualcóyotl after movie stars from the golden age of Mexican cinema. He fixates on the larger-than-life María Félix and the dedication of a movie theater to her in the former shantytown turned modern slum. He describes a vulgar affair "where prolonged whistling reaffirms the lack of the custom of applauding as a mark of civilization, or proof that the director understood uncannily well the spirit of Mahler or Stravinsky," wizards of orchestration who transplanted elements of folk culture into highbrow cultural music. In the essay, the crowd whistles in numb adulation at a celluloid star, whom they have only seen "interspersed with police dramas" on tiny televisions. María Félix becomes a collective fetish. Mimicking a newspaper headline, Monsiváis declares: "THE ENTIRE TOWN ADMIRES CLOSE UP THE SOUGHT-AFTER ARTIST FROM THE MEXICAN CINEMA, THE PEERLESS MARIA FELIX. The humble people follow her every move, and surely they admire her. How could they not? Beautiful, famous, rich, and sought-after." Kids chase after her Rolls Royce as she rolls out of the slums and into the sunset. Monsiváis declares, "Nezahualcóyotl has internationalized." In order to capture the broader meaning of this desire in the aftermath of Echeverría's failed populism and the decadence of the post-revolutionary national project (represented by the golden age of Mexican cinema), he recalls a scene from a bar in the Zona Rosa. "A drunk would get up from his table every ten or fifteen minutes and shout a slurred 'María Félix will never be poor'" before passing out again. "Of course not," Monsiváis explains, "she belongs to an extinct genre of the stars and the disappeared world of prosperity, and thus she models her delight and casts her gaze (which demands idolatrous discipline) upon that eminently popular auditorium, whose solitary dressing room and whose stunned emotional distance in response to the gesture spares us the need for any kind of sociological commentary." This is "the historical fatalism of the country according to the chambers of commerce: María Félix will never be poor, and the people of Nezahualcóyotl will never trade places with her."[54] The clairvoyant who lays down the inevitable conclusion is, of course, "a drunk," with all the prescience of Bolaño's Lalo Cura.

The political capture of this captured public on the small screen that Monsiváis showcases is still big business, and not just in terms of the attempts to buy content and influence at Televisa outlined above. The sets and signals still matter too. During Mexico's national transition to digital-only broadcasts, the PRI-dominated regime gave out more than 10 million new TV sets to the poor, especially in politically contested areas, such as the state of México, where the PRI candidate won the governor's race a by a razor-thin margin in 2017.[55] The machinery may be aging, but the resonance of narratives of violence that contradict the designs of those who would control popular media is more relevant than ever.

These lamentations may look like small beer in an environment in which more than 150,000 people have been killed; 30,000 have been forcibly disappeared; torture and rape have become routine; and drug kingpins like El Chapo have become more popular than sports heroes or movie stars. The moral outrage over murderers in the crime pages of the 1930s and 1940s and the blind adoration of old-fashioned movie stars on the small screen in the 1970s seem almost camp by contrast. But elite critics often miss the desire by ordinary people to speak and be heard, or at least to see people who speak like them and voice their concerns, which the crime pages and other popular media provided almost intuitively. There have always been serious social inequities and dislocations that people care more about than the latest child murderer, political scandal, or inane act of beneficence by the rich and famous, but they have had few channels to express these concerns in a corporatist political system with a highly insulated elite.

Getting the democratic aspects of the crime pages right—looking for the participatory space, social experience, and subtle subversions of the powerful and entitled they encourage, rather than stopping at their more obvious exploitative, fantastical, or lynch mob aspects—is as relevant in the current era of the neoliberal drug war as it was under the "perfect dictatorship." Think of the demonstrations in support of El Chapo after his 2015 escape, complete with satirical ballads and "I Want to Have Your Baby, Chapo"

T-shirts, or the outpouring of emotion on display in Culiacán during the wake for famed *sicario* (hitman) Pancho Chimal in April 2017.[56] On the surface, there is more than a little nostalgia for the paternalism of these mafia bosses and more than a little blind adulation. Indeed, there are parents in Sinaloa who hope that their daughters will attract and marry a narco with a shiny truck and a fat billfold (the full patriarchal package). But the same myths also show the inability of the government or even the gringos to contain these legendary men, despite trotting out new rhetoric and resources. The ability to shout at a reporter or to shove a cameraperson or a municipal official out of the way in order to sing the praises of wanted men who trample hierarchical social codes like blades of grass under their ostrich-skin boots, whether in physical demonstrations or in social media echo chambers, is a form of power, a way of talking back to a political system that has failed the majority. And there's a clear separation between the myths of the narcos and their actual crimes. The same forums where the picaresque achievements of the narcos are celebrated are full of sorrowful lamentations on the injustice of particular murders, concerns about the involvement of the authorities in many acts of violence, and a pervasive feeling of abandonment. After more than ten years of horrific violence, there's a growing sense of "we have suffered while they have done nothing," where the "we" is expanding and the "they" is contracting.

One of the most striking aspects of the present wave of violence is that it has affected everyone, certainly not equally but in ways that have crossed barriers of class, ethnicity, and geography like never before. This shared experience presents a unique opportunity to do a kind of social history of the present, and that's what many of the keener local journalists seem to be doing.

Human Fragments over Master Narratives

In his reporting for the Sinaloa-based weekly *Ríodoce* and in his numerous compilations, Javier Valdez Cárdenas created a new genre of testimonial literature that is closer to the kinds of personal testimonies collected during the revolutions and dirty wars of the 1970s and 1980s than to conventional crime journalism. While the stories are hyperdescriptive and violent, and they often don't offer the reader a periscope to see out of the constrained agency of their

protagonists, they are also undeniably human, and they offer a unique perspective on how ordinary people try to make the best of the limited moral
choices offered to them during waves of violence. The stories in *Levantones*, for
example, reveal many small acts of courage and solidarity, often done at considerable personal risk: a bus driver who helps a kidnapped man to get home,
a young woman who shouts a warning to a stranger about to be jumped by
hitmen, an older brother who trades himself to kidnappers in exchange for his
little brother's life, municipal employees who go on strike to save a colleague
from corrupt officials who have targeted him for murder, and so on.

The latter story involves a forensic dentist who is kidnapped and held by
local police after he refuses a bribe from a family member of a dead *pistolero*,
who wants to carry him off before the examination is complete. After his fellow employees camp out in front of the jail, Valdez explains, "the dentist was
set free 'for lack of evidence.' But his colleagues knew that if the other staff
member hadn't continued to follow him when he was taken by the armed
group then this public servant would be dead. And if they hadn't turned up
to demand his release at the ministerial headquarters, he would be a prisoner
in the Culiacán jail." But it's not a one-off thriller or triumph-over-adversity
narrative either, and Valdez concludes the story accordingly: "Now he's
among children and their happy shouting. He's no longer in the middle of
cadavers and threats. But, yes, he's still in a city that wrecks itself, that falls,
exhausted and overtaken. On streets, medians, sidewalks, and corners, the
cenotaphs grow and multiply, traces of the violence, as if it were a dead city,
a great cemetery."[57]

There's also a lot of life and desire in this "dead city," and Valdez shows
how the ever-present danger and the mythos of the narco in Culiacán worm
their way into ordinary people's expectations and fantasies. In "You're Going
to Cry," he tells the story of a suburban woman who abandons her husband
and children without warning one night, and takes up with a sicario, with
whom she falls madly in love, obsessed in equal parts by his fancy lifestyle
and by the raw masculinity of the violent life he leads. One day, she wakes up
and questions the affair, wondering how she has fallen so far so fast. The man
tells her: "I've never left a woman and I won't do it with you. If you go, there'll
be no problem, just don't take anything with you. That way you'll know that
you wanted me, that it wasn't for the money." Valdez describes the tragic
denouement:

She took her car and went back to her old life and her kids, but she didn't want anything to do with her husband, and they divorced within a couple of months. One of her closest friends recounted that one time she was sitting in a chair in the living room of her house, in a working-class housing development in the northern part of Culiacán, in December of 2012, when she came across the crime section of a newspaper.

And she saw him. He was the same dude. First, she was hypnotized, her eyes glued to the page of the newspaper, his photo, his frozen gaze. She was leaving, already beating a hasty retreat. And then the girl started to cry.[58]

This is a story about loyalty and betrayal, money and sex, and the life of a drug trafficker and his girl. But it isn't about a narco showing off partially nude models sipping champagne, stroking his pet tiger, or ordering around a small army of faceless gunmen. It's a story about a man and a woman with very normal doubts about the meaning and trajectory of their lives, plunked down in a universe in which a parallel reality of violence, money, and power constantly loom in the background. Valdez begs us to question the smile on the face of a teenage assassin, who is killed after he can't stop bragging about his first hit; he asks us to see the pain and sickness behind it, to see him as a person, not a zombie. He shows us unlikely romances, impossible career choices, stonewalling bureaucrats, and the blackest of black humor, all shaped by the omnipresent reality of the narco and its exaggeration of the human weaknesses we all share. Valdez, who also wrote about the high politics of organized crime and its relationship to broader structures of power in Sinaloa, seems to suggest that if we don't get this ordinary reality, then we have no hope of understanding the broader phenomenon or the people behind it.

Much of this critique boils down to the apparent pressure to come up with a theory of the whole—whether it's journalists trying to communicate "Mexico" to a foreign audience or scholars and journalism practitioners trying to synthesize the data in huge categories like "violence in Mexico" or "el narco" into overdetermined packages. In the particular scenario of supporting a vibrant Mexican press and finding a way forward during the current wave of violence, Bolaño's counsel would seem to be to ditch the master narratives, both past and present, for now and focus on careful, relevant, and empathetic human fragments. While it might appear counterintuitive at first blush—editors, readers, and policy makers often demand both compact capsules and grand narratives—Bolaño's success in bringing a new and conscientious audience to Ciudad Juárez should buoy efforts toward a thicker description of the experience.

Master narratives, moreover, are not limited to all-encompassing theories or hypotheses. They are also about certainty and focus. Take, for example, *A Narco History*, a riveting and stylish contemporary history of the drug war in the United States and Mexico by novelist Carmen Boullosa and historian Mike Wallace. The authors begin their study with the kidnapping and presumed murder of forty-three Ayotzinapa students in Iguala, Guerrero, on October 22, 2014. The incident provoked a massive public outcry and revealed layers of corruption and violence in contemporary Mexico that have little to do with international drug trafficking. The authors qualify that they are relating "a" history not "the" history of the kidnapping, and they list a variety of sources. But they then proceed to dramatize what amounts to a slight variation in the Mexican government's official account, and they lump together the opposing views that promote the theory that "the students were in fact captured by the army, taken to the battalion's barracks, and there killed and burned in the military's professional grade crematorium." The authors argue: "We do not find this narrative persuasive, given the large number of people who would have had to participate in such a mammoth conspiracy, and the as of yet complete absence of evidence for such an approach." It all sounds reasonable, and the authors concede that if this theory were to be proven, it would have "immense consequences."[59] Unfortunately, that's not the only alternative theory of what happened, nor is it really a "theory," because it doesn't explain *why* the army would have done this. The plausible reasons range from the spectacular (large-scale global drug trafficking on passenger buses overseen by the army) to the banal (random local political thuggery backed by some federal officials), but they have yet to be investigated in a serious and independent fashion.

Indeed, since the book went to press, a committee of international experts has released a comprehensive report, completely discrediting the official account. It shows that the government misstated the most basic facts, including the number of buses involved and the number of places from which students were taken; that the chronologies of the events do not make sense or correlate from witness to witness; that many of the government's witnesses were known criminals and their confessions likely coerced; that the students arrived long after the campaign event for the mayor's wife; that law enforcement at all levels tracked their movements throughout the evening; that the forensic evidence is entirely inconclusive; and many, many other troubling details. The experts did not posit an alternative theory of the case. Their main conclusion was that there has yet to be a real investigation, and a real investigation would necessarily probe the role of the Mexican Army and other federal agencies.[60] Unhappy with the results, the federal government declined to extend the experts' mandate and even opened a criminal investigation against the executive secretary of the Inter-American Commission on Human Rights, Emilio Álvarez Icaza, the official in charge of coordinating the commission's investigation of the Ayotzinapa case and four other cases of government involvement in the forced disappearance of young people in Mexico. The government dropped the investigation against Álvarez Icaza weeks later in the face of diplomatic pressure.[61]

Even setting aside this misguided attempt to shut down the investigation, shouldn't the Mexican government's account merit a hefty degree of skepticism? Surely, the federal government's interest in restricting culpability to local and state officials and to the local drug cartel is fairly obvious, to say nothing of the fact that government agents have been implicated in a sizable portion of the 27,000 forced disappearances that the government itself acknowledges, half of which have happened under the present administration. The point here is not just that *A Narco History* was instantly outdated, that the authors got the story wrong, or that they caricatured those with whom they disagree, including the victims' families (all of which are sadly true). The real problem is one of focus, which they didn't have: they manufactured specific alternative theories from a very fluid situation and then argued the case with criminological precision and in a thrilling narrative. By mimicking and attempting to outdo the official criminal investigation, they fell into a similar trap as the investigators—the Iguala massacre was not a one-off crime, but rather part of a much larger wave of violence that is multifactorial and cannot be reduced to a simple narrative. There was, however, (and there remains) a social universe in which the incident was possible, and perhaps even likely.

John Gibler's *Una historia oral de la infamia* seeks to reconstruct the environment in which the massacre unfolded. He presents dozens of personal testimonials from survivors, victims' family members, Ayotzinapa teachers, and local witnesses to various parts of the Iguala events, in their own words. Gibler frames the exercise as active listening, exploring how the gestures of soliciting, recording, and trying to understand the perspective of the poor and marginalized can empower them and reveal a broader range of truths. But it's not just a representational or interpretive exercise. Gibler draws specific conclusions from their stories. He challenges in particular the government's account of the disposal of the students' bodies at the Cocula trash dump, citing a formidable array of eyewitness testimonies far more consistent than those cited in the official account.[62] But the significance of the social universe he re-creates—the worldviews, values, fears, and expectations of the communities involved—will likely transcend the specific findings of fact about that infamous October night. They help us to understand how something like the Iguala massacre was possible and what it means to those most affected.

In a famous 1919 essay, H. G. Wells noted "a very great increase in the possible vividness of [the] mental impact" of reporting on the suffering of others, thanks to "the printing of pictures, and to the cinematograph, the gramophone, and similar means of intense world-wide information and suggestion." Wells worked this sanguine assessment into a cautionary tale about the technological boom in the decade preceding World War I and the unfathomable destruction left in its wake. Technological marvels "render possible such a reasoned coordination of human affairs as has never hitherto been conceivable," but they also "enlarge and intensify the scope and evil of war and of international hostility as to give what was formerly a generous aspiration more and more of the aspect of an imperative necessity."[63]

The only other period in modern history when one could make a similar claim about revolutions in communications technology and their lethal misappropriation, of course, is the one that just ended. The internet generation began with sunny proclamations about global civil society, the eradication of poverty, and the flourishing of democracy—all facilitated by instant and enlightened global communications. Specific to Mexico and the United States, this meant the end of the one-party regime, a more just and humane migration accord, and mutually beneficial economic integration. Globally, the period has produced indiscriminate warfare, the largest refugee crisis since World War II, exploding inequality, and broadcast beheadings, propagandized and intensified online. In our binational backyard, it's a similar story—war and mass displacement, the resurgence of the PRI, the revival of harsh nativism, and more war, this one as dirty as ever and facilitated at every turn by new technologies.

There are signs of hope. One need look no further than the global reaction to the Iguala massacre and to the civil society awakening it has ignited in Mexico. Upper middle-class women in Mexico City carrying placards demanding "Bring Them Back Alive," a wheat field in Norway cut into a giant "43," die-ins at universities and forty-three-second moments of silence in legislatures across the globe, and even sympathetic questions about "the missing students" from US immigration judges—all of these gestures testify to "the vividness of [the] mental impact" the story has produced. But the lesson from the likes of Rodríguez Nieto and Turati, Valdez Cárdenas and Gibler is that the lasting impact comes less from the speed and spectacle of the media or its ability to "solve" a case than from the slowness and ethnographic detail of the reporting and its ability to expose the environment in which a case makes sense. And the lesson from Bolaño is that the fetishization of the narrator—an authoritative voice delimiting the broader social claims and horizons of a story—makes it all too easy to ignore the truths right in front of our faces, whether they come from the crime pages or partisan activists, drunks or madmen.

Notes

1. Rodríguez Nieto, *La fábrica del crimen* and *The Story of Vicente*.
2. Washington Valdez, *Cosecha de mujeres*; Rodríguez, Montané, and Pulitzer, *Daughters of Juárez*; González Ramírez, *Huesos en el desierto* and *The Femicide Machine*.
3. Inter-American Court of Human Rights, Case of González et al. ("Cotton Field") v. Mexico, Judgment of November 16, 2009 (Preliminary Objection, Merits, Reparations, and Costs), http://www.corteidh.or.cr/docs/casos/articulos/seriec_205_ing.pdf; and Rubio-Marín and Sandoval, "Engendering the Reparations Jurisprudence."
4. Staudt, *Violence and Activism*; Gaspar de Alba and Guzmán, *Making a Killing*; Monárrez Fragoso et al., *Violencia contra las mujeres*; Bowden, *Murder City*; Driver, *More or Less Dead*.

5. "Informe de las acciones de la PGR en los homicidios de mujeres en CD. Juárez, Chih.," http://www.pgr.gob.mx/Temas%20Relevantes/Casos%20de%20Interes/Muertas%20de%20Juarez/Informe%20Final.asp# (accessed Sept. 8, 2017).

6. See Christopher Hooks, "Q&A with Molly Molloy: The Story of the Juarez Femicides Is a 'Myth,'" *Texas Observer*, Jan. 9, 2014; Alice Driver's reply: "Femicide in Juárez Is Not a Myth," *Texas Observer*, Sept. 28, 2015; and Powell, *This Love*.

7. For example, one of the victims was sixteen-year-old Rubí Frayre, killed in 2008. Her mother, Marisela Escobedo Ortiz, tracked down the apparent murderer in Zacatecas. The well-known assassin was arrested and charged, but then released on a technicality. Escobedo took her protest to the state capital in 2010. On the evening of December 16, she was holding a placard in the Plaza Hidalgo when a gunman jumped out of a car, chased her across the street, and shot her in the head on the steps of the statehouse. The whole thing was captured by security cameras and posted on YouTube. "Video del asesinato de Marisela Escobedo," Dec. 17, 2010, https://www.youtube.com/watch?v=7AM3G0D-hZA; "A dos años de la muerte de Marisela Escobedo, persiste exigencia de justicia," *Proceso*, Dec. 8, 2012. The man likely responsible for both killings, Sergio Rafael Barraza, died in a shootout with police in 2012. "Cierran casos de asesinatos de Marisela Escobedo y su hija," *Animal Político*, Nov. 23, 2012.

8. "Bolaño-Mania: Hymn to a Dead Chilean," *Economist*, Nov. 20, 2008; Andrews, *Roberto Bolaño's Fiction*; Sarah Kerr, "The Triumph of Roberto Bolaño," *New York Review of Books*, Dec. 18, 2008.

9. Rodríguez Nieto, *The Story of Vicente*, ch 1.

10. Marcela Turati, "Me, the Women, and War," address at the International Women's Day breakfast hosted by the Joan B. Kroc Institute for Peace and Justice, University of San Diego, Mar. 8, 2016. A selection of the reporting she cited in this talk can be found in Páez Varela, *La guerra por Juárez*. See also Turati, *Fuego cruzado*.

11. See, for example, "Masacre en San Fernando: Lo que la PGR le oculta a las familias," *Proceso*, Aug. 22, 2015; Guillermoprieto et al., *72 migrantes*, and the interactive portal http://masde72.org/creditos (accessed Sept. 8, 2017).

12. "Mexico's San Fernando Massacres: A Declassified History," Digital National Security Archive, doc. 11, Aug. 26, 2011, http://nsarchive.gwu.edu/NSAEBB/NSAEBB445/docs/20100826.pdf.

13. Habermas, *Structural Transformation*; Schudson, *Why Democracies Need*; Hallin and Mancini, *Comparing Media Systems*.

14. "La periodista Carmen Aristegui, despedida de la cadena MVS," *El País*, Mar. 16, 2015; "La periodista Carmen Aristegui, voz crítica del poder en México, es despedida por MVS," *SinEmbargo*, Mar. 15, 2015; "'Guillotina' a Carmen Aristegui por parte de MVS," *Zócalo*, Mar. 16, 2015.

15. *Reforma*, May 11, 2012. See also "Paga millones Peña Nieto a López Dóriga y Beteta por 'apoyos informativos,'" *Proceso*, May 12, 2012.
16. Everard Meade, "El Chapo's Capture Is Latest Fiction Masking an Inconvenient Truth," *Times of San Diego*, Jan. 17, 2016.
17. "La PGR compró a prestanombres el malware espía Pegasus," *Proceso*, July 28, 2017; "Mexican Spy Scandal Escalates as Study Shows Software Targeted Opposition," *Guardian*, June 30, 2017.
18. See, for example, Rodríguez Castañeda, *Prensa vendida*; Orme, *Culture of Collusion*; Ochoa Campos, *Reseña histórica*.
19. Guerrero and Márquez Ramírez, "The 'Captured Liberal' Model."
20. Márquez Ramírez, "Estudio introductorio."
21. Lomnitz, *Deep Mexico*, 228–63.
22. Rodríguez Castañeda, *Prensa vendida*, 218.
23. Lawson, *Building the Fourth Estate*, chs. 1 and 5; Hughes, *Newsrooms in Conflict*.
24. For more on the term "tyrannofilia," see Lilla, *Reckless Mind*.
25. "The Panama Papers: Politicians, Criminals and the Rogue Industry That Hides Their Cash," International Consortium of Investigative Journalists, 2015, https://panamapapers.icij.org (accessed Sept. 8, 2017).
26. Artículo 19, "Periodistas asesinados en México," 2017, https://articulo19.org/periodistasasesinados (accessed Sept. 8, 2017).
27. Valdez Cárdenas, *Narcoperiodismo*, ch. 1.
28. Del Palacio Montiel, "En Veracruz se aprende a vivir"; "Attacks on Journalists in Veracruz, Mexico: An Interactive Report on Recent Trends," Trans-Border Institute, http://sites.sandiego.edu/tbi-foe/attacks-on-journalists-in-veracruz (accessed Nov. 10, 2017).
29. Granados Chapa, *Buendía*; Aguilar Camín, *Los días de Manuel Buendía*; Bartley and Bartley, *Eclipse of the Assassins*.
30. Valdez Cárdenas, *Levantones*, ch. 4.
31. "Soy el número 16: El hombre que cuenta su secuestro con una animación," *BBC Mundo*, July 6, 2015.
32. Valdez Cárdenas, *Narcoperiodismo*, ch. 9; Francisco Goldman, "Who Killed Rubén Espinosa and Nadia Vera?," *New Yorker*, Aug. 14, 2015; "Caso Narvarte: CDHDF enumera los errores e irregularidades cometidos en la investigación," *Animal Político*, June 22, 2017; "¿A quién protege Mancera y la PGJ en el caso Narvarte? Cuestionan a dos años del multihomicidio," *Proceso*, July 31, 2017.
33. "Asesinan al periodista de *Ríodoce*, Javier Valdez," *Ríodoce*, May 15, 2017; "Así fue el asesinato de Javier Valdez según peritos," *El Debate*, May 23, 2017.
34. "¿A quién va a delatar 'El Mini Lic'?," *El Debate*, July 31, 2017.
35. Patrick Timmons, "Life Imitating News: The Murder of Mexican Journalist Javier Valdez," *NACLA*, May 30, 2017; and "El origen del asesinato de Javier Valdez," *Zeta Tijuana*, May 30, 2017.

36. Ameglio Patella, *Gandhi*, 184–85.

37. Preston and Dillon, *Opening Mexico*, 37–38.

38. McLuhan and Fiore, *The Medium Is the Message*. Perhaps the most important case study is of the EZLN in Chiapas, its "war of position" in media and other representations, and its politicization of culture over a simpler materialist critique. Morton, "Structural Change"; Bruhn, "Antonio Gramsci"; and Figueroa-Ibarra and Martínez-Zavala, "Ejército Popular Revolucionario." For an excellent series of examples of the Gramscian perspective in post-revolutionary Mexico, see Joseph and Spenser, *In from the Cold*. More specific to media and journalism, see Caldeira, *City of Walls*.

39. Henck, "Subcommander and the Sardinian."

40. Grillo, *El Narco*, ch. 1.

41. *Criminalia* 1, no. 1 (Sept. 1933).

42. Monsiváis, "Red News," 149. For a contemporary version of this perspective, see Lara Klahr and Barata, *Nota roja*.

43. Leñero, "Prólogo," xxv–xxix.

44. García, *El Imparcial*, 19–22, 30, 39; Saborit, *El mundo ilustrado*.

45. *El Imparcial*, Sept. 10, 1907; Arroyo and Casanova, "The Casasolas," 204.

46. Posada, "Las bravísimas calaveras de Mora y de Morales," 430.

47. *La Prensa*, Apr. 23–29, 1929; Monsiváis, "Red News," 149; Piccato, *History of Infamy*. For a more detailed recounting from the contemporary press, see Ortega Ramírez, *Crimen, terror y páginas*, 174–75, 176–79.

48. *La Prensa*, July 22, 1933.

49. Proponents included 104 men and 14 women; opponents 30 men and 1 woman. This count is based on my survey of the opinions published in *La Prensa* from the initial article through the end of the survey, July 23–Aug. 22, 1933. The paper did not publish an official tally.

50. Bartra, "Seduction of the Innocents," 303–5; and Rubenstein, *Bad Language*, 3–7.

51. Sierra Guzmán, *El enemigo interno*.

52. Enciso, "1976: Alberto Sicilia Falcón," 365–66.

53. Monsiváis, *Los mil*, ch. 13.

54. Carlos Monsiváis, "María Félix nunca será pobre," *Proceso*, Nov. 5, 1976.

55. "Free TVs in Mexico Are Seen as Having Political Strings Attached," *New York Times*, June 4, 2015; "As Elections Approach, Mexico Is Handing Out Free Digital TVs to Millions of Voters," *Vice News*, Dec. 4, 2014; and "Morena, PAN y PRD denuncian: En el Edomex hubo una 'elección de estado' para imponer a Del Mazo," *Sinembargo*, June 5, 2017.

56. "Marchan en Culiacán a favor de 'El Chapo,'" *El Universal*, July 7, 2015; "¿Quién era el Pancho Chimal?," *El Debate*, Apr. 15, 2017; "Con plomo y banda se despiden de 'Pancho Chimal' en Culiacán," *Milenio*, Apr. 17, 2017.

57. Valdez Cárdenas, *The Taken*, 128–29.

58. Valdez Cárdenas, *The Taken*, 185.

59. Boullosa and Wallace, *Narco History*, ch. 1.

60. Grupo Interdisciplinario de Expertos Independientes, *Informe Ayotzinapa: Investigación y primeras conclusiones de las desapariciones y homicidios de los normalistas de Ayotzinapa* (2015), http://www.casede.org/BibliotecaCasede/ Informe_AyotziGIEI.pdf (accessed Sept. 8, 2017).

61. "Álvarez Icaza regresará a México por la 'crisis de derechos humanos,'" *El País*, Jan. 5, 2016; "Presentan denuncia por fraude contra Emilio Álvarez Icaza," *Excélsior*, Mar. 15, 2016; "PGR archiva denuncia contra Emilio Álvarez Icaza por presunto fraude," *El Financiero*, Apr. 5, 2016; and "El grupo de expertos da por rota su confianza en el gobierno en el caso Ayotzinapa," *El País*, Apr. 7, 2016.

62. Gibler, *Una historia oral*.

63. Wells, "Idea of the League of Nations."

14 | # Front Lines and Back Channels

The Fractal Publics of El Blog del Narco

PAUL K. EISS

I n April 2013, a striking book made its appearance in a bilingual edition in bookstores in Mexico and abroad: *Dying for the Truth: Undercover inside the Mexican Drug War.*[1] The anonymous authors were identified on the cover only as "the fugitive reporters of Blog del Narco." The books were hard to miss: they came tied with garish yellow crime scene tape, which served both as a deterrent to the prying eyes of underage readers and as a morbid attention getter, advertising the work's gory contents to potential buyers. To open the book is indeed to confront an unrelenting spectacle of slaughter. *Dying for the Truth* consists of a selection and summary of Blog del Narco posts in its first year of existence, early 2010 to early 2011. Like those posts, it is copiously illustrated with gruesome photographs of corpses in whole or in parts, often exhibiting signs of deliberate and sadistic mutilation. The book is a compilation of narrative accounts—of gun battles, executions, and other events of a particularly violent year in the so-called drug war—and what might be called the "primary sources" of that war: the images themselves, photographs of scrawled messages left behind by the killers, and transcribed video interrogations of torture victims in the moments before their execution. From the moment of unraveling the police tape that binds the volume, the reader feels, and is surely meant to feel, as if they are thumbing through a police file as much as a journalistic account.

But *Dying for the Truth* is more than that: it is meant to present El Blog del Narco as a personal and political cause, one worth dying for. Hence *Dying for the Truth* begins with an origin story, relating how the blog was the outcome of a chance encounter between a young journalist and a computer scientist in early 2010. They shared how their families had been directly affected by the violence and discussed politicians' and officeholders' indifference to, or complicity in, the escalating carnage; they discussed the silence of mainstream media that were either intimidated by direct threats or "in bed with" both the government and the cartels. After talking they decided to "leave indifference behind, to yank open a window and enable citizens, with no shades or blinds, to observe the harsh reality around them." They made a secret pact, one concealed even from close friends and family: they would join their journalistic and technical skills to create a blog that would share "unfiltered, uncensored news about the government's war with the narco-gangsters, about the shootouts, decapitations, and other bloody acts taking place on a daily basis."[2] From the outset, in contrast with a traditional news reporting organization, anonymity was to be a hallmark of the blog. Its creators have carefully protected the identities of bloggers; they have concealed their own identities as well, sharing only scant personal details via a few anonymous interviews.[3] Only around the time of the publication of *Dying for the Truth* in April 2013 would one of the founders provide personal information of any kind, identifying herself to a reporter for the *Guardian* via a pseudonym—Lucy—and a sparse personal description: "Who am I? I'm in my mid-20s, I live in northern Mexico, I'm a journalist. I'm a woman, I'm single, I have no children. And I love Mexico."[4]

As the framing of *Dying for the Truth* makes clear, El Blog del Narco was meant to respond not only to the violence of the drug war, but in particular to the conflict's silencing effect on the mainstream press—a development that is only too well known.[5] In contemporary Mexico, violence against journalists, from threats to kidnappings to disappearances and executions, is commonplace; several organizations, including the Committee to Protect Journalists, Artículo 19, and Reporters Without Borders, have dedicated substantial efforts to documenting the violence and harassment faced by reporters—not just the dozens killed or disappeared, but the constant attacks and threats, which according to Artículo 19 occurred on average once every six-teen hours in the first half of 2017, a 23 percent increase over a similar period in 2016.[6]

In 2010, the year of the blog's founding, several high-profile attacks on journalists resulted in extraordinary public statements by major news edi-tors, contributing to a sense of crisis. In March, after the kidnapping of eight journalists over a two-week period in Reynosa, *Milenio* editor Ciro Gómez Leyva published an opinion column declaring, "Every day, it is becoming impossible to pursue journalism in more and more parts of Mexico. Journal-ism is dead in Reynosa. . . . I have nothing more to say." Gómez then left half of his column blank, entitling it "the day that journalism died."[7] After the killing of two of its reporters in September, the largest-circulation newspaper in Ciudad Juárez, *El Diario*, published a front-page piece denouncing the attacks on journalists and the government's lack of protection for, and even hostility toward, the press. It went on to recognize the traffickers as the de facto authorities of Ciudad Juárez, asking them: "What do you want from us? Tell us what it is that you want us to publish or that you want us to stop pub-lishing, so we can know how to proceed."[8] In May 2012, after the offices of *El Mañana de Nuevo Laredo* suffered a grenade attack, the editors similarly declared their intention to "abstain, as long as necessary, from publishing any information relating to the violent conflicts taking place in our city and other regions in the country."[9] Episodes of violence against journalists, like other acts of aggression in the unfolding conflict, have been left not only unpunished, but unprosecuted and uninvestigated by police and the govern-ment; indeed, some reports have indicated that a substantial proportion of the acts of violence and harassment have been committed by government or security forces themselves.[10]

As such episodes and statements make clear, the climate of repression, threat, and impunity in the context of the "drug war" has left the main-stream news organizations at least in some regions effectively silenced—or at least highly constrained—in their coverage relating to drug-related vio-lence. Such constraint is often termed *autocensura* (self-censorship), which reflects a situation that is unlike direct, state-sponsored censorship but no less consequential in shaping and limiting coverage. Moreover, the federal government has undertaken several measures that explicitly aim to shape news coverage relating to drug trafficking, albeit through "voluntary" agreements with the media.[11] In 2011, President Felipe Calderón arrived at an accord with some sixty media groups, perhaps most notably Televisa and TV Azteca but also involving some major newspapers like *El Universal* and *Excélsior*, which established "editorial criteria" for news coverage of violence related to trafficking. They were to avoid serving the "propagandistic aims" of the narcos by not portraying them as "victims or public heroes." They were to avoid the republication of messages left by traffickers, whether in the form of painted signs left at crime scenes (*narcomensajes*) or large, publicly exhibited banners (*narcomantas*), and were even to avoid using the nicknames of cartel leaders.[12] In a similar spirit, President Enrique Peña Nieto in 2013 issued his own policy called the "Nueva narrativa en material de seguridad" (New narrative on security issues). In it, officials and the press were enjoined to contextualize and narrate events in such a way as to hold traffickers entirely responsible for the violence and to sustain the legitimacy of all government measures against them.[13]

The upsurge of trafficking-related violence and of media censorship in its varied forms along with the simultaneous rise of internet access and social media use in Mexico has, as Monroy-Hernández and Palacios argue, presented a "perfect trifecta for the emergence of Blog del Narco"—a website, or rather an "entire ecosystem of websites," with several domain names, all of them connected to a single email address located in Monterrey, Mexico.[14] The blog made its appearance in March 2010 with spectacular cell-phone video footage of the aftermath of a gun and grenade battle between the Gulf cartel and the Zetas in Tamaulipas. While police refused to confirm that anything had happened, the video showed damaged vehicles, remnants of trucks and homes destroyed by explosions, and bodies lying in the street. The blog's promise and premise of anonymity attracted photographs and eyewitness accounts of drug-related violence not only from the general public, but from soldiers, police officers, journalists, and even cartel gunmen. Its penchant for such attention-getting coverage of the front line of the drug war, featuring images and information not available in official or mainstream sources, soon won over a vast audience of readers. The overwhelming majority of blog posts have been concerned in some way with cartel-related violence; the most frequent topic of blog posts has been the finding of bodies of execution victims, which one study found accounted for 41 percent of all posts on the blog.[15] Along with accounts and photographs of kidnappings, executions, and piles of severed body parts, the blog also provides access to videos of the interrogation, torture, and execution of captured cartel members by members of rival groups.[16]

El Blog del Narco clearly was intended as a forum not only for glimpses of raw footage from the front lines of the drug war, but also for something akin to investigative journalism, drawing on a wide range of anonymous back-channel sources and informers not available in other venues. Hence the coverage of the spate of violence over the course of the first year of the blog's existence tried to make sense of the confusing plethora of killings on the front lines by placing them in the context of an emerging alliance of the Gulf and Sinaloa cartels against the Zetas, whom the former aimed to eject from the plazas they controlled along trafficking routes, principally in northern Mexico.[17] The blog published well-sourced coverage of the assassination of Tamaulipas gubernatorial candidate Rodolfo Torre Cantú by a gang of Zeta hitmen, who ambushed Torre Cantú's motorcade, killing him and several of his staff and bodyguards. Posts at the Blog del Narco included photographs of the scene in the immediate aftermath of the killings, but also information that could have only been provided by those involved: on the planning of the attack and its staging and on the personal involvement of Zeta leader Heriberto Lazcano Lazcano, who emerged from one of the attackers' trucks to personally supervise the execution of Torre Cantú. In July the blog published videos of a Zeta beating and interrogating a policeman in Durango. Before his own execution at the end of the video, the policeman asserted that the head of a federal penitentiary in Gómez Palacio, Durango, knowingly housed cartel gunmen in that prison, and they regularly left there at night to commit crimes, including killings, in the area of Torreón, Coahuila. Within days, the publicity garnered by the post led the Mexican attorney general to arrest the director of the penitentiary and dozens of prison guards for their presumed involvement.[18]

Through such high-profile posts, El Blog del Narco swiftly established itself as Mexico's premier venue for drug war content and the model for a certain kind of digitally enabled citizen journalism. By 2012, the site had some 25 million monthly visitors, more online readers than many mainstream Mexican and international newspapers, like *Milenio, La Jornada*, or the *Miami Herald*.[19] One commentator called it "the most important website in Mexico."[20] At one point, the blog had more than 100,000 followers on

Twitter.[21] Yet the blog's meteoric rise was accompanied by the equally swift appearance of a host of problems. Initially established on Google's free blogging platform, the sheer size of the site and its posts, including substantial numbers of videos and photographs—in addition to complaints from the Mexican government regarding the site's content—led Google Mexico to limit access to the blog and its archives (the vast majority of previous posts became unavailable for consultation). Under pressure to generate revenues to fund the site's increasing size and presence, given its heavy demands on server space and bandwidth, the blog began selling advertising space to automobile companies and the like. But such efforts, perhaps in part owing to the controversial nature of the site, seem not to have generated sufficient funds to resolve continuing problems of access.[22] To such problems were added the hundreds of cyber attacks the blog suffered since its formation, in some cases taking it offline for days at a time.[23]

Most consequentially, the Blog del Narco became the target of a host of public criticisms, beginning with condemnation of the graphic nature of the images and videos posted on the site. Defending themselves against the charge of doing so for shock value, the editors of Blog del Narco claimed instead that they did so to provide readers with a glimpse of the "undistorted reality" of Mexico's drug war and also to help relatives recognize and reclaim the bodies of their loved ones, many of them *sicarios* (hitmen).[24] Perhaps most tellingly, the blog's creators were targeted by the mainstream press for their journalistic ethics or lack thereof. In the first year of the blog's appearance, Carlos Lauría, director of the Committee to Protect Journalists, declared that while all media outlets have "social responsibilities" and act in service to the public, Blog del Narco was not truly "journalistic"; it was produced "without any ethical considerations."[25] For some, the blog committed cardinal sins that made it unworthy of being considered journalism. It did not sufficiently contextualize the material presented on the blog, drew on anonymous sources, and published unsubstantiated rumors and material submitted by criminals.[26]

One trenchant line of critique concerned the editors' denunciations of the generalized complicity of mainstream media with the government or narcos, and their presentation of the blog as a citizen response to a news vacuum in Mexico. Thus *Proceso* reporter and Periodistas de a Pie founder Marcela Turati took exception to Lucy in 2013: "I don't agree with her statement that what she does is the journalism that is not being done by anyone else in Mexico. . . . her function was to act as an administrator; put up information from others, post videos that she received. . . . That's not journalism because that is not doing your own reporting." Citing the blog's debt to the many brave Mexican journalists who published the results of their investigations without hiding their identity, Turati characterized Lucy's claim as a "kind of statement [that] can only be made by someone who does not know the world of journalism or is just seeking publicity."[27]

Such criticism extended to the integrity of the blog's self-presentation as a venue for anonymous—and autonomous—citizen journalism from the front lines of conflict. In April 2013, around the time of Lucy's appearance and *Dying for the Truth*'s publication, reporters from *Fronteras Desk* and *Borderland Beat* published articles alleging that a large proportion of the anonymous posts at El Blog del Narco were lifted directly from mainstream journalistic sources—newspapers like *El Universal, Milenio, Reforma, El Sol, Proceso, Diario, Vanguardia*—and even government press releases, that is, precisely the kind of "mainstream" and even official sources that the editors of the Blog del Narco tended to disparage. Such articles, critics alleged, were published without source credits as to authorship or the original venue of publication, and apparently without the consent of the original authors, though sometimes with changed titles and added photographs.[28] Some media observers see this approach as making the blog comparable to a news aggregator like Huffington Post or Yahoo News, albeit one that does not adequately recognize or credit its dependence on mainstream news outlets.[29] In their defense, the editors of El Blog del Narco stated that the blog "never made the claim of being journalism per se, but an information-gathering resource" and, moreover, that writers for the blog had no desire to be named and hence endangered for their work, making the site an invaluable "repository of material from journalists, police, and ordinary citizens who wanted to remain anonymous."[30] Yet such defenses seemed to do justice neither to the blog's evident entry, in many of its posts, into the domain of investigative journalism, nor to the fact that much of its reposted material had already been published as the work of publicly identified journalists (seeming to invalidate the argument about protective anonymity, at least in the case of republished material).

But more than through the vicissitudes of technical issues or public reception or media critique, Blog del Narco has been seriously affected—like most Mexican news organizations—by the direct physical threats posed in the context of drug war violence, whether leveled by traffickers or agents of the government. While initially the blog featured a user comment section, the editors decided to close it down after receiving threats from purported cartel members. In September 2011 in Nuevo Laredo, Tamaulipas, several people who had written reports for the blog on trafficking-related violence were identified by Zeta hitmen, who killed and brutally disfigured them, hanging their bodies from a bridge. The Zetas left a computer keyboard and mouse near the bodies, as well as signs, one of which stated: "This is what will happen to all the internet snitches. Be warned: we are watching you." In another episode, the blog received photos of nine corpses with threatening messages written on their skin: "You are next BDN [Blog del Narco]."[31]

The threats came to a climax in May 2013 when the editors of El Blog del Narco found themselves unexpectedly and at great peril on the front lines and in the headlines. According to Lucy, she received a phone call from her collaborator, who simply said "run": a signal they had prepared to indicate imminent danger, presumably that they had been discovered and were in immediate peril. Fleeing first to the United States and then to Spain, she ceased posting to the blog, describing her fears of discovery and feelings of isolation in a final interview via Skype with a reporter from the *Guardian*. She related that after the warning from her colleague, she had heard no more from him, and her efforts to contact or locate him had been fruitless. Her greatest fear, she said, was that she would soon see him on the internet in a video like the ones that Blog del Narco had posted, interrogated under torture, perhaps executed or decapitated: "I don't want to think the worst but I can't help it."[32] Since then, Lucy has disappeared from the internet, and the Blog del Narco has radically decreased the number of its posts and its media presence—even as a host of other sites and platforms, like *Valor por Tamaulipas*, *Valor por Michoacán*, and a number of other regional or national internet and social media venues have taken on many of the features earlier associated with Blog del Narco.

What preliminary conclusions might be drawn from this brief narrative of a blog's rise and fall? What are the implications of Blog del Narco for the changing circumstances of journalism in contemporary Mexico? One above all: at least for a time, El Blog del Narco became the consummate manifestation—albeit in forms specific to the situation in contemporary Mexico—of what media studies scholar Henry Jenkins has called a "convergence culture": a conjunction of technological developments (rising access to the internet, digital technology, social media) and sociopolitical factors (the violence and political pressures associated with the so-called drug war).[33] Against *Dying for the Truth*'s origin story—the demise of traditional "mainstream" journalism and the rise of digitally mediated "citizen" journalism—we find a different story of convergence, in which El Blog del Narco has remained highly dependent on the traditional media that provide much of its material, even as many journalists of the traditional media have become dependent on the unique resources provided by El Blog del Narco and other digital venues.

Beyond this convergence of old and new media, and beyond the participatory and collective aspects of media consumption at Blog del Narco—both defining features of Jenkins's discussion of convergence in contemporary media culture—there are two kinds of convergence that seem particular to this case. First, against a simple narrative of news media being "silenced" by cartel violence and state censorship or self-censorship, Blog del Narco shows another kind of convergence where such violence and pressure have also generated the context and impetus for a new form of news media production, arguably of a reach equal to or even greater than conventional mass media journalism. In other words, the convergence of censorship and repression with the rise of the internet and social media access has had the paradoxical effect of producing new kinds of media production across multiple platforms. The second particular convergence, which has been manifested not so much in the content of Blog del Narco but in its public or publics, takes us from the front lines of the blog to its back channels.

Back Channels

In the introduction to *Dying for the Truth* the creators of Blog del Narco made clear their determination to continue blogging despite direct threats against them by "narcoterrorists." They stated their refusal to succumb for one reason above all others: "Because we want a better Mexico." They were acting on behalf of all the "decent and hard-working people" of Mexico, who despite negative stereotypes were "simply poor people who break our backs working." The warfare between trafficking groups and between those groups and security forces had "destroyed the lives of millions of innocent men, women and children." Hence, facing the indifference of the Mexican government and the mainstream media, the blog's creators decided "as victims, as Mexicans, and as human beings" to act on behalf of those good Mexican people. Though El Blog del Narco, they knew, was monitored by traffickers and by government officials, NGOs, and the police, "we had no target audience other than the Mexican people."[34]

Such statements reflected a clear determination of the creators of the Blog del Narco to define themselves in relation to, and in fact in service to, a legitimate public that they identified as its "target audience": honorable, hard-working, victimized, betrayed, but above all "Mexican." Framed in this way, *Dying for the Truth* was an implicit response to those who criticized the blog for its potentially corrupting effect on those who viewed it or its potential association with the traffickers themselves: a free "public relations" platform for the cartels.[35] Some critics even insinuated that the Blog del Narco was owned or bankrolled by one or another of the drug-trafficking organizations.[36] The willingness of the Blog del Narco to reproduce messages from the traffickers had transformed it, in the eyes of some observers, from the Blog del Narco to the Narcos' Blog: "nothing more," in one commentator's view, "than a platform for narco traffickers to boast about their killings of some anonymous civilians and their threats against others."[37]

The concerns of such critics—and the blog editors' desire to clearly exclude traffickers from their "target audience"—to some degree reflected more generalized anxieties about the advent and increasing prestige of diverse forms of cultural expression in Mexico that some have called "narcoculture."[38] Popular literary and cultural forms like *narcoliteratura* and narco-themed telenovelas, musical genres like *narcocorrido* and *corrido alterado*, popular religious cults venerating Santa Muerte and especially Jesús Malverde—all have attracted censorious rhetoric from politicians and public figures for their glorification, glamorization, or sanctification of the easy money, profligate lifestyle and violence of the traffickers.[39] Censorship measures, against narcocorridos in particular, have been undertaken in the states of Sinaloa, Chihuahua, and Baja California[40]—perhaps not so much as policies targeting the cartels themselves as measures of cultural defense against the presumably corrupting effects of narcoculture on its consuming public.

More recently and more acutely, the dangers of narcoculture have seemed to loom in the deliberate use of digital and social media by the Mexican traffickers themselves, particularly where such usage has taken public and highly visible forms. The use of such media to issue "narco-propaganda," often in the form of videos, publicly displayed banners (*mantas*), and messages left near the remains of murder victims—all of which digitally circulate on the internet—has been a signature aspect of the most recent phase of the drug war, triggering repeated denunciations and occasional attempts at government censorship or media self-censorship.[41] Hitmen have been surprisingly public on the platforms Myspace, YouTube, Facebook, and Snapchat, posting on their activities and building online followings.[42] Surely the best-known celebrity of this type was Broly Banderas, a Caballeros Templarios gunman who avidly posted handsome, pouting (albeit gun-toting and bloodstained) photographic self-portraits from various crime scenes. Banderas built an audience of 7,000 Facebook followers before disappearing from the internet for reasons unknown.[43] Adepts in social media have entered into the employ of some traffickers, helping to locate informers or to carry out "virtual kidnappings," which involve simulating kidnappings through the infiltration of victims' phones or social media accounts.[44]

It was in this charged context that the authors of *Dying for the Truth* took pains to define their target audience as the "decent and hard-working people of Mexico," an entity whose interests, they claimed, directly opposed those of the narcoterrorists. They made clear that they did accept photographs and information from sources affiliated with the traffickers but that they refused to publish photographs, like images of the traffickers partying with pop stars, that served only to glorify the narcos or their lifestyle. Their aim, they insisted, was not only to "show the undistorted reality of the situation" but—in terms that seemed to converge with official anti-narcoculture rhetoric—to "put a halt to the glamorization of drug kingpins by Mexican children, young adults, and the entertainment industry." And their efforts, the editors claimed, had helped to reverse the corrupting of some sectors of the public by both narcoculture and official complacency. Every day, former dealers sent them emails stating that they had "stopped selling drugs because they didn't want their relatives to see them decapitated on [El Blog del Narco]." Most important, citizens reported that due to the blog's unfiltered coverage, they were "now forming their own opinions about the drug war, rather than accepting the standard government story."[45]

Responding to criticism of their publication of narcomensajes and videos, the editors insisted that doing so was essential to their own kind of journalistic ethic. The steady flow of "exclusive news" that such posts represented strengthened a bond of trust with the blog's reading audience and—through the editors' determination to publish messages from all groups—defined the blog's "objectivity."[46] Pressed on this point in one early interview, an editor of the blog responded: "We don't insult them. We don't say one specific group is the bad one."[47] Several years later, Lucy maintained a consistent line on this, responding to a question whether, after the blog posted a narcomanta from one cartel, it was obliged to publish mantas from all: "Exactly. You have to be objective. Or rather, even with the narcos you have to be objective."[48]

Yet such statements were belied by the diverse ways in which traffickers, or those sympathetic to them, sometimes seemed to find ways to turn the features of Blog del Narco to their own purposes. The creators of the blog initially included comment sections and chat windows in their posts as a way to encourage the formation of an online community, to share information and views regarding the drug war and other topics.[49] But, as Monroy-Hernández and Palacios have noted, this feature of the website also attracted many comments—presumably by affiliates of one or another trafficking group—praising or insulting rival cartels. Online participants, whether affiliated with the traffickers or not, provided a steady stream of "vicious and often inhumane comments" about the victims of the violence.[50]

While eventually the comment and chat features were discontinued, apparently in response to threats the blog received,[51] the material published for informational purposes—photographs, narcomensajes, mantas, videos, and the like—sometimes doubled as publicity for the trafficking groups, facilitating their messages to rival groups and serving as public relations to a wider readership. On one occasion, Zetas sent a flyer to the people of Tamaulipas, disassociating themselves from acts of violence in the region, blaming their rivals the Gulf cartel, and soliciting informers to contact them (the phone number was not published in the blog).[52] In another incident, the kidnappers of the wife of cartel leader Héctor Beltrán Leyva sent a photograph to the blog of their blindfolded victim along with a handwritten sign taunting Beltrán Leyva;[53] the photograph eventually became the cover image of

Dying for the Truth. In May 2012, shortly after a pile of forty-nine decapitated and dismembered bodies of Honduran migrants was found near Reynosa, a video was posted to the blog by the killers, showing the disposition of the bodies and messages crediting the murders to the Zetas. In response, the Zetas posted images of their own narcomantas to the blog, distancing themselves from the killings, which they claimed was a frame job.[54] In May 2015, after the massacre of forty-two Jalisco Nueva Generación cartel members by federal security forces in Ecuandureo, Michoacán, the group issued a video—immediately posted to Blog del Narco—calling for community self-defense groups in the state, which they had helped by ridding the area of "Templar rats," to join with them in avenging the deaths and attacking "the corrupt narcogovernment."[55]

As these examples demonstrate, regardless of the target audience of the Blog del Narco, the public with which it interacts is painted not in white and black but in shades of gray. And there are others among the blog's contributors and users who fall outside its presumed target audience. Police and security agents have shared photographs and information with the blog as part of their own tactics of self-representation and bravado (for example, images of cartel hitmen killed in engagements with police and security forces). Moreover, given the rich flow of information, particularly the comments by users involved in the trafficking groups, the Blog del Narco's Facebook and Twitter feeds have acquired many followers that the editors might not have hoped for—the Mexican Defense Department, the FBI, and the US Drug Enforcement Administration, among others.[56] Several security agencies, including the US Department of Homeland Security and Mexico's Centro de Investigación y Seguridad Nacional, have had staff dedicated to harvesting and analyzing posts on the Blog del Narco and other sites.[57] Such operations may have played a role in the editors' September 2011 decision to eliminate the comment and chat functions and to erase prior posts, comments, and forums from the blog.[58]

It was against such shades of gray and in denial of the convergence of multiple groups, some quite unsavory, in its audience of contributors and users that the authors of *Dying for the Truth* presented their narrative in black and white. At the end of the introduction, the "fugitive reporters" shared with readers the one message they wished to convey, in the event that they were "not here tomorrow or next week or next month." Their message was, first, to not fear those in power but especially that "we are Mexico, we are good, and there are more of us."[59] This message of hopeful patriotism was meant to justify the ends and means of the blog and perhaps to chart a future course for "us"—defined as the country's good, hard-working citizens. But it also performed the ideological work of excluding an implied "them"—if not several "thems"—whose presence and participation in the blog had been absolutely essential to its existence and functioning, yet were just as essential to deny.

Fractal Publics

In a study of digital messaging in the context of drug war violence—so-called narcomensajes, narcomantas, and narcovideos—I argued that through their recirculation in forums like Blog del Narco, such "narcomedia" were "encouraging the emergence of challenges and alternatives to Mexico's beleaguered public sphere."[60] The circulation of these messages, and the debates that surrounded them, indeed demonstrate the emergence of new "counterpublics"—a term derived from scholarly debates around the concept of the public sphere, which Nancy Fraser has defined as "spaces of withdrawal and regroupment . . . [and] bases and training grounds for agitational activities directed toward wider publics."[61] The term "counterpublics" seems to reflect the convergence of groups with very different and sometimes diametrically opposed interests and stakes in venues like Blog del Narco. Such counterpublics, I have argued elsewhere, might in the best of cases facilitate critiques and even political mobilizations that could "undercut the very binaries and ideological assumptions of the 'drug war.'"[62]

Yet the concept of counterpublics fails to capture what is so striking about how the authors of *Dying for the Truth* defined their target audience: by gesturing toward those who were to be included in their "public" but just as much toward others who, though part of the universe of blog users, were to be excluded: clearly narco traffickers, but also police, government authorities, and a mainstream press that was bought off or cowed into silence. That a public might be defined by exclusion as much as inclusion is, of course, no recent development. It is arguably foundational for the traditional (bourgeois, masculinist, Eurocentric) concept of the public sphere, which emerged in forms that claimed universality even as they were predicated on a thoroughgoing set of gender, class, and racial exclusions. A variety of critiques—most notably on feminist grounds—have exposed the normative dimensions of the concept of "the public" both in projected opposition to a "private" sphere but also against the notion of others, who are excluded on the basis of their presumed unreason, passion, inferiority, corruption, or unrestrained pursuit of self-interest. The legitimate "public" is thus typically articulated or imagined against entities that fall outside its bounds, whether into the domain of the "private" or into the various categories for illegitimate collective actors: the "crowd," the "mob," "gangs," "terrorists," and the like.[63]

Such distinctions are ideologically fraught. They are characteristic not only of social or political actors in the public realm, but also of many scholarly analyses of communications and the public sphere. Analysts of social media, for instance, tend to distinguish in sharply normative terms the usage of social media by "citizens" and "governments" from their usage by narco traffickers. The former, as legitimate public or political actors, appropriately employ the resources of social media and the internet for public safety and security; the latter, as enemies of the public, are presented as abusing social media and the internet for opposing and illegitimate ends. In a study of the use of information and communication technology (ICT) for "violence prevention" in Brazil, Colombia, and Mexico, Muggah and Diniz acknowledge the use of digital and social media by traffickers and gangs. But they sharply distinguish ICTs according to their function in securing security and safety. Hence, in their typology of ICTs, Blog del Narco is classified unambiguously as a "horizontal citizen to citizen violence reduction ICT."[64]

To categorize Blog del Narco in this way is not just to obscure the kinds of ambiguity and ambivalence that have been defining features of its operation and reception. It is also to engage in a kind of ideological work that converges with that of the authors of *Dying for the Truth*, as they retrospectively clarified the blog's target public through a set of inclusions and exclusions. Applying such distinctions categorically invokes what linguistic anthropologist Susan Gal has identified as a language "ideology," which has persistently identified a distinction between the public and private realms of life ever since the emergence of a doctrine of "separate spheres" in the eighteenth and nineteenth centuries, at least in Europe and the United States. Gal argues that "public" and "private" are not "particular places, domains, spheres of activity or even types of interaction" nor are they "descriptions of the social world in any direct way; they are rather tools for arguments about and in that world."[65]

Gal categorizes the binary public-private opposition as a "fractal distinc-tion" that is invoked communicatively in various domains. Such invocations perform or enact the distinction "recursively" in different contexts, with the meaning of the distinction varying according to context. The house, as a domestic space, is figured as "private" in relation to the "public" space of the street outside; yet within it, the living room becomes "public" space relative to other rooms.[66] The meaning of the private-public distinction changes according to the context of its recursive iteration, yet communicating actors repeatedly invoke the distinction as a means to order spaces, bodies, and cultural frameworks—in ways, Gal argues, that are socially constitutive of capitalism and liberal politics. As she stresses, this "fractal recursivity" involves not only consequential ideological statements about the actions, bodies, and contexts differentiated in public-private terms, but also equally consequential erasures: "forms of forgetting, denying, ignoring, or forcibly eliminating those distinctions or social facts that fail to fit the picture of the world presented by an ideology."[67]

In the controversial case of El Blog del Narco, the "public" demonstrates a similar kind of fractal recursivity—though not so much in the context of a repeated distinction between "public" and "private" realms as via a resolute differentiation between what is to be allowed inside the "public" and what is declared to be outside its bounds. For the anonymous authors of *Dying for the Truth* and for advocates of the blog more generally, its "good," "hard-working" Mexican audience is the public, who are arrayed against the narco terrorists, corrupt government officials, and even mainstream reporters, all of whom act against the public good. But critics of the blog enact their own fractal distinctions: government officials have inverted the terms, defining themselves and their activities in terms of service to the public good and ally-ing the communicative practices of the blog and similar entities with the criminality of the narcos whose messages they reproduce. Media critics of the blog have applied the distinction to yet another realm, distinguishing ethical and responsible journalistic practice—defined as driven by a set of mandates to provide a certain kind of information to the public—from a blog that seems to some to be abdicating those responsibilities by serving the pri-vate interests and goals of the narcos. Even the trafficking groups have entered the same ideological terrain, principally through the issuance of messages or mantas, often posted on the blog and other platforms, criticizing rival trafficking groups and the "narcogovernment" for their despicable actions against the "pueblo."[68] In so doing they also invoke an imagined public—one that erases their own crimes and groups them with the victims of other cartels or government misdoings, even as it places other trafficking groups, security forces, and officials outside the bounds.

To consider the fractal publics and back channels of Blog del Narco is to consider how and why the blog became so significant, at least for a time, in debates in Mexico over the press and the public sphere in the time of the so-called drug war. Blog del Narco is not just reflective of wider debates over the public sphere. Rather, it has been on the front line of those debates, in a context in which the lines were drawn and redrawn and every act of differentiation and erasure seemed to invite rebuttal—in the process projecting a new configuration of the Mexican public against its enemies. Of course, El Blog del Narco is not the only front line. To recall the conclusion of the introduction of *Dying for the Truth*, though altering its meaning: "We are Mexico. . . . There are more of us."

Notes

1. Blog del Narco, *Dying for the Truth*.
2. Blog del Narco, *Dying for the Truth*, 3.
3. Raul Gutierrez, "Leaking Secrets, Leaking Blood," *Boing Boing*, Sept. 14, 2010, http://boingboing.net/2010/09/14/narco.html.
4. Rory Carroll, "'They Stole Our Dreams': Blogger Reveals Cost of Reporting Mexico's Drug Wars," *Guardian*, Apr. 4, 2013, https://www.theguardian.com/world/2013/apr/03/mexico-blog-del-narco-drug-wars.
5. Gibler, *To Die in Mexico*.
6. Javier Garza Ramos, "Being a Journalist in Mexico Is Getting Even More Dangerous," *Washington Post*, Feb. 18, 2016, https://www.washingtonpost.com/posteverything/wp/2016/02/18/being-a-journalist-in-mexico-is-getting-even-more-dangerous; Artículo 19, "Primer semestre de 2017: 1.5 agresiones diarias contra periodistas en México," Aug. 17, 2017, https://articulo19.org/informese mestral2017; "Mexico," Reporters Without Borders, https://rsf.org/en/mexico (accessed June 15, 2016).
7. Moncada, *Oficio de muerte*; Ciro Gómez Leyva, "Dos reporteros de *Milenio*: El día que el periodismo murió," *Periodistas en Línea*, Mar. 4, 2010, http://www.periodistasenlinea.org/04-03-2010/23252.
8. "¿Qué quieren de nosotros?," *El Diario*, Sept. 19, 2010, http://diario.mx/Local/2010-09-19_cfaade06/_que-quieren-de-nosotros?.

9. "Decide *El Mañana de Nuevo Laredo* no publicar información de violencia," *El Mañana*, May 13, 2012, http://www.elmanana.com/decideelmananade-nuevolaredonopublicarinformaciondeviolencia-1620921.html.

10. Gloria Leticia Díaz, "El gremio: Informar desde el temor," *Proceso*, Aug. 8, 2010.

11. Eiss, "Narcomedia."

12. José Gil Olmos, "Y los medios se amordazan," *Proceso*, Mar. 27, 2011.

13. Luis Prados, "El gobierno mexicano impone una nueva 'narrativa' sobre la violencia," *El País*, May 5, 2013, http://internacional.elpais.com/internacional/2013/05/05/actualidad/1367787128_023117.html; César Cepeda, "Imponen en NL nueva 'narrativa' en seguridad," *Reporte Indigo*, Sept. 5, 2013, http://www.reporteindigo.com/reporte/monterrey/imponen-en-nl-nueva-narrativa-en-seguridad.

14. Monroy-Hernández and Palacios, "Destabilizing Demographics."

15. Monroy-Hernández and Palacios, "Destabilizing Demographics."

16. Carroll, "They Stole Our Dreams."

17. Blog del Narco, *Dying for the Truth*.

18. Blog del Narco, *Dying for the Truth*, 171–77.

19. Blog del Narco, *Dying for the Truth*; J. W. Fabian, "Google Kills Blog del Narco," *Advantage Mexico*, Oct. 28, 2011, http://www.advantagemexico.com/news/5064/google_kills_blog_del_narco.

20. Melissa del Bosque, "Why Blog del Narco Has Become the Most Important Website in Mexico," *Guardian*, Apr. 3, 2013, https://www.theguardian.com/world/2013/apr/03/mexico-drugs-blog-del-narco.

21. Monroy-Hernández and Palacios, "Destabilizing Demographics."

22. Fabian, "Google."

23. Blog del Narco, *Dying for the Truth*; Del Bosque, "Why Blog del Narco."

24. Blog del Narco, *Dying for the Truth*, 5.

25. Olga R. Rodríguez, "Narco-Blogger Foils Censors," Associated Press, Aug. 13, 2010, http://www.telegram.com/apps/pbcs.dll/article?AID=/20100813/news/8130523.

26. Juan Carlos Romero Puga, "El Blog del Narco: La renuncia al periodismo," *Letras Libres*, Sept. 1, 2011, http://www.letraslibres.com/blogs/polifonia/el-blog-del-narco-la-renuncia-al-periodismo; Homero Campa, "El 'Blog del Narco' y la veinteañera que lo maneja," *Proceso*, Apr. 28, 2010.

27. Ronnie Lovler, "Mexico Drug Wars Website Provokes Controversy," International Media Support, June 22, 2013, https://www.mediasupport.org/mexico-drug-wars-website-provokes-controversy.

28. Michael Marizco, "Is 'The Most Important Website In Mexico' Stealing Work from Mexican Journalists?," *Fronteras Desk*, Apr. 12, 2013, http://www.fronterasdesk.org/content/most-important-website-mexico-stealing-work-mexican-journalists; Chivis Martínez, "Mexico's Blog del Narco: A Case of Stealing the

Work of Others?," *Borderland Beat*, Apr. 13, 2013, http://www.borderlandbeat. com/2013/04/mexicos-blog-del-narco-case-of-stealing.html.

29. Monroy-Hernández and Palacios, "Destabilizing Demographics."

30. Martínez, "Mexico's Blog del Narco."

31. Juan Manuel Reyes Cruz, "Torturan y cuelgan a pareja en puente de Nuevo Laredo," *Excélsior*, Sept. 13, 2011, http://www.excelsior.com.mx/2011/09/13/ nacional/768068; Fabian, "Google"; Blog del Narco, *Dying for the Truth*, ix; Del Bosque, "Why Blog del Narco"; Carroll, "They Stole Our Dreams."

32. Rory Carroll, "Blog del Narco: Author Who Chronicled Mexico's Drugs War Forced to Flee," *Guardian*, May 16, 2013, http://www.theguardian.com/ world/2013/may/16/blog-del-narco-mexico-drug-war.

33. Jenkins, *Convergence Culture*.

34. Blog del Narco, *Dying for the Truth*, 1–5.

35. Romero Puga, "El Blog del Narco"; Campa, "El 'Blog del Narco.'"

36. Blog del Narco, *Dying for the Truth*, 5.

37. Romero Puga, "El Blog del Narco."

38. Cabañas, "Imagined Narcoscapes."

39. Wald, *Narcocorrido*; Roush, "Santa Muerte"; Gómez Michael and Park, "Cult of Jesús Malverde."

40. Pablo Ordaz, "Sinaloa declara la guerra contra el 'narcocorrido,'" *El País*, May, 20, 2011, http://elpais.com/diario/2011/05/20/cultura/1305842408_850215.html.

41. Campbell, "Narco-Propaganda"; Eiss, "Narcomedia."

42. Womer and Bunker, "Sureños Gangs"; Robert Muggah, "The Rise of Cyber Cartels and Digital Gangs," OpenCanada, Feb. 2, 2015, https://www.opencanada.org/ features/the-rise-of-cyber-cartels-and-digital-gangs; Joseph Cox, "Mexico's Drug Cartels Love Social Media," *Vice*, Nov. 4, 2013, http://www.vice.com/read/ mexicos-drug-cartels-are-using-the-internet-to-get-up-to-mischief.

43. Lucio R., "Where in the World Is Broly Banderas?," *Borderland Beat*, Mar. 29, 2015, http://www.borderlandbeat.com/2015/03/what-happened-to-broly-banderas.html.

44. Priscila Mosqueda, "Mexican Drug Cartels Are Using Social Media Apps to Commit Virtual Kidnappings," *Vice*, Sept. 17, 2014, http://www.vice.com/ read/mexican-cartels-are-using-social-media-apps-to-commit-virtual-kidnappings-917.

45. Blog del Narco, *Dying for the Truth*, 5.

46. Blog del Narco, *Dying for the Truth*, 3.

47. Rodríguez, "Narco-Blogger."

48. Campa, "El 'Blog del Narco.'"

49. Beltrán, "Mexico's Fearscapes."

50. Monroy-Hernández and Palacios, "Destabilizing Demographics."

51. Fabian, "Google."

52. Blog del Narco, *Dying for the Truth*, 41–43.

53. Blog del Narco, *Dying for the Truth*, 73–77; Campa, "El 'Blog del Narco.'"

54. "Texto íntegro de narcomantas firmadas por los Zetas," Blog del Narco, May 2012, http://www.blogdelnarco.com/2012/05/texto-integro-de-narcomantas-firmadas.html; Marcela Turati, "Cadáveres en pos de identidad," *Proceso*, June 1, 2014.

55. "El CJNG amaga con vengar a caídos en Ecuandureo," *Proceso*, May 28, 2015, http://www.proceso.com.mx/405621/el-cjng-amaga-con-vengar-la-muerte-de-caidos-en-ecuandureo.

56. Ben Bodnar, "In Mexico, Alternative Media Steps In," Rendon Group, Feb. 23, 2011, http://www.rendon.com/in-mexico-alternative-media-steps-in.

57. Carmen Álvarez, "Los narcoblogs, bajo lupa de Estados Unidos," *Excélsior*, Jan, 17, 2012.

58. Beltrán, "Mexico's Fearscapes," 85.

59. Blog del Narco, *Dying for the Truth*, 5.

60. Eiss, "Narcomedia," 85.

61. Fraser, "Rethinking the Public Sphere," 68; Asen and Brouwer, introduction to their *Reconfigurations*.

62. Eiss, "Narcomedia," 95.

63. Cody, "Publics and Politics," 40, 41.

64. Muggah and Diniz, "Digitally Enhanced," 11.

65. Gal, "Semiotics," 79, 80.

66. Gal, "Semiotics," 82.

67. Gal, "Language Ideologies Compared," 27.

68. Eiss, "Narcomedia."

Bibliography

Archives

Baja California

Archivo Histórico de Tijuana (AHT)
Hemeroteca

Guerrero

Archivo Histórico del Estado de Guerrero (AHEG)
Archivo Paucic (AP)

London

London School of Economics Library
National Archives, Foreign Office (NA/FO)

Mexico City

Archivo General de la Nación (AGN)
Archivo Histórico de la Suprema Corte de Justicia de la Nación (AHSCJN)
Archivo Histórico del Distrito Federal (AHDF)
Archivo J. Y. Limantour (AL)
Archivo Plutarco Elías Calles (APEC)
Archivo Rafael Chousel (RC)
Centro de Estudios de Historia de México Carso (CEHM)
Centro de Estudios sobre la Universidad (CEU)
Colección Cuartel General del Sur (CCGS)

Colección Lafragua (CL)
Colección Particular Miguel Ángel Granados Chapa (MAGC)
Direccióon Federal de Seguridad, Versión Pública (DFS/VP)
Dirección General de Investigaciones Políticas y Sociales (DGIPS)
Fideicomiso Archivos Plutarco Elías Calles y Fernando Torreblanca
Fondo Francisco Bulnes (FFB)
Presidentes Adolfo López Mateos (ALM)
Presidentes Adolfo Ruiz Cortines
Presidentes Gustavo Diaz Ordaz (GDO)
Presidentes Lázaro Cárdenas del Río (LCR)
Presidentes Manuel Avila Camacho
Presidentes Miguel Alemán Valdés (MAV)
Sociedad Cooperativa Editora de Periódicos (SCEP)

Puebla

Archivo del Congreso del Estado de Puebla (ACEP)

Washington, DC

National Archives and Records Administration

Books and Articles

Acevedo Valdés, Agustín. *Historia de la caricatura en México*. Mexico City: Milenio, 2011.
Adler, Ilya. "Media Uses and Effects in Large Bureaucracies: A Case Study in Mexico." Ph.D. diss., University of Wisconsin, Madison, 1986.
Aguayo, Sergio. *La charola: Una historia de los servicios de inteligencia en México*. Mexico City: Grijalbo, 2001.
———. *1968: Los archivos de la violencia*. Mexico City: Grijalbo, 1999.
Aguilar, Gabriela, and Ana Cecilia Terrazas. *La prensa en la calle: Los voceadores y la distribución de periódicos y revistas en México*. Mexico City: Grijalbo, 1996.
Aguilar, José Antonio, and Rafael Rojas. *El republicanismo en hispanoamérica: Ensayos de historia intelectual y política*. Mexico City: Universidad Nacional Autónoma de México, 2002.
Aguilar Camín, Héctor. *Los días de Manuel Buendía: Testimonies*. Mexico City: Océano, 1985.
———. *La guerra de Galio*. Mexico City: Cal y Arena, 1991.
Agundis, Teódulo Manuel. *El verdadero Jorge Pasquel: Ensayo biográfico sobre un caracter?* Mexico City: N.p., 1956.
Agustín, José. *Tragicomedia mexicana*. Mexico City: Planeta, 1990.
———. *Tragicomedia mexicana: La vida en México de 1970 a 1982*, vol. 2. Mexico City: Planeta, 1992.

Alegre, Robert F. *Railroad Radicals: Gender, Class, and Memory in Cold War Mexico*. Lincoln: University of Nebraska Press, 2013.

Alexander, Ryan. "Fortunate Sons of the Mexican Revolution: Miguel Alemán and His Generation, 1920–1952." Ph.D. diss., University of Arizona, 2011.

Ameglio Patella, Pietro. *Gandhi y la desobedencia civil*. Mexico City: Plaza y Valdés, 2002.

Anderson, Jon Lee. *Che Guevara: A Revolutionary Life*. New York: Grove, 2010.

Andrews, Catherine, ed. *La tradición constitucional en México, 1808–1940*. Mexico City: Archivo General de la Nación, 2017.

Andrews, Chris. *Roberto Bolaño's Fiction: An Expanding Universe*. New York: Columbia University Press, 2016.

Anduiza Pimentel, Marcel. "Squatter Movements in Acapulco: The 'Civic Revolt' and the PRI's Corporatist Morass, 1955–1967." Paper delivered at the American Historical Association annual meeting, Chicago, 2012.

Annino, Antonio, Luis Castro Leiva, and François-Xavier Guerra, eds. *De los imperios a las naciones: Iberoamerica*. Mexico City: Zaragoza IberCaja, 1994.

Anuario estadístico compendiado de los Estados Unidos Mexicanos. Mexico City: Talleres Gráficos de la Nación, 1942–1974.

Arenas Guzmán, Diego. *Historia de la cámara de diputados de la XXVI legislatura federal*. Vol. 4, *La revolución tiene la palabra: Actas del "diario de debates" de la cámara de diputados, del 14 de septiembre de 1912 al 19 de febrero de 1913*. Mexico City: Inherm, 1963.

———. *El periodismo en la Revolución Mexicana*. Mexico City: Instituto Nacional de Estudios Históricos de la Revolución Mexicana, 1966.

Armistrad, Robert Thomas. "The History of *Novedades*." Ph.D. diss., University of Texas, Austin, 1964.

Arroyo, Sergio Raul, and Rosa Casanova. "The Casasolas: An Everyday Epic." In *Mexico: The Revolution and Beyond: Photographs by Agustín Víctor Casasola, 1900–1940*, ed. Pablo Ortiz Monasterio. New York: Aperture Foundation, 2003.

Asen, Robert, and Daniel C. Brouwer, eds. *Reconfigurations of the Public Sphere and Counterpublics and the State*. Albany: State University of New York Press, 2001.

Astorga, Luis. *Drogas sin fronteras*. Mexico City: Grijalbo, 2003.

Aviña, Alexander. *Specters of Revolution: Peasant Guerrillas in the Cold War Mexican Countryside*. New York: Oxford University Press, 2014.

Bakhtin, Mikhail. *Rabelais and His World*. Bloomington: Indiana University Press, 1984.

Bakker, Gerben. "Trading Facts: Arrow's Fundamental Paradox and the Origins of Global News Networks." In *International Communication and Global News Networks: Historical Perspectives*, ed. Peter Putnis, Chandrika Kaul, and Jürgen Wilke, 9–54. New York: Hampton Press / International Association for Media and Communication Research, 2011.

Balderas Martínez, Orlando. "José de León Toral: Proceso histórico-jurídico (1928–1929)." B.A. thesis, Universidad Nacional Autónoma de México, n.d.

Baqueiro López, Oswaldo. *La prensa y el estado*. Mexico City: ISSTEY, 1992.

Barajas, Rafael. *El país de "El Ahuizote": La caricatura mexicana de oposición durante el gobierno de Sebastián Lerdo de Tejada (1872–1876)*. Mexico City: FCE, 2005.

———. *El país de "El Llorón de Icamole": La caricatura mexicana de combate y libertad de imprenta durante los gobiernos de Porfirio Díaz y Manuel González (1877–1884)*. Mexico City: FCE, 2007.

———. *El sexenio me da risa: La historieta no oficial*. Mexico City: Grijalbo, 1994.

———. *Sólo me río cuando me duele: La cultura del humor en México*. Mexico City: Planeta, 2009.

———. "The Transformative Power of Art: Mexico's Combat Cartoonists." *NACLA Report on the Americas* 33:6 (2000): 6–41.

Bartley, Russell H., and Sylvia Erickson Bartley. *Eclipse of the Assassins: The CIA, Imperial Politics, and the Slaying of Mexican Journalist Manuel Buendía*. Madison: University of Wisconsin Press, 2015.

Bartra, Armando. "The Seduction of the Innocents: The First Tumultuous Moments of Mass Literacy in Post-revolutionary Mexico." In *Everyday Forms of State Formation: Revolution and the Negotiation of Rule in Modern Mexico*, ed. Gilbert Joseph and Daniel Nugent, 301–25. Durham, NC: Duke University Press, 1994.

Bates, John M. "From State Monopoly to a Free Market of Ideas? Censorship in Poland, 1976–1989." In *Censorship and Cultural Regulation in the Modern Age*, ed. Beate Müller. Amsterdam: Rodopi, 2004.

Baudrillard, Jean. *En América*. Barcelona, Spain: Anagrama, 1987.

Bazant, Mílada. "Lecturas del Porfiriato." In *Historia de la lectura en México*, ed. Seminario de Historia de la Educación en México. Mexico City: Colegio de México, 1988.

Beardsell, Peter. *A Theatre for Cannibals: Rodolfo Usigli and the Mexican Stage*. Rutherford, NJ: Associated University Presses, 1992.

Becerra Acosta, Manuel. *Dos poderes*. Mexico City: Grijalbo, 1984.

Beltrán, Edith. "Mexico's Fearscapes: Where Fantasy Personas Engage in Citizenship." In *Fear and Fantasy in a Global World*, ed. Susana Araujo, Marta Pacheco Pinto, and Sandra Bettencourt, 75–98. Leiden: Brill, 2015.

Bernal, Rafael. *The Mongolian Conspiracy*. Trans. Katherine Silver. New York: New Directions, 2013.

Blanco Moheno, Roberto. *La corrupción en México*. Mexico City: Bruguera Mexicana, 1979.

———. *Memorias de un reportero*. Mexico City: Libro Mex, 1965.

Blanquel, Eduardo. "Setenta años de la entrevista Díaz-Creelman." *Vuelta* 17 (Apr. 1978): 28–33.

Blog del Narco. *Dying for the Truth: Undercover inside the Mexican Drug War by the Fugitive Reporters of Blog del Narco*. Port Townsend, WA: Feral House, 2013.

Bobbio, N. "La democracía y el poder invisible." In *El futuro de la democracía*, ed. N. Bobbio and trans. J. Moreno. Madrid: Plaza and Janes, 1985.

Bohmann, Karin. *Medios de comunicación y sistemas informáticos en México*. Mexico City: CONACULTA, 1994.

Bolaño, Roberto. *2666*. Trans. Natasha Wimmer. New York: Farrar, Straus and Giroux, 2013.

Borrás, Leopoldo. *Historia de periodismo mexicano, del ocaso porfirista al derecho a la información*. Mexico City: Universidad Nacional Autónoma de México, 1983.

Bortz, Jeffrey Lawrence. *Los salarios industriales en la Ciudad de México, 1939–1975*. Mexico City: FCE, 1984.

Boullosa, Carmen, and Mike Wallace. *A Narco History: How the United States and Mexico Jointly Created the "Mexican Drug War."* Oakland, CA: Nomadic Press, 2015.

Bourdieu, Pierre. *Language and Symbolic Power*. Cambridge: Polity, 2011.

Bowden, Charles. *Murder City: Ciudad Juarez and the Global Economy's New Killing Fields*. New York: Nation Books, 2010.

Bresnahan, Rosalind. "Reclaiming the Public Sphere in Chile under Dictatorship and Neoliberal Democracy." In *Making Our Media: Global Initiatives toward a Democratic Public Sphere*, vol. 1, ed. Clemencia Rodríguez, Dorothy Kidd, and Laura Stein. Cresskill, NJ: Hampton, 2009.

Brewster, Claire. "The Student Movement of 1968 and the Mexican Press: The Cases of *Excélsior* and *Siempre*." *Bulletin of Latin American Research* 21:2 (Apr. 2002): 171–90.

Bringas, Guillermina, and David Mascareño. *Esbozo histórico de la prensa obrera en México*. Mexico City: Universidad Nacional Autónoma de México, 1988.

———. "Un siglo de publicaciones periódicas obreras en México." *Revista Mexicana de Sociología* 42:2 (1980): 907–46.

Brocca, Victoria. *Nota roja 60's: La crónica policiaca en la Ciudad de México*. Mexico City: Diana, 1993.

Bruhn, Kathleen. "Antonio Gramsci and the Palabra Verdadera: The Political Discourse of Mexico's Guerrilla Forces." *Latin American Politics and Society* 41:2 (July 1999): 29–55.

Brunk, Samuel. "Zapata and the City Boys: In Search of a Piece of the Revolution." *Hispanic American Historical Review* 73 (1993): 32–65.

Buffington, Robert. *A Sentimental Education for the Working Man: The Mexico City Penny Press, 1900–1910*. Durham, NC: Duke University Press, 2015.

Bulnes, Francisco. *El verdadero: Díaz y la revolución*. Mexico City: Nacional, 1960.

Bunker, Steven, and Victor Macías González. "Consumption and Material Culture in the Twentieth Century." In *A Companion to Mexican History and Culture*, ed. William Beezley, 83–118. Oxford: Blackwell, 2011.

Burkholder de la Rosa, Arno Vicente. "Construyendo una nueva relación con el estado: El crecimiento y consolidación del diario *Excélsior* (1932–1968)." *Secuencia* 73 (2009): 84–110.

———. "Forging a New Relationship with the State: The Growth and Consolidation of *Excélsior* Newspaper (1932–1968)." *Secuencia* 73 (Jan.–Apr. 2009): 89.

———. "El olimpo fracturado: La dirección de Julio Scherer García en *Excélsior* (1968–1976)." *Historia Mexicana* 59:4 (Apr.–June 2010): 1339–99.

———. "El periódico que llegó a la vida nacional: Los primeros años del diario *Excélsior* (1916–1932)." *Historia Mexicana* 58:4 (2009): 1369–1418.

———. *La red de los espejos: Una historia del diario "Excélsior," 1916–1976*. Mexico City: Fondo de Cultura Económica, 2016.

Cabañas, Miguel A. "Imagined Narcoscapes: Narcoculture and the Politics of Representation." *Latin American Perspectives* 41:2 (2014): 3–17.

Cabrera, Luis (Lic. Blas Urrea). "El balance de la revolución." In his *Veinte años después*. Mexico City: Botas, 1938.

Cabrera Acevedo, Lucio. *La Suprema Corte de Justicia durante el fortalecimiento del Porfiriato (1882–1888)*. Mexico City: Suprema Corte de Justicia de la Nación, 1991.

———. *La Suprema Corte de Justicia: La revolución y el constituyente de 1917*. Mexico City: Suprema Corte de Justicia, 1994.

Cabrera Acevedo, Luis. *Obras políticas*. Mexico City: Nacional, 1921.

Cabrera López, Patricia. *Una inquietud de amanecer: Literatura y política en México, 1962–1987*. Mexico City: Universidad Nacional Autónoma de México, 2006.

Cacho, Lydia, et al. *La ira de México: Siete voces contra la impunidad*. Mexico City: Debate, 2016.

Cadava, Geraldo L. *Standing on Common Ground: The Making of a Sunbelt Borderland*. Cambridge, MA: Harvard University Press, 2013.

Caldeira, Teresa. *City of Walls: Crime, Segregation, and Citizenship in São Paulo*. Berkeley: University of California Press, 2001.

Calmon Alves, Rosental. "From Lapdog to Watchdog: The Role of the Press in Latin America's Democratization." In *Making Journalists: Diverse Models, Global Issues*, ed. Hugh de Burgh, 183–202. London: Routledge, 2005.

Camp, Roderic Ai. "Education and Political Recruitment in Mexico: The Alemán Generation." *Journal of Interamerican Studies and World Affairs* 18:3 (Aug. 1976): 295–321.

———. *Intellectuals and the State in Twentieth-Century Mexico*. Austin: University of Texas Press, 1985.

Campbell, Howard. "Narco-Propaganda in the Mexican 'Drug War': An Anthropological Perspective." *Latin American Perspectives* 41:2 (2014): 60–77.

Cano Andaluz, Aurora. "*El Dictamen* de Veracruz, *El Informador* de Guadalajara y *El Porvenir* de Monterrey: Tres empresas periodísticas durante la presidencia de Plutarco Elías Calles (1924–1928)." In *Rompecabezas de papel: La prensa y el periodismo desde las regiones de México, siglos XIX y XX*, ed. Celia del Palacio Montiel. Guadalajara: Porrúa, 2006.

Cárdenas Gutiérrez, Salvador. *El juez y su imagen pública*. Mexico City: Suprema Corte de Justicia, 2006.

Carey, Elaine. *Plaza of Sacrifices: Gender, Power, and Terror in 1968*. Albuquerque: University of New Mexico Press, 2005.

Castaño, Luis. *El régimen legal de la prensa en México*. Mexico City: Arpe, 1958.

Castelán Rueda, Roberto. *La fuerza de la palabra impresa: Carlos María Bustamante y el discurso de la modernidad*. Mexico City: Fondo de Cultura Económica, 1997.

Castellaños, José J. *México engañado: Por que la prensa no informa*. Mexico City: N.p., 1983.

Celis de la Cruz, Martha. "Vicente García Torres." In *Tipos y caracteres: La prensa mexicana (1822–1855): Memoria del coloquio celebrado los días 23, 24 y 25 septiembre de 1998*, 147–59. Mexico City: Universidad Nacional Autónoma de México, 2001.

Cerwin, Herbert. *These Are the Mexicans*. New York: Reynal and Hitchcock, 1947.

Clark de Lara, Belem, and Elisa Speckman Guerra, eds. *La república de las letras*. Vol. 2, *Publicaciones periódicas y otros impresos*. Mexico City: Universidad Nacional Autónoma de México, 2005.

Cline, Howard. *Mexico: Revolution to Evolution, 1940–1960*. New York: Greenwood, 1962.

Cockcroft, John D. *Precursores intelectuales de la Revolución Mexicana (1900–1913)*. Mexico City: Siglo Veintiuno, 1985.

Cody, Francis. "Publics and Politics." *Annual Review of Anthropology* 40:1 (2011): 37–52.

Cole, Richard Ray. "The Mass Media of Mexico: Ownership and Control." Ph.D. diss., University of Minnesota, 1972.

Cole, Richard, and Albert Hester, eds. *Mass Communication in Mexico: Proceedings of the March 11–15, 1974, Seminar in Mexico City*. Mexico City: International Communication Division, 1975.

Comité 68 Pro Libertadores Democráticas. *Los procesos de México*. Mexico City: Comité 68 Pro Libertadores Democráticas, 2008.

Condés Lara, Enrique. *Represión y rebelión en México (1959–1985)*. Vol. 2, *Los años dorados del priato y los pilares ocultos del poder; 1968 y el fin de una etapa; Los acólitos del diablo*. Mexico City: Miguel Ángel Porrúa, 2007.

Cook, Timothy E. *Governing the News: The News Media as a Political Institution*. Chicago: University of Chicago Press, 2001.

Corchado, Alfredo. *Midnight in Mexico: A Reporter's Journey through a Country's Descent into Darkness*. New York: Penguin, 2014.

Cordero y Bernal, Rigoberto. *Maximino Ávila Camacho*. Puebla, Mexico: N.p., 2012.

Cordero y Torres, Enrique. *Diccionario biográfico de Puebla*. Puebla: Centro de Estudios Historicos, 1972.

——. *Historia del periodismo en Puebla, 1820–1946*. Puebla: Bohemia Poblana, 1947.

Cosío Villegas, Daniel. *Historia moderna de México*. Vols. 9 and 10. Mexico City: Hermes, 1983.

——. *El Porfiriato: Vida política interior*. 2 vols. Mexico City: Hermes, 1972.

——. "The Press and Responsible Freedom in Mexico." In *Responsible Freedom in the Americas*, ed. Angel del Río, 272–80. Garden City, NY: Doubleday, 1955.

——. *La República Restaurada, la vida política*. Mexico City: Hermes, 1955.

——. *El sistema político mexicano: Los posibilidades de cambio*. Mexico City: Joaquín Mortiz, 1973.

Cossío, José Ramón. *La justicia prometida: El poder judicial de la federación, de 1900 a 1910*. Mexico City: FCE, 2014.

——. *La teoría constitucional de la Suprema Corte de Justicia*. Mexico City: Fontamara, 2008.

Coudart, Laurence. "Función de la prensa en el México independiente: El correo de lectores de *El Sol*." *La Revista Iberoamericana* 72:214 (Jan.–Mar. 2006): 93–104.

Covo, Jacqueline. "La prensa en la historiografía mexicana: Problemas y posibilidades." *Historia Mexicana* 42:3 (Jan.–Mar. 1993): 689–710.

Crónica de la publicidad en Mexico. Mexico City: Clio, 2002.

Cross, John. *Informal Politics: Street Vendors and the State in Mexico City*. Stanford, CA: Stanford University Press, 1998.

Cruz García, Ricardo. *Nueva era y la prensa en el maderismo: De la caída de Porfirio Díaz a la decena trágica*. Mexico City: Universidad Nacional Autónoma de México, 2013.

Cumberland, Charles C. *Madero y la Revolución Mexicana*. Mexico City: Siglo Veintiuno, 1977.

Curley, Robert. "Anticlericalism and Public Space in Revolutionary Jalisco." *The Americas* 65:4 (Apr. 2009): 511–33.

Curran, James, and Myung-Jin Park, eds. *De-Westernizing Media Studies*. London: Routledge, 2000.

Darnton, Robert. *Censors at Work: How States Shaped Literature*. New York: Norton, 2014.

——. *The Devil in the Holy Water; or, The Art of Slander from Louis XIV to Napoleon*. University Park: Penn State University Press, 2010.

——. "An Early Information Society: News and the Media in Eighteenth-Century Paris." *American Historical Association* 105:1 (2000): 1–35.

——. *The Forbidden Best-Sellers of Pre-Revolutionary France*. New York: Harper-Collins, 1996.

——. "What Is the History of Books?," *Daedalus* 111:3 (1982): 65–83.

Davis, Diane. *Urban Leviathan: Mexico City in the Twentieth Century*. Philadelphia: Temple University Press, 2010.

De Burgh, Hugh, ed. *Making Journalists: Diverse Models, Global Issues*. London: Routledge, 2005.

De la Garza Toledo, Enrique. *La democracía de los telefonistas*. Mexico City: Plaza y Valdés, 2002.

Del Castillo Troncoso, Alberto. *Ensayo sobre el movimiento estudiantil de 1968: La fotografía y la construcción de un imaginario*. Mexico City: Instituto Mora, 2012.

——. "Fotoperiodismo y representaciones del movimiento estudiantil de 1968: El caso de *El Heraldo* de México." *Secuencia* 60 (Sept.–Dec. 2004): 137–74.

——. "El movimiento estudiantil de 1968 narrado en imagenes." *Sociológica* 23:68 (Sept.–Dec. 2008): 63–114.

——. *Rodrigo Moya: Una visión crítica de la modernidad*. Mexico City: CONACULTA, 2006.

——. "La visión de los vencidos: El movimiento estudiantil de 1968 visto desde la izquierda, el caso de la revista *Por Qué?*" In *Caminar entre fotones: Formas y estilos de la mirada documental*, ed. R. Monroy Nasr and A. del Castillo, 149–78. Mexico City: INAH, 2013.

Del Palacio Langer, Julia. "Agrarian Reform, Oil Expropriation, and the Making of National Property in Post-revolutionary Mexico." Ph.D. diss., Columbia University, 2014.

Del Palacio Montiel, Celia. "En Veracruz se aprende a vivir con miedo: La construcción social de la violencia a través de los periódicos de Veracruz en México (2005–2011)." *Comunicação y Informação* 15:1 (2012).

——. "La prensa católica en México." In *Catolicismo social en México: Las instituciones*, ed. Manuel Castellanos, 2:161–83. Mexico City: IMDOSOC-AIH, 2005.

Del Palacio Montiel, Celia, ed. *Rompecabezas de papel: La prensa y el periodismo desde las regiones de México, siglos XIX y XX*. Guadalajara: Porrúa, 2006.

——. *Siete regiones de la prensa en México, 1792–1950*. Guadalajara: CONACYT, 2006.

——. *Violencia y periodismo regional en México*. Mexico City: Juan Pablos, 2015.

Del Río, Eduardo. *Rius para principiantes*. Mexico City: Grijalbo Mondadori, 2008.

De María y Campos, Armando. *El teatro de Género Chico en la Revolución Mexicana*. Mexico City: INRM, 1956.

Díaz, María Elena. "The Satiric Penny Press for Workers in Mexico, 1900–1910: A Case Study in the Politicization of Popular Culture." *Journal of Latin American Studies* 22:3 (1990): 497–526.

Díaz del Castillo, Bernal. *Historia verdadera de la conquista de la Nueva España*. Madrid: Carmelo Sáenz de Santa María, 1982.

Díaz Redondo, Regino. *La gran mentira, ocurrió en Excélsior, el periódico de la vida nacional*. Mexico City: Libros para Todos, 2002.

Domínguez, Jorge. *To Make a World Safe for Revolution: Cuba's Foreign Policy*. Cambridge, MA: Harvard University Press, 1989.

Doyle, Kate. *Investigative Journalism and Access to Information in Mexico*. Center for Latin American Studies Working Paper (Berkeley: University of California, 2011).

Driver, Alice. *More or Less Dead: Feminicide, Haunting, and the Ethics of Representation in Mexico*. Tucson: University of Arizona Press, 2015.

Dumas, Claude, and Zamudio Vega. "El discurso de oposición en la prensa clerical conservadora de México en la época de Porfirio Díaz (1876–1910)." *Historia Mexicana* 39:1 (1989): 243–65.

Durand Ponte, Victor Manuel. "La cultura política en nueve ciudades mexicanas." *Revista Mexicana de Sociología* 54:1 (Jan.–Mar. 1992): 289–322.

Editor and Publisher International Yearbook. New York: Editor and Publisher, 1981.

Eiss, Paul K. "The Narcomedia: A Reader's Guide." *Latin American Perspectives* 41:2 (2014): 78–98.

Enciso, Froylán. "1976: Alberto Sicilia Falcón." In *El Libro Rojo: Continuación*, vol. 3, ed. Gerardo Villadelángel Viñas. Mexico City: Fondo de Cultura Económica, 2008.

Enríquez, Antonio. *Dictadura presidencial o parlamentarismo democrático: Estudio crítico de nuestro sistema federal, y proposiciones de reforma a la constitución, mediante la creación del parlamentarismo y de la república central*. Mexico City: A. Enríquez, 1913.

Erlandson, E. H. "The Press of Mexico, with Special Consideration of Economic Factors." Ph.D. diss., Northwestern University, 1963.

Esquivel Hernándeze, José Luis. *El Norte: Lider sin competencia*. Monterrey: Cerda, 2003.

Fallaw, Ben. "The Politics of Press Freedom during the Maximato: The Case of the *Diario de Yucatán*." Unpublished article in author's possession.

———. *Religion and State Formation in Post-Revolutionary Mexico*. Durham, NC: Duke University Press, 2013.

Farah, Douglas. *Dangerous Work: Violence against Mexico's Journalists and Lessons from Colombia*. Washington, DC: Center for International Media Assistance, 2012.

Fernández Christlieb, Fatima. *Los medios de difusión masiva en México*. Mexico City: Juan Pablos, 1982.

Fernández Meléndez, Jorge. *Nadie supo nada: La verdadera historia del asesinato de Eugenio Garza Sada*. Mexico City: Grijalbo, 2006.

Ferrer, Eulalio. *Cartas de un publicista*. Mexico City: Diana, 1966.

Figueroa-Ibarra, Carlos, and Lorena Martínez-Zavala. "The Ejército Popular Revolucionario: Occupying the Cracks in Mexico's Hegemonic State." *Latin American Perspectives* 40:5 (July 2013): 153–64.

Forment, Carlos A. *Democracy in Latin America*. Chicago: University of Chicago Press, 2003.

Fowler, Will, ed. *Forceful Negotiations: The Origins of the Pronunciamiento in Nineteenth-Century Mexico*. Lincoln: University of Nebraska Press, 2011.

Fraser, Nancy. "Rethinking the Public Sphere: A Contribution to the Critique of Actually Existing Democracy." *Social Text* 25–26 (1990): 56–80.

Fregoso Peralta, Gilberto, and Enrique Sánchez Ruiz. *Prensa y poder en Guadalajara*. Guadalajara: UAG, 1993.

Freije, Vanessa. "Exposing Scandals, Guarding Secrets: Manuel Buendía, Columnismo, and the Unraveling of One-Party Rule in Mexico, 1965–1984." *The Americas* 72:3 (June 2015): 377–409.

Fromm, Erich, and Michael Maccoby. *Social Character in a Mexican Village: A Sociopsychoanalytical Study*. London: Prentice Hall, 1970.

Frutos, Luz María. "Prensa lozana." *Historia Mexicana* 1:1 (July–Sept. 1951).

Fuentes, Carlos. *The Death of Artemio Cruz*. New York: Farrar, Straus and Giroux, 1991.

Fuentes Díaz, Vicente. *Guerrero: Un pasado aciago, un porvenir promisirio*. Mexico City: Camara de Diputados, 2000.

Fuentes para la historia de la Revolución Mexicana. Vol. 2, *La caricatura política*. Mexico City: Fondo de Cultura Económica, 1974.

Gal, Susan. "Language Ideologies Compared." *Journal of Linguistic Anthropology* 15:1 (2005): 23–37.

———. "A Semiotics of the Public/Private Distinction." *Differences: A Journal of Feminist Cultural Studies* 13:1 (2002): 77–95.

Gamboa, Féderico. *Impresiones y recuerdos*. Buenos Aires: Arnoldo Moen, 1893.

Gamiño Muñoz, Rodolfo. *Guerrilla, represión, y prensa en la década de los setenta en México: Invisibilidad y olvido*. Mexico City: Instituto Mora, 2011.

———. "Prensa oficialista y acción guerrillera en la década de 1970: El caso de la Liga Comunista 23 de Septiembre." *Antropología* 94 (2012): 118–19.

Gantús, Fausta. Caricatura y poder político: Crítica, censura repesión en la Ciudad de México, 1876–1888. Mexico City: Instituto Mora, 2009.

García, Clara Guadalupe. *El Imparcial: Primer periódico moderno de México*. Mexico City: Centro de Estudios Históricos del Porfiriato, 2003.

García Cantú, Gastón. *El pensamiento de la reacción mexicana: Historia documental*. Vol. 2, *1860–1926*. Mexico City: Empresas, 1965.

Garcíadiego, Javier. "La prensa durante la Revolución Mexicana." In *Las publicaciones periódicas y la historia de México: Ciclo de conferencias*, ed. Aurora Cano Andaluz. Mexico City: Universidad Nacional Autónoma de México, 1995.

García Márquez, Gabriel. *El coronel no tiene quien le escriba*. 1961. Barcelona: Delbolsillo, 2015.

García Rubio, Claudia I. "Radiografía de la prensa diaria en México en 2010." *Comunicación y Sociedad* 20 (July–Dec. 2013): 65–93.

Gaspar de Alba, Alicia, and Georgina Guzmán, eds. *Making a Killing: Femicide, Free Trade, and La Frontera*. Austin: University of Texas Press, 2010.

Gibler, John. *Una historia oral de la infamia: Los ataques contra los normalistas de Ayotzinapa*. Mexico City: Grijalbo, 2016.

———. *To Die in Mexico: Dispatches from Inside the Drug War*. San Francisco: City Lights, 2011.

Gibson, Edward L. *Boundary Control: Subnational Authoritarianism in Federal Democracies*. Cambridge: Cambridge University Press, 2013.

Gillingham, Paul. "Maximino's Bulls: Popular Protest after the Mexican Revolution, 1940–1952." Past and Present 206:1 (Feb. 2010): 175–211.

———. "'We Don't Have Arms, but We Do Have Balls': Fraud, Violence and Popular Agency in Elections." In *Dictablanda: Politics, Work, and Culture in Mexico, 1938–1968*, ed. Paul Gillingham and Benjamin T. Smith, 147–79. Durham, NC: Duke University Press, 2014.

———. "Who Killed Crispín Aguilar? Violence and Order in the Post-revolutionary Countryside." In *Violence, Coercion, and State-Making in Twentieth-Century Mexico: The Other Half of the Centaur*, ed. Wil Pansters, 91–112. Stanford, CA: Stanford University Press, 2013.

Gillingham, Paul, and Benjamin T. Smith. "The Paradoxes of Revolution." In *Dictablanda: Politics, Work, and Culture in Mexico, 1938–1968*, ed. Paul Gillingham and Benjamin T. Smith, 1–43. Durham, NC: Duke University Press, 2014.

Gillingham, Paul, and Benjamin T. Smith, eds. *Dictablanda: Politics, Work, and Culture in Mexico, 1938–1968*. Durham, NC: Duke University Press, 2014.

Gil Mendieta, Jorge, Samuel Schmidt, and Alejandro Arnulfo Ruiz León. *Estudios sobre la red política de México*. Mexico City: Universidad Nacional Autónoma de México, 2005.

Giron Barthe, Nicole. "El entorno editorial." In *Empresa y cultura en tinta y papel (1800–1860)*, ed. Laura Beatriz Suárez de la Torre and Miguel Angel Casto. Mexico City: Instituto Mora, 2001.

Gitlin, Todd. *The Whole World Is Watching: Mass Media in the Making and Unmaking of the New Left*. Berkeley: University of California Press, 2003.

Gómez Arias, Alejandro. *Memoria personal de un país*. Mexico City: Grijalbo, 1990.

Gómez Estrada, José Alfredo. *Gobierno y casinos: El origen de la riqueza de Abelardo L. Rodríguez*. Mexico City: Instituto Mora, 2007.

Gómez Michael, Gerardo, and Jungwon Park. "The Cult of Jesús Malverde: Crime and Sanctity as Elements of a Heterogeneous Modernity." *Latin American Perspectives* 41:2 (2014): 202–14.

Gómez-Quiñones, Juan. *Porfirio Díaz, los intelectuales y la revolución*. Mexico City: El Caballito, 1981.

González Casanova, Pablo. *La democracia en México*. Mexico City: Era, 1983.

———. *Democracy in Mexico*. Trans. Danielle Salti. Oxford: Oxford University Press, 1970.

González de Bustamante, Celeste. *Muy buenas noches: Mexico, Television, and the Cold War*. Lincoln: University of Nebraska Press, 2012.

González de Bustamante, Celeste, and Jeannine E. Relly. "Professionalism under Threat of Violence." *Journalism Studies* 17:6 (2016): 684-702.

———. "Silencing Mexico: A Study of Influences on Journalists in the Northern States." *International Journal of Press/Politics* 19:1 (2014): 108-31.

González Marín, Silvia. "La prensa y el poder político en el gobierno del General Lázaro Cárdenas." In *Las publicaciones periódicas y la historia de México*, ed. Aurora Cano Andaluz. Mexico City: Universidad Nacional Autónoma de México, 1995.

———. *Prensa y poder político: La elección presidencial de 1940 en la prensa Mexicana*. Mexico City: Siglo Veintiuno, 2006.

González Ramírez, Sergio. *The Femicide Machine*. Cambridge, MA: MIT Press, 2012.

———. *Huesos en el desierto*. Barcelona, Spain: Anagrama, 2005.

Gosse, Van. *Where the Boys Are: Cuba, Cold War America and the Making of a New Left*. New York: Verso, 1993.

Granados Chapa, Miguel Ángel. "Aproximación a la prensa mexicana." *Revista Mexicana de Ciencia Política* 69 (1972): 49–50.

———. *Buendía: El primer asesinato de la narcopolítica en México*. Mexico City: Grijalbo, 2013.

———. *Excélsior y otros temas de comunicación*. Mexico City: Ediciones el Caballito, 1980.

———. *Nava Sí! Zapata No!: La hora de San Luis Potosí: Cronica de una lucha que triunfó*. Mexico City: Grijalbo, 1992.

Grillo, Ioan. *El Narco: Inside Mexico's Criminal Insurgency*. New York: Bloomsbury, 2012.

Guardino, Peter. *The Time of Liberty: Popular Political Culture in Oaxaca, 1750–1850*. Durham, NC: Duke University Press, 2005.

Guerra, Elisa Speckman. "Las posibles lecturas de la república de las letras: Escritores, visiones y lectores." In *La república de las letras: Asomos a la cultura escrita del México decimonónico*, ed. Belem Clark de Lara and Elisa Speckman Guerra, 47–72. Mexico City: Universidad Nacional Autónoma de México, 2005.

Guerra, François-Xavier. *México: Del antiguo régimen a la revolución*. Mexico City: Fondo de Cultura Económica, 1988.

Guerra, François-Xavier, et al. *Los espacios públicos en Iberoamérica: Ambigüedades y problemas, siglos XVIII–XIV*. Mexico City: Centro Francés de Estudios Mexicanos y Centroamericanos, 1998.

Guerrero, M. A., and Mireya Márquez Ramírez. "The 'Captured-Liberal' Model: Media Systems, Journalism and Communication Policies in Latin America." *International Journal of Hispanic Media* 7 (2014).

Guillermoprieto, Alma, et al. *72 migrantes*. Mexico City: Almadía, 2010.

Gutiérrez Espíndola, José Luis. *Prensa obrera*. Mexico City: El Caballito, 1983.

Habermas, Jürgen. *The Structural Transformation of the Public Sphere*. Cambridge, MA: MIT Press, 1991.

Hale, Charles A. *The Transformation of Liberalism in Late Nineteenth-Century Mexico*. Princeton, NJ: Princeton University Press, 1989.

Hallin, Daniel C. "Media, Political Power, and Democratization in Mexico." In *De-Westernizing Media Studies*, ed. James Curran and Myung-Jin Park, 85–97. London: Routledge, 2000.

Hallin, Daniel C., and Paolo Mancini. *Comparing Media Systems: Three Models of Media and Politics*. Cambridge: Cambridge University Press, 2004.

Hayes, Joy Elizabeth. *Radio Nation: Communication, Popular Culture, and Nationalism in Mexico, 1920–1950*. Tucson: University of Arizona Press, 2000.

Heitman, John Russell. "The Press of Mexico: Its History, Characteristics, and Content." Ph.D. diss., Northwestern University, 1948.

Henck, Nick. "The Subcommander and the Sardinian: Marcos and Gramsci." *Mexican Studies/Estudios Mexicanos* 29:2 (Summer 2013): 428–58.

Henderson, Timothy, and David LaFrance. "Maximino Ávila Camacho of Puebla." In *State Governors in the Mexican Revolution, 1910–1952*, ed. J. Buchenau and W. Beezley. Lanham, MD: Rowman and Littlefield, 2009.

Herman, Edward S., and Noam Chomsky. *Manufacturing Consent: The Political Economy of the Mass Media*. New York: Pantheon, 2003.

Hernández, Keith. "Between War and Writing: Urban Catholics in the Mexican Public Sphere during the Cristero Period, 1925–1930." B.A. thesis, Columbia University, 2007.

Hernández Chávez, Alicia. *La mecánica cardenista*. Mexico City: Colegio de México, 1979.

Herrera Calderón, Fernando, and Adela Cedillo Cedillo, eds. *Challenging Authoritarianism in Mexico: Revolutionary Struggles and the Dirty War, 1964–1982*. New York: Routledge, 2012.

Hodges, Donald Clark, and Ross Gandy. *Mexico under Siege: Popular Resistance to Presidential Despotism*. London: Zed, 2002.

Hughes, Sallie. *Newsrooms in Conflict: Journalism and the Democratization of Mexico*. Pittsburgh, PA: University of Pittsburgh Press, 2006.

Hughes, Sallie, and Mireya Márquez Ramírez. "Examining the Practices That Mexican Journalists Employ to Reduce Risk in a Context of Violence." *International Journal of Communication* 11 (2017): 499–521.

Hutchinson, Linda. *Irony's Edge: The Theory and Politics of Irony*. New York: Routledge, 1995.

———. *A Theory of Parody: The Teachings of Twentieth-Century Art Forms*. Champaign: University of Illinois Press, 2000.

Ibargüengoitia, Jorge. *Autopsias rápidas*. Mexico City: Vuelta, 1988.

———. *Instrucciones para vivir en México*. Mexico City: Joaquín Mortiz, 1990.

Ibarra de Anda, F. *El periodismo en México, lo que es y lo que debe ser: Un estudio del periódico y del periodista mexicanos y de las posibilidades de ambos para el future*. Mexico City: Mundial, 1934.

Iber, Patrick. *Neither Peace nor Freedom: The Cultural Cold War in Latin America*. Cambridge, MA: Harvard University Press, 2015.

Jenkins, Henry. *Convergence Culture: Where Old and New Media Collide*. New York: New York University Press, 2006.

Jiménez de Ottalengo, Regina. "Un periódico mexicano, su situación social y sus fuentes de informacion: Una ilustración de la teoría de la dependencia en el ámbito de la comunicación." *Revista Mexicana de Sociología* 36:4 (Oct.–Dec. 1974): 767–806.

Johnson, John J. *Latin America in Caricature*. Austin: University of Texas Press, 1980.

Johnson, Julie Greer. *Satire in Colonial Spanish America: Turning the New World Upside Down*. Austin: University of Texas Press, 1993.

Johnson, Thomas, and Barbara Kaye. "Cruising Is Believing? Comparing Internet and Traditional Sources on Media Credibility Measures." *Journalism and Mass Communication Quarterly* 75:2 (1998): 325–40.

Joseph, Gilbert, and Daniela Spenser, eds. *In from the Cold: Latin America's New Encounter with the Cold War*. Durham, NC: Duke University Press, 2008.

Katz, Friedrich. *La guerra secreta en México*. Mexico City: Era, 1985.

———. *The Life and Times of Pancho Villa*. Stanford, CA: Stanford University Press, 1998.

Keller, Renata. "Don Lázaro Rises Again: Heated Rhetoric, Cold Warfare, and the 1961 Latin American Peace Conference." In *Beyond the Eagle's Shadow: New Histories of Latin America's Cold War*, ed. Virginia Garrard-Burnett, Mark Atwood Lawrence, and Julio E. Moreno, 129–50. Albuquerque: University of New Mexico Press, 2013.

———. "A Foreign Policy for Domestic Consumption: Mexico's Lukewarm Defense of Castro, 1959–1969." *Latin American Research Review* 47:2 (Summer 2012): 100–119.

———. *Mexico's Cold War: Cuba, the United States, and the Legacy of the Mexican Revolution*. Cambridge: Cambridge University Press, 2017.

Klahr, Marco Lara, and Francesc Barata. *Nota roja: La vibrante historia de un genero y una nueva manera de informar*. Buenos Aires: Random House Mondadori, 2009.

Knight, Alan. *The Mexican Revolution*. 2 vols. Lincoln: University of Nebraska Press, 1990.

Koestler, Arthur. *Los somnámbulos*. Mexico City: Salvat, 1994.

Krauze, Enrique. *Mexico: Biography of Power*. New York: HarperCollins, 1997.

Lafaye, Jacques. *Quetzalcóatl y Guadalupe: La formación de la conciencia nacional en México*. Mexico City: FCE, 1995.

LaFrance, David. *Revolution in Mexico's Heartland: Politics, War, and State Building in Puebla, 1913–1920*. Wilmington, DE: SR Books, 2003.

Landes, Joan B. *Women and the Public Sphere in the Age of the French Revolution*. Ithaca, NY: Cornell University Press, 1988.

Lawson, Chappell H. *Building the Fourth Estate: Democratization and the Rise of a Free Press in Mexico*. Berkeley: University of California Press, 2002.

Leal, Luis. "El contenido literario de *La Orquesta*." *Historia Mexicana* 7:3 (Jan.–Mar. 1958): 329–67.

Lear, John. *Picturing the Proletariat: Artists and Labor in Revolutionary Mexico, 1908–1940*. Austin: University of Texas Press, 2016.

Lempérière, Annick. Intellectuels, état, et société au Mexique: Les clercs de la nation (1910–1968). Paris: L'Harmattan, 1992.

Leñero, Vicente. *Los periodistas*. Mexico City: Mortiz, 1978.

———. "Prólogo: La belleza del crimen." In *El Libro Rojo: Continuación*, vol. 1, ed. Gerardo Villadelángel Viñas. Mexico City: Fondo de Cultura Económica, 2008.

Lenti, Joseph Umberto. "Collaboration and Conflict: Organized Labor, Business, and the State in Post-Tlatelolco Mexico." Ph.D. diss., University of Arizona, 2012.

Lettieri, Michael. "A Model Dinosaur: Power, Personal Networks, and the Career of Rubén Figueroa." *Mexican Studies/Estudios Mexicanos* 31:2 (2015): 305–42.

———. "Wheels of Government: The Alianza de Camioneros and the Political Culture of PRI Rule, 1929–1981." Ph.D. diss., University of California, San Diego, 2014.

Lewis, Oscar. *Life in a Mexican Village: Tepoztlán Restudied*. Urbana: University of Illinois Press, 1963.

Libertad de expresión en venta. Mexico City: Article 19 and Fundar, 2015.

Lilla, Mark. *The Reckless Mind: Intellectuals in Politics*. New York: New York Review of Books, 2016.

Limantour, José Yves. *Apuntes sobre mi vida pública (1982–1911)*. Mexico City: Porrúa, 1965.

Loaeza, Soledad. "Gustavo Díaz Ordaz: Las insuficiencias de la presencia autoritaria." In *Gobernantes mexicanos*, ed. Will Fowler, 287–335. Mexico City: Fondo de Cultura Económica, 2008.

Lombardo de Ruiz, Irma. *De la opinión a la noticia: El surgimiento de los géneros informativos en México*. Mexico City: Kiosko, 1992.

Lomnitz, Claudio. *Deep Mexico, Silent Mexico: An Anthropology of Nationalism*. Minneapolis: University of Minnesota Press, 2006.

———. *The Return of Comrade Ricardo Flores Magón*. New York: Zone, 2014.

———. "Ritual, rumor y corrupción en la formación del espacio nacional en México." *Revista Mexicana de Sociologia* 58:2 (Apr.–June 1996): 21–51.

Loret de Mola, Rafael. *Denuncia: Presidente sin palabra*. Mexico City: Grijalbo, 1995.

Loseff, Lev. *On the Beneficence of Censorship: Aesopian Language in Modern Russian Literature*. Munich: O. Sagner in Kommission, 1984.

Luquín, Eduardo. *Análisis espectral del mexicano*. Mexico City: Costa-Amic, 1961.

Macías González, Victor Manuel. "El caso de una beldad asesina: La construcción narrativa, los concursos de belleza y el mito nacional posrevolucionario (1921–1931)." *Historia y Grafía* 13 (1999): 113–54.

Maldonado Aranda, Salvador. "Between Law and Arbitrariness: Labour Union Caciques in Mexico." In *Caciquismo in Twentieth-Century Mexico*, ed. Alan Knight and Wil Pansters, 227–48. London: Institute for the Study of the Americas, 2005.

Márquez Ramírez, Mireya. "Estudio introductorio: El impacto de la violencia criminal en la cultura periodística posautoritaria: La vulnerabilidad del periodismo regional en México." In *Violencia y periodismo regional en México*, ed. Celia del Palacio Montiel, 15–48. Mexico City: Juan Pablos, 2015.

Martínez de la Vega, Francisco. *Aliento y lastre del periodismo.* Mexico City: El Día, 1966.

Martínez S., José Luis. *La vieja guardia: Protagonistas del periodismo mexicano.* Mexico City: Plaza and Janes, 2006.

Marván Laborde, Ignacio. *Nueva edición del diario de debates del Congreso Constituyente, 1916–1917.* Mexico City: Suprema Corte de Justicia, 2005.

McLuhan, Marshall, and Quentin Fiore. *The Medium Is the Message: An Inventory of Effects.* Berkeley, CA: Gingko, 2002.

Medel y Alvarado, León. *Historia de San Andrés Tuxtla.* 3 vols. Xalapa: Gobierno del Estado de Veracruz, 1993–1994.

Mejía Barquera, Fernando. *La industria de la radio y la televisión y la política del estado mexicano.* Mexico City: Fundación Manuel Buendía, 1989.

Mejido, Manuel. *Con la maquina al hombre.* Mexico City: Siglo Veintiuno, 2011.

Méndez Reyes, Jesús. "La prensa opositora al maderismo, trinchera de la reacción: El caso del periódico *El Mañana.*" *Estudios de Historia Moderna y Contemporánea de México* 21 (2001).

Middlebrook, Kevin. *The Paradox of Revolution: Labor, the State, and Authoritarianism in Mexico.* Baltimore, MD: Johns Hopkins University Press, 1995.

Miguel de Mora, Juan. *Por la gracia del señor presidente: México la gran mentira.* Mexico City: Editores Asociados, 1975.

Miller, Arthur H., Edie N. Goldenburg, and Lutz Erbring. "Type-Set Politics: The Impact of Newspapers on Public Confidence." *American Political Science Review* 73:1 (Mar. 1979): 67–84.

Miquel, Angel. *Disolvencias: Literatura, cine y radio en México (1900–1950).* Mexico City: FCE, 2005.

Moheno Tabares, Querido. *¿Hacia dónde vamos? Bosquejo de un cuadro de instituciones políticas adecuadas al pueblo mexicano.* Mexico City: I. Lara, 1908.

Monárrez Fragoso, Julia, et al. *Violencia contra las mujeres e inseguridad ciudadana en Ciudad Juárez.* Mexico City: El Colegio de la Frontera Norte, Miguel Ángel Porrúa, 2010.

Moncada, Carlos. *Oficio de muerte: Periodistas asesinados en el país de la impunidad.* Mexico City: Grijalbo, 2012.

Mondragón, Magdalena. *Los presidentes: Dan Risa.* Mexico City: N.p., 1948.

Monroy-Hernández, Andrés, and Luis Daniel Palacios. "Destabilizing Demographics: Blog del Narco and the Future of Citizen Journalism." *Georgetown Journal of International Affairs* 15:2 (2014): 81–92.

Monsiváis, Carlos. *A ustedes les consta: Antologia de la crónica en México*. Mexico City: Era, 1980.

———. "La crónica y el reportaje como géneros periodísticos." In *Periodismo: Una visión desde Nuevo León*, ed. José de la Luz Lozano and Samuel Flores Longoria, 33–45. Monterrey, Mexico: Gobierno de Nuevo León, 1989.

———. *Los mil y un velorios: Crónica de la nota roja en México*. Mexico City: Debate, 2016.

———. "Red News: The Crime Pages in Mexico." In his *Mexican Postcards*, ed. John Kraniauskas. New York: Verso, 1999.

Montgomery, Louise F. "Stress on Government and Mexican Newspapers' Commentary on Government Officials, 1951–1980." Ph.D. diss., University of Texas, 1983.

Morales Moreno, Humberto. *El poder judicial de la federación en el siglo XX: Una breve historia institucional, 1895–1996*. Mexico City: Suprema Corte de Justicia, 2007.

Moreno, Julio. *Yankee Don't Go Home! Mexican Nationalism, American Business Culture, and the Shaping of Modern Mexico, 1920–1950*. Chapel Hill: University of North Carolina Press, 2003.

Morley, Jefferson. *Our Man in Mexico: Winston Scott and the Hidden History of the CIA*. Lawrence: University of Kansas Press, 2011.

Morton, Adam David. "Structural Change and Neoliberalism in Mexico: 'Passive Revolution' in Global Political Economy." *Third World Quarterly* 24:4 (Aug. 2003): 631–53.

Mraz, John. *Looking for Mexico: Modern Visual Culture and National Identity*. Durham, NC: Duke University Press, 2009.

Muggah, Robert, and Gustavo Diniz. "Digitally Enhanced Violence Prevention in the Americas." *Stability: International Journal of Security and Development* 2:3 (2013): 108–31.

Müller, Beate. "Censorship and Cultural Regulation: Mapping the Territory." In *Censorship and Cultural Regulation in the Modern Age*, ed. Beate Müller. Amsterdam: Rodopi, 2004.

Narváez, Rubén. *La sucesión presidencial: Teoría y práctica del tapadismo*. Mexico City: Instituto Mexicano de Sociologia Política, 1981.

Nava Martínez, Othón. "Origen y desarrollo." In *Empresa y cultura en tinta y papel (1800–1860)*, ed. Laura Beatriz Suárez de la Torre and Miguel Angel Casto. Mexico City: Instituto Mora, 2001.

Navarro, Aaron W. *Political Intelligence and the Creation of Modern Mexico, 1938–1954*. University Park: Penn State University Press, 2010.

Nerone, John. *The Media and Public Life: A History*. Cambridge: Polity, 2015.

———. *Violence against the Press: Policing the Public Sphere in US History*. Oxford: Oxford University Press, 1994.

Nesvig, Martin Austin. *Ideology and Inquisition: The World of the Censors in Early Mexico*. New Haven, CT: Yale University Press, 2009.

Newcomer, Daniel. *Reconciling Modernity: Urban State Formation in 1940s León, Mexico.* Lincoln: University of Nebraska Press, 2004.

Niblo, Stephen R. *Mexico in the 1940s: Modernity, Politics, and Corruption.* Wilmington, DE: Scholarly Resources, 1999.

Nichols, John Spicer. "Coyotes of the Press: Professionalization of Mexican Journalists." Ph.D. diss., University of Minnesota, 1979.

Nolan, Sidney David. "Relative Independence of Two Mexican Dailies: A Case Study of *El Norte* and *El Porvenir* of Monterrey." M.A. thesis, University of Texas, Austin, 1965.

Notkin, Benjamin. "History Unheard: The Decline of Local History in San Andrés Tuxtla." B.A. honors thesis, University of Pennsylvania, 2013.

Novo, Salvador. *La vida en México en el periodo presidencial de Lázaro Cárdenas.* Mexico City: Consejo Nacional para la Cultura y las Artes, 1994.

Ochoa Campos, Moises. *Reseña histórica del periodismo mexicano.* Mexico City: Porrúa, 1968.

O'Dogherty Madrazo, Laura. *De urnas y sotanas: El Partido Católico Nacional en Jalisco.* Mexico City: Consejo Nacional para la Cultura y las Artes, 2001.

Olcott, Jocelyn. "Empires of Information: Media Strategies for the 1975 International Women's Year." *Journal of Women's History* 24:4 (Winter 2012): 24–48.

Orme, William A., Jr., ed. *A Culture of Collusion: An Inside Look at the Mexican Press.* Boulder, CO: Lynne Reiner, 1996.

Orozco, José Clemente, and Robert C. Stephenson. *José Clemente Orozco: An Autobiography.* New York: Dover, 2001.

Ortega Ramírez, Patricia, ed. *Crimen, terror y páginas: Antología.* Mexico City: El Nacional, 1990.

Ortiz Bullé Goyri, Alejandro. "Origines y desarrollo del teatro de revista en México (1869–1953)." In *Un siglo de teatro en México,* ed. David Olguín, 40–53. Mexico City: FCE, 2011.

Ortiz Marín, Ángel Manuel. *Los medios de comunicación en Baja California.* Mexicali, Mexico: UABC, 2006.

Ortiz Monasterio, José. *Historia y ficción: Los dramas y novelas de Vicente Riva Palacio.* Mexico City: Instituto Mora, 1993.

Ossorio, León. *El pantano: (Apuntes para la historia) un libro acusador.* Mexico City: N.p., 1954.

Padilla, Tanalís. *Rural Resistance in the Land of Zapata: The Jaramillista Movement and the Pax Priísta, 1940–1962.* Durham, NC: Duke University Press, 2008.

Páez Varela, Alejandro, ed. *La guerra por Juárez: El sangriento corazón de la tragedia nacional.* Mexico City: Planeta, 2009.

Palti, Elías José. "Los diarios y el sistema político mexicano en tiempos de la República Restaurada (1867–1876)." In *Construcciones impresas: Panfletos, diarios y revistas en la formación de los estados nacionales en América Latina, 1820–1920,* ed. Paula Alonso, 167–82. Buenos Aires: Fondo de Cultura Económica, 2004.

———. *La invención de una legitimidad: Razón y retórica en el pensamiento mexicano del siglo XIX: Un estudio sobre las formas del discurso político*. Mexico City: FCE, 2005.

———. "La Sociedad Filarmónica del Pito: Ópera, prensa y política en la República Restaurada (México, 1867–1876)." *Historia Mexicana* 52:4 (Apr.–June 2003): 941–78.

Pansters, Wil G. *Politics and Power in Puebla: The Political History of a Mexican State, 1937–1987*. Amsterdam: CEDLA, 1990.

Parada Gay, Francisco. *Breve reseña histórica de la Suprema Corte de Justicia*. Mexico City: Murguía, 1929.

Pascual García, Francisco. *Código penal para el distrito y territorios federales: Sobre delitos del fuero común y para toda la republica sobre delitos contra la federación, seguido de las leyes que le han reformado en muchos de sus artículos*. Mexico City: Herrero Hermanos Sucesores, 1906, 1907, 1910.

Paxman, Andrew. "Cooling to Cinema and Warming to Television: State Mass Media Policy, 1940–1964." In *Dictablanda: Politics, Work, and Culture in Mexico, 1938–1968*, ed. Paul Gillingham and Benjamin T. Smith, 299–320. Durham, NC: Duke University Press, 2014.

———. *Jenkins of Mexico: How a Southern Farm Boy Became a Mexican Magnate*. Oxford: Oxford University Press, 2017.

Paz, Octavio. *Hoguera que fue*, comp. Felipe Gálvez. Mexico City: Universidad Autónoma Metropolitana, 1986.

———. "Libertad de imprenta." B.A. thesis, Escuela Nacional de Jurisprudencia, 1911.

Pellicer de Brody, Olga, and Jose Luis Reyna. *Historia de la Revolución Mexicana, período 1952–1960: El afianzamiento de la estabilidad política*. Mexico City: El Colegio de México, 1978.

Pensado, Jaime M. *Rebel Mexico: Student Unrest and Authoritarian Political Culture during the Long Sixties*. Stanford, CA: Stanford University Press, 2013.

Pérez-Rayón, Nora. "La prensa liberal en la segunda mitad del siglo XIX." In *La república de las letras*, ed. Belem Clark de Lara and Elisa Speckman Guerra. Vol. 2, *Publicaciones periódicas y otros impresos*, 175–70. Mexico City: Universidad Nacional Autónoma de México, 2005.

Perzabal, Carlos. *De las memorias de Manuel Marcué Pardiñas*. Mexico City: Rino, 1997.

Piccato, Pablo. "Altibajos de la esfera pública." In *Independencia y revolución: Pasado, presente y futuro*, ed. Gustavo Leyva, 240–91. Mexico City: Fondo de Cultura Económica and Universidad Autónoma Metropolitana, 2010.

———. *Congreso y revolución: El parlamentarismo en la XXVI legislatura*. Mexico City: Instituto Nacional de Estudios Históricos de la Revolución Mexicana, 1992.

———. *A History of Infamy: Crime, Truth, and Justice in Mexico*. Berkeley: University of California Press, 2017.

———. "Murders of Nota Roja: Truth and Justice in Mexican Crime News." *Past and Present* 223 (May 2014): 195–231.

———. "Pistoleros, Ley Fuga, and Uncertainty in Public Debates about Murder in Twentieth- Century Mexico." In *Dictablanda: Politics, Work, and Culture in Mexico, 1938–1968*, ed. Paul Gillingham and Benjamin T. Smith, 321–41. Durham, NC: Duke University Press, 2014.

———. "The Public Sphere and Liberalism in Mexico: From the Mid-Nineteenth Century to the 1930s." In *Latin American History: Oxford Research Encyclopedias*, ed. William H. Beezley. Oxford: Oxford University Press, 2016.

———. "Public Sphere in Latin America: A Map of the Historiography." *Social History* 35:2 (2010): 165–92.

———. *The Tyranny of Opinion: Honor in the Construction of the Mexican Public Sphere*. Durham, NC: Duke University Press, 2010.

———. "'Ya saben quién': Journalism, Crime, and Impunity in Mexico Today." In *Mexico's Struggle for Public Security: Organized Crime and State Responses*, ed. Susana Berruecos and George Philip, 75–70. London: Palgrave Macmillan, 2012.

Pilcher, Jeffrey M. *Cantinflas and the Chaos of Mexican Modernity*. Wilmington, DE: Scholarly Resources, 2001.

Pineda Soto, Adriana. "La prensa religiosa y el estado liberal en el siglo XIX: La perspectiva michoacana." In *Rompecabezas de papel: La prensa y el periodismo desde las regiones de México, siglos XIX y XX*, ed. Celia del Palacio Montiel, 74–96. Guadalajara: Porrúa, 2006.

Posada, José Guadalupe. "Las bravísimas calaveras de Mora y de Morales." In *José Guadalupe Posada, ilustrador de la vida mexicana*. Mexico City: Fondo Editorial de la Plástica Mexicana / Consejo Nacional para la Cultura y las Artes, 1992.

Powell, Robert Andrew. *This Love Is Not For Cowards: Salvation and Soccer in Ciudad Juárez*. New York: Bloomsbury USA, 2013.

Pozas Horcasitas, Ricardo. *La democracía en blanco: El movimiento médico en México, 1964–1965*. Mexico City: Siglo Veintiuno, 1993.

Preston, Julia and Dillon, Samuel. *Opening Mexico*. New York: Farrar Straus Giroux, 2004.

Prieto, Guillermo. *Obras completas*, ed. Boris Rosen Jélomer. Mexico City: Consejo Nacional para la Cultura y las Artes, 1994.

Pruneda, Salvador. *La caricatura como arma política*. Mexico City: Instituto Nacional de Estudios Históricos de la Revolución Mexicana, 2003.

Quezada, Abel. *Antes y después de Gardenia Davis*. Mexico City: J. Mortiz, 1991.

Quintana, Alejandro. *Maximino Ávila Camacho and the One-Party State: The Taming of Caudillismo and Caciquismo in Post-Revolutionary Mexico*. Lanham, MD: Rowman and Littlefield, 2010.

Rama, Ángel. *The Lettered City*. Durham, NC: Duke University Press, 1996.

Ramón Garmabella, José, and Renato Leduc. *Renato por Leduc: Apuntes de una vida singular.* Mexico City: Oceano, 1982.

Ramírez, Guillermo H. *Los gangsters del periodismo.* Durango, Mexico: N.p., 1944.

Ramírez, Paul. "Enlightened Publics for Public Health: Assessing Disease in Colonial Mexico." *Endeavour* 37:1 (Mar. 2013): 3–12.

Rath, Thomas. *Myths of Demilitarization in Post-revolutionary Mexico, 1920–1960.* Chapel Hill: University of North Carolina Press, 2013.

———. "Paratroopers under the Volcano: Animal Disease, Sovereignty, and Scandal in Cold War Mexico." Unpublished manuscript in author's possession.

Reich, Peter L. "Recent Research on the Legal History of Modern Mexico." *Mexican Studies/Estudios Mexicanos* 23 (2007): 181–93.

Ríos Zúñiga, Rosalina. "Contención del movimiento: Prensa y asociaciones cívicas en Zacatecas, 1824–1833." *Historia Mexicana* 52:1 (2002): 103–61.

———. "Una retórica para la movilización popular: *El Cometa*, periódico político literario de zacatecas, 1832." *Historia Mexicana* 58:2 (2008): 753–801.

Riva Palacio, Raymundo. "A Culture of Collusion: The Ties That Bind the Press and the PRI." In *A Culture of Collusion: An Inside Look at the Mexican Press*, ed. William A. Orme Jr., 21–32. Boulder, CO: Lynne Reiner, 1996.

———. "The Nightmare of Tlatelolco." In *1968: Year of Media Decision*, ed. Robert Giles and Robert W. Snyder, 103–11. New Brunswick, NJ: Transaction, 2001.

Robles, Emilio. *Retrato hablado: De los que hacen periodismo en Sonora.* Mexico City: Garabatos, 1999.

Rodman, Selden. *Mexican Journal: The Conquerors Conquered.* London: Feffer and Simons, 1958.

Rodríguez, Teresa, Diana Montané, and Lisa Pulitzer. *The Daughters of Juárez: A True Story of Serial Murder South of the Border.* New York: Atria, 2008.

Rodríguez Baños, Roberto. *Libertad de expresión.* Mexico City: Departamento Editorial Secretaría de la Presidencia, 1975.

Rodríguez Castañeda, Rafael. *Prensa vendida: Los periodistas y presidentes: 40 años de relaciones.* Mexico City: Grijalvo, 1993.

Rodríguez Kuri, Ariel. "El discurso del miedo: *El Imparcial* y Francisco I. Madero." *Historia Mexicana* 40:4 (1991): 697–740.

Rodríguez Munguía, Jacinto. *La otra guerra secreta: Los archivos prohibidos de la prensa y el poder.* Mexico City: Random House Mondadori, 2007.

Rodríguez Nieto, Sandra. *La fábrica del crimen.* Mexico City: Planeta, 2012.

———. *The Story of Vicente, Who Murdered His Mother, His Father, and His Sister: Life and Death in Juárez.* New York: Verso, 2015.

Rojas, Rafael. *La escritura de la independencia: El surgimiento de la opinión pública en México.* Mexico City: Taurus, Centro de Investigación y Docencia Económicas, 2003.

———. "Una maldición silenciada: El panfleto político en el México independiente." *Historia Mexicana* 47:1 (1997): 35–67.

Ronfeldt, David R. *Atencingo: The Politics of Agrarian Struggle in a Mexican Ejido.* Stanford, CA: Stanford University Press, 1973.

Ross, Stanley. "El historiador y el periodismo mexicano." *Historia Mexicana* 14:3 (Jan.–Mar. 1965): 347–82.

Roush, Laura. "Santa Muerte, Protection, and Desamparo: A View from a Mexico City Altar." Special edition of *Latin American Research Review* 49 (2014): 129–48.

Rubenstein, Ann. *Bad Language, Naked Ladies, and Other Threats to the Nation: A Political History of Comic Books.* Durham, NC: Duke University Press, 1998.

Rubin, Jeffrey. *Decentering the Regime: Ethnicity, Radicalism, and Democracy in Juchitán, Mexico.* Durham, NC: Duke University Press, 1997.

Rubio-Marín, Ruth, and Clara Sandoval. "Engendering the Reparations Jurisprudence of the Inter-American Court of Human Rights: The Promise of the Cotton Field Judgment." *Human Rights Quarterly* 33:4 (Nov. 2011): 1062–91.

Rugeley, Terry. *The River People in Flood Time: The Civil Wars in Tabasco, Spoiler of Empires.* Stanford, CA: Stanford University Press, 2014.Ruiz Castañeda, María del Carmen, Luis Reed Torres, and Enrique Cordero y Torres, eds. *El periodismo en México: 450 años de historia.* Mexico City: Editorial Tradición, 1974.

Russell, Philip. *The History of Mexico: From Pre-Conquest to Present.* Hoboken, NJ: Taylor and Francis, 2010.

Saborit, Antonio. *El mundo ilustrado de Rafael Reyes Spíndola.* Mexico City: Grupo Carso, 2003.

Salado Álvarez, Victoriano. *Memorias: Tiempo viejo, tiempo nuevo.* Mexico City: Porrúa, 1985.

Sánchez García, Alfonso. *El Plumaje del Mosco: Páginas autobiográficas.* Toluca: Universidad Autónoma del Estado de México, 2001.

Sánchez González, Agustín. *Diccionario biográfico ilustrado de la caricatura mexicana.* Mexico City: Limusa, 1997.

Sánchez Rivera, Roberto, Aurora Cano Andaluz, and Arturo Martínez Nateras. "Los libros y la prensa." In *Diálogos sobre el 68*, ed. Silvia González Marín, 115–46. Mexico City: Universidad Nacional Autónoma de México, 2003.

Sánchez Ruíz, Enrique E. "Los medios de comunicación masiva en México, 1968–2000." In *Una historia contemporánea de México*, ed. Ilán Bizberg and Lorenzo Meyer, 403–54. Mexico City: Colegio de México, 2005.

Sánchez Sierra, Juan Carlos. "Crisis mística, educación y juventud: La formación del periodismo en la revista *Política*, 1960–1967." *Estudios de Historia Moderna y Contemporánea de México* 45 (2013): 97–144.

———. "Periodismo heróico, moral y virilidad revolucionaria: La juventud y la mujer en la revista *Por Qué?* 1968–1974." *Secuencia* 94 (Jan.–Apr. 2016): 240–72.

Santos, Gonzalo N. *Memorias.* Mexico City: Grijalbo, 1984.

Scherer García, Julio. *Estos años.* Mexico City: Océano, 1995.

———. *Los presidentes.* Mexico City: Grijalbo, 1986.

———. *La tercer memoria*. Mexico City: Grijalbo, 2007.

———. *Vivir*. Mexico City: Grijalbo, 2012.

Scherer García, Julio, and Carlos Monsiváis. *Parte de guerra*. Vol. 1, *Tlatelolco 1968: Documentos del general Marcelino García Barragán: Los hechos y la historia*. Mexico City: Nuevo Siglo, 1999.

———. *Tiempo de saber: Prensa y poder en México*. Mexico City: Aguilar, 2003.

Schmidt, Samuel. "Elite Lore in Politics: Humor versus Mexico's Presidents." *Journal of Latin American Lore* 16:1 (1990): 91–108.

———. *Seriously Funny: Mexican Political Jokes as Social Resistance*. Tucson: University of Arizona Press, 2014.

Schudson, Michael. *Why Democracies Need an Unlovable Press*. Cambridge: Polity, 2008.

Schuger, Deborah. Censorship and Cultural Sensibility: The Regulation of Language in Tudor-Stuart England. University Park: University of Pennsylvania Press, 2006.

———. "Civility and Censorship in Early Modern England." In *Censorship and Silencing: Practices of Cultural Regulation*, ed. Robert Post. Los Angeles, CA: Getty Research Institute, 1998.

Secanella, Petra María. *El periodismo político en México*. Mexico City: PRISMA, 1983.

Serna Rodríguez, Ana María. *Un análisis de los casos relativos a la libertad de imprenta: Los juicios de amparo de Filomeno Mata*. Mexico City: Suprema Corte de Justicia, 2013.

———. *La justicia durante el Porfiriato y la revolución, 1898–1914: Casos que motivan la interposición del amparo relacionados con la libertad de expresión y los delitos de difamación, calumnia e injurias*. Mexico City: Suprema Corte de Justicia, 2010.

———. "Periodismo, estado y opinión pública en los inicios de los años veinte (1919–1924)." *Secuencia* 68 (May–Aug. 2007): 57–85.

———. "Prensa y sociedad en las décadas revolucionarias (1910–1940)." *Secuencia* 86 (Jan.–Apr. 2014): 111–44.

———. "La vida periodística mexicana y el movimiento estudiantil de 1968." *Signos Históricos* 31 (2014): 116–59.

Servín, Elisa. "Propaganda y guerra fría: La campaña anticomunista en la prensa mexicana del medio siglo." *Signos Históricos* 11 (Jan.–June 2004): 9–39.

Sewell, William H. *Logics of History: Social Theory and Social Transformation*. Chicago: University of Chicago Press, 2005.

Shapira, Yoram. *Mexican Foreign Policy under Echeverría*. Beverly Hills, CA: Sage, 1978.

Sherman, John W. *The Mexican Right: The End of Revolutionary Reform, 1929–1940*. Westport, CT: Praeger, 1997.

Sierra, Justo. *Evolución política del pueblo mexicano*. Mexico City: Ayacucho, 1977.

———. *Obras completas*. Mexico City: Universidad Nacional Autónoma de México, 1948.

Sierra Guzmán, Jorge Luis. *El enemigo interno*. Mexico City: Plaza y Valdés, 2003.

Sloan, Kathryn A. *Death in the City: Suicide and the Social Imaginary in Modern Mexico*. Berkeley: University of California Press, 2017.

Sluis, Ageeth. *Deco Body, Deco City: Female Spectacle and Modernity in Mexico City, 1900–1939*. Lincoln: University of Nebraska Press, 2016.

Smith, Benjamin T. *Pistoleros and Popular Movements: The Politics of State Formation in Post-revolutionary Oaxaca*. Lincoln: University of Nebraska Press, 2009.

———. *The Mexican Press and Civil Society, 1940-1976: Stories from the Newsroom, Stories from the Street*. Chapel Hill: University of North Carolina Press, 2018.

———. "Who Governed? Grassroots Politics in Mexico under the Partido Revolucionario Institucional, 1958–1970." *Past and Present* 225 (2014): 227–71.

Snodgrass, Michael. *Deference and Defiance in Monterrey: Workers, Paternalism, and Revolution in Mexico, 1890–1950*. Cambridge: Cambridge University Press, 2003.

———. "The Golden Age of Charrismo: Workers, Braceros, and the Political Machinery of Post-revolutionary Mexico." In *Dictablanda: Politics, Work, and Culture in Mexico, 1938–1968*, ed. Paul Gillingham and Benjamin T. Smith, 175–95. Durham, NC: Duke University Press, 2014.

Sosenski, Susana. "El niño consumidor: Una construcción publicitaria de mediados de siglo XX." In *Ciudadanos inesperados: Espacios de formación de la ciudadanía ayer y hoy*, ed. Paula López Caballero and Ariadna Acevedo, 191–222. Mexico City: Centro de Investigación y de Estudios Avanzados, 2012.

Sosenski, Susana, and Ricardo López León. "La construcción visual de la felicidad y la convivencia familiar en México: Los anuncios publicitarios en la prensa gráfica (1930–1970)." *Secuencia* 92 (May 2015): 194–225.

Sotelo Mendoza, Humberto. *Crónica de una autonomía anhelada*. Puebla: Universidad Autónoma de Puebla, 2004.

Staudt, Kathleen. *Violence and Activism at the Border: Gender, Fear, and Everyday Life in Ciudad Juárez*. Austin: University of Texas Press, 2008.

Stevens, Evelyn. "Legality and Extra-Legality in Mexico." *Journal of Interamerican Studies and World Affairs* 12 (Jan. 1970): 62–75.

———. *Protest and Response in Mexico*. Cambridge, MA: MIT Press, 1974.

Streitmatter, Roger. *Voices of Revolution: The Dissident Press in America*. New York: Columbia University Press, 2001.

Taylor, William B. *Shrines and Miraculous Images: Religious Life in Mexico before the Reforma*. Albuquerque: University of New Mexico Press, 2010.

Torres Puga, Gabriel. *Opinión pública y censura en Nueva España: Indicios de un silencio imposible, 1767–1794*. Mexico City: Colegio de México, 2010.

Torres Ramírez, Blanca. *Hacia la utopía industrial*. Mexico City: Colegio de México, 1984.

Toussaint Alcaraz, Florence. *Escenario de la prensa en el Porfiriato*. Mexico City: Fundación Manuel Buendia, 1989.

———. *Periodismo, siglo diez y nueve*. Mexico: Universidad Nacional Autónoma de México, 2006.

Trejo Delarbre, Raúl. *Crónica del sindicalismo en México (1976–1988)*. Mexico City: Siglo Veintiuno, 1990.

———. *Mediocracía sin mediaciones, prensa, television y elecciones*. Mexico City: Cal y Arena, 2001.

———. *La prensa marginal*. Mexico City: El Caballito, 1975.

Treviño, Blanca Estela. "Los bandidos de río Frío, de Manuel Payno: Una lectura." In *La república de las letras: Asomos a la cultura escrita del México decimonónico*, ed. Belem Clark de Lara and Elisa Speckman Guerra, 1:153–63. Mexico City: Universidad Nacional Autónoma de México, 2005.

Trevizo, Dolores. *Rural Protest and the Making of Democracy in Mexico, 1968–2000*. University Park: Penn State University Press, 2011.

Trujillo Muñoz, Gabriel. *La canción del progreso: Vida y milagros del periodismo bajacaliforniano*. Tijuana: Instituto Municipal de Arte y Cultura, 2000.

Turati, Marcela. *Fuego cruzado: Las victimas atrapadas en la guerra del narco*. Mexico City: Grijalbo Mondadori, 2011.

Underwood, Robert Bruce. "A Survey of Contemporary Newspapers of Mexico." Ph.D. diss., University of Missouri, 1965.

Uribe-Uran, Victor M. "The Birth of a Public Sphere in Latin America during the Age of Revolution." *Society for Comparative Studies in Society and History* 42:2 (Apr. 2000): 425–57.

Valdez Cárdenas, Javier. *Levantones: Historias reales de desaparecidos y víctimas del narco*. Madrid, Spain: Aguilar, 2012.

———. *Narcoperiodismo: La prensa en medio del crimen y la denuncia*. Madrid, Spain: Aguilar, 2016.

———. *The Taken: True Stories of the Sinaloa Drug War*. Trans. Everard Meade. Norman: University of Oklahoma Press, 2017.

Valencia Castrejón, Sergio. *Poder regional y política nacional en México: El gobierno de Maximino Avila Camacho en Puebla (1937–1941)*. Mexico City: Instituto Nacional de Estudios Históricos de la Revolución Mexicana, 1996.

Valencia Ríos, Alfonso. *Historia de El Dictamen*. Xalapa: Editorial del Gobierno del Estado, 1979.

Vargas Llosa, Mario. *Desafíos a la libertad*. Madrid, Spain: Aguilar, 1994.

Vasconcelos, José. *El desastre*. Mexico City: Botas, 1951.

Vaughan, Mary Kay. *Portrait of a Young Painter: Pepe Zúñiga and Mexico City's Rebel Generation*. Durham, NC: Duke University Press, 2014.

Velarde, Victor. *Siete dibujantes con una idea*. Mexico City: Libros y Revistas, 1954.

Velasco Valdés, Miguel. *Historia del periodismo mexicano: Apuntes*. Mexico City: Librería de Manuel Porrúa, 1955.

Volpi, Jorge. *La imaginación y el poder: Una historia intelectual de 1968*. Mexico City: Era, 1998.

Wald, Elijah. *Narcocorrido: A Journey into the Music of Drugs, Guns, and Guerrillas.* New York: Rayo, 2001.

Walker, Louise E. "Spying at the Drycleaners: Anonymous Gossip in 1973 Mexico City." *Journal of Iberian and Latin American Research* 19:1 (2013): 52–61.

———. *Waking from the Dream: Mexico's Middle Classes after 1968.* Stanford, CA: Stanford University Press, 2013.

Washington Valdez, Diana. *Cosecha de mujeres: Safari en el desierto mexicano.* Mexico City: Océano, 2005.

Weldon, Jeffrey A. "El presidente como legislador, 1917–1930." In *El poder legislativo en las décadas revolucionarias, 1908–1934*, ed. Pablo Piccato, 117–46. Mexico City: Instituto de Investigaciones Legislativas-Cámara de Diputados, 1997.

Wells, H. G. "The Idea of the League of Nations, Part I." *Atlantic Monthly* 123:1 (Jan. 1919): 106–15.

White, D. Anthony. *Siqueiros: A Biography.* Encino, CA: Floricanto Press, 1994.

White, Luise. "Telling More: Lies, Secrets, and History." *History and Theory* 39 (2000): 11–22.

Williford, Miriam. *It's the Image That Counts: Cartoon Masters for Latin American Study.* Gainesville, FL: Latin American Studies Association, 1976.

Womer, Sarah, and Robert J. Bunker. "Sureños Gangs and Mexican Cartel Use of Social Networking Sites." *Small Wars and Insurgencies* 21:1 (2010).

Wright-Rios, Edward. *Searching for Madre Matiana: Prophecy and Popular Culture in Modern Mexico.* Albuquerque: University of New Mexico Press, 2014.

Zolov, Eric. "Expanding Our Conceptual Horizons: The Shift from an Old to a New Left in Latin America." *A Contra Corriente* 5:2 (Winter 2008): 47–73.

———. "Jorge Carreño's Graphic Satire and the Politics of 'Presidentialism' in Mexico during the 1960s." *Estudios Interdisciplinarios de América Latina y el Caribe* 17:1 (2006): 13–38.

———. *Refried Elvis: The Rise of Mexican Counterculture.* Berkeley: University of California Press, 1999.

Contributors

Rafael Barajas, also known as **El Fisgón**, is a cartoonist for *La Jornada* and the author of several books on the history of cartoons and satire in Mexico.

Roderic Ai Camp is a professor of government at Claremont McKenna College. He is the author of some thirty books on Mexican politics, including works on intellectuals, journalists, businessmen, the church, and the military.

Paul K. Eiss is an associate professor of anthropology and history at Carnegie Mellon University. He is the author of *In the Name of El Pueblo: Place, Community, and the Politics of History in Yucatán.*

Vanessa Freije is an assistant professor of international studies at the University of Washington. Her current project is a monograph entitled "Scandalous Democracy: Journalists and Citizenship in Mexico, 1962–1988."

Javier Garza Ramos is a journalist in Torreón, Mexico, the host of the Reporte100 newscast, and a contributor to *El País, Washington Post, Animal Político, Esquire,* and *Nexos.* He is the former editorial director of *El Siglo de Torreón* and has been a Knight Fellow at the International Center for Journalists in Washington, DC.

Paul Gillingham is an associate professor of history at Northwestern University and the author of *Cuauhtémoc's Bones: Forging National Identity in Modern Mexico.*

Renata Keller is an assistant professor of Latin American history at the University of Nevada, Reno, and the author of *Mexico's Cold War: Cuba, the United States, and the Legacy of the Mexican Revolution.*

Michael Lettieri is an independent consultant on Mexican politics and human rights issues. He is the author of "A Model Dinosaur: Power, Personal Networks, and the Career of Rubén Figueroa."

Judith Matloff is a journalist and international consultant on safety training for media workers. She teaches conflict reporting at the Columbia Graduate School of Journalism; her most recent book is *No Friends but the Mountains: Dispatches from the World's Violent Highlands.*

Everard Meade is the director of the Trans-Border Institute at the University of San Diego, specializing in human rights, migration, and violence against journalists. He is the translator of Javier Valdez Cárdenas's *The Taken: True Stories of the Sinaloa Drug War.*

Andrew Paxman is a historian and journalist who teaches at the Centro de Investigación y Docencia Económicas in Mexico City and Aguascalientes. He has co-authored a biography of Emilio Azcárraga, founder of Televisa; his most recent work is *Jenkins of Mexico: How a Southern Farm Boy Became a Mexican Magnate.*

Pablo Piccato is a professor of history and Latin American studies at Columbia University, specializing in crime, journalism, and the public sphere. His most recent work is *A History of Infamy: Crime, Truth, and Justice in Mexico.*

Jacinto Rodríguez Munguía is a journalist and researcher. He has held fellowships at Harvard University and the University of Texas, Austin, and is the author of *La otra guerra secreta: Los archivos prohibidos de la prensa y el poder.*

Ana María Serna Rodríguez is a faculty member at the Instituto de Investigaciones Dr. José Luis Mora. She is the author of *Se solicitan reporteros: Historia oral del periodismo mexicano en la segunda mitad del siglo XX*.

Benjamin T. Smith is a reader of history at the University of Warwick. His most recent work is *The Mexican Press and Civil Society, 1940-1976: Stories from the Newsroom, Stories from the Street*.

Index

Page numbers in italic text indicate illustrations.